Activating Critical Thinking to Advance the Sustainable Development Goals in Tourism Systems

Activating Critical Thinking to Advance the Sustainable Development Goals in Tourism Systems focuses on the role of critical thinking and inquiry in the implementation of the 2030 Sustainable Development Goals (SDGs) in tourism systems. The impetus for the development of this book emerged from the declaration by the United Nations (UN) General Assembly of 2017 as the International Year of Sustainable Tourism for Development. This declaration purposely positions tourism as a tool to advance the universal 2030 Agenda for Sustainable Development and the 17 SDGs, thus mutually serving as an opportunity and responsibility to appraise from a critical lens what the SDGs signify and how they can be understood from multiple perspectives.

The chapters in the book foster the next phase of sustainable tourism scholarship that actively considers the interconnections of the UN's SDGs to tourism theory and praxis, and activates critical thinking to analyze and advance sustainability in tourism systems. It articulates the need for the academy to be more intrinsically involved in ongoing iterations of multilateral accords and decrees, to ensure they embody more critical and inclusive transitions toward sustainability, as opposed to market-driven, neoliberal directives. The contributions in this book encourage various worldviews challenging, shaping, and more critically reflecting the realities of global communities as related to, and impacted by, sustainable tourism development.

The chapters in this book were originally published as a special issue of the *Journal of Sustainable Tourism*.

Karla A. Boluk, Ph.D., is an Associate Professor in the Department of Recreation and Leisure Studies at the University of Waterloo, Canada. Utilizing a critical lens, she investigates ways to sustainably engage and empower communities, positioning tourism as a mechanism for the creation of positive change.

Christina T. Cavaliere, Ph.D., is a conservation social scientist. Her research involves the human dimensions of socio-ecological systems including tourism impacts and biocultural conservation. She serves as an Assistant Professor at Colorado State University, USA, and has experience working with universities, communities, businesses, non-governmental organizations, and multilateral institutions on six continents.

Freya Higgins-Desbiolles, Ph.D., is a Senior Lecturer in Tourism Management at the University of South Australia. Her work focuses on human rights and justice issues in tourism. She has worked with communities, non-governmental organizations, and businesses that seek to harness tourism for sustainable and equitable futures.

Activating Critical Thinking to Advance the Sustainable Development Goals in Tourism Systems

Edited by
Karla A. Boluk, Christina T. Cavaliere and Freya Higgins-Desbiolles

Routledge
Taylor & Francis Group

LONDON AND NEW YORK

First published 2021
by Routledge
2 Park Square, Milton Park, Abingdon, Oxon, OX14 4RN

and by Routledge
52 Vanderbilt Avenue, New York, NY 10017

Routledge is an imprint of the Taylor & Francis Group, an informa business

© 2021 Taylor & Francis

British Library Cataloguing-in-Publication Data
A catalogue record for this book is available from the British Library

ISBN: 978-0-367-69139-4 (hbk)
ISBN: 978-0-367-69140-0 (pbk)
ISBN: 978-1-003-14054-2 (ebk)

Typeset in Myriad Pro
by codeMantra

Publisher's Note
The publisher accepts responsibility for any inconsistencies that may have arisen during the conversion of this book from journal articles to book chapters, namely the inclusion of journal terminology.

Disclaimer
Every effort has been made to contact copyright holders for their permission to reprint material in this book. The publishers would be grateful to hear from any copyright holder who is not here acknowledged and will undertake to rectify any errors or omissions in future editions of this book.

Contents

Citation Information

The chapters in this book were originally published in the *Journal of Sustainable Tourism*, volume 27, issue 7 (May 2019). When citing this material, please use the original page numbering for each article, as follows:

Chapter 1
A critical framework for interrogating the United Nations Sustainable Development Goals 2030 Agenda in tourism
Karla A. Boluk, Christina T. Cavaliere and Freya Higgins-Desbiolles
Journal of Sustainable Tourism, volume 27, issue 7 (May 2019) pp. 846–864

Chapter 2
A pedagogical framework for the development of the critical tourism citizen
Karla A. Boluk, Christina T. Cavaliere and Lauren N. Duffy
Journal of Sustainable Tourism, volume 27, issue 7 (May 2019) pp. 865–881

Chapter 3
Overcommitted to tourism and under committed to sustainability: The urgency of teaching "strong sustainability" in tourism courses
Debbie Cotterell, Robert Hales, Charles Arcodia and Jo-Anne Ferreira
Journal of Sustainable Tourism, volume 27, issue 7 (May 2019) pp. 882–902

Chapter 4
No sustainability for tourism without gender equality
Daniela Moreno Alarcón and Stroma Cole
Journal of Sustainable Tourism, volume 27, issue 7 (May 2019) pp. 903–919

Chapter 5
Assessing gender representation in knowledge production: A critical analysis of UNWTO's planned events
Catheryn Khoo-Lattimore, Elaine Chiao Ling Yang and Jess Sanggyeong Je
Journal of Sustainable Tourism, volume 27, issue 7 (May 2019) pp. 920–938

Chapter 6
Gender and sustainability – exploring ways of knowing – an ecohumanities perspective
Kumi Kato
Journal of Sustainable Tourism, volume 27, issue 7 (May 2019) pp. 939–956

Chapter 7

The land has voice: Understanding the land tenure – sustainable tourism development nexus in Micronesia
T. S. Stumpf and C. L. Cheshire
Journal of Sustainable Tourism, volume 27, issue 7 (May 2019) pp. 957–973

Chapter 8

Critical discourse analysis and the questioning of dominant, hegemonic discourses of sustainable tourism in the Waterberg Biosphere Reserve, South Africa
Andrew Lyon and Philippa Hunter-Jones
Journal of Sustainable Tourism, volume 27, issue 7 (May 2019) pp. 974–991

Chapter 9

Rethinking the ideology of responsible tourism
Elisa Burrai, Dorina-Maria Buda and Davina Stanford
Journal of Sustainable Tourism, volume 27, issue 7 (May 2019) pp. 992–1007

Chapter 10

Sustaining precarity: Critically examining tourism and employment
Richard N. S. Robinson, Antje Martins, David Solnet and Tom Baum
Journal of Sustainable Tourism, volume 27, issue 7 (May 2019) pp. 1008–1025

Chapter 11

Rethinking decent work: The value of dignity in tourism employment
Anke Winchenbach, Paul Hanna and Graham Miller
Journal of Sustainable Tourism, volume 27, issue 7 (May 2019) pp. 1026–1043

Chapter 12

Constructing sustainable tourism development: The 2030 agenda and the managerial ecology of sustainable tourism
C. Michael Hall
Journal of Sustainable Tourism, volume 27, issue 7 (May 2019) pp. 1044–1060

Chapter 13

Can tourism help to "end poverty in all its forms everywhere"? The challenge of tourism addressing SDG1
Regina Scheyvens and Emma Hughes
Journal of Sustainable Tourism, volume 27, issue 7 (May 2019) pp. 1061–1079

Chapter 14

The critical capacities of restaurants as facilitators for transformations to sustainability
Freya Higgins-Desbiolles and Gayathri Wijesinghe
Journal of Sustainable Tourism, volume 27, issue 7 (May 2019) pp. 1080–1105

For any permission-related enquiries please visit:
http://www.tandfonline.com/page/help/permissions

Contributors

DANIELA MORENO ALARCÓN University Complutense of Madrid, Spain.

CHARLES ARCODIA Griffith University, Australia.

TOM BAUM University of Strathclyde Business School, UK.

KARLA A. BOLUK University of Waterloo, Canada.

DORINA-MARIA BUDA Leeds Beckett University, UK.

ELISA BURRAI Leeds Beckett University, UK.

CHRISTINA T. CAVALIERE Colorado State University, USA.

C. L. CHESHIRE University of Hawaii at Manoa, USA.

STROMA COLE University of the West of England, UK.

DEBBIE COTTERELL Griffith University, Australia.

LAUREN N. DUFFY Clemson State University, USA.

JO-ANNE FERREIRA Southern Cross University, Australia.

ROBERT HALES Griffith University, Australia.

C. MICHAEL HALL University of Canterbury, New Zealand.

PAUL HANNA University of Surrey, UK.

FREYA HIGGINS-DESBIOLLES University of South Australia, Australia.

EMMA HUGHES Massey University, New Zealand.

PHILIPPA HUNTER-JONES University of Liverpool Management School, UK.

KUMI KATO Wakayama University, Japan.

CATHERYN KHOO-LATTIMORE Griffith University, Australia.

ANDREW LYON University of Chester, UK.

ANTJE MARTINS The University of Queensland, Australia.

GRAHAM MILLER University of Surrey, UK.

RICHARD N. S. ROBINSON The University of Queensland, Australia.

JESS SANGGYEONG JE Griffith University, Australia.

REGINA SCHEYVENS Massey University, New Zealand.

DAVID SOLNET The University of Queensland, Australia.

DAVINA STANFORD Leeds Beckett University, UK.

T. S. STUMPF Humboldt State University, USA.

ANKE WINCHENBACH University of Surrey, UK.

GAYATHRI WIJESINGHE University of South Australia, Australia.

ELAINE CHIAO LING YANG Griffith University, Australia.

A critical framework for interrogating the United Nations Sustainable Development Goals 2030 Agenda in tourism

Karla A. Boluk, Christina T. Cavaliere and Freya Higgins-Desbiolles

ABSTRACT

Research in the area of sustainable tourism continues to grow, however a lack of understanding regarding necessary action inhibits progress. McCloskey's (2015) critique regarding the failure of the MDGs, as a direct result of a lack of critical consciousness, and understanding of the structural contexts of poverty and under-development, provided the impetus for our work. McCloskey (2015) signals the important role of education in fostering transitions to sustainability. As such, we have applied our critical lens to the 2030 United Nations Sustainable Development Goals. Our paper offers tools for critically thinking through the potential for the SDGs to help shape the tourism industry for more sustainable, equitable, and just futures. We positioned six themes to serve as a conceptual framework for interrogating the SDG agenda in tourism; arising from our considerations of both reformist and radical pathways to sustainable transitions in tourism: critical tourism scholarship, gender in the sustainable development agenda, engaging with Indigenous perspectives and other paradigms, degrowth and the circular economy, governance and planning, and ethical consumption. We address these core themes as essential platforms to critique the SDGs in the context of sustainable tourism development, and highlight the cutting edge research carried out by our contributors in this special issue.

Introduction

Balancing socio-economic interests with the planet's finite ecological systems is a fundamental goal of sustainability. While significant environmental damage continues (e.g. Klein, 2010), there has been momentum and progress towards sustainability pathways in tourism (e.g. sustainability initiatives in hotels see Sloan, Legrand, & Chen, 2013). Tourism is multifaceted and highly impactful despite claims that it is a benign industry (e.g. Hall, 2008). As humanity transitions from the Holocene to the Anthropocene (Gren & Huijbens, 2014), the need to re-examine and re-enact systems thinking to transition socio-economic paradigms has become increasingly urgent due to habitat loss, threats to biodiversity and climate change. The conservation of our cultural and environmental diversity is indispensable for continued livelihood development and well-being and is fundamental to tourism.

The inherent relationship between sustainability and tourism has received increasing scholarly attention, since concerns about carrying capacity were expressed by O'Reilly (1986). Bramwell and Lane (1993) were the first to define sustainable tourism as

[...] a positive approach intended to reduce the tensions and friction created by the complex interactions between the tourism industry, visitors, the environment and the communities which are host to holidaymakers. It is an approach which involves working for the long-term viability and quality of both natural and human resources. It is not anti-growth, but it acknowledges that there are limits to growth. (p. 2)

The authors refer to the work of Inskeep (1991) and Krippendorf (1987) as scholars offering tangible ways in which stakeholders involved in tourism may reduce the impacts of tourism operations. However, contemporary scholars have pointed out that this is not yet fully realised in tourism despite increased public awareness of sustainability issues (Moscardo & Hughes, 2018), drawing attention to the elusiveness of the goal of sustainability (e.g. Higgins-Desbiolles, 2010). Such intangibility seems to inhibit behavioural change and action among both the tourism industry and tourists.

The United Nations World Tourism Organization (UNWTO) declared 2017 a "watershed moment" with its official International Year of Sustainable Tourism for Development which proposed "making tourism a catalyst for positive change" (UNWTO, 2017a, p. i). This declaration positions tourism as a tool to advance the universal 2030 Agenda for Sustainable Development, including the 17 Sustainable Development Goals (2015–2030) (SDGs) and 169 targets (UN, 2019). Such a claim needs to be met with considered critical thinking and analysed from a diversity of approaches and perspectives. It is important to understand that it was the failure of the Millennium Development Goals (MDGs), with their 2015 deadline that necessitated the development of the Sustainable Development Goals (SDGs). McCloskey explained that:

One of the reasons that new goals are necessary and the MDGs failed to meet all of their targets was the absence of a critical consciousness that considered the structural causes of poverty [...] Above all, we have failed to relate the dominant neoliberal economic model to persistent levels of poverty and climate change. (2015, p. 186)

In response to this declaration, the papers presented in this special issue (SI) consider through a critical lens how the SDGs may be understood and realised from multiple worldviews and disciplinary perspectives. The UN's 17 SDGs have received limited specific attention from tourism sustainability scholars (Bramwell, Higham, Lane, & Miller, 2017) which is surprising given the international applicability of the SDGs and their origin from a globally recognised intergovernmental organisation. Clearly, the academy must work more critically to reflect the realities of global communities, as related to, and impacted by, sustainable tourism development. Through this SI we seek to foster the next phase of sustainable tourism scholarship that actively considers the interconnections of the UN's SDGs to tourism theory and praxis, and to activate critical thinking to analyse and advance sustainability in tourism systems. We also seek to articulate the need for the academy to be more intrinsically involved in ongoing iterations of multilateral accords and decrees to ensure they embody more critical and inclusive transitions toward sustainability as opposed to market-driven, neoliberal directives. This SI focuses on the functions that tourism systems serve in furthering sustainable livelihoods specifically through an examination of the essential role that critical thinking must play in education and multilateral directives and initiatives.

Critical thinking can be emancipatory. It lies at the heart of democracy (Giroux, 2011) and embodies a process of discovering, acknowledging, and checking implicit assumptions to ensure inclusive and informed decision-making (Brookfield, 1987). Sustainable tourism necessitates critical thinking; requiring deeper explorations of the dynamics of power, privilege, hegemony, and hierarchical structures (Mowforth & Munt, 1998). Barriers to sustainability are increasingly identified with inequitable distribution of resources, privatisation of the commons, and wealth accumulating to a small elite (Büscher & Fletcher, 2017). This realisation demonstrates that it is particularly important for all stakeholders to be involved in tourism planning and decision-making, including travellers, the industry, governments, communities, workers and the academy (Beaumont & Dredge, 2010). Neglecting adequate stakeholder involvement may lead to irreparable harm such as tourism conflicts and public opposition; ultimately risking an unsustainable future (Hall, 2008). Jamal and Stronza (2009) stress the importance of nature as a key stakeholder in sustainability that requires a voice.

Throughout the SI authors have positioned examples of ways to deconstruct power and to view tourism systems from multiple worldviews (e.g. marginalised and under-represented populations) through mobilising critical interrogation. Accordingly, contributions provide evidence for the need to work to build critical understandings of the processes and dynamics of tourism and the vital necessity for training, learning, and action, aiming for goals ranging from reform of current practices to alternatives and agendas that are more radical. We can imagine alternatives through engagement with underused paradigms such as Indigenous perspectives, ethics of care, feminist ecology, and radical eco-socialism, which may serve as vital entry points into alternate ways of being, knowing, and doing. The tourism academy has more to offer in this vital work and the analysis of the UN SDGs agenda towards 2030 is an optimum opportunity to apply critical thinking to move past the status quo to more radical and transformative approaches. Seizing tourism as a platform for imaginative and transformative action is the unfinished work we take up here.

In an era of neoliberalism and conservatism, engaging in critical thinking is essential (Giroux, 2014). Critical thinking aids us in illuminating the environmental, social and economic injustices that are perpetuated by and within the tourism industry. In this paper, we present six general themes which arise from our considerations of both reformist and radical pathways to sustainable transitions in tourism: critical tourism scholarship, gender in the sustainable development agenda, engaging with Indigenous perspectives and other paradigms, degrowth and the circular economy, governance and planning, and ethical consumption. We address these core themes as essential platforms to critique the SDGs in the context of sustainable tourism development. Our six themes, present a conceptual framework for interrogating transformed futures in tourism. Critical tourism scholarship provides the skill for deep critical thinking that supports open and emancipatory approaches. These innovative approaches can be supported through the open-mindedness that comes from engaging with diverse views and voices from women, Indigenous peoples, and others that will underscore there are many ways of being, knowing and doing in tourism. The final three core themes confront neoliberal capitalism as it prevents achieving sustainability and the SDG agenda. The six themes provide entry ways into thinking through both the problematic nature of the current tourism industry, as well as possible alternatives already evident. As we address each of these six core themes we take the opportunity to briefly highlight key contributions from authors of this SI.

While this SI is focused on the SDGs, it does so from a critical positioning. Elsewhere, the UN SDGs have been critiqued for their universalising tendencies, a concern that the agenda remains set in the neoliberal mould, the development role assigned to the private sector and a concern that it will allow for little more than "business as usual" (see Scheyvens, Banks, & Hughes, 2016). Perhaps the most critical question of all is: who will drive sustainability forward as choices get more difficult in a resource-constrained world and as climate change impacts compound? The roles of the multiple stakeholders in tourism are vital but as the body of this article will demonstrate there are power struggles and power vacuums that impact their capacity to support and to secure the SDG agenda.

Critical tourism scholarship

Critical tourism scholars have expressed concerns regarding the socio-cultural impacts of tourism, generated by the tourist gaze (Urry, 1990). Hollinshead (1992, p. 43) referred to such encounters as an "objectifying" gaze, thus raising questions about the ability of the industry to promote equality (Turner & Ash, 1975), concerns about power (Bianchi, 2009), and apprehensions regarding the lack of morality demonstrated by consumers and producers (Weeden & Boluk, 2014). Furthermore, concerns regarding the lack of local representation in tourism decision-making

(Freire-Mederios, 2013), apprehensions regarding gender equality (e.g. Ferguson & Alarcon, 2015), environmental fears challenging the notion of sustainability (e.g. Higgins-Desbiolles, 2018), environmental justice (Higgins-Desbiolles & Powys Whyte, 2013), the postcolonial nature of the industry (e.g. Hall & Tucker, 2004), and aid in poverty alleviation (Scheyvens, 2011) have been articulated. The real and various impacts generated by tourism urge critical scholars and practitioners to reimagine a sector that can give back to the communities in which tourism takes place.

Concerns, regarding the impacts of neoliberalism on academic spheres are evidenced in the literature, in the themes that run through international conferences, university campuses, and in tourism practices. Therefore, critically reflecting on the ways in which neoliberalism affects our work, teaching and engagement with the broader community is needed to acknowledge, navigate, and resist neoliberal pressures. Neoliberal rhetoric has shaped a particular ideology valuing a market-driven education (Fletcher & Piemonte, 2017). Specifically, neoliberal structures prioritise the financial outcomes of higher education (Giroux, 2004), and consider the academy as an enterprise (Fletcher & Piemonte, 2017). As such, what matters in the neoliberal knowledge economy is securing grants and contracts, and the ability for scholars to present themselves and their teaching/research programs in ways that compete to attract domestic and international students (Ali, 2009). Furthermore, the various quantitative metrics by which scholars are evaluated prioritise individualism, productivity and profit maximisation. Such measurements, breeds self-commodification (Gahman, 2016). This has significantly undermined the contemporary possibilities in fostering, and at times modelling critical thinking.

Joseph (2012) refers to several disciplines (such as feminist studies, ethnic and racial studies, and postcolonial studies) that may be undervalued in traditional classical discipline streams (e.g. anthropology, psychology, sociology, geography, business) thus pushed to the margins under neoliberalism. Tourism studies may be another field ignored and/or perceived as less rigorous by non-tourism/leisure/recreation/hospitality/events scholars who are unable/unwilling to value its contribution. However, non-major and critical disciplines facilitate "spaces to engage discussions about social inequalities and cultural hierarchies" (Joseph, 2012, p. 254). Such considerations have clearly been taking place in the tourism scholarship. For example, from the producer perspective Mowforth, Charlton, and Munt (2008) challenge the benefits derived by tourism establishing that the rights of local people are neglected. This is echoed by Lovelock's (2008) work on the ethical decision-making behaviour of travel agents who favour the rights of their clients to travel, above the human rights of host communities. From a consumer perspective, Mostafanezhad (2014) argued that volunteer tourism perpetuates geopolitical discourses of North-South relations and naturalises political, economic and social inequality. Furthermore, Groulx, Boluk, Lemieux, and Dawson (2019) examined the ethical challenges faced by last chance travellers visiting climate-threatened destinations, finding that most visitors are unwilling to engage in carbon offsetting.

The pedagogical emphasis in tourism studies on management and business fields (e.g. Hollinshead, 2009; Tribe, 2000, 2008) has shifted priorities. Specifically, the weight placed on workforce training echoes concerns expressed by scholars such as Freire (1970) and Giroux (2004). Such orientations, influenced by neoliberal agendas, have paid limited attention to the development of critical thinking, the original priority of tertiary institutions (Johnson & Morris, 2010; Kincheloe, 2008). Training critical pedagogues has been usurped with the profit driven nature of the tourism industry. This challenges the possibilities of tourism functioning as a social force (Higgins-Desbiolles, 2006). The importance of instilling the skills of critical thinking was expounded in Boluk, Cavaliere and Duffy's (this SI) work in their presentation of a framework to support the delivery and development of critical thinking in the classroom and beyond. Cotterell, Hales, Arcodia and Ferreira's (this SI) work revealed the use of weak conceptualisations of sustainability that act to support "business as usual". Limited engagement with the SDGs in tourism courses led to their development of a number of indicative critical questions assisting instructors in their incorporation of the SDGs.

The call for a "critical turn" in tourism studies to better respond to contemporary problems (Ateljevic, Morgan, & Pritchard, 2013) recognised "the future success of tourism rides not only on our ability to harness and channel its positive impacts, but also to come to terms with tourism's negative impacts by taking responsibility for positive change" (Caton, Schott, & Daniele, 2014, p. 125). Accordingly, the opportunity of tourism as a tool for education (Pritchard, Morgan, & Ateljevic, 2011), social justice (Boluk & Carnicelli, 2019; Carnicelli & Boluk, 2017) and business productivity (Belhassen & Caton, 2011; Boluk, 2011), human rights (e.g. Cole, 2010; Higgins-Desbiolles & Blanchard, 2010), peace building, and citizenship (e.g. Bianchi & Stephensen, 2014; Blanchard & Higgins-Desbiolles, 2013) has been noted in the scholarship. An emerging interest in recognising the importance of criticality in tourism has been embraced in networks such as BEST EN, social movements such as TEFI, and conferences such as Critical Tourism Studies.

This section has established that critical tourism scholars have signalled the crucial impacts generated by the tourism industry. Furthermore, the neoliberal emphasis has prioritised vocational training over the development of skills which could equip students to think critically. This is problematic given the array of sustainability concerns that students will face in their professional lives. Interestingly, critical thinking is largely absent from the descriptions of the United Nation's 17 SDGs as a way to realise the goals. We argue that critical thinking must be activated in order to respond to contemporary concerns in relation to sustainability. In activating critical thinking, it may become apparent whose voices are prioritised, whose are neglected, and which stakeholders should be actively facilitated to participate in processes and decision-making in order to have full and fair representation and empowerment. Even more significant, such inclusivity and openness will be an antidote to groupthink; avoiding this will be essential to address the challenges we now confront.

Gender in the sustainable development agenda

Women are essential to the achievement of sustainable development. Research has demonstrated that gender inequalities result in economic costs, social inequities and ecological damage (Shiva, 2009). Stevens (2010) has asked if "[...] gender equity is the 'missing link' of sustainable development" (p. 1). Similarly, women are essential to implementing the SDGs in tourism. When tourism is developed in a community, women may experience some of the worst negative impacts that tourism may bring. Moreno Alarcón, and Cole (this issue) note that employment for women in tourism does not take into account the need to redistribute unpaid care work, or reduce the gender pay gap or combat sexual harassment and that patriarchal structures, are often reinforced by tourism policy, such as viewing water work as women's work. Additionally, women are a significant component of the tourism workforce, both in the formal and informal sectors. Women often experience the vulnerabilities that feature in tourism work, particularly in front-line hospitality positions (e.g. cleaning, serving) including seasonality, low wages, precarious conditions, and sexual harassment (Poulston, 2008). Without focused planning, women may find their personal, social, economic, and environmental conditions of living materially damaged by tourism developments within their communities. Most importantly, women's leadership of tourism development and decision-making brings unique and invaluable wisdom to the process and underpins sustainability. This is the reason that such emphasis has been given to gender in development policies and planning and explains the inclusion of SDG 5 "Achieve gender equality and empower all women and girls" in the 17 UN SDGs.

While SDG 5 is concerned with achieving gender equality and empowering all women and girls, this is indeed essential for achieving all 17 SDGs. As a result, "gender analysis, once confined to the margins of development theory, has over the last ten years penetrated both the thinking and the operations of international development institutions" (Miller & Razavi, 1998, p. 4). The United Nations has organised world conferences on women and periodic reviews of progress in an effort to advance a gender equality agenda globally (See UN Women, n.d.). Recently, the 'Fourth World Conference on Women' held in Beijing declared: "Women's empowerment and their full participation on the basis of equality in all spheres of society, including participation in the decision-making process and access to power, are fundamental for the achievement of equality, development and peace" (Beijing Declaration, 1989).

In addition to considerations of gender in development, it is also important to understand the influence of feminism as an evolving social movement of significant power. There have been a number of "waves" of feminism (see Munro, 2013), as well as various paradigms that hold significance for critically interrogating tourism and shaping it towards justice. These allow structures of power and oppression to be addressed in a more transformative approach than the efforts undertaken to incorporate gender analysis in development. Evidence of the impacts of feminism theory on tourism scholarship are clear. There is evolving interest in the lived lives of women in tourism and the ways patriarchal and hierarchical structures work to oppress women, women of colour and others (though the fourth wave of feminism does not yet seem evident in tourism as we have not seen the "call-out culture" of the #MeToo era addressed; see Munro, 2013). Thus, there is a need for holistic considerations of what a feminist approach to development, tourism and the SDG agenda might offer as tools to advance critical thinking and action in tourism.

Gender analysis of tourism emerged from the discussions of gender in development. Enloe (1989) wrote a key critical text *Making feminist sense of international politics* which offered a chapter called *"On the beach: Sexism and tourism"* (pp. 19–41). This book applied the feminist ethos (second wave feminism) that the "personal is political" to endeavours such as tourism and thereby revealed how initiatives such as tourism development can be built on the oppression and exploitation of women. Margaret Swain edited a SI of *Annals of Tourism* on *Gender in Tourism* in 1995, marking a pivotal moment in tourism studies. Additionally, Sinclair (1997) edited a volume that examined the interfaces between gender, work and tourism through comparisons across international contexts to consider the ways in which tourism, patriarchal systems, and capitalism constrained and enabled women's empowerment. The tourism literature during this time addressed issues such as: the inequalities of tourism development; gender in tourism experiences of both the tourists and the hosts; gender in marketing and representation; gender in sex tourism; gender and international political economy; and gender in tourism research. For Swain's (1995) *Gender in Tourism* volume, gender referred to: "[...] a system of culturally constructed identities, expressed in ideologies of masculinity and femininity, interacting with socially constructed relationships in divisions of labour and leisure, sexuality, and power between women and men" (pp. 258–9).

Recent work on the tourism and gender interface focuses on gender and sexualities in tourism (Pritchard, 2007) or gender issues in the tourism academy (Chambers et al., 2017). Women in the tourism academy have gathered their voices using new technologies such as creative commons to co-author a report on the "gender gap" in the academy (Munar & Waiting for the Dawn, 2015) and to create social media networks such as "Women Academics in Tourism" on Facebook. There is much more focus needed on the gender in development segment and the knowledge gained from feminist activism to confront power if SDG 5 is to be realised within the domain of tourism development. More than two decades ago, Swain (1995) asserted that gender in tourism is "both a scholastic and a political endeavour" (p. 264). Realising SDG 5 requires renewed commitment on both fronts within the tourism academy.

A recent event suggests that the gender domain is a critical arena for action to attain sustainable development in tourism. In response to the 2017 *International Year of Sustainable Tourism for Development,* the UNWTO set out key priorities for action addressing SDG 5 of a very limited nature: "gender analysis and monitoring of work conditions" and "training and capacity building for women and youth" (2017). This approach was criticised by the non-government organisation

Equality in Tourism (EiN) who stated: "it depicts a limited framing of gender issues as related to economic empowerment, leaving out discussions of political empowerment and broader questions on structural inequalities" (2017). This NGO was established in 2014 to advocate for "gender equality in the tourism industry" and to "help ensure women enjoy an equal share in the tourism industry" (EiN, n.d.). Since its establishment, it has attempted to influence policy and has supported a small number of projects. Its criticism of the UNWTO's engagement with SDG 5 suggests what a feminist approach offers in terms of guiding sustainability analysis to issues of power, justice and structural inequalities.

This SI presents three cutting-edge articles that advance critical thinking on gender, tourism and sustainable development. First, Moreno Alarcón and Cole highlight that gender issues are central to all 17 SDGs. Second, Khoo-Lattimore, Chiao, Yang and Sanggyeong Je offer a critical analysis of UNWTO planned events, finding that the tourism industry is missing out through the marginalisation of gender and diversity approaches; they question if the UNWTO may be engaging in "gender greenwashing". Third, Kato uses feminist ecology in her study of women Japanese traditional divers and the ways they know and protect the marine environment and continue culture practices. Feminist approaches and gender analysis alert us to the need to think critically and seek out a diverse lens from which to view the tourism phenomenon.

Engaging with Indigenous perspectives and other paradigms

The problems that necessitate the SDGs and efforts to reorient the globe's economies to more sustainable pathways may be attributed to the mono-cultural approach to modernisation and development since the 1960s (see Shiva, 1993). Mowforth and Munt (1998) described this as economic globalisation infiltrating and incorporating all countries into the global capitalist system. Transporting a host of negative impacts that collectively are catalysts to unsustainability; they demonstrated that tourism accompanies and supports this process (Mowforth & Munt, 1998). Analysts such as David Harvey have argued that the need for endless capital accumulation and economic growth is what drives the spread and imposition of this system, despite negative social, ecological, and political consequences (Harvey 2005, p.181).

As this capitalist form of globalisation was taking hold, simultaneously Indigenous Peoples from around the world had collectively acted to assert their rights through the United Declaration on the Rights of Indigenous Peoples (UNDRIP) and other instruments (Blaser, 2004). Most had experienced the impacts of colonisation which may be viewed as the early beginnings of the western model of modernisation and development. As a result, Indigenous voices have marked a vocal point of resistance to imposition of this mono-cultural approach. Many Indigenous communities have confronted the unsustainable practices of modernising societies as their colonisation practices have inflicted dispossession and/or exploitation for several hundred years (Blaser, 2004). Resistance is more pronounced in recent, more resource-constrained times, including the iconic battle against oil pipelines such as at Standing Rock in the USA and against large dams in Brazil's Amazonia, but also against tourism developments such as the recent struggle of the Maasai in Tanzania against land expropriation for foreign-owned game reserves (see Patinkin, 2013).

Indigenous approaches may also offer a positive alternative to the unsustainable trajectories of modernist development models. Mäori academic Stewart-Harawira (2005, pp. 250–251) argued that "a deep understanding of the interconnectedness of all existence is not only fundamental to Indigenous ontologies but has been empirically demonstrated in the studies of leading quantum physicists such as David Bohm". Stewart-Harawira (2005) presented a sustained argument that traditional Indigenous ontologies can offer alternatives that could result in a transformed global order. Learning from her work, we would argue that Indigenous communities' values and lifeways may better integrate many of the SDG goals as in Indigenous worldviews, people co-exist in webs of interrelationships and responsibilities to other people, other species and the total "environment". These worldviews represent an alternative and a challenge to the myopic, instrumental and exploitative approach of globalising capitalism.

As more scientists and other experts have come to respect and value the accumulated wisdom of the millennia of insights Indigenous peoples have gathered, Indigenous knowledges, and particularly traditional ecological knowledges are increasingly being engaged in collaborative projects to address such issues as global environmental change (i.e. Whyte, 2013). However, it would be problematic for non-Indigenous experts to try to appropriate Indigenous knowledges and lifeways to resolve the ecological, social and even ontological crises that monolithic modernisation has brought to our societies. Indigenous peoples assert their Indigenous rights, including over Indigenous knowledges, and so the only appropriate way this knowledge can be tapped is through respectful collaborations that are developed through Indigenous processes and protocols (see UN, 2008).

The insights that may be gleaned from this analysis is that diversity is required for sustainable futures. Accordingly, respect for local rights and local lifeways are essential for building consensus and collaborations on pathways forward. We also note that Indigenous rights have manifested in the tourism phenomenon and provide important insights for the sustainable development of the industry. The case of the Kuna Indigenous peoples of Panama offer the lessons of a Statute on Tourism that stipulated the only tourism allowed in their communities would be controlled by and benefit the Kuna peoples (Snow & Wheeler, 2000). While not fully and effectively implemented in practice, this declaration of Kuna rights and authority has shown that Indigenous peoples can practice and participate in tourism in self-determining ways (Pereiro et al., 2012).

The values of other traditions and civilisations also play a role in challenging imposed, monocultural development models enacted in tourism. An early contribution was offered by Sohail Inayatullah (1995) who in his work on "rethinking tourism" offered an Islamic perspective on tourism. Another illustrative case is how the 'fair trade in tourism' phenomenon emerged in South Africa out of a black empowerment ethos underpinning the effort to build a post-Apartheid future for the country, and alleviate poverty (e.g. Boluk, 2011). Rural sociologist David Barkin has presented models of tourism development for Mexico that challenge the corporatised growth-pole strategies pursued by the Mexican government at destinations such as Cancun, including a strategy for rural tourism development based on engagement between rural communities and urban schools that assist in building rural-urban bonds and solidarity (2001). Barkin advocated a form of social tourism "more conducive to the country's needs and to those of its people" and that can be "an instrument to promote decentralized development" (2001, p. 43). Such examples show how sustainable practices are fostered through diverse worldviews and paradigms and how local authority is essential in securing local needs through tourism. One of the most important developments which has emerged in part from Indigenous leadership is the growing recognition of the "rights of Mother Nature". This gained global status with the "Universal Declaration of Rights of Mother Earth" (2010) and is realising meaningful implementation in jurisdictions such as New Zealand (i.e. Daly, 2017) and most recently with a Sami Parliament (Sami Parliament of Sweden, 2018).

In this SI, the work presented by Stumpf and Cheshire provided rich insights into the Indigenous Micronesian views of land, relationships and community thereby revealing that Indigenous perceptions of poverty differ greatly from western views. Their findings established several disconnects between understandings of sustainable development and often held views on land as commodified physical spaces removed from cultural meaning which are important in Micronesian societies. Lyon and Hunter-Jones' contribution provides a critical approach to examining discourses related to sustainable tourism development through the case of the Watersberg Biosphere Reserve in South Africa revealing that South Africa's black population have still not been positioned as equals post-apartheid. They revealed how top-down decisions support unequal power dynamics impeding the realisation of sustainability.

Degrowth and the circular economy

There is a need to transform the dominant approach of infinite growth of consumption and production due to the impossibilities of operating within a finite Earth system. The neoliberal economic growth perspective is prevalent across many industries, including tourism. SDG 8 focuses on the promotion of "sustained, inclusive and sustainable economic growth", along with an emphasis on "full and productive employment and decent work for all" (UN, 2019). While ongoing economic development is essential in many parts of the world for people to attain a decent standard of living, an overarching goal of continued growth is not possible based on ecosystem capacities. Target 8.4 recognises a need to "endeavour to decouple economic growth from environmental degradation" (UN, 2019) urging developed countries to take the lead. An addiction to growth has been identified as a central problem in tourism (Higgins-Desbiolles, 2018).

Conceptualisations of post-capitalistic politics, degrowth and tourism can be linked through identifying the need to downsize global patterns of consumption and production (Büscher & Fletcher, 2017). Kallis et al. (2018) argues that the concept of degrowth is being increasingly utilised among scholars who debunk growth-based economic development. They also highlight the need for "radical political and economic reorganization" to enact reductions in resource and energy usage (Kallis et al., 2018, p. 291). Unsurprisingly, degrowth conflicts with the premises of SDGs 12, 8 and 14, which view growth as success.

A goal of critical citizenship is to create a society that questions and analyses consumption (Johnson & Morris, 2010). According to Salleh (2010), the pervasive drive toward growth-based economics is responsible for overconsumption and therefore, climate change and biodiversity loss are the direct products of capitalist overproduction. An emphasis on prioritising economic growth and acquisition of corporate wealth has superseded socio-cultural and environmental interests in communities, and biocultural conservation (Assadourian, 2012; Cavaliere, 2017a). Engaging with other worldviews can support understandings of economic alternatives to capitalism and "business as usual" approaches that are driving dynamics leading to biocultural extinction. Doing so can serve to encourage connection with the non-human world and progressive paradigms that support regeneration and biocultural conservation (Cavaliere, 2017b).

A critical examination of traditional market driven contexts entrenched in pro-growth rhetoric is essential for realising sustainable systems in the long-term. Thus, analysis of the current conceptualisation of responsible tourism can assist in diagnosing the issues of contemporary capitalism (Burrai, Buda & Stanford, this issue). Degrowth analysis suggests a need for focus instead on social system-based innovations that result in wellbeing (Hall & Gössling, 2013). Notions of new approaches to sustainable production and consumption from post-capitalist social movements is quintessential to making radical transitions for improved livelihoods (Cavaliere, 2017a). Authors within this SI have identified issues of contention arising from neoliberal agendas and discourses that define progress as synonymous with the growth-based economy (Robinson, this issue). Critical perspectives are offered that call for the recognition that the dominant environmental-economic narrative in relation to sustainability must be reconfigured to include focus on social sustainability (Robinson, this issue). Social equity, decent working conditions and quality jobs are required to alleviate poverty and promote sustainable livelihood development (Bramwell et al., 2017). A critical lens is required to more deeply understand how to achieve this as decoupled from a sole focus on economic growth.

Responsible consumption and production, a specific focus of SDG 12, are imbedded within the antithetical discourse promoting the continuation of the market driven neoliberal regime.

Bramwell and Lane (2011) cautioned the weak support or acceptance of alternative policy paradigms that recognise different sustainability paradigms such as degrowth. In addition, many of the articles in this SI reveal the roles that leading international organisations, state agencies, destination managers, corporate actors and academic institutions play in reinforcing continual economic growth that is resulting in environmental and social devastation (Hall, 2019, this issue).

Shifts towards alternatives can be further understood through in-depth ecological impact analysis of the tourism system. The concept of bioregionalism is linked to wellbeing and notions of degrowth (Cavaliere, 2017a). Snyder (2010) noted that bioregionalism demonstrates ways that specific places ground understandings of the natural world and include elements such as biota, elevations and watersheds. A focus on locality is important in tourism research if the "cultural troupe of western ethnocentric perspectives are to be challenged, re-constituted and re-told" (Jamal & Hollinshead, 2001, p. 76). An additional lens to be considered involves the consideration of notions of biocapacity (Zappile & Cavaliere, 2018). Biocapacity is another way of measuring the resources available to continue fulfilling human and socio-ecological needs. Ecological footprint and biocapacity provide an understanding of the supply and demand of the biosphere's ecosystem services and can be "less biased than the monetary valuations, which are affected by market price variability and individuals' preferences" (Mancini et al., 2018, p. 234).

Finally, we introduce the concept of the circular economy. This concept serves as acounter to the current approach of the linear economy, and describes the "redesign of processes and cycling of materials" (Murray, Skene and Haynes, 2017, p. 369). However, currently academic business and sustainable literature is not engaged in this discussion (Murray et al., 2017) and the concept of the circular economy has also been largely ignored by the tourism academy. Scheyvens et al. (2016) noted some inclusion of philosophical literature as related to the Chinese state-controlled economy however not so for business models in the Western free market economy. However, there are initial indications that there is an understanding of the need for multistakeholder partnerships for transitions to new economic approaches within the UN system. A joint meeting was held between experts from the Economic and Financial Committee of the United Nations General Assembly and the Economic and Social Council to focus on accelerating implementations of multiple SDGs from 9 to 18 July 2018 (UNDESA, 2018). This meeting resulted from in-depth reviews of SDG 12 and 13 by the United Nations High-Level Political Forum. The outcomes from the meeting focused on the articulation of the transition to a circular economy (UNDESA, 2018). Attainment of sustainable tourism development will require ongoing critical engagement focused on challenging pro-growth dynamics and advocating for inclusion of multistakeholder perspectives.

Governance and planning

Tourism is now a globalised activity and so planning and governance have become more complicated. Tourism ranges from the local to the global, from the individual to the societal, and from the immediate impacts of activities to the longer terms of environmental change in the age of the Anthropocene. These temporal, geo-spatial and sociological aspects make tourism impacts a highly complex endeavour to address. Because of these complexities, a variety of paradigms or platforms have been applied to tourism analysis (see Macbeth, 2005). Additionally, systems thinking is an evolving approach to build understanding and enable better management (Hall, 2008).

The neoliberal ideologies and practices discussed in the preceding section have added to the complexity in efforts to implement sustainability. Neoliberalism promotes freeing the market from governmental regulation based on arguments that this results in greater economic efficiencies, maximisation of resource use and beneficial outcomes for all through a "trickle-down effect" of free enterprise. Harvey (2007) stated: "The corporatization, commodification, and privatization of hitherto public assets have been signal features of the neoliberal project" (p. 35). This has had particular impacts on tourism, for instance by transitioning national parks from dedication to con-servation priorities and public benefit to commercialised tourism ones. Additionally, power is now more diffuse and so policy is no longer limited to "public policy". As a result, Hall (2011) suggested there are now four categories of governance, ranging from political hierarchies (state governance), to markets (recognising the power of private economic actors and their associations), to networks (through public-private partnerships and associations), to communities (governance arising from the local level with direct public involvement). In Hall's contribution to this SI, he examines the managerial ecology of tourism and the SDGs. He explains managerial ecology as involving: "the instrumental application of science and economic utilitarian approaches and in the service of resources utilization and economic development" (p. X). Such approaches offer little of the changes that are required to transition to more sustainable futures and underscore arguments that the SDG agenda allows for continuation of "business as usual" (Scheyvens et al., 2016).

However, extreme cases as found at the Galapagos Islands, Machu Picchu, Mount Everest, Majorca, Barcelona, and Venice have shown that regulation of tourism impacts is essential and that neoliberalism's laissez faire approach to tourism management is not conducive to securing long-term sustainability. In 2017, cases of over-tourism became obvious and concerns grew about how to address such issues. Particular phenomena, such as Airbnb and Uber, representing the disruptive forces of technological change raised particular concerns for the negative impacts they might bring to destinations. Jurisdictions around the world are turning back to regulation to manage these tensions illuminated by the over-tourism phenomenon. Interventions have included: tourist information to change tourist behaviour, changes in zoning regulations, caps on visitation, tourist levies and even temporary closures. While neoliberalism has overseen a steady diminution of governments' role in tourism governance and a concomitant expansion of private sector power, these recent developments suggest the pendulum may swing back again as governments are forced to again govern for the public good.

Additionally, a concern with the precarity of working conditions for the tourism and hospital-ity workforce is growing as market forces are driving structural changes that foster technological disruptions and a new "gig economy", with Uber impacts creating a new concept of uberisation (Nurvala, 2015). There are movements to secure fair work, award rates and a living wage for the workers in the tourism and hospitality sector. One Australian report indicated that 84% of Australian fast food restaurants underpaid their workers (Crellin, 2016). This situation represents serious inequity in the tourism and hospitality spheres that undermine the sector's contributions to sustainability and directly relate to SDG 8 focused on decent work and SDG 10 on reduced inequalities. Robinson's article in this SI addresses issues of precarity for workers in tourism and hospitality. Furthermore, Winchenbach, Hanna and Miller offer conceptual explorations of the value of dignity and the importance of identity in tourism employment in this SI which builds understanding of what creates positive work in tourism.

Addressing such issues is a matter for tourism businesses and their commitments to imple-menting sustainability are of primary importance. Recent work by Campos, Hall, and Backlund (2018) addressed the role of powerful multinational corporations in implementing sustainable, fair and inclusive practices. Examining the case of one of the largest Scandinavian tour operators, Apollo, they argued:

> Powerful players in the industry, such as large tour operators, have the ability to enable greater sustainability and more inclusive forms of tourism. But if more coercive institutional pressures, in the form of laws, regulations and incentives, are not enacted to accelerate this process, it risks perpetuating a limited adoption of inclusive practices in the mass tourism industry (p. 19).

There has been a growing realisation that tourism policy and planning research must become more attentive to power dynamics. Dredge and Jamal (2015) have advocated more critical deconstructions of the political and economic structures that shape tourism policy and planning.

Higgins-Desbiolles (2018) has argued that the "structural context set by powerful corporations, subservient governments and consumerized citizenry needs to be understood" (p. 158). Jamal and Camargo (2018) have argued that justice is a "key principle of good governance" (p. 205). These works indicate that critically challenging power dynamics and pursuing shared decision-making are important aspects in the pursuit of sustainability.

Ethical consumption

SDG 12 focuses on responsible consumption and production patterns. SDG12 is one of only three SDGs (along with SDG 8 and SDG 14) explicitly recognising the role of the tourism industry. In fact, SDG 12 positions tourism as a leader suggesting that sustainability in tourism has implications for a global shift towards more sustainable practices. Perhaps echoing the absence of the tourism industry in the articulation of the 17 SDGs, limited evidence in the tourism scholarship identifies the industry as a trailblazer supporting sustainability. Rather, tourism is more commonly associated with trepidations regarding how it is practiced; this is articulated by Weeden and Boluk (2014) who argued despite the documentation of the negative impacts generated by tourism, neither producers nor consumers have responded convincingly to urgent responsibility concerns. Discussions of sustainability are often embedded in discussions of sustainable growth (Tyrvainen, Uusitalo, Silvennoinen, & Hasu, 2014). As aforementioned, conceptualisations and implementation of degrowth strategies present both opportunities and challenges that need to be critically considered.

Unambiguously, tourism sustainability has been discussed in the literature since initial concerns regarding carrying capacity (O'Reilly, 1986). Sustainability in tourism has not been addressed holistically as its emphasis is usually on greening efforts (which mutually recognise cost savings). In relation to SDG 12, contemporary consumption has been regarded as a source of harm and political practice (Harrison, Newholm, & Shaw, 2005). Evidence of impairment may be related to Marx's (1867) notion of commodity fetishism, where consumers demonstrate limited knowledge of the goods they consume thus causing damage to environments, cultures, animals, and peoples. Commodity fetishism is recognised in the discourse of behavioural addiction specifically "binge flying", reflecting the rising appetite for holidaying (Cohen, Higham, & Cavaliere, 2011). Supporting neoliberal rhetoric, tourism provides an opportunity to commodify and package experiences for the primary benefit of wealthy and privileged tourists; for example, touring Antarctica in an attempt to capture spaces of last chance tourism, touring the other in poverty porn through slum tourism, and child exploitation in "volunteer" capacities through orphanage tourism (Higgins-Desbiolles, 2018, p. 158). Such examples draw attention to the superficial encounters and potential social-cultural damage created by the tourism industry. Drawing on Fiji as a case study, Scheyvens and Hughes (this SI) challenged the notion that tourism may be a vehicle to support sustainable development. Specifically, the authors examine some of the critiques of tourism as a tool for "end[ing] poverty in all its forms everywhere" as stipulated in SDG 1 and ultimately highlight that the eradication of poverty would require herculean efforts in an industry that caters to the hedonic interests of holiday seekers.

Newholm (2000) reminded us that individuals increasingly express their responsibility via their consumption and the related self-image construction resulting as this is one of society's major time-consuming activities. As such, the above tourism experiences are often positioned and marketed as opportunities to conserve the environment and make a contribution to local communities which often times allows western travellers to position themselves as moral beings and/or reconcile their guilt (see Butcher, 2006).

In addition to commodity fetishism, a "bucket list" mentality of accumulating an impressive list of visited travel destinations has been documented in the literature. For example, McKay (2014) described a bucket list mentality in her interpretation of addicted or dedicated adventure rafters seeking ultimate white-water such as the Ash River in South Africa. Taylor, Grimwood, and Boluk (2018) argued that enhanced captive elephant welfare is hindered by Western tourists' bucket list mentality in Thailand. Specifically, they identify the bucket list mentality as representing a narrow-mindedness among tourists to simply engage in experiences in order to tick them off their lists. Such lists then provide the impetus to act upon desires given that this is interpreted as *the* experience to engage in. This constructed discourse supports an egocentric mentality blocking the process of grappling with any critical concerns about the welfare impacts of their actions. Such examples of addictive behavioural tendencies recognise the hedonic behaviours asserted by Marx (1867) and adverse impacts for tourism.

There are examples however where consumers participate in driving alternative approaches by supporting businesses that implement sustainability. Higgins-Desbiolles and Wijesinghe's contribution (this SI) addressed the ways restaurant patrons support sustainability agendas by choosing sustainable restaurants and how such restaurants support: "implementation of specific SDGs; using food as a way to unite and empower people; educating their stakeholders about environmental and community impacts of sustainability practices; and indeed, even critical questioning" (p.x) of sustainability. However, such restaurants still must support an economic bottom-line and the patrons are often engaging in prestige consumption so critical questioning of such transitions to ethical consumption remain essential.

Relationships between consumption and identity challenge the acceptance of sustainability in tourism. We are reminded of Mowforth and Munt's (1998) argument that sustainable tourism was the industry's way to rationalise the consumption of the environment, commodifying it for the tourists' gaze and enforcing its preservation as an exclusive amenity for advantaged tourists. The discussion analysing consumption and production in the tourism industry highlights a lack of criticality in research addressing sustainability in tourism (Budeanu, Miller, Moscardo, & Ooi, 2016). These observed gaps provided the impetus to this SI, which inspired the collection of articles mobilising critical thinking as a way to assess current attainments in sustainability of tourism systems. In doing so, we seize the opportunity presented by the UN's 2030 SDGs framework to consider the tourism industry as it currently is, and also what it could be.

Conclusion

As noted in the introduction to this article, McCloskey (2015) offered a considered critique of the failure of the MDGs which he attributed to a lack of critical consciousness to the structural contexts of poverty and under-development. His remedy was "development education" which would draw the public into the consideration of sustainability and the structural causes of poverty; entailing "persuading the development sector as a whole to take a larger view of the development process" (McCloskey, 2015, p. 192). He urged understanding of the structural impacts of neoliberalism rather than band-aid solutions of development aid. This work alerted us to the role of education in fostering transitions to sustainability as we applied a critical lens to the 2030 UN SDG agenda. McCloskey's critique reinforces the necessity to situate our analyses of tourism within a wider context of holistic sustainable development and avoiding a myopic focus of merely sustaining tourism (Higgins-Desbiolles, 2018).

This article has offered tools for critically thinking through the potential for the SDGs to help shape the tourism industry for more sustainable, equitable and just futures. We positioned six themes to serve as a conceptual framework for interrogating the SDG agenda in tourism. (1) Critical tourism scholarship is essential in fostering the critical thinking skills required to holistically interrogate tourism development. (2) Gender in development and feminism must underpin our work to empower women for equal contributions to all roles in tourism essential for co-creating sustainable futures. Feminist thinking also foregrounds issues of oppression and justice prompting us to ask critical questions of who benefits and who is excluded. (3) Indigenous and alternative paradigms bring other values to the fore and widen the array of possibilities we consider. (4) Degrowth and transitions to a circular economy presents alternative paradigms under development which provide evidence that there are viable alternatives to the pervasive pro-growth neoliberal model of capitalism. (5) Considerations of ethical consumption and production remind us that tourism is not only a business and development sector but also a moral sphere; accordingly, all stakeholders have ethical responsibilities that must be further examined. (6) Issues and mechanisms of governance are essential to shape tourism's future into a form that is equitable, inclusive, just, ecologically compatible and thereby sustainable. Thus, our analysis indicates how this critical framework assists in interrogating and influencing the way the UN SDG agenda is enacted in the domain of tourism.

This SI presents cutting edge research from diverse contributing authors and perspectives that challenge us to deepen and widen our critical lens specifically as we strive to decouple the challenges, limitations, and opportunities in achieving the SDGs. We propose that one essential component to furthering sustainability is through the application of critical thinking within our multilateral covenants. This may allow for a propulsion toward transitions for sustainable livelihoods for all. In order to combat injustice, question positions of power, subvert corporate domination and give rights to those without voices (human and non-human) we must first challenge political and economic structures to circumvent business as usual approaches that currently control socio-ecological processes. This SI broadens the discussion and considerations of the role and value of critical thinking to further tourism sustainability via the SDGs.

Further research is required to deepen the understanding of how activating critical thinking could contribute to the redistribution of power, attaining equity, new economic paradigms and biocultural conservation that can enact benchmarking toward realising inclusive sustainability within the tourism system. While this SI is the first to call on scholars to consider how critical thinking may propel sustainability in tourism systems, in specific reflection of the UN's 2030 SDGs, we do not expect, and indeed we hope, it will not be the last. With this SI, we would like to call on scholars to critically reflect on the SDGs and challenge how tourism may be a conduit for enhanced sustainability. Our intention is for this SI to inspire future empirical and philosophical inquiry into the role of critical thinking for furthering sustainability not only in relation to the UN SDG agenda but also beyond 2030. As demonstrated here, critical thinking enables interrogation of our assumptions of ways of being, knowing and doing tourism in order to envision radical pathways to a fairer and more sustainable future for all.

Acknowledgements

We would like to thank the editors of the *Journal of Sustainable Tourism*, and particularly Professor James Higham, for his support and guidance during the development of this Special Issue. We also thank the authors for their contributions and the many reviewers who provided their advice and expertise.

Disclosure statement

No potential conflict of interest was reported by the authors.

References

Ali, S. (2009). Black feminist praxis: Some reflections on pedagogies and politics in higher education. *Race, Ethnicity and Education, 12*(1), 79–88. doi:10.1080/13613320802650998

Assadourian, E. (2012). The path to degrowth in overdeveloped countries. In E. Assadourian & M. Renner (Eds.), *State of the world 2012: Moving toward sustainable prosperity* (pp. 22–37). Washington, DC: Island Press.

Ateljevic, I., Morgan, N., & Pritchard, A. (Eds.). (2013). *The critical turn in tourism studies: Creating an academy of hope*. London: Routledge.

Beaumont, N., & Dredge, D. (2010). Local tourism governance: A comparison of three network approaches. *Journal of Sustainable Tourism, 18*(1), 7–28. doi:10.1080/09669580903215139

Beijing Declaration. (1989). *Fourth World Conference on Women*. Retrieved from http://www.un.org/womenwatch/daw/beijing/platform/declar.htm.

Belhassen, Y., & Caton, K. (2011). On the need for critical pedagogy in tourism education. *Tourism Management, 32*(6), 1389–1396. doi:10.1016/j.tourman.2011.01.014

Bianchi, R. V. (2009). The 'critical turn' in tourism studies: A radical critique. *Tourism Geographies, 11*(4), 484–504. doi:10.1080/14616680903262653

Bianchi, R., & Stephensen, M. (2014). *Tourism and citizenship rights, freedoms and responsibilities in the global order*. London: Routledge.

Blanchard, L., & Higgins-Desbiolles, F. (2013). Peace matters, tourism matters. In L. Blanchard & F. Higgins-Desbiolles (Eds.), *Peace through tourism promoting human security through international citizenship* (pp. 19–33). London: Routledge.

Blaser, M. (2004). Life projects: Indigenous peoples' agency and development. In M. Blaser, H. A. Feit, & G. McRae (Eds.), *In the way of development: Indigenous peoples, life projects and globalization* (pp. 26–46). London: Zed.

Boluk, K. (2011). Fair Trade Tourism South Africa: A pragmatic poverty reduction mechanism? *Tourism. Planning and Development, 8*(3), 237–251. doi:10.1080/21568316.2011.591152

Boluk, K., & Carnicelli, S. (2019). Tourism for the emancipation of the oppressed: Towards a critical tourism educa- tion drawing on Freirean philosophy. *Annals of Tourism Research, 76*, 168–179. doi:10.1016/j.annals.2019.04.002

Bramwell, B., Higham, J., Lane, B., & Miller, G. (2017). Twenty-five years of sustainable tourism and theJournal of Sustainable Tourism: Looking back and moving forward. *Journal Ofsustainable Tourism, 25*(1), 1–9.

Bramwell, B., & Lane, B. (1993). Sustainabletourism:Anevolvingglobalapproach. *Journal of SustainableTourism,1*,1-5.

Bramwell, B., & Lane, B. (2011). Critical research on the governance of tourism and sustainability. *Journal of Sustainable Tourism, 19*(4–5), 411–421. doi:10.1080/09669582.2011.580586

Budeanu, A., Miller, G., Moscardo, G., & Ooi, C. S. (2016). Sustainable tourism, progress, challenges and opportunities: Introduction to special volume. *Journal of Cleaner Production, 111*(Part B), 16285–16294. doi:10.1016/j.jclepro.2015.10.027

Büscher, B., & Fletcher, R. (2017). Destructive creation: Capital accumulation and the structural violence of tourism. *Journal of Sustainable Tourism, 25*(5), 651–667. doi:10.1080/09669582.2016.1159214

Butcher, J. (2006). Response to building a decommodified research paradigm in tourism: The contribution of NGOs by Stephen Wearing, Matthew McDonald and Jess Ponting. *Journal of Sustainable Tourism, 14*(3), 424–455.

Campos, M. J. Z., Hall, C. M., & Backlund, S. (2018). Can MNCs promote more inclusive tourism? Apollo tour opera- tor's sustainability work. *Tourism Geographies, 20*, 630–652.

Carnicelli, S., & Boluk, K. (2017). The promotion of social justice: Learning for transformative education. *Journal of Hospitality, Leisure, Sport & Tourism Education (JoHLSTE), 21*(Part B), 126–134. doi:10.1016/j.jhlste.2017.01.003

Caton, K., Schott, C., & Daniele, R. (2014). Tourism's imperative for global citizenship. *Journal of Teaching in Travel & Tourism, 14*, 123–128. doi:10.1080/15313220.2014.907955

Cavaliere, C. T. (2017a). *Cultivating climate consciousness: Agritourism providers' perspectives of farms, food and place.* (Doctor of Philosophy Dissertation). Retrieved from University of Otago: http://hdl.handle.net/10523/7476

Cavaliere, C. T. (2017b). Foodscapes as alternate ways of knowing: Advancing sustainability and climate conscious- ness through tactile space. In S. Slocum & C. Kline (Eds), *Linking Urban and rural tourism: Strategies for sustain- ability*. Oxfordshire, United Kingdom: CABI International.

Chambers, D., Munar, A. M., Khoo-Lattimore, C., & Biran, A. (2017). Interrogating gender and the tourism academy through epistemological lens. *Anatolia, 28*(4), 501–513. doi:10.1080/13032917.2017.1370775

Cohen, S. A., Higham, J. E. S., & Cavaliere, C. T. (2011). Binge flying behavioural addiction and climate change. *Annals of Tourism Research, 38*(3), 1070–1089. doi:10.1016/j.annals.2011.01.013

Crellin, Z. (2016, 11 March). *84% of Australian fast food restaurants underpay workers*. International Business Times. Retrieved from http://www.ibtimes.com.au/84-australian-fast-food-restaurants-underpay-workers-two-melbourne-underpaid-employees-over-9000.

Daly, M. (2017, 16 March). New Zealand's Whanganui River gets the legal rights of a person. The Sydney Morning Herald Online. Retrieved from https://www.smh.com.au/environment/new-zealands-whanganui-river-gets-the-legal-rights-of-a-person-20170316-guz43n.html.

Dredge, D., & Jamal, T. (2015). Progress in tourism planning and policy: A post-structural perspective on knowledge production. *Tourism Management, 51*, 285–297. doi:10.1016/j.tourman.2015.06.002

Enloe, C. (1989). *Bananas, beaches and bases: Making feminist sense of international politics*. Berkeley: University of California Press.

Equality in Tourism (n.d.). Our Vision. Retrieved from http://equalityintourism.org/our-vision/

Equality in Tourism. (2017). Equality in Tourism responds to UNWTO Discussion Paper on International Year of sustainable tourism for development 2017. Retrieved from http://equalityintourism.org/equality-in-tourism-responds-to-unwto-discussion-paper-on-the-occasion-of-the-international-year-of-sustainable-tourism-for-development-2017/.

Ferguson, L., & Alarcon, D. M. (2015). Gender and sustainable tourism: Reflections on theory and practice. *Journal of Sustainable Tourism, 23*(3), 401–416. doi:10.1080/09669582.2014.957208

Fletcher, E. H., & Piemonte, N. M. (2017). Navigating the paradoxes of neoliberalism: Quiet subversion in mentored service-learning for the pre-health humanities. *Journal of Medical Humanities, 38*(4), 397–407. doi:10.1007/s10912-017-9465-1

Freire, P. (1970). *The pedagogy of the oppressed*. New York: Herder and Herder.

Freire-Medeiros, B. (2013). *Touring Poverty*. New York: Routledge.

Gahman, L. (2016). Dismantling neoliberal education: A lesson from the Zapatistas. *Roar Magazine*. Retrieved from https://roarmag.org/essays/neoliberal-education-zapatista-pedagogy/

Giroux, H. A. (2011). *On Critical Pedagogy*. New York: Bloomsbury

Giroux, H. A. (2004). Public pedagogy and the politics of neo-liberalism: Making the political more pedagogical. *Policy Futures in Education, 2*(3), &4), 494–503. doi:10.2304/pfie.2004.2.3.5

Giroux, H. A. (2014). Thinking dangerously in an age of political betrayal. Truthout, opinion piece. Retrieved from https://truthout.org/articles/henry-a-giroux-thinking-dangerously-in-an-age-of-political-betrayal/

Gren, M., & Huijbens, E. H. (2014). Tourism and the anthropocene. *Scandinavian Journal of Hospitality and Tourism, 14*(1), 6–22. doi:10.1080/15022250.2014.886100

Groulx, M., Boluk, K., Lemieux, C. J., & Dawson, J. (2019). Place stewardship among last chance tourists. *Annals of Tourism Research, 75*, 202–212. doi:10.1016/j.annals.2019.01.008

Gruenewald, D. A. (2003). Foundations of place: A multidisciplinary framework for place-conscious education. *American Educational Research Journal, 40*(3), 619–654.

Hall, C. M. (2008). *Tourism planning: Policies, processes and relationships* (2nd ed.). Harlow: Pearson Prentice Hall.

Hall, C. M. (2011). A typology of governance and its implications for tourism policy analysis. *Journal of Sustainable Tourism, 19*(4-5), 437–457. doi:10.1080/09669582.2011.570346

Hall, C. M., & Gössling, S. (2013). *Sustainable culinary systems: Local foods, innovation, tourism and hospitality*. London, UK: Routledge.

Hall, C. M., & Tucker, H. (2004). *Tourism and postcolonialism: Contested discourses, identities and representations*. New York: Routledge.

Harrison, R., Newholm, T., & Shaw, D. (2005). *The ethical consumer*. London: Sage Publications.

Harvey, D. (2005). *A brief history of neoliberalism*. Oxford: Oxford University Press.

Harvey, D. (2007). Neoliberalism as creative destruction. *Annals of American Academy of Political and Social Science, 610*, 22–44.

Higgins-Desbiolles, F. (2006). More than an industry: Tourism as a social force. *Tourism Management, 27*(6), 1192–1208. doi:10.1016/j.tourman.2005.05.020

Higgins-Desbiolles, F. (2010). The elusiveness of sustainability in tourism: The culture-ideology of consumerism and its implications. *Tourism and Hospitality Research, 10*(2), 116–129. doi:10.1057/thr.2009.31

Higgins-Desbiolles, F. (2018). Sustainable tourism: Sustaining tourism or something more? *Tourism Management Perspectives, 25*(1), 157–160. doi:10.1016/j.tmp.2017.11.017

Higgins-Desbiolles, F., & Blanchard, L. (2010). Challenging peace through tourism: Placing tourism in the context of human rights, justice and peace. In O. Moufakkir, & I. Kelly (eds.). Tourism Progress and Peace (pp.35–47). Oxford: CABI.

Higgins-Desbiolles, F., & Powys Whyte, K. (2013). No high hopes for hopeful tourism: A critical comment. *Annals of Tourism Research, 40*, 428–433. doi:10.1016/j.annals.2012.07.005

Hollinshead, K. (1992). White gaze, 'Red people' – Shadow visions: the disidentification of 'Indians' in cultural tourism. *Leisure Studies*, *11*(1), 43–64. doi:10.1080/02614369100390301

Hollinshead, K. (2009). *Tourism and the social production methodologies*. Amsterdam: Elsevier.

Inayatullah, S. (1995). Rethinking tourism: Unfamiliar histories and alternative futures. *Tourism Management*, *16*(6), 411–415. doi:10.1016/0261-5177(95)00048-S

Inskeep, E. (1991). *Tourism Planning: An Integrated and Sustainable Development Approach*. New York: Can Nostrand Reinhold.

Jamal, T., & Camargo, B. A. (2018). Tourism governance and policy: Whither justice? *Tourism Management Perspectives*, *25*(1), 205–208. doi:10.1016/j.tmp.2017.11.009

Jamal, T., & Hollinshead, K. (2001). Tourism and the forbidden zone: The underserved power of qualitative inquiry. *Tourism Management*, *22*(1), 63–82. doi:10.1016/S0261-5177(00)00020-0

Jamal, T., & Stronza, A. (2009). Collaboration theory and tourism practice in protected areas: Stakeholders, structuring and sustainability. *Journal of Sustainable Tourism*, *17*(2), 169–189. doi:10.1080/09669580802495741

Johnson, L., & Morris, P. (2010). Towards a framework for critical citizenship education. *The Curriculum Journal*, *21*(1), 77–96. doi:10.1080/09585170903560444

Joseph, C. (2012). Internationalizing the curriculum: Pedagogy for social justice. *Current Sociology*, *60*(2), 239–257. doi:10.1177/0011392111429225

Kallis, G., Kostakis, V., Lange, S., Muraca, B., Paulson, S., & Schmelzer, M. (2018). Research on degrowth. *Annual Review of Environment and Resources*, *43*(1), 291–316. doi:10.1146/annurev-environ-102017-025941

Kincheloe, J. L. (2008). *Critical pedagogy primer* (2nd ed.). New York, NY: Peter Lang.

Klein, R. A. (2010). The cruise sector and its environmental impact. In C. Schott (Ed.), *Tourism and the implications of climate change: Issues and actions* (pp. 113–130). Bingley: Emerald.

Lovelock, B. (2008). Ethical travel decisions travel agents and human rights. *Annals of Tourism Research*, *35*(2), 338–358. doi:10.1016/j.annals.2007.08.004

Macbeth, J. (2005). Towards an ethics platform for tourism. *Annals of Tourism Research*, *32*(4), 962–984. doi:10.1016/j.annals.2004.11.005

Mancini, M. S., Galli, A., Coscieme, L., Niccolucci, V., Lin, D., Pulselli, F. M., … Marchettini, N. (2018). Exploring ecosystem services assessment through ecological footprint accounting. *Ecosystem Services*, *30*, 228–235. doi:10.1016/j.ecoser.2018.01.010

Marx, K. (1867). The fetishism of commodities and the secret thereof. *Capital: A Critique of Political Economy*, *1*, 71–83.

McCloskey, S. (2015). Viewpoint: From MDGs to SDGs: We need a critical awakening to succeed. In S. McCloskey (Ed.), *Policy and practice: A development education review* (pp. 186–194). Carson, CA: Center for Global Education.

McKay, T. J. M. (2014). White water adventure tourism on the Ash River, South Africa. *African Journal for Physical, Health Education, Recreation and Dance*, *20*(1), 52–75.

Miller, C., & Razavi, S. (1998). *Gender analysis: Alternative paradigms. Gender in development monograph series, 6*. New York: United Nations Development Program.

Munar, A. M., & Waiting for the Dawn. (2015). The gender gap in the tourism academy. Retrieved from http://www/tourismeducationfutures.org/about-tefi/gender-equity-in-the-tourism-ac.

Munro, E. (2013). Feminism: A fourth wave? *Political Insight*, *4*(2), 22–25. doi:10.1111/2041-9066.12021

Moscardo, G., & Hughes, K. (2018). All aboard! Strategies for engaging guests in corporate responsibility programmes. *Journal of Sustainable Tourism*, *26*(7), 1257–1272. doi:10.1080/09669582.2018.1428333

Mostafanezhad, M. (2014). Volunteer tourism and the popular humanitarian gaze. *Geoforum*, *54*, 111–118. doi:10.1016/j.geoforum.2014.04.004

Mowforth, M., Charlton, C., & Munt, I. (2008). *Tourism and responsibility: Perspectives from Latin America and the Caribbean*. London: Routledge.

Mowforth, M., & Munt, I. (1998). *Tourism and sustainability: New tourism in the Third World*. London: Routledge.

Murray, A., Skene, K., & Haynes, K. (2017). The circular economy: An interdisciplinary exploration of the concept and application in a global context. *Journal of Business Ethics*, *140*(3), 369–380. doi:10.1007/s10551-015-2693-2

Newholm, T. (2000). Consumer exit, voice, and loyalty: Indicative, legitimation, and regulatory role in agricultural and food ethics. *Journal of Agricultural and Environmental Ethics*, *12*(2), 153–164. doi:10.1023/A:1009590630426

Nurvala, J.-P. (2015). 'Uberisation' is the future of the digitalised labour market. *European View*, *14*(2), 231–239. doi:10.1007/s12290-015-0378-y

O'Reilly, A. M. (1986). Tourism carrying capacity: Concept and issues. *Tourism Management*, *7*(4), 254–258.

Patinkin, J. (2013). *Battle over the Serengeti pits Maasai against Dubai. Christian Science Monitor*. Retrieved from https://www.csmonitor.com/World/Africa/2013/0430/Battle-over-the-Serengeti-pits-Maasai-against-Dubai.

Pereiro, X., De León, C., Mauri, M. M., Ventocilla, J., & Del Valle, Y. (2012). *Los turistores kunas: Antropología del turismo étnico en Panamá*. Palma, Spain: Universitat de les Illes Balears.

Poulston, J. (2008). Metamorphosis in hospitality: A tradition of sexual harassment. *International Journal of Hospitality Management*, *27*(2), 232–240. doi:10.1016/j.ijhm.2007.07.013

Pritchard, A. (2007). *Tourism and gender: Embodiment, sensuality and experience*. Wallingford: CABI.

Pritchard, A., Morgan, N., & Ateljevic, I. (2011). Hopeful tourism: A new transformative perspective. *Annals of Tourism Research, 38*(3), 941–963. doi:10.1016/j.annals.2011.01.004

Salleh, A. (2010). Climate strategy: Making the choice between ecological modernisation or living well. *Journal of Australian Political Economy, 66*, 118–143.

Sami Parliament of Sweden endorses the Universal Declaration of Rights of Mother Earth. (2018). Retrieved from http://www.naturensrattigheter.se/2018/05/29/the-sami-parliament-of-sweden-endorses-the-universal-declaration-of-rights-of-mother-earth/

Scheyvens, R. (2011). *Tourism and poverty*. New York: Routledge.

Scheyvens, R., Banks, G., & Hughes, E. (2016). The private sector and the SDGs: The need to move beyond 'business as usual'. *Sustainable Development, 24*(6), 371–382. doi:10.1002/sd.1623

Shiva, V. (1993). *Monocultures of the mind: Perspectives on biodiversity and biotechnology*. London: Zed Books.

Shiva, V. (2009). Development, ecology and women. In D. Clowney & P. Mosto (Eds.), *Earthcare: An anathology in environmental ethics* (pp. 273–282). Lanham: Bowman and Littlefield.

Sinclair, M. T. (1997). *Gender, work and tourism*. London: Routledge.

Sloan, P., Legrand, W. & Chen, J. (2013). *Sustainability in the hospitality Industry:Principles of Sustainable Operations* (2nd ed.). London: Routledge.

Snow, S. G., & Wheeler, C. L. (2000). Pathways in the periphery: Tourism to Indigenous communities in Panama. *Social Science Quarterly, 81*(3), 732–749.

Snyder, G. (2010). *The practice of the wild*. Berkeley, CA: Counterpoint Press.

Stevens, C. (2010). *Are women the key to sustainable development? Sustainable Development Insights, 003*. Boston: Boston University.

Stewart-Harawira, M. (2005). *The new imperial order: Indigenous responses to globalisation*. London: Zed books.

Swain, M. B. (1995). Gender in tourism. *Annals of Tourism Research, 22*(2), 247–266. doi:10.1016/0160-7383(94)00095-6

Taylor, M., Grimwood, B., & Boluk, K. (2018). Caring for animal welfare: Volunteer tourists and captive elephant well-being in Thailand. In B. S. R., Grimwood, H., Mair, K., Caton, & M. Muldoon (Eds.), *Tourism and wellness. Travel for the good of all?* (pp. 71–94). Lanham: Lexington Books.

Tribe, J. (2000). Balancing the vocational: The theory and practice of liberal education in tourism. *The International Journal of Tourism and Hospitality Research (the Surrey Quarterly Review), 2*, 9–26.

Tribe, J. (2008). Tourism: A critical business. *Journal of Travel Research, 46*(3), 245–255. doi:10.1177/0047287507304051

Turner, L., & Ash, J. (1975). *The golden hordes: International tourism and the pleasure periphery*. London: Constable.

Tyrvainen, L., Uusitalo, M., Silvennoinen, H., & Hasu, E. (2014). Towards sustainable growth in nature-based tourism destinations: Clients' views of land use options in Finnish Lapland. *Landscape and Urban Planning, 122*, 1–15. doi:10.1016/j.landurbplan.2013.10.003

UN. (2008). United Nations Declaration on the Rights of Indigenous Peoples. Retrieved from http://www.un.org/esa/socdev/unpfii/documents/DRIPS_en.pdf.

UN. (2019). Sustainable development goals. Retrieved from http://www.undp.org/content/undp/en/home/sustainable-development-goals.html

UN Women. (n.d). World conferences on women. Retrieved from http://www.unwomen.org/en/how-we-work/intergovernmental-support/world-conferences-on-women.

UNWTO. (2017a). *Discussion paper on the occasion of the international year of sustainable tourism for development*. Madrid: UNWTO.

UNWTO. (2017b). Discussion paper on sustainable tourism for development. Retrieved from http://media.unwto.org/content/unwto-news-1-special-international-year-sustainable-tourism-development-edition.

United Nations Department of Economic and Social Affairs [UNDESA]. (2018). Experts explore potential of global transition to circular economy. Retrieved from https://www.un.org/development/desa/en/news/intergovernmental-coordination/potential-of-transition-to-circular-economy.html

Universal Declaration of Rights of Mother Earth. (2010). World people's conference on climate change and the rights of mother earth, Cochabamba, Bolivia. Retrieved from http://therightsofnature.org/universal-declaration/.

Urry, J. (1990). *The tourist gaze: Leisure and travel in contemporary societies*. Thousand Oaks, CA: Sage Publications.

Weeden, C., & Boluk, K. (Eds.). (2014). *Managing ethical consumption in tourism*. London: Routledge.

Whyte, K. P. (2013). On the role of traditional ecological knowledge as a collaborative concept: A philosophical study. *Ecological Processes, 2*(7), 2–7. https://doi-org.access.library.unisa.edu.au/10.1186/2192-1709

Zappile & Cavaliere, 2018 Zappile, T. & Cavaliere, C. T. (2018). Mobilizing the private sector in tourism: A conceptual framework of corporate social environmental responsibility towards improvements in bio-cultural conservation and biocapacity. In *Sustainability and Development Conference*. Ann Arbor, Michigan, USA: University of Michigan. Retrieved from https://umsustdev.org/wp-content/uploads/2018/11/SDCSubmission194.pdf

A pedagogical framework for the development of the critical tourism citizen

Karla A. Boluk, Christina T. Cavaliere and Lauren N. Duffy

ABSTRACT

The Sustainable Development Goals (SDGs) are an international frame-work to improve global wellbeing, and SDG 4 Quality Education serves as a substructure to achieve sustainability. However, absent from the SDGs is explicit reference to critical thinking which is needed to con-tend with structures of power. Similarly, tertiary education systems glo-bally are facing challenges due to appropriation by neoliberal agendas favouring capitalism over cogitation. Accordingly, the aim of this paper is to propose a framework for bringing criticality to sustainable tourism education to strengthen SDG 4 and empower future decision- makers as Critical Tourism Citizens (CTC). A definition of a CTC is presented to further critical citizenship scholarship in tourism. This paper examines the role of criticality in advancing sustainability in tourism. Supported by empirical qualitative data, we propose a pedagogical framework that aids critical examination of tourism systems to advance sustainability in relation to the SDGs. The framework is positioned within current schol-arship on global citizenship and critical citizenship education to propel theory into praxis.

Introduction

Universities have long been associated with cultivating spaces for critical thought, dialogue and debate, and introspection. Neoliberalism within higher education is now increasingly elevating the priorities of research metrics, external funding and job-readiness (Giroux, 2016). Current man-agerial, business-oriented foci in recreation, events, tourism and hospitality programs tend to overshadow criticality. This compromises the development of students who can contribute to the critique of the tourism phenomenon (Ayikoru, Tribe, & Airey, 2009; Dredge et al., 2012; Fullagar & Wilson, 2012; McLaren & Jaramillo, 2013; Tribe, 2005, 2008). The emphasis on prioritiz-ing economic growth and acquisition of wealth has superseded socio-cultural and environmental interests in local communities, which lie at the heart of the sustainable tourism agenda (Assadourian, 2012).

Building on the Millennium Development Goals, the United Nations' (UN) *Transforming our World 2030 Agenda for Sustainable Development* outlines 17 Sustainable Development Goals (SDGs). The SDGs present recommendations centered on achieving social and environmental justice and offer direction for addressing complex sustainability challenges. The preamble notes the importance of the SDGs embedded into everyday discourse if they are to be realized (UN, 2015). Yet surveys indicate that knowledge of the SDGs is poor; an international study investigating awareness of the SDGs in 24 countries (over 56,000 people) discovered that only 1% of informants were 'very' familiar and 36% did 'not know them at all' (Lampert & Papadongonas, 2016, p. 10).

The ability to think critically through complex issues of sustainability is also needed (Holdsworth & Thomas, 2015; Kearins & Springett, 2003). This notion is reflective of the evolution from *education about sustainability* that implied content coverage, to *education for sustainability* (EfS), requiring individuals to develop "skills in critical inquiry and systematic thinking to explore the complexity and implications of sustainable development" (Holdsworth & Thomas, 2015, p. 138). Researchers within EfS have presented the importance of values and morality in their programs (Sibbel, 2009; Springett, 2005).

Critical tourism studies focus on under explored issues of power, justice, equity, representation and access (Ateljevic, Morgan, & Pritchard, 2013). Within tourism education, growing interest in critical tourism scholarship has translated into calls for more critical, and transformative approaches across curricula and classrooms (see Belhassen & Caton, 2011; Boluk & Carnicelli, 2019; Cotterell, Arcodia, & Ferreira, 2017; Crossley, 2017; Farber Canziani, Sönmez, Hsieh, & Byrd, 2012; Fullagar & Wilson, 2012; Jamal, Taillon, & Dredge, 2011; McKercher & Prideaux, 2011; McLaren & Jaramillo, 2013; Moscardo, 2015; Schwarzin, 2013; Sheldon, Fesenmaier, & Tribe, 2008; 2011). Crossley (2017) notes, "there is general consensus that tourism education has remained largely insulated from these radical and potentially transformative academic currents" (p. 428).

Thus, this paper is premised on three ideas. First, there is an intersection between sustainable tourism and critical tourism studies, deemed *critical sustainable tourism*. Issues of sustainability cannot be solved without a critical lens that recognizes influences of power, poverty, inequality and ideology in tourism. Secondly, this paper reflects upon the presence of critical thinking and critical pedagogy and responds to calls for criticality in research approaches in tourism (e.g., Tribe, 2008) and for criticality in tourism education (e.g., Boluk & Carnicelli, 2019; Crossley, 2017; Fullagar & Wilson, 2012). While critical thinking reflects skills that allow for a more systematic process of reasoning, critical pedagogy is the explicit engagement with critical inquiry that seeks to undercover power structures (Burbules & Berk,1999; Huckle, 2017). Third, this paper builds on the work of Bricker, Black, and Cottrell (2012) who recognized the connections between the former MDGs and sustainable tourism development. In line with Freire's (1970) work on *conscientization*, the authors propose that students must mutually recognize injustices and inequalities to be able to address macro and micro level challenges of sustainability in tourism.

Our paper proposes a framework for bringing criticality to sustainable tourism education to strengthen SDG 4 and empower future decision makers as *Critical Tourism Citizens* (CTC). A CTC is defined as one who through a critical disposition is mutually empathetic and willing to lead change, equipped with the understandings, skills, and capacity to acknowledge power and challenge the status quo to creatively and responsibly, progress sustainability within tourism. Our definition of the CTC responds to calls to bring criticality to the tourism classroom, particularly in the context of EfS and building on the work of Crossley (2017) and Blanchard and Higgins-Desbiolles (2013). Supported by empirical qualitative data collected through Brookfield's (1987) *Critical Incident Questionnaire* (CIQ) distributed in three North American tourism classes, the framework includes five strategies for teaching critical thinking and critical perspectives: (a) Critical Topics, (b) Critical Dialogue (c) Critical Reflection, (d) Critical Positionality and (e) Critical Praxis. Such strategies build on Crossley's (2017) work articulating a three-movement approach which comprises bringing criticality to the classroom; the conscious-raising of structural oppression through critical pedagogy; and an explicit undertaking of positionality. The strategies also build upon Blanchard and Higgins-Desbiolles' (2013) work using Freire's notion of critical consciousness and engagement.

Our paper positions the framework within the literature on *global citizenship* and *critical citizenship education*. Contemporary definitions of citizenship broadly infer ideas of what it means to be a good citizen, whereby critical citizenship education focuses on the development of an ideal and committed citizen (Johnson & Morris, 2010). Adding a component of citizenry underscores the responsibility of this conscious-raising endeavor that needs to be followed into praxis. Once students are introduced to critical sustainability issues affecting tourism, critical thinking skills and the underlying causes of unsustainable practices, they can become part of a community "oriented towards social action" (Jamal et al., 2011, p. 136).

Literature review

To achieve sustainability or sustainable tourism in practice, we must start with education. SDG 4 is described as "ensur[ing] inclusive and quality education for all and promoting lifelong learning" (UN Educational, Scientific, and Cultural Organization [UNESCO], 2018, p. 43). The 10 targets expressed within SDG 4 focus on equitable educational access, improvements of literacy rates, support for teachers, and capacity building of vocational skills. Target 4.7 is of particular importance to this paper:

> By 2030, ensure that all learners acquire the knowledge and skills needed to promote sustainable development, including, among others, through education for sustainable development and sustainable lifestyles, human rights, gender equality, promotion of a culture of peace and non-violence, global citizenship and appreciation of cultural diversity and of culture's contribution to sustainable development (UNESCO, 2017, p. 2).

Target 4.7 reflects the need to focus on sustainable development education, emphasizing social and environmental justice issues. The 2017/18 *Global Education Monitoring Report* found 51% of reporting countries have policy reflecting the inclusion of sustainable development education, 33% of whom have focused curricula and only 7% include the topic in teacher training. Indeed, "in many countries, teachers are poorly prepared to teach topics related to target 4.7" (UNESCO, 2018, p. 43). Such statistics do little to describe what is being done to teach sustainability. Education plays an important role in addressing challenges presented in the SDGs including sustainability. As Boyle (2017) states, we "can no longer afford a 'wait and see' attitude'" (p. 389). Therefore, we need to rethink how we teach sustainability in classrooms. The following sections consider the importance of critical thinking, pedagogy and citizenry as a means for developing critical tourism citizens.

Critical teaching for sustainability

Critical thinking is the ability to contemplate one's thoughts as a metacognitive activity (Paul & Binker, 1990) that is "purposeful, reasoned and goal directed" (Halpern, 2014, p. 4). Reflecting the development of analytical skills critical thinking allows one to trace logic and reasoning; it does not require engagement with a critical issue. The term *critico-creative thinking* is sometimes used interchangeably with critical thinking to emphasize focus on the creative process of identifying alternatives to problems (Fisher, 2001). In contrast, critical pedagogy is rooted in critical inquiry focusing on teaching to question and challenge dominant ideologies to create social transformation (McLaren, 2003). For a review of the differences between critical thinking and critical pedagogy, see Burbules and Berk (1999) and Huckle (2017).

The outcomes of critical pedagogy can include instilling learners with a political and ethical consciousness, an understanding of power dynamics and the creation of students who can bring about social action (Crossley, 2017; McLaren & Jaramillo, 2013). According to Giroux (2011, p. 3) education has the potential to be emancipatory and is "fundamental to democracy." Democracy is an instructional tool and theory about discourse, learning and politics (Freire, 1970) supporting exchange, questioning and self-criticism (Giroux, 2004b). Current critical pedagogues seek to challenge messages arising in higher education regarding the reinforcement of capitalism and re-instill possibilities of democratic social values in the classroom (Johnson & Morris, 2010; Kincheloe, 2008). Scholars such as Springett (2005), and Sibbel (2009) note the importance of connecting EfS to values and moral imperatives central for critical pedagogy.

Fostering critical citizenship through education

Citizenship education reinforces nationalistic qualities and reflects a broader notion of what it means to be a 'good citizen' (Althof & Berkowitz, 2006; Johnson & Morris, 2010). Understood through the principles of democratic citizenship Sherrod, Flanagan, and Youniss (2002) noted, a key element is to "move beyond one's individual self-interest and to be committed to the well-being of some larger group of which one is a member" (p. 265). Recent discussions of citizenship education adhere to Dewey's tenets of democracy where citizens deliberate respectfully and engage in problem solving. There is emergence of *critical citizenship education* aiming to question before consuming (Johnson & Morris, 2010). Individuals need to be "educated to be critical" through engagement with discussions supported in learning environments (Puolimatka, 1996, p. 329). In their application of critical citizenship to higher education curricula in South Africa, Costandius and Bitzer (2015) indicate that as a type of educational pedagogy:

> Critical citizenship encourages critical reflection on the past and the imaging of a possible future shaped by social justice to prepare people to live together in harmony in diverse societies. Critical citizenship education is therefore specifically aimed at the transformation of thinking on a personal level towards a wider public good. (p. 11)

The authors illustrate that critical citizenship education bridges the modern ideas of citizenship to criticality and interlinks awareness of political processes and power structures.

Limited scholarship has examined the notion of *critical citizenship education* within the field of tourism, although two notable studies have engaged with global citizenship. Blanchard and Higgins-Desbiolles (2013) draw on Freire's notion of critical consciousness with examples of peace in literature that evidence the "awakening of critical consciousness through the act of travel" (p. 27). They developed a *Peace Through Tourism* course that links critical thinking to global citizenship. Further, Bianchi and Stephenson (2014) examined ethical implications of the continued growth in tourism and challenged the assumption that international travel is inherently democratic and beneficial to all, considering negative impacts to those not part of capitalist mobility. They introduced new interpretations of global citizenship through 'ethical' or 'responsible' forms of travel, supporting social and/or environmental movements, giving rise to a new 'active citizen.' The authors question whether such forms of tourism nurture a sense of global civic responsibility in tourists; if so, tourism could be a tool for reconciliation and social justice. Both examples shed light on discussions concerning criticality specific to emerging *global* citizenship in tourism.

Global citizenship is defined as "awareness, caring, and embracing cultural diversity while promoting social justice and sustainability, coupled with a sense of responsibility to act" (Reysen & Katzarska-Miller, 2013, p. 1). Higgins-Desbiolles' (2006) encouraged broader thinking regarding tourism's role in global communities and Higgins-Desbiolles and Blanchard (2010) discuss prioritizing desires of tourism business at the cost of perpetuating human and environmental inequality. While global citizenship is clearly a goal of the Tourism Education Futures Initiative (TEFI) it is not explicit in the values put forth by TEFI (stewardship, knowledge, professionalism, ethics and mutuality). In 2013 TEFI7 mutually considered the capacity of tourism education as contributing to global citizenship and creating graduates who "can lead lives of consequence" (Paddison & Dredge, 2014, p. 210). Blanchard and Higgins-Desbiolles (2013) examined the role of tourism as achieving peace, promoting international relations and global citizenship and Urban (2013) highlighted the peace-building potential of tourism in Japan. Drawing on Freire's (1970) urgency to rectify the dichotomy between the oppressor and oppressed, Urbain (2013) concluded that raising awareness about atrocities and encouraging shared responsibility may lead to global citizenship.

TEFI7 also provided the groundwork for Caton, Schott, and Daniele (2014, p. 124) who argue that technologies provide insight into others' suffering, creating a "moral problem for all who live in privilege"; as such, global citizenship reflects a common humanity to promote change. Gretzel et al. (2014) drew on a case study of a leadership development program with the goal to create a network of global leaders for sustainability. Butcher (2017) draws on Dower's (2003) ideas that global citizenship reflects political concerns that span borders related to climate change and development. Butcher (2017) challenges the moral and political framework of global citizenship, suggesting problems volunteer tourists encounter that do little to prompt critical reflection and action. This contradicts Bianchi and Stephenson's (2014) notion that responsible travel may support active citizenship. Current studies draw attention to the need for awareness around cultural diversity, responsibility and sustainability in pedagogical activities to support global citizenship. However, an emphasis on critical citizenship is absent. Accordingly, building on the limited scholarship, this paper empirically explores the development of a CTC through critical pedagogy.

Integrating critical education into sustainable tourism studies is essential as students identify as consumers/travelers and future producers/professionals who may contribute to decision-making processes to advance sustainability. While raising awareness of the material relations of power and ideological forces students may understand their agency in shaping sustainable tourism agendas. Pedagogy may provide a language of both critique and possibility, mutually encouraging political and moral practice (Giroux, 2004b). It is imperative that educators and students (Freire, 1970), practice critiquing and assessing claims (Puolimatka, 1996) while also providing space for self-development.

As a political practice, pedagogy can draw attention to relationships between power and knowledge. Pedagogy can be influenced by hegemonic forces that direct what constitutes valid knowledge from identities reproduced through the socialization of education (Dadds, 2001). Educators need a critical consciousness to engage students in discussions of politics that make the "workings of power visible and accountable" (Giroux, 2004b, p. 502). As a moral practice, pedagogy may recognize what it means to invest in public life and concerns about the future. This may encourage students to locate themselves in public discourse (Giroux, 2004a). Morally committed citizens are needed to confront propensities concerning apathy, corruption and exploitation (Puolimatka, 1996). Educating critical citizens includes equipping one with the tools needed to make rational decisions; moral integrity and awareness of power that can drive transformations for a sustainable society. A CTC can mobilize learnings by actively participating in public policy and influencing positions of power promoting sustainability within tourism.

Methodology

This paper proposes a framework for bringing criticality to sustainable tourism education to strengthen SDG 4 and empower future decision makers as CTCs. Specifically, qualitative data collected from undergraduate students who completed an adapted version of Brookfield's (1987) CIQ is presented. The CIQ was administered six times in three North American university tourism classes during September–December 2016 (total $N = 72$). Brookfield's (1987) CIQ is a five-question evaluation tool encouraging student reflection on learning experiences through probing about moments they felt most engaged, distanced, affirmed, confused and surprised. The authors developed a sixth question, requiring reflection on actions students took to improve their learning. Limited scholarship has employed the CIQ to explore critical thinking and/or enhance critical

Figure 1. Strategies for fostering critical tourism citizens.

reflection, albeit, Gilstrap and Dupree (2008) who identified the CIQ as an effective tool to "assess student critical thinking" in situ, and as a formative assessment for educators highlighting opportunities to enhance teaching methods (p. 410; also see Glowacki-Dudka & Barnett, 2007). Keefer's (2009) research analyzed the CIQ after four years of organizational and academic use and notes the CIQ "should be adaptable based on learner and instructor needs (p. 181)." Thus, the CIQ was a method of data collection to study effective teaching methods and a strategy for bringing criticality to the classroom through critical reflection. The CIQ was also used to analyze how the researchers understand the role of criticality in sustainable tourism education.

Data were generated in a cross-institutional context. The first course focused on tourism and community development through a service-learning approach with a partner responsible for integrating new immigrants to the community. Students planned a welcoming event for newcomers and presented social action plans responding to community needs. The second course focused on ethical topics of international tourism and used a scenario-based learning approach challenging students to consider different perspectives related to environmental and social justice issues. The third course focused on analysis of tourism economics and included critical engagement with micro and macro impacts of implementing sustainable tourism development. Each course began with an explicit lesson on critical thinking, co-constructed by the authors, approaching topics that required questions of power structures through critical reflection using the CIQ. The researchers coordinated three class activities allowing similar content to be shared reinforcing the fundamentals of EfS and principles of sustainable tourism. The researchers mutually focused on critical thinking skill development and critical pedagogical practice.

The research team engaged in open, axial and selective coding that began during data collection; though not driven inherently by grounded theory and constant comparative analysis (see Glaser & Strauss, 1967), the process of implementing the CIQ required reflection and analysis after each round of data collection. It is incumbent upon the educator to share an overview of how students reflected on the CIQ. This process involved ongoing dialogue among the researchers throughout the semester for a deeper understanding of what criticality within sustainable tourism studies encompasses. The researchers engaged in inductive open coding of the data in their respective classes (January–July 2017). Research meetings about initial individual analysis (April–September 2017) provided opportunities to discuss similarities and differences in the data. The data were individually revisited to explore areas of overlap (axial coding) before exchanging data sets for cross analysis (September 2017). In a selective analysis process, the researchers cross-analyzed data (October 2017–January 2018) and identified themes under three areas: evidence reflecting critical thinking and transformational learning, consideration of factors leading to critical thinking and the utility of the CIQ.

In the final round of selective coding (October 2017–January 2018), the team had in-depth conversations regarding factors leading to critical thinking evidenced in the data. It was the identification of these factors, which led to the development of the pedagogical framework. Figure 1 identifies strategies, evident across data, to teach critical thinking within sustainable tourism studies. Over a two-year period, the framework resulted from ongoing individual and cross analysis of the CIQ data, continual researcher communication regarding teaching practice, deep educator-researcher reflexive practice and a cumulative literature review (August 2016–February 2018). The inductive nature of this study and the framework presented informs the basis of theory building around the ideas of critical sustainable tourism education.

The framework serves to support educators, engage students in a critical examination of EfS, and illustrates the role of critical thinking and use of critical pedagogy in transforming sustainable tourism education. The strategies are cyclic and continuous, and can be simultaneously considered and enacted. The framework is designed to foster a CTC. The following sections provide empirical evidence from the CIQs that contributed to the development of the framework strategies.

Fostering critical tourism citizens

Critical topics

Addressing sustainability in tourism places an important responsibility on graduates. Students should not merely be aware of contemporary tourism issues but should view industry concerns with a critical lens, anticipate problems that may arise and identify their accountability in responding to sustainability challenges. Boluk, Cavaliere, and Higgins-Desbiolles (2017) call for papers proposed a number of indicative themes in relation to the UN's 17 SDGs. The data revealed the impact of exposing students to an array of critical sustainable tourism topics, providing insight into tourism impacts which afforded opportunities to formulate ideas and practice responses to pressing global problems. For example, one student learned *"climate change is such a big issue, yet we keep traveling to places like the Arctic which makes it worse."* This reflection recognizes the importance of introducing pertinent critical sustainability topics, creating opportunities for considering one's personal agency.

The introduction of critical topics requires a twofold willingness from both educators and students. Educators bare a responsibility to bring forth difficult topics to the curriculum. This creates mutual discomfort yet encourages student engagement with their own critical ideas (and those of their peers, educators, scholars, media), providing opportunities to discuss topics that counter the positive status quo image of tourism. Challenging the conditions of the tourism industry was commonly recognized in student CIQ reflections *"I have learned that tourism isn't always the answer, during our council meeting I learned from my peers that tourism could potentially generate more harm to Brazil than help."* Another student shared *"I have given deeper thought into the impact of tourism and how outside sources affect the industry."* Other students considered, seemingly for the first time, that *"tourism isn't always the answer."* One student said *"in my other classes it has been stressed why tourism is important and has not been informative about the cons of tourism as well. This class has taught me about some of the negative aspects, making me think about what can be done."* Educators must provide opportunities to see how the industry intersects with other socio-ecological systems and analyze positive and negative impacts, comprehending reality versus market messages and the quality of life for local destination stakeholders monopolized by corporations. These are imperative components to understanding sustainability. Students need to be accountable and willing to engage in topics that are thought provoking and challenge their assumptions. Some students demonstrated an openness to exploring alternative ways of thinking *"my viewpoints on so many issues are changing! This class has been an eye opener!"*

Contemporary politics, specifically the right-wing populist movements and related political parties that are gaining traction in North and South America and in EU member states, coupled with the rise of the spread of misinformation that requires readers to engage in critical consumption, further complicate educational spaces. This provides a particularly challenging backdrop albeit an essential time to confront competing discourses. An appreciation for the interplay between politics and tourism is crucial, as tourism is political. The influence of right-wing political administration on destination attitudes may result in boycotts into the U.S.; right-wing narratives regarding 'unsafe' places to travel may also signal concerns, misinformation and influence choices of American travelers. This is demonstrated in travel bans and changes in visa entry processes that reduce mobility for individuals. Thus, introducing topics in the classroom around travel as a right or a privilege, implications of travel policy, and the intersection with human rights issues such as the refugee crisis and immigration are important. Our data revealed that these topics encouraged students to consider *"how much politics are connected to the course,"* *"how relatable the topics are to real life,"* and these topics generated a *"deeper understanding of international travel and how current events will impact the industry."* Specifically, one student drew a parallel between the instability in Syria and tourism, *"the Syrian [crisis] surprised me on how much it links to tourism. I didn't link this together before."* EU membership and the implications of Brexit is another example of the relationship between politics and tourism as one student reflected *"just how bad the Brexit situation is."*

Novice learners are challenged to identify essential topics to master (Young & Olutoye, 2015); contemporary issues are essential to the curriculum. Introducing an array of critical topics may encourage thought around opportunities for the tourism industry to be a conduit for equity, agency and sustainability. Such topics can draw awareness to complex problems requiring systems thinking and necessitates dialogue.

Critical dialogue

The incorporation of critical topics provides a platform to imagine potential creative solutions to address contemporary challenges facing the tourism industry and practice how one may effectively present ideas. As Crossley (2017) contends, critical content should be "accompanied by an equally important creative and dialogical pedagogical context" to which learners can be nurtured (p. 429; also see Schwarzin, 2013). The importance of critical dialogue was apparent in the data. For example, *"the group discussions have been really helpful in learning others' points of view, but also helping me articulate my own."* Another student stressed *"the group discussions helped me with the development of my own ideas."* The importance of student interaction was shared, *"I liked the group work and then discussions because it allowed me to express my thoughts and learn how my class members felt as well as my instructor."* Engaging in dialogue was particularly important to this student:

> I really liked coming together as a group and talking about what we had just read. I think the class discussions made the quality of our group's conversation even better. Normally in groups there is a lot of listening and people bringing up their isolated thoughts, but yesterday I noticed there was a lot of back and forth and that really promoted critical thinking within the group.

Critical dialogue is a pivotal strategy required to foster a CTC. A learning goal for the incorporation of critical dialogue may be to assess divergent viewpoints regarding critical tourism topics to develop an informed perspective. This requires an iterative process, critical engagement with the literature, among the learners, with the teacher (Freire, 1970) and stakeholders.

Encouraging critical dialogue provides space to practice and engage in oral articulation of opinions and to contemplate one's thinking (Paul & Binker, 1990), but also to learn the language of the tourism profession. The practice of critical dialogue requires a skill set including curiosity and inquiry, quietude and active listening, suspending assumptions, expressing one's viewpoint, and reflection. Student reflections noted a culmination of skills required in engaging in critical dialogue to understand the attitudes of others, "*it was interesting to see how other […] perspectives were either similar or different to my perspective.*" Providing the space to dialogue led to this reflection, "*I'm not as scared of public speaking and dialogue as I thought and I'm more open-minded and see things from different angles.*" Another student explained, "*The entire class engaged in an open discussion about topics especially when we broke into groups. Not many college classes encourage open discussion and, in this case, it was incredibly beneficial.*" An important outcome of providing a safe space for students to practice dialoguing is particularly relevant to progressing sustainability.

Reflection and inquiry refer to metacognition which is a primer for facilitating critical thinking (Schon, 1983). Students must reflect on the process of unpacking their thinking and can be facilitated via a Socratic approach whereby educators provide questions not answers, and thus model inquiry and facilitate critical thinking. Modelling questions categorized as procedural (those with a right or wrong answer), preference (those with no correct answer), and judgment (questions requiring critical reflection to obtain the best answer; Paul & Elder, 2006) are important in facilitating critical thinking. A Socratic paradigm aids in the analysis of information "requiring clarity, logical consistency, and self-regulation" (Oyler & Romanelli, 2014, p. 1). Socratic tactics may be challenging from the educator's perspective as to not impede the direction of the discussion and from the student's perspective to avoid groupthink. A Socratic approach may facilitate self-generated knowledge and an ability to regulate thinking which may aid in recognizing one's role in responding to sustainability challenges. Although critical dialogue could generate uncomfortable feelings, such practice will foster critical engagement.

Given the challenging political milieu educators may consider the way in which dialogue activities are deployed. Small group activities may be useful and include student research on topics alternative to their position. While sustainable development has been used as a popular conceptual framework in tourism, the tourism industry is mostly absent from the SDGs (albeit 8, 12, 14) and while the broadly written approach may lend to open interpretation across fields, the size and impact of the industry highlights the importance of sustainability considerations. Identifying critical topics will foster an opportunity to consider meanings of concepts, prioritized interests, and opportunities to deconstruct the origins of sustainable tourism. The maintenance of the status quo in sustainability is commonly ordered by capitalistic interests concerned with maintaining a linear economy, rendering environmental and socio-cultural interests as secondary (Springett, 2005). Acknowledging the nuances of the SDGs and considering different perspectives is essential to challenge the status quo and actively progress sustainability. Explicit in students' reflections was their openness to listen to alternative perspectives and engage in dialogue. Scholars have noted the difficulty in teaching interdisciplinary topics calling for critical and systems thinking to effectively address the complexities (Capra, 1996; Coops et al., 2015). That is, "the more we study the major problems of our time, the more we come to realize that they cannot be understood in isolation. They are systematic problems and are interconnected and interdependent" (Capra, 1996, p. 4).

Critical reflection

Active reflection of the educator and learner is a necessary component to invoke an emphasis on participation in one's own learning process. Identifying the importance for reflexivity in tourism pedagogy is not new. Fullagar and Wilson (2012) highlighted the implications of "narrow criticality" which may "run the risk of becoming unreflexive about power-knowledge," and halt opportunities for "thinking and acting" (p. 2). Critical reflexivity creates opportunities to consider ways to address sustainability challenges. Jamal et al. (2011) concur with Tribe (2002) regarding the need to educate reflective practitioners who can promote sustainability.

The five strategies proposed in our framework are intended to be cyclic (see Figure 1), yet critical reflection may occur as an outcome of the discussion of critical topics. Reflection may emerge from critically reading and engaging with critical discourse (Mezirow, 1998). Through critical positionality, one can critically reflect on how and why they think a certain way. One student reflected *"This was kind of eye opening for me because it's a reminder that not everyone shares the same views as myself. I have always struggled to understand how we can be so eager to help certain groups in society but are quick to discriminate and judge others."* Another student said this, *"when my group member played devil's advocate, this really made me examine my answer before I contributed."*

An additional aspect of supporting critical reflection requires intentionally building in time within the curriculum to practice this skill. Brookfield (2012) suggests that facilitating intentional silence may support learner's engagement. Planning for time to support intentional debriefing is crucial for the learner to be able to participate in active critical reflection. Purposely creating space for critical reflection led to the following *"seeing class material coincide with my daily life, watching the news and seeing the relevance to class."* Another student said, *"the moment I felt most engaged during class was when we discussed current events and relatable issues within our specific community [...] the relatable examples made it a lot easier to understand."* This demonstrates the importance of practicing this reflective skill set and provides evidence that in-class learnings hold implications beyond class.

Mezirow's (1998) research supports notions that active reflection requires time and is a challenging process that ultimately impacts one's behaviors in the future (critical praxis). A reflection highlighted *"This class has changed my perspectives on the value of being involved in the community. I am more aware and more likely to volunteer and be involved as a result of this class."* Another student shared *"the thing that surprised me the most was at the Networking Event this weekend. I was surprised with how well we were able to communicate with our family, even though there was a language barrier."* Critical reflection was also noted when some members of the university community said they would not support a fundraising activity for Syrian refugees:

> I have been surprised that people can be willing to help, but have a limitation on what they may help with. What's worse, not only are people not willing to help anyone in need, but they may not show willingness to even listen to opposing opinions. For me, one of the most important parts about my education is learning that there are other opinions, and these may be different to my own.

The relationship between critical reflection and capitalist driven proliferation of economic growth is important. Awareness between time-space compression and mindless consumption can further sustainability (Dickinson & Peeters, 2012). Capitalism and neoliberalism support production and consumption, yet quiet contemplation may facilitate critical reflection. One student shared, *"Every time we have discussions that make us think critically about the way power works, we are performing a subversive act."* This strategy is a reminder to purposefully build time into the curriculum for active reflection, intentional silence, and deliberate debriefing. Engaging with difficult topics may require deeper paradigm shifts and students must have time to process these changes.

Brookfield (2012) presents several teaching tools that support active reflection. For example, *Chalk Talk* is an activity that emphasizes the need for the educator to plan time and space for the learner to engage in active and intentional critical reflection. One student explains *"I found critical thinking most helpful because I get to use my brain and be more challenged but helpful to know what's going on in the world and how my peers feel about it."* The use of the CIQ required the researchers to plan time for critical reflection and debriefing in a structured approach. The researchers' experiences with active critical reflection allowed for awareness to balance content while reflecting on the approach to time. The CIQ requires time for both independent and group reflection and allows the educators to provide feedback about their process of critical reflection, brought forth from the instrument.

Critical positionality

The strategy of critical positionality builds on research which notes that critical thinking helps to move individuals along a continuum from weak to strong adoptions of sustainability. This 'holds up a mirror' to themselves with the contradicting discourses of consumption and sustainability (Kearins & Springett, 2003; Springett, 2005). This framework strategy brings awareness to privilege, position, and power. Critically considering our own positionality as instructors fosters an effort to co-explore ways of confronting diverse power dynamics, model critical thinking (Brookfield, 1987) and challenges hierarchies between students and teachers (Freire, 1970). Although the emphasis of this paper is not to specifically reflect on our own positionality, one way for instructors to share their insights in the classroom may be to also complete CIQs throughout the term, alongside students and share these responses with students.

The following student excerpt elucidates this strategy: *"I felt most engaged when we were discussing the premise of invisible power because I am very interested in post structuralism and how society is shaped through power dynamics."* This awareness allows for deeper investigation into the perspective of the other, opportunities to understand bias and various forms of oppression. The following illustrates the process of critically engaging with one's positionality: *"Learning about different cultures and differences between countries. The different "norms" that each country has that we may not have previously considered."*

Through implementation of this strategy, an educator may encourage students to consider their perspectives, providing space to pivot following reflection: *"What surprised me is how often people are marginalized for no apparent reason. I find we are very quick to judge without knowing the circumstances that one has been through in their lives and we tend to target the things about people that they have no control over."* The ability to change one's vantage point following reflection on one's privilege or lack thereof, and to embrace the practice of flexibility of perception, can strengthen understandings of the other. Critical positionality helps students develop empathy, humility and understanding of their own position and that of others. Brookfield (1995) argues that to critically reflect we must 'hunt our assumptions' about the world. Through this process we can build a deeper respect for diverse perspectives and encourage reduction in predominant Western-centric perspectives that dominate discourse, international policy and teaching materials.

Winter (2009, p. 23) explains how tourism's key concepts remain influenced by Western Europe and North American perspectives; "The Western-centric modus operandi of research and teaching which endures today means the geographic, cultural and racial biases in the field remain a common blind-spot." Teaching for critical positionality brings forth the educator's and learner's biases and assumptions which in turn may reframe worldviews. Another student shared how the consideration of ethics allowed for a more thorough understanding of tourism impacts *"I thought about the ethics of tourism because I can see how it has negative impacts, and I also see the positives."* After a classroom activity that encouraged consideration of critical positionality a student shared *"Getting to think about what is ethical and what is not, made me feel most engaged."*

From a more philosophical perspective and imperative for achieving sustainability, we need to critically position ourselves within the realities of the violence of capitalism (Žižek, 2008). One student reflected *"How unethical society can be, especially when money is involved. It's sickening how little people care about one another versus how much profit they will get."* Radical views contend with the role that multilateral international organizations serve in proliferation of capitalism and assaults on nature and culture (Salleh, 2010). Another student reflected *"I found it confusing that people don't think about how the locals feel about tourism."* Through critical positionality we may be able to encourage engagement with the impacts of capitalistic structures on bio-cultural conservation. Another student shared, *"This week's lesson made me realize a different side of sustainability other than just affecting the environment.*" The reflections shared here suggest that teaching for critical positionality is imperative to furthering actions toward holistic sustainability.

Critical praxis

Inherent in our framework for the development of a CTC is that it moves from theory to praxis, or as Freire (1970) described, an "authentic union" of critical reflection and action (p. 48; also see Johnson & Morris, 2010). Therefore, in bringing forth critical topics, engaging in critical dialogue and reflection, and recognizing one's positionality, a foundation is built to apply abstract critical theory to real world situations. This is premised on the idea that justice requires action (Freire, 1970) and all human behavior is either in support of, or in opposition to dominant ideology and social order (Giroux, 1983). A student reflected on awareness around the lack of engagement in the community, "*I felt puzzled with all the ways [my state] can be sustainable and yet I feel like no one is taking action to do so.*" Tourism educators must provide opportunities for translating critic-ality in the classroom to criticality in practice, to create professionals who are prepared to enact against injustices (Jamal et al., 2011) with sustainability in mind.

Often the development of tourism curricula is thought to be a balance of how it embodies critical thinking and a liberal arts education, as well as how it responds to the neoliberal push of developing 'skills' necessary in the 21st century workforce (Belhassen & Caton, 2011). This strat-egy considers how students bridge work skills through the cognitive and emotive responses to critical issues in the classroom to tangible ways they behave and creates responsible actions to complex, real world sustainability challenges. Tribe (2002) argued for ethical decision-making in tourism, and likewise, value-based hospitality curricula have been offered (e.g., TEFI, BEST Educators Network; Sheldon et al., 2011). Philosophical acceptance and adoption of values is necessary and a CTC is delimited to actions in industry and personal practice as values and eth-ics transcend these spheres. Cultivating motivations and capacities for activism is imperative for the development of a CTC (Boluk & Carnicelli, 2015). A student expressed the urge to engage after hearing others share their critical positionalities "*I was surprised how much a simple 15-minute group presentation in class could strike a chord and empower me to work towards a change in larger society.*" Critical praxis is focused on challenging students to consider how to enact solu-tions. A student shared, "*Maybe not surprising, but I was very interested in these discussions on dif-ferent topics and applying them both internationally and in [my state].*" Educators should provide tools, so students may modify existing systems, or build radical alternative systems (e.g., Lotz-Sisitka et al., 2015).

Arguably, this is the most difficult task, as it requires action steps that may force students to uncomfortably confront how they behave in their own lives. This is aptly demonstrated by a stu-dent who commented that their "*view of mass tourism has changed drastically and sometimes pre-vents the idea of me partaking in traveling.*" Certain pedagogies such as experiential and service learning, may place action steps in context. Exposing students to tourism challenges within their own communities encourages reflection on how they can participate in more sustainable practi-ces and decision-making. A student noted gaining "*knowledge on how to help the different groups*" and how to "*reach out to these communities.*" Critical praxis increases willingness to take home the responsibility of addressing these issues. After exposure to tools to critique 'best prac-tices' in sustainable tourism development, a student explained "*how easy it would be to apply best practices to [our community] if only us, as a group of local inhabitants, would put forth the effort.*"

Critical praxis requires developing a vision of how things should look if guided by values such as justice, equity, respect, and stewardship while creatively exploring possible solutions and plans for change. The SDGs are ideal topics that enable critical dialogue and move students towards action of working sustainability into praxis. The SDGs are meant to be problem-solved, in need of solutions and real actions, to address desired outcomes. If the SDGs are utilized as critical topics and the framework is implemented, students can develop skills for enactment in the field. To do so, they must draw from inductive reasoning and think laterally while considering ideas that may be radical. Finally, they should act, practicing responsible behaviors through continuous adaptation to effect change.

Discussion

SDG 4 sets the stage for achieving other SDGs, and classrooms provide the optimal backdrop to critique the language used, imagine creative responses to challenges, and encourage students to consider their role in advancing the goals. This research has illuminated the absence of critical thinking throughout the presentation of the 17 SDGs. This is particularly evident in SDG 4 and the expressed targets. The troubled milieu of tertiary systems confronted with neoliberal agendas favoring capitalism over critical thinking provided the impetus for this research. To this end, this paper introduced a framework that uses critical pedagogy to encourage a sense of criticality that can then question these very systems. Our pedagogical framework confronts neoliberal structures and illustrates how education may be emancipatory (Giroux, 2011) building on the foundations of democracy (Giroux, 2004b).

Students must recognize injustices and inequalities to address macro and micro challenges of sustainability in tourism. Our framework builds on current scholarship on critical citizenship education and global citizenship. This research supports Freire's (1970) theory on *conscientization* as he held imperative that educators and students practice critiquing and assessing claims (Puolimatka, 1996) while also providing space for self-development. Our framework provides strategies for educators to implement Freire's work. In presenting the definitions and current scholarship in pedagogical activities to support global citizenship, we recognized a relationship between global citizenship, sustainability and responsibility, and the absence of critical thinking. This led to our development of a CTC definition and framework including bringing forth critical topics, facilitating critical discussions, providing time for critical reflection in relation to one's positionality, and encouraging action to further sustainability.

Bringing the SDGs to the classroom is crucial given that global knowledge of the SDGs is poor (Lampert & Papadongonas, 2016) and doing so could enhance students' appreciation regarding how the SDGs intersect with their field of inquiry. Sustainable tourism may help address issues in relation to poverty (SDG1), hunger (SDG2), water and sanitation (SDG6), reducing inequality (SDG10) developing clean energy sources (SDG7), enhancing well-being (SDG3), improving gender equality (SDG5) and in considering one's own consumption and production (SDG12) practices. The framework proposes critical reflection which may elicit self-critique (Giroux, 2004b) regarding one's behaviours and claims (Puolimatka, 1996). Students also need to consider their positionality and roles within the neoliberal system and make informed decisions that translate theory to action (critical praxis). If such criticality is strengthened, a CTC, one who recognizes collective agency (Giroux, 2004b) is fostered and equipped to make responsible decisions. The CTC framework assists actualizing Target 4.7 to "ensure that all learners acquire the knowledge and skills needed to promote sustainable development' and promote 'global citizenship'." Since the SDGs do not include critical processes in which the targets should be actualized specifically in relation to education, pedagogy or teaching, we must start in our classrooms to develop citizens who may confront complex sustainability challenges.

Conclusion

This study adopts a critical sustainable tourism lens and responds to the call made by Boluk et al. (2017) to reflect on the role of criticality to advance the sustainable development of tourism systems. Specifically, we have drawn attention to SDG 4 Quality Education because as we see it, to achieve sustainability or sustainable tourism in practice, we must start with education. We argue that mobilizing SDG 4 could help realize all SDGs. Recognizing the absence of critical thinking in the description of SDG 4 and the limited detail explaining critical processes in which the targets could be actualized has been our point of departure for this contribution. Our paper builds on the work of Bricker et al. (2012) who recognized the connections between the former MDGs and sustainable tourism development.

Our paper responds to calls for criticality in research approaches in tourism (e.g., Tribe, 2007, 2008) and for criticality in tourism education (e.g., Boluk & Carnicelli, 2019; Crossley, 2017; Fullagar & Wilson, 2012) by proposing a five strategy framework (see Figure 1) derived from our analysis of CIQs (Brookfield, 1987) administered in three North American tourism classrooms. Importantly, the strategies presented aim to equip instructors for preparing students to be critical thinkers in order to address complex sustainability issues. We have argued that the implementation of our framework may serve to strengthen SDG 4 and empower future decision makers as *Critical Tourism Citizens* (CTC). The described strategies build on Crossley's (2017) work articulating a three-movement approach which comprises fundamental skill development of critical thinking; the conscious-raising of structural oppression through critical pedagogy; and an explicit undertaking of positionality. The strategies also build upon Blanchard and Higgins-Desbiolles' (2013) work using Freire's notion of critical consciousness and engagement. Our definition of the CTC responds to calls to bring criticality to the tourism classroom, particularly in the context of EfS and builds on the work of Crossley (2017) and Blanchard and Higgins-Desbiolles (2013). Our paper mutually positions the framework and CTC definition within the literature on *global citizenship* and *critical citizenship education*.

Critical pedagogy has been criticized as being abstract (Ellsworth, 1989). In response, our framework illustrates tangible strategies for teaching critical thinking. As such, future research should interrogate our new framework for its utility in tracking critical thinking and could include analysis of syllabi, curriculum design, and instructional methods supporting EfS and criticality. Sharing resources may provide educators with evidence to highlight specific examples drawing on alternative stakeholder discourses for critical perspectives (Fullagar & Wilson, 2012). Engaging in criticality requires mutual commitment from students and educators. It necessitates that educators are mindful, self-aware, and open to considering the unique experiences of their students and *care* enough to push students outside of their comfort zones. Caring may be driven by a passion to be part of the change and involves time and reflexivity. Time however, in a neoliberal context, is not on our side and capitalism has influenced administrators to prioritize student recruitment and vocational training perpetuating the status quo. With 2030 set as the deadline for achieving the SDGs it is incumbent upon us all to consider our agency in achieving the goals. Educators have a responsibility, in line with social justice scholarship (e.g., Freire, 1970). If we frame curricular and co-curricular meetings with students and time spent writing on pedagogy to progress SDG 4, we may be successful in achieving this goal. As such, with our new framework, the definition of the CTC, and in the lead up to 2030, the authors' challenge tourism educators to consider pedagogical practices and scholarship through the lens of Quality Education that embodies criticality.

Disclosure statement

No potential conflict of interest was reported by the authors.

References

Althof, W., & Berkowitz, M. W. (2006). Moral education and character education: Their relationship and roles in citizenship education. *Journal of Moral Education*, 35(4), 495–518. doi:10.1080/03057240601012204

Assadourian, E. (2012). The path to degrowth in overdeveloped countries. In E. Assadourian & M. Renner (Eds.), *State of the world 2012: Moving toward sustainable prosperity* (pp. 22–37). Washington, DC: Island Press.

Ateljevic, I., Morgan, N., & Pritchard, A. (Eds.). (2013). *The critical turn in tourism studies: Creating an academy of hope.* London: Routledge.

Ayikoru, M., Tribe, J., & Airey, D. (2009). Reading tourism education: Neoliberalism unveiled. *Annals of Tourism Research, 36*(2), 191–221. doi:10.1016/j.annals.2008.11.001

Belhassen, Y., & Caton, K. (2011). On the need for critical pedagogy in tourism education. *Tourism Management, 32*(6), 1389–1396. doi:10.1016/j.tourman.2011.01.014

Blanchard, L., & Higgins-Desbiolles, F. (2013). Peace matters, tourism matters. In L. Blanchard and F. Higgins-Desbiolles (Eds.), *Peace through tourism promoting human security through international citizenship* (pp. 19–33). London: Routledge.

Boluk, K., & Carnicelli, S. (2015). Activism and critical reflection through experiential learning. *Journal of Teaching in Travel & Tourism, 15*(3), 242–251. doi:10.1080/15313220.2015.1059304

Boluk, K., & Carnicelli, S. (2019). Tourism for the emancipation of the oppressed: Towards a critical tourism education drawing on Freirean philosophy. *Annals of Tourism Research, 76*, 168–179. doi:10.1016/j.annals.2019.04.002

Boluk, K., Cavaliere, C., & Higgins-Desbiolles, F. (2017). Critical thinking to realize sustainability in tourism systems: Reflecting on the 2030 sustainable development goals. *Journal of Sustainable Tourism, 25*(9), 1201–1204. doi:10.1080/09669582.2017.1333263

Boyle, A. (2017). Integrating sustainability in the tourism curriculum: dilemmas and directions. In P. Benckendorff & A. Zehrer (Eds.), *Handbook of Teaching and Learning in Tourism* (pp. 389 – 401). Northampton, MA: Edward Elgar.

Bianchi, R. V., & Stephenson, M. L. (2014). *Tourism and citizenship: Rights, freedoms and responsibilities in the global order.* London: Routledge.

Bricker, K. S., Black, R., & Cottrell, S. (Eds.). (2012). *Sustainable tourism and the millennium development goals.* Burlington: Jones & Bartlett Publishers.

Brookfield, S. (1987). *Developing critical thinkers: Challenging adults to explore alternative ways of thinking and acting.* San Francisco, CA: Jossey-Bass.

Brookfield, S. (1995). *Becoming a critically reflective teacher.* San Francisco, CA: JosseyBass.

Brookfield, S. (2012). *Teaching for critical thinking tools and techniques to help students question their assumptions.* San Francisco, CA: Jossey-Bass.

Burbules, N., & Berk, R. (1999). Critical thinking and critical pedagogy: Relations, differences, and limits. In T. Popkewitz & L. Fendler (Eds.), *Critical theories in education.* New York: Routledge.

Butcher, J. (2017). Citizenship, globalcitizenship and volunteer tourism: A critical analysis. *Tourism Recreation Research, 42*(2), 129–138.

Capra, F. (1996). *The web of life: A new scientific understanding of living systems.* New York, NY: Random House.

Caton, K., Schott, C., & Daniele, R. (2014). Tourism's imperative for global citizenship. *Journal of Teaching in Travel & Tourism, 14*, 123–128. doi:10.1080/15313220.2014.907955

Coops, N. C., Marcus, J., Construt, I., Frank, E., Kellett, R., Mazzi, E., … Sipos, Y. (2015). How an entry-level, interdisciplinary sustainability course revealed the benefits and challenges of a university-wide initiative for sustainability education. *International Journal of Sustainability in Higher Education, 16*(5), 729–747. doi:10.1108/IJSHE-04-2014-0059

Costandius, E., & Bitzer, E. (2015). *Engaging higher education curricula: A critical citizenship perspective.* Stellenbosch: Sun Media.

Cotterell, D., Arcodia, C., & Ferreira, J. A. (2017). Teaching for strong sustainability in university tourism courses. In P. Benckendorff & A. Zehrer (Eds.), *Handbook of teaching and learning in tourism* (pp. 373–388). Northampton, MA: Edward & Elgar.

Crossley, É. (2017). Criticality in tourism education. In P. Benckendorff & A. Zehrer (Eds.), *Handbook of teaching and learning in tourism* (pp. 427–438). Northampton, MA: Edward & Elgar.

Dadds, M. (2001). The politics of pedagogy. *Teachers and Teaching, 7*(1), 43–58. doi:10.1080/713698759

Dickinson, J. E., & Peeters, P. (2014). Time, tourism consumption and sustainable development. *International Journal of Tourism Research, 16*(1), 11–21. doi:10.1002/jtr.1893

Dower, M. (2003) Developing sustainable rural tourism. *Thematic guide one.* Athens: European Summer Academy for Sustainable Rural Development.

Dredge, D., Benckendorff, P., Day, M., Gross, M. J., Walo, M., Weeks, P., & Whitelaw, P. (2012). The philosophic practitioner and the curriculum space. *Annals of Tourism Research, 39*(4), 2154–2176. doi:10.1016/j.annals.2012.07.017

Ellsworth, E. (1989). Why Doesn't This Feel Empowering? Working Through the Repressive Myths of Critical Pedagogy. *Harvard Educational Review, 59*(3), 297–325. doi:10.17763/haer.59.3.058342114k266250

Farber Canziani, B., Sönmez, S., Hsieh, Y., & Byrd, E. T. (2012). A learning theory framework for sustainability education in tourism. *Journal of Teaching in Travel & Tourism, 12*(1), 3–20. doi:10.1080/15313220.2012.650052

Fisher, A. (2001). *Critical thinking an introduction.* Cambridge, UK: Cambridge University Press.

Freire, P. (1970). *Pedagogy of the oppressed.* New York: Continuum.

Fullagar, S., & Wilson, E. (2012). Critical pedagogies: A reflexive approach to knowledge creation in tourism and hospitality studies. *Journal of Hospitality and Tourism Management, 19*(1), 1–6. doi:10.1017/jht.2012.3

Gilstrap, D. L., & Dupree, J. (2008). Assessing learning, critical reflection, and quality educational outcomes: The Critical Incident Questionnaire. *College & Research Libraries, 69*(5), 407–426. doi:10.5860/0690407

Giroux, H. A. (1983). *Theory and resistance in education: A pedagogy for the opposition.* Westport, CT: Bergin & Garvey.

Giroux, H. A. (2004a). Critical pedagogy and the postmodern/modern divide: Towards a pedagogy of democratization. *Teacher Education Quarterly, 31*(1), 31–47.

Giroux, H. A. (2004b). Public pedagogy and the politics of neo-liberalism: Making the political more pedagogical. *Policy Futures in Education, 2*(3 & 4), 494–503. doi:10.2304/pfie.2004.2.3.5

Giroux, H. A. (2011). *On critical pedagogy.* New York, NY: Continuum.

Giroux, H. A. (2016). Disposable futures: Neoliberalism's assault on higher education. *Límite, 11*(35), 7–17.

Glaser, B. G., & Strauss, A. L. (1967). *The discovery of grounded theory.* Chicago: Aldine.

Glowacki-Dudka, M., & Barnett, N. (2007). Connecting critical reflection and group development in online adult education classrooms. *International Journal of Teaching and Learning in Higher Education, 19*(1), 43–52.

Gretzel, U., Davis, E. B., Bowser, G., Jiang, J., & Brown, M. (2014). Creating global leaders with sustainability mindsets: Insights from the RMSSN summer academy. *Journal of Teaching in Travel & Tourism, 14*(2), 164-183.

Halpern, D. F. (2014). *Critical thinking across the curriculum: A brief edition of thought & knowledge.* New York, NY: Routledge.

Higgins-Desbiolles, F. (2006). More than an industry: Tourism as a social force. *Tourism Management, 27*(6), 1192–1208. doi:10.1016/j.tourman.2005.05.020

Higgins-Desbiolles, F., & Blanchard, L. (2010). Challenging peace through tourism: Placing tourism in the context of human rights, justice and peace. In O. Moufakkir and I. Kelly (Eds.), *Tourism progress and peace* (pp. 35–47). Oxford: CABI.

Holdsworth, S., & Thomas, I. (2015). Framework for introducing education for sustainable development into university curriculum. *Journal of Education for Sustainable Development, 9*(2), 137–159. doi:10.1177/0973408215588246

Huckle, J. (2017). Becoming critical: A challenge for the Global Learning Programme? *International Journal of Development Education and Global Learning, 8*(3), 63–84.

Jamal, T., Taillon, J., & Dredge, D. (2011). Sustainable tourism pedagogy and academic community collaboration: A progressive service-learning approach. *Tourism and Hospitality Research, 11*(2), 133–147. doi:10.1057/thr.2011.3

Johnson, L., & Morris, P. (2010). Towards a framework for critical citizenship education. *The Curriculum Journal, 21*(1), 77–96. doi:10.1080/09585170903560444

Kearins, K., & Springett, D. (2003). Educating for sustainability: Developing critical skills. *Journal of Management Education, 27*(2), 188–204. doi:10.1177/1052562903251411

Keefer, J. M. (2009). *The critical incident questionnaire (CIQ): From research to practice and back again.* Paper presented at the Adult education research conference, Chicago, IL (pp. 176–182). Retrieved from http://newprairiepress.org/aerc/2009/papers/31

Kincheloe, J. L. (2008). *Critical pedagogy primer* (2nd ed.). New York, NY: Peter Lang.

Lampert, M., & Papadongonas, P. (2016). *Towards 2030 without poverty* (pp. 1–36). Amsterdam: Glocalities. Retrieved from https://www.glocalities.com/reports/towards-2030-without-poverty.html

Lotz-Sisitka, H., Wals, A. E., Kronlid, D., & Mcgarry, D. (2015). Transformative, transgressive Social Learning: Rethinking Higher Education Pedagogy in Times of Systemic Global Dysfunction. *Current Opinion in Environmental Sustainability, 16* , 73–80.

McKercher, B., & Prideaux, B. (2011). Are tourism impacts low on personal environmental agendas? *Journal of Sustainable Tourism, 19*(3), 325–345. doi:10.1080/09669582.2010.524702

McLaren, P. (2003). Critical Pedagogy: A look at the major concepts. In A. Darder, M. Baltodano, & R. D. Torres (Eds.), *The critical pedagogy reader* (pp. 69–97). New York, NY: Routledge.

McLaren, P., & Jaramillo, N. E. (2013). Forward: Dialectical thinking and critical pedagogy – towards a critical tourism studies. In I. Ateljevic, N. Morgan, & A. Pritchard (Eds.), *The critical turn in tourism studies: Creating an academy of hope* (pp. xvii–xl). New York, NY: Routledge.

Mezirow, J. (1998). On critical reflection. *Adult Education Quarterly, 48*(3), 185–198. doi:10.1177/074171369804800305

Moscardo, G. (2015). The importance of education for sustainability in tourism. In G. Moscardo & P. Benckendorff (Eds.), *Education for sustainability in tourism: A handbook of processes, resources, and strategies* (pp. 1–24). New York, NY: Springer.

Oyler, D. R., & Romanelli, F. (2014). The fact of ignorance revisiting the Socratic method as a tool for teaching critical thinking. *American Journal of Pharmaceutical Education, 78*(7), 1–9.

Paddison, B., & Dredge, D. (2014). TEFI7-Tourism Education for global citizenship: Educating for lives of consequence. *Journal of Teaching in Travel & Tourism, 14*, 210–214. doi:10.1080/15313220.2014.907960

Paul, R. W., & Binker, A. J. A. (1990). *Critical thinking: What every person needs to survive in a rapidly changing world.* Rohnert Park, CA: Center for Critical Thinking and Moral Critique.

Paul, R., & Elder, L. (2006). *The thinkers guide to the art of Socratic questioning*. Dilton Beach, CA: The Foundation for Critical Thinking.

Puolimatka, T. (1996). Democracy, education and the critical citizen. *Philosophy of Education Archive, 329*, 338.

Reysen, S., & Katzarska-Miller, I. (2013). A model of global citizenship: Antecedents and outcomes. *International Journal of Psychology, 48*(5), 858–870. doi:10.1080/00207594.2012.701749

Salleh, A. (2010). From metabolic rift to "metabolic value": Reflections on environmental sociology and the alternative globalization movement. *Organization & Environment, 23*(2), 205–219. doi:10.1177/1086026610372134

Schon, D. A. (1983). *The reflective practitioner*. New York, NY: Basic Books.

Schwarzin, L. (2013). To act as though the future mattered. In I. Ateljevic, N. Morgan, & A. Pritchard (Eds.), *The critical turn in tourism studies: Creating an academy of hope* (pp. 135–148). New York, NY: Routledge.

Sheldon, P. J., Fesenmaier, D. R., & Tribe, J. (2011). The tourism education futures initiative (TEFI): Activating change in tourism education. *Journal of Teaching in Travel & Tourism, 11*(1), 2–23. doi:10.1080/15313220.2011.548728

Sherrod, L. R., Flanagan, C., & Youniss, J. (2002). Dimensions of citizenship and opportunities for youth development: The what, why, when, where, and who of citizenship development. *Applied Developmental Science, 6*(4), 264–272. doi:10.1207/S1532480XADS0604_14

Sibbel, A. (2009). Pathways towards sustainability through higher education. *International Journal of Sustainability in Higher Education, 10*(1), 68–82. doi:10.1108/14676370910925262

Springett, D. (2005). 'Education for sustainability' in the business studies curriculum: A call for a critical agenda. *Business Strategy and the Environment, 14*(3), 146–159. doi:10.1002/bse.447

Tribe, J. (2007). Critical tourism: Rules and resistance. In I. Ateljevic, A. Pritchard, & N. Morgan (Eds.), *The critical turn in tourism studies: Innovative research methodologies* (pp. 29-40). New York: Elsevier.

Tribe, J. (2002). Education for ethical tourism action. *Journal of Sustainable Tourism, 10*(4), 309–324. doi:10.1080/09669580208667170

Tribe, J. (2005). Tourism, knowledge and the curriculum. In D. Airey & J. Tribe (Eds.), *An international handbook of tourism education* (pp. 47–60). New York, NY: Routledge.

Tribe, J. (2008). Tourism: A critical business. *Journal of Travel Research, 46*(3), 245–255. doi:10.1177/0047287507304051

United Nations (UN). (2015). *Transforming our world: The 2030 agenda for sustainable development*. New York, NY: United Nations Publication.

UNESCO. (2017). Measurement strategy for SDG Target 4.7. Retrieved from file:///C:/Users/kboluk/Desktop/gaml4-measurement-strategy-sdg-target4.7.pdf

UNESCO. (2018). Global Education Monitoring Report Summary 2017/18: Accountability in our Education: Meeting our commitments. Retrieved from https://releifweb.int/sites/reliefweb.int/files/resources/259338e.pdf

Urbain, Y. (2013). Awareness-raising and global citizenship through peace tourism. In L. Blanchard & F. Higgins-Desbiolles (Eds.), *Peace through tourism promoting human security through international citizenship* (pp. 144–155). London: Routledge.

Winter, T. (2009). Asian tourism and the retreat of Anglo-western centrism in tourism theory. *Current Issues in Tourism, 12*(1), 21–31. doi:10.1080/13683500802220695

Young, D. A., & Olutoye, O. A. (2015). *Handbook of critical incidents and essential topics in pediatric anesthesiology*. Cambridge: University Printing House.

Žižek, S. (2008). *Violence: Six sideways reflections*. London: Picador.

Overcommitted to tourism and under committed to sustainability: The urgency of teaching "strong sustainability" in tourism courses

Debbie Cotterell, Robert Hales, Charles Arcodia and Jo-Anne Ferreira

ABSTRACT

With the tourism sector being urged to contribute to the UN's 2030 Sustainable Development Goals (SDGs), tourism educators need to develop industry leaders with "strong sustainability" mindsets. "Sustainable development" has long been contested as a weaker form of sustainability due to its "pro-growth" emphasis. Research suggests that tourism students are graduating with narrow understandings of sustainability, partly due to course designs based on weaker conceptualisations of sustainability and a lack of holistic, critical and systemic thinking. The purpose of this paper is to analyse – using content analysis – the strength of sustainability conceptualisations underpinning international undergraduate sustainable tourism courses, which has not previously been carried out. Results indicate that sustainable tourism courses do not include "very strong" conceptualisations of sustainability, and that sustainability pedagogy and approaches such as systems and holistic thinking are not widely used. This paper argues that stronger conceptualisations and sustainability skills are essential. A framework is also suggested to assist tourism educators to use critical reflective thinking in conjunction with the SDGs to assist the development of more complex ways of thinking and acting towards achieving global sustainable tourism outcomes. The discussion concludes with suggestions for further research to ensure stronger sustainable tourism curricula.

Introduction

The current global "overtourism crisis" has induced a growing sense of urgency to create a more sustainable tourism industry (Seraphin, Sheeran, & Pilato, 2018). Universities have a pivotal role in providing graduates with an education that will empower them and promote the greatest impact in the tourism industry. This requires graduates with strong conceptualisations of sustainability (Boyle, Wilson, & Dimmock, 2015; Sterling & Thomas, 2006), key sustainability skills such as critical thinking and systems thinking (Phelan et al., 2015), as well as a holistic knowledge of the United Nation's (UN) 2030 SDGs (2017). The SDGs are a set of 17 global goals and related targets designed to meet some of the world's most pressing issues such as climate change, poverty, health and peace (Sustainable Development Solutions Network, 2017). Previous research in tourism education has focused on how sustainability is embedded in Australian tourism curricula (e.g. Wilson & von der Heidt, 2013) and general graduate sustainability capabilities within Australian universities (e.g. Thomas & Day, 2014), however, there are few indications of the extent to which "very strong sustainability" conceptualisations and key sustainability skills are embedded into sustainable tourism courses (Cotterell, Arcodia, & Ferreira, 2017). Tourism courses have traditionally been based on the triple bottom line approach and/or sustainable growth, which some believe does not represent the strongest approach to sustainability (Springett, 2010). If student learning is based on potentially "weak" conceptualisations of sustainability it is then not surprising to discover that students are graduating without the ability to think in complex ways about the phenomena. Indeed, they are often limited to a surface level, and less holistic understanding of sustainability (Camargo & Gretzel, 2017; McKercher & Prideaux, 2011). Other studies have found that tourism lecturers' conceptualisations of sustainability also vary, with the majority displaying weak to moderate conceptualisations (Boyle et al., 2015; Cotterell, Ferriera, Hales, & Arcodia, 2018). This may, in turn, have contributed to the design of sustainable tourism courses with weaker conceptualisations of sustainability and also of graduating students' ability to practice sustainability. Stronger conceptualisations include a focus on critical, holistic and systemic thinking. Critical thinking is "the art of thinking about thinking in an intellectually disciplined manner" (Paul, 2005, p. 28) which ultimately encourages students to develop a higher order thinking process. Whilst critical thinking is one of the distinguishing features of university education, and in particular, sustainable development (Howlett, Ferriera, & Blomfield, 2016) other forms of thinking such as holistic thinking and systems thinking appear to have limited uptake in universities (Thomas & Day, 2014). Systemic thinking, or systems thinking, is about identifying connections and relationships in order to better understand complex situations (Senge, 2006). Similarly, holistic thinking considers the impact one's decisions have on a whole (system) (Sterling, 2003), which is essential for understanding the complexity of sustainability within the tourism industry. Curriculum guidelines associated with sustainability from a range of sources indicate the importance of holistic and systemic thinking (and critical thinking), transdisciplinary knowledge, environmental and sustainability skills and ethical practice in teaching the concepts and practice of sustainability (Phelan et al., 2015; Sustainable Development Solutions Network, 2017).

In addition, the 17 SDGs have now added an extra layer of complexity to an already crowded curricula, with international pressure on nations, including Australia, to work towards achieving these goals (World Tourism Organisation and United Nations Development Plan, 2017). The tourism industry is being asked to play a key role in achieving sustainability goals related to economic growth, responsible consumption and life below water (UN, 2017). However, the term sustainable development has long been contested as a weak form of sustainability due to the emphasis on growth and development (Neumayer, 2003). The rise of the SDGs as a tool for curriculum development follows on from sustainability imperatives such as Education for Sustainability (EfS) (Springett, 2010; Sterling & Thomas, 2006), the call for strong sustainability (Davies, 2013) inclusion of sustainability in developing key graduate skills (Thomas & Day, 2014) and the UNESCO (2014) Decade of Education for Sustainable Development. The SDGs are claimed to firstly provide students with the knowledge and skills to redefine the role of business (Sustainable Development Solutions Network, 2017). Secondly, SDGs provide a critical, holistic and systemic framework because of the integrated nature of 17 SDGs, with the achievement of one goal dependent on actions taken towards achieving other goals (Nilsson, Griggs, & Visbeck, 2016). Although there has been some research examining the role of SDGs within universities (Sustainable Development Solutions Network, 2017) and tourism (e.g. Jones, Hillier, & Comfort, 2017), there is growing interest (and limited published research) in examining how the SDGs can be implemented in sustainable tourism curricula.

Further research is essential in order to advance knowledge on how tourism educators can equip graduates with ways of thinking critically, systemically and holistically about how a stronger, more holistic sustainable tourism industry can be generated over time and thus assist with achieving the SDGs by 2030. Previous research focuses on embedding sustainability into the Australian business curricula and lacks insight into sustainable tourism curricula from an international perspective. In addition, it is now timely to examine if and how the SDGs are being embedded. This study addresses a number of research gaps by addressing three research questions. The first ascertains the conceptualisations of sustainability that are currently used in university undergraduate sustainable tourism courses internationally. The second examines whether university undergraduate sustainable tourism courses are designed to equip graduates with essential and relevant sustainability skills necessary for more complex ways of thinking about sustainability. The third addresses whether key SDGs are evident in sustainable tourism curricula.

This study has both academic and practical importance. Academically, the paper challenges the sustainability conceptualisations currently employed by tourism educators and contributes to the literature by providing a questioning strategy to drive tourism education towards a strong conceptualisation of sustainability, and towards inclusion of the SDGs. The study also aims to go beyond previous business curricula research focused on the Australian context by focusing internationally on sustainable tourism courses. This study therefore contributes to practical knowledge about ways in which educators around the world can develop stronger conceptualisations of sustainability and utilise these in their teaching.

To clarify the terminology used in this paper, the term "course" has been used to describe the subjects found within an undergraduate degree programme. For example, an undergraduate programme such as "International Tourism Management BSC (Hons)" might have over 30 core (and optional) courses, otherwise referred to as modules, topics, units, or subjects. These "courses" that make up a degree programme have outlines, descriptions or profiles that are documents that give an overview for the student to understand the content of that individual subject/course. In this study, the term "course profile" is used.

Literature review

Sustainability in higher education

Almost 500 universities around the world have now signed the Talloires Declaration (TD), which is a promise to care for the environment (University Leaders for a Sustainable Future, 2016a). The focus of the sustainability assessment criteria by the University Leaders for a Sustainable Future (ULSF), however, tends to focus on the extent to which sustainability is embedded into certain courses as well as campus greening. Furthermore, their definition of sustainability refers to universities that are "ecologically sound, socially just and economically viable, and that they will continue to be so for future declaration" (University Leaders for a Sustainable Future, 2016b, para. 4). Other evaluations of the sustainability pedagogy in universities also show a similar picture of triple bottom line frameworks to drive the process of sustainability in universities (Boyle, Wilson, & Dimmock, 2014). This suggests that many university course designs are also using the "triple-bottom line" approach, which is a weaker form of sustainability (Neumayer, 2003; Springett, 2010).

There has also been a third-wave of sustainability that focuses more on teaching and pedagogy rather than the previous waves of integrating environment into curricula and campus greening (Wals & Blewitt, 2010). This aligns with Sterling's work on the need for a change in the teaching and learning of sustainability that includes pedagogies such as trans-disciplinary learning and problem learning (Sterling, cited in Wals & Blewitt, 2010). However, such approaches often face resistance from staff, as seen in an investigation into how well sustainability is embedded in first-year Australian university tourism business courses (Wilson & von der Heidt, 2013). Their study identified limited uptake of transformational approaches to teaching and learning about sustainability due to curriculum crowding and limited knowledge of the conceptualisation of sustainability (Wilson & von der Heidt, 2013). Their study also notes limited evidence of Education for Sustainability (EfS) underpinning business courses. EfS is an approach which enables students to make behavioural changes in their own lives that will then translate into effective sustainable management skills in the industry. As opposed to education about sustainability (EaS) which encompasses teaching and learning about sustainability, EfS prepares students to become change-agents in the industry (Springett, 2010) by facilitating transformative change which is essential given the future sustainability of the tourism industry.

Conceptualisations of sustainability

The concept "sustainability" first appeared in a book that discussed the future of humankind called *Blueprint for Survival* in 1972. There is also a US reference to a "no-growth economy" in 1974 with a first reference in a UN document in 1978 (Kidd, 1992). Since then, the concept has been in a constant state of evolution with increasingly unclear and varied definitions and under-standings proposed and debated (Higgins-Desbiolles, 2010; McCool, Butler, Buckley, Weaver, & Wheeler, 2013). One of the most frequently cited definitions from Brundtland's "Our Common Future" is "[meeting] the needs of the present without compromising the ability of future gener-ations to meet their own needs" (World Commission, 1987, p. 393). The term "sustainable devel-opment," however, is contradictory as while "sustainable" includes concepts of steady state, "development" includes notions of growth. There is similar contradiction within the meaning of sustainable tourism and the terms sustainable tourism and sustainable tourism development are used interchangeably by the United Nations World Tourism Organisation (UNWTO, 2017). Sustainable tourism is defined as "tourism that takes full account of its current and future economic, social and environmental impacts, addressing the needs of visitors, the industry, the environment and host communities" (UNWTO, 2017, para. 1). While for some, sustainable tourism means continued growth, for others it means a halt to mass tourism (Weaver, 2005). This is one of the reasons why the "triple bottom line" approach to sustainable tourism is often criticized as a weaker form of sustainability; because economic aspects appear to dominate ecological and social aspects (Hunter, 1997; Springett, 2010). Nevertheless, the continuing need for sustainable development has forced the tourism industry to make changes to the way in which destinations manage and plan for sustainable tourism (Dwyer, Forsyth, & Dwyer, 2010, p. 739).

A study of sustainable tourism researchers showed a variation of understandings of the phe-nomena among even the experts in the field (see Miller, 2001). Definitions of sustainability can be understood by placing different conceptions on a scale. A simple understanding of sustainability is "anthropocentrism" which takes the view that the environment can be used in a beneficial way to humans as they are the dominant species on the planet (Weaver, 2008). Weak sustainability is based on the notion that it is economically acceptable for natural capital to be replaced by man-made capital in the interest of balancing the triple bottom line. This is referred to as the "substitutability" paradigm (Neumayer, 2003). On the opposite end of the scale is "ecocentrism" which is based on the notion that as humans use the environment for their own benefit, they must sustain and support it for future use (Kopnina, 2013). One of the first sustainability continu-ums/scale shows the two extremes sitting on a continuum and highlights the differences between weak (resource exploitative position) and strong sustainability (extreme preservationist position) (Pearce, 1993; Solow, 1993; Springett, 2003). Despite modifications to Pearce's sustainability spec-trum, it is still relevant and debated today with alternatives such as "extended anthro-pocentricism" being suggested as less biased and having a more practical application in the tourism industry (Dwyer, 2017). A summary of the literature on sustainability conceptualisations showing the variation from very weak to very strong conceptualisations can be seen in Table 1.

Table 1. Conceptualisations of sustainability ranging from very weak to very strong.

	Sustainability position				
	Very weak	Weak	Moderate	Strong	Very strong
Core concepts	Economic growth: Anthropocentric; Resource Exploitative; Business as usual Model	Sustainable growth; Sustainable development; Resource conservationist; Triple bottom line Model; Ethical awareness; Tourism systems; Multi-disciplinary	Combination of strong and weak principles; Sustainable growth/develop-ment; Ethical values; Business focus; Triple bottom line model	New ecological paradigm; Resource preservationist; Strong sustain-ability model; Integrity; Systems thinking	Anti-economic growth; Eco-centric; Utilization of natural resources is minimized; Strong sustainability model; Ecological integrity; Societal ethics and val-ues; Cross-disciplinary; Science and ecology based;
	Keeping self/business going	Environmental domain	Three broad domains of economic, social and environmental	Beyond three domains	Complex system of adaptive management and systems thinking
Scale	1	2	3	4	5

Source: Adapted from previous categorisation by ALTC (2010); Dunlap, Van Liere, Mertig, and Jones (2000), Hunter (1997), Neumayer (2003), Pearce (1993), Springett (2010), SANZ (2009).

Strong sustainability emphasises the need for preservation of the natural environment with a strong focus on justice for the environment as well as social considerations (Springett, 2010). Despite the widespread acceptance of ecological principles underpinning strong sustainability, government and business sectors tend to adopt conceptualisations and practices of sustainability that are much weaker (Dovers, 2005; SANZ, 2009). A recent study of over 100 tourism experts revealed that the majority of responses discussing "tourism growth" largely represented views from the dominant social paradigm which supports anthropocentrism (Becken, 2017). Recent and regular reports of the global overtourism crisis (e.g. Venice, Barcelona, Lisbon, Kyoto, Ko Phi Phi Leh) confirm this approach to the world being overcommitted to tourism and under committed to sustainability. This is concerning given the focus of the SDGs.

The predominance of weaker conceptualisations of sustainability is highly likely to have an impact on lecturers' and consequently students' concepts of sustainability and sustainable tourism. The importance of educating people on worldviews that embody the "strongly sustainable" end of the spectrum has thus been argued by several authors (Boyle et al., 2015; Springett, 2010). One justification for such a position can be found in climate change, which according to SANZ (2009) requires responses that are ecosystem centric in order to return to safer carbon dioxide levels. This also requires a holistic framework that recognizes the complex and fragile sustainability system rather than viewing individual parts of economic, environmental, social, cultural, political or even spiritual domains (Tilbury, 1995). These variations in defining sustainability further explain the complexities of teaching and learning about the phenomenon as well as embedding it into a university curriculum. In order to teach about this complex phenomenon, tourism scholars need to teach the art of critical thinking (Howlett et al., 2016) as well as holistic thinking, systems thinking, transdisciplinary knowledge, environmental and sustainability skills and ethical practice (Phelan et al., 2015; Sustainable Development Solutions Network, 2017).

Generic sustainability skills and competencies

In addition to the conceptualisations of sustainability underpinning teaching and learning and their incorporation into curricula, there is continuing discussion surrounding the sustainability attributes and skills of graduates. In the tourism curricula space, discussion has centred on the need to develop students' vocational and philosophical skills (e.g. Tribe, 2002) in order to develop more job-ready graduates (Wang, Ayres, & Huyton, 2013). This idea was further developed by Dredge et al. (2012) who placed emphasis on the importance of having a curriculum that encourages both capabilities and knowledge in sustainable tourism curricula with a stronger focus on skills whilst not affecting core knowledge. The Tourism Education Futures Initiative (TEFI) devised a framework for a new curriculum to promote global citizenship that consists of five pillars representing key values that include: Mutuality, Ethics, Professionalism, Knowledge and Stewardship. One of the core values "Stewardship" is underpinned by the ability to manage sustainability and complex adaptive systems by acting in responsible ways (Dwyer, 2017; Sheldon, Fesenmaier, Woeber, Cooper, & Antonioli, 2008). This framework is a useful model to promote holistic ways of thinking about sustainability; however, some researchers have found these values impractical to incorporate into curriculum design (Faber Canziani, Sonmez, Hsieh, & Byrd, 2012). In addition, the Office for Learning and Teaching (OLT) put forward five sustainability standards by which students could be assessed in terms of their sustainability skills. These include (1) keeping self/business going; (2) environmental domain; (3) three broad domains of economic, social and environmental; (4) beyond three domains; (5) complex system of adaptive management and systems thinking (cited in von der Heidt & Lamberton, 2015). Although no longer in use, these serve as a very efficient and useful way to measure outcomes of university sustainable tourism courses ranging from weak to very strong conceptualisations (see Table 1).

Another approach is to use threshold learning concepts. The Australian Government Office for Learning and Teaching's current academic standards for higher education programs in environment and sustainability are based on minimum threshold learning outcomes (TLOs) which graduates are expected to meet. In order to equip graduates with the skills necessary for a future career, the TLOs focus on four key areas: transdisciplinary knowledge, systemic understanding, environmental and sustainability skills, and ethical practice (Phelan et al., 2015). For a Bachelor degree, students should demonstrate "transdisciplinary knowledge" which includes "holistic systems thinking and complexity" as well as "systemic understanding" which encompasses an understanding of diverse approaches including varying conceptualisations and "different frameworks for knowing" (p. 13). This is also supported by other studies (e.g. Connell, Remington, & Armstrong, 2012; Wiek, Withycombe, & Redman, 2011). Systems/holistic thinking is also seen as a key factor in sustainability curricula (Fisher & McAdams, 2015; Rieckmann, 2012) and has recently been referred to as an important cognitive ability to aid students in learning about complex topics such as climate change (Roychoudhury, Shepardson, & Hirsch, 2017).

While thinking holistically and systemically are central skills, another key component is "thinking critically and creatively in designing and evaluating sustainable alternatives and envisioning sustainable futures" (Phelan et al., 2015, p. 13). Various researchers have emphasized the need for sustainability curricula to develop graduates who can understand sustainability from an interdisciplinary approach and to be critical and reflective thinkers (Howlett et al., 2016; Sipos, Battisti, & Grimm, 2008). According to Dewey (cited in Howlett et al., 2016), critical thinking is reflective thinking as it encourages students to use reflection whilst considering a situation in order to make a reasoned argument. A further useful practice for tourism teachers is critically reflective practice (CRP) which uses a more student-centred and transformative classroom approach, particularly useful for sustainable tourism curricula (Fullagar & Wilson, 2012; Wilson, 2010). Furthermore, research suggests that transformative approaches are experiential and participatory active learning that prompts self-reflection acts as a pathway to creating transformative learning and change with the tourism curricula space (Boluk & Carnicelli, 2015). Despite the notion of critical thinking being used widely within higher education, it is unclear if universities are actually educating their students to be critical thinkers. With the recent addition of the SDGs to the tourism curricula space, how can tourism academics encourage students to think critically and reflectively about sustainability? This is an area of tourism research that needs further consideration.

Sustainable development goals

The tourism sector is now encouraged to contribute towards achieving the Global Goals for Sustainable Development (World Tourism Organisation and United Nations Development Plan, 2017). The tourism industry is explicitly mentioned in three of the goals including: Goal 8 Promoting sustainable economic growth; Goal 12 Ensuring sustainable consumption and production; and Goal 14 Conserving and sustainably using the oceans for sustainable development (UN, 2017). Additionally, the UNWTO has acknowledged tourism can be used as a powerful tool to contribute to all 17 goals such as combatting climate change (Goal 13), and empowering women (Goal 5). However, multiple goals are relying on economic growth from the tourism industry to help, for example, end hunger (Goal 1), build sustainable industrialization (Goal 9) and sustainable and safe cities (Goal 11). As previously discussed, the term "development" includes notions of pro-growth which is seen as contradictory to the notion of sustainability making the SDGs potentially focused on a less-than-strong approach to achieving "sustainability." A counterpoint is that although Goal 8 is about economic growth some of the sub-goals under this heading do refer to inclusive growth (UN, 2017).

Tourism can be used as a powerful tool to end poverty and promote sustainable use of oceans and forests whilst maintaining biodiversity, but only if it is underpinned by a "strong" conceptualisation of sustainability. The importance of achieving the SDGs internationally requires many stakeholders to collaboratively integrate the complexity of sustainability into the tourism industry, and ultimately challenge whether underlying conceptualisations of sustainability in the industry are based on weak or strong interpretations (Cotterell, Hales, Arcodia, & Ferreira, 2018; Hák, Janoušková, & Moldan, 2016). Universities play a role in this by educating students on not only the goals but through critically and holistically learning how to achieve the goals in a very complex and uncertain world (Sustainable Development Solutions Network, 2017). Due to the newness of the goals, it would not be expected that the SDGs have been built into existing tourism curriculum design. However, given the overlap with the UN's preceding Millenium Development Goals (MDGs), it would be expected that the core principles of key SDGs directly related to tourism should underpin current sustainable tourism courses.

In summary, there is a risk that tourism courses are still teaching sustainability using the triple bottom line and a balanced approach to managing a business or destination (Boyle et al., 2015). Despite the business focus, tourism students need to be challenged with alternative viewpoints such as eco-centric or even deep ecological worldviews in order to encourage holistic and stronger understandings of sustainability. It appears, therefore, that there are still variations in conceptualisations of holistic or strong forms of sustainability that are potentially discipline-related and need to be explored further (Cotterell, Arcodia, & Ferreira, 2015). More attention is needed in designing curricula that helps students to develop key sustainability skills (such as critical thinking and systems thinking). Embedding SDGs that are aligned with strong sustainability understandings and holistic objectives is important not only for achieving the SDGs but to also advance deeper forms of sustainable tourism.

Methodology

This study forms part of a larger research project that explores the current approaches to teaching and learning about "strong sustainability" addressing a central question on *how can conceptualisations of strong sustainability amongst university students be strengthened?* The purpose of this study was to explore the conceptualisations of sustainability contained in university sustainable tourism course outlines/profiles internationally. Textual analysis was used to analyse the main characteristics in the communication of texts or messages (Frey, Botan, & Kreps, 1999). There are four major approaches to textual analysis: rhetorical criticism, interaction analysis, performance studies and content analysis. Content analysis aims to analyse the messages embedded in texts (Frey et al., 1999). There are two types of content analysis: quantitative analysis where key themes are recorded and counted; and qualitative analysis where the focus is more on the meanings of the messages that emerge (Bryman & Bell, 2011). This study used both a qualitative and quantitative content analysis approach to reveal the strength of the concept of sustainability adopted, as well as the keywords representing sustainability skills and SDGs embedded in the sustainable tourism course profiles.

Data collection and analysis

The collection of data for the content analysis involved accessing a number of sustainable tourism course profiles ($n = 60$) from international universities (Asia $n=$ 5, Australia and NZ $n=$ 21, Europe $n=$ 18, N. America $n = 14$, Central America $n=$ 2). The key universities targeted were selected using a combination of the world ranking of the top 100 tourism programs (Severt, Tesone, Bottorff, & Carpenter, 2009), and the top 50 university rankings by journal articles as an indicator of high-performing universities (Lee, Au, Li, & Law, 2014) as well as the QS world rankings (QS, 2017). University public websites, a tourism industry forum, as well as email requests to sustainable tourism lecturers were used to obtain a selection of course profiles. The majority (75%) of selected course profiles contained sustainability/sustainable tourism in the course title. Other tourism courses (25%), were also selected as long as they had a sustainability focus, for example, "destination management," "tourism management," "impacts of tourism." Course profiles containing insufficient evidence for analysis of key criteria were rejected, for example too short in length with insufficient detail on either sustainability conceptualisations or sustainability skills. The selected course profiles ranged in length (and detail) averaging 8 pages and ranging from 2 pages ($n=$ 3) to 20+ pages ($n=$ 2) with 85% containing 4 pages or more. The course profiles were then subjected to content analysis to determine the following:

Strength of sustainability conceptualisations

In order to answer the first research question regarding the conceptualizations of sustainability currently used in university undergraduate tourism courses, a qualitative content analysis was undertaken. The purpose of this was to establish the nature of the concept of sustainability currently being integrated into university tourism education and in particular, the extent to which "strong sustainability" is underpinning course design. Course profiles were reviewed for evidence of the core principles of strong sustainability. A review of the literature on weak and strong sustainability has been adapted and modified to identify these core conceptualisations (see Table 1). The literature ranges from journal articles, government reports as well as the five sustainability achievement standards used as a framework for graduate skills by the Australian Government's Australian Learning and Teaching Council (ALTC, 2010). Although no longer in use, they match the existing literature supporting the differences between weak and strong conceptualisations of sustainability. These conceptualisations of sustainability were measured using a five-point scale. As a qualitative analysis of the content was conducted, the researcher was looking for key themes regarding sustainability. Although keywords (and synonyms) from Table 1 were used in the search, the researcher manually analysed the documents to identify the overarching key theme as it was expected that there might be some cases that show overlap. As such the researcher made a judgment by placing the course on a scale from 1 to 5. For example, some courses may show evidence of being based on strong sustainability but are underpinned predominantly by the triple bottom line model, which categorised their curriculum design as moderate. This procedure was cross-checked by other members of the research team to ensure data accuracy.

Sustainability skills

The level of sustainability skills embedded within the course was also analysed using keywords from sustainability education literature (i.e. critical, holistic and systems thinking) as well as the threshold learning outcomes (TLOs) for environment and sustainability. Despite the TLOs being designed by the Australian Government Office for Learning and Teaching, these graduate skills were still deemed relevant internationally as they are part of a project which was assessed by the chair of the UNESCO (2014) Decade of Education for Sustainable Development giving assurance that the TLOs meet both national and international best practice (Phelan et al., 2015, p. 10). The course profiles were content-analysed quantitatively using NVivo to search for keywords and themes relating to the four key areas (transdisciplinary knowledge, systemic understanding, skills for environment and sustainability, and ethical practice) as well as holistic thinking, critical thinking and systems thinking. In addition to keyword searches, the researcher used judgment by manually reading and assessing course profiles to ensure data accuracy, which was then cross-checked with other members of the research team. This allowed for the extent to which courses demonstrate the ability for graduates to be equipped with essential and relevant vocational skills necessary to be identified.

Sustainable development goals

Finally, in order to answer the last research question relating to the extent to which the SDGs underpin sustainable tourism course design, a quantitative textual analysis of keywords was conducted. Keywords used in the search were taken from a detailed report on the framework for the SDGs and targets for the 2030 Agenda for Sustainable Development (UN, 2017) as well as existing keywords deemed relevant by Monash University and Sustainable Development Solutions Network (SDSN) Australia/Pacific (2017, p. 36). NVivo was used to analyse the frequency of relevant words within the course profiles. The keyword list was limited to concepts that did not lose their meaning out of context when analysed independently and were deemed relevant to tourism curricula. For example, keywords for SDG 1 End Poverty, such as "Africa," "Class," "Poor," "developing countries," "Third World," and "income" were not deemed important if searched with a positive outcome. Instead, the search focused on keywords such as "land tenure," "pro-poor policies," "wealth distribution," "equal rights." Approximately 20-25 of the most relevant keyword/phrases were used per SDG. The results of the analysis are presented below using the three key areas as previously outlined.

Evidence of moderate conceptualisations of sustainability in university tourism courses

The analysis of the selected sustainable tourism course profiles revealed 77% of profiles showed evidence of only moderate conceptualisations of sustainability (Figure 1 below). The main reason for this was the distinct focus on the triple bottom line – balancing the economic, environmental and social elements of sustainability with little evidence of strong sustainability. Some course profiles did show some evidence of moving beyond these three domains, for example mentioning a cultural domain; however, little to no discussion of, for example, new ecological paradigm, systems thinking and other strong core principles were identified.

A repetitive focus on the triple bottom line prevented courses being classified as having a strong sustainability conceptualisation. Two courses designed by an Australian university showed a combination of moving beyond the three domains whilst still mentioning the triple bottom line throughout. A further four courses showed traces of strong sustainability but overall the main focus was still classified as moderate due to their economic business focus.

There were a small number of courses (*n*= 4) demonstrating weak sustainability, however, it must be noted that two courses were strongly focused on sustainable development or other

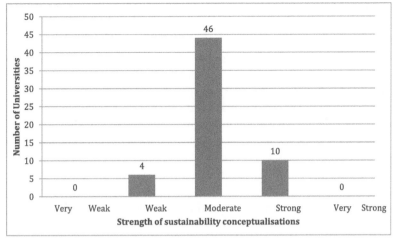

Figure 1. Strength of sustainability conceptualisations underpinning international sustainable tourism courses.

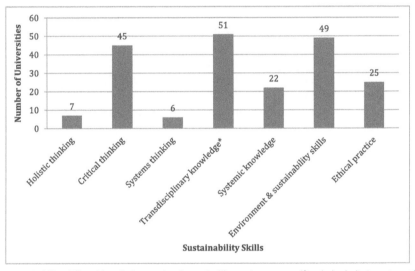

Figure 2. Key sustainability skills evident in international sustainable tourism courses (*excludes holistic systems thinking).

sub-topics, for example, environmental planning and climate change in relation to sustainable tourism, hence the strong focus on only the environmental domain which is deemed a weak sustainability position. It was interesting to see that only ten universities (10%) – located in N. America (*n*= 6), UK (*n*= 2) and New Zealand (*n*= 2) – had courses designed on clearly defined "strong sustainability" principles. These courses moved beyond the triple bottom line and demonstrated on a more holistic and varied approach.

"Critical thinking" over "systems thinking"

Following the analysis of the core principles of sustainability underpinning the course designs, a further investigation into some of the keywords representing sustainability skills present in the documents was conducted (see Figure 2 below). Despite most courses showing moderate conceptualisations of sustainability, limited sustainability skills were evident in the course profiles. Some of the minimum learning outcomes for university graduates in programs related to environment or sustainability are in relation to holistic thinking, systemic understanding, critical thinking and ethical practice (Phelan et al., 2015). In this study, a small number (21%) made reference to the term "holistic," whilst 75% referred to critical thinking in their course outlines. Overall, only six courses (10%) referred to "systems thinking" which is deemed by some as a key skill needed in order to think deeply about complex phenomenon such as sustainability (Connell et al., 2012; Senge, 2006; Sterling, 2003; Wiek et al., 2011).

A further analysis of the course profiles revealed that overall only two of the four sustainability skill areas appear visible in the course designs: "transdisciplinary knowledge" and "skills for environment and sustainability." It must be noted though that whilst "transdisciplinary knowledge" was reported in 85% of course profiles, this includes a "broad and coherent knowledge of key environment and sustainability issues and an appreciation of different frameworks for exploring these issues" (p. 18). This encompasses three sub TLOs including: (1.1) a broad knowledge of environments at various scales and interdependencies; (1.2) key sustainability challenges and their drivers; and (1.3) holistic thinking and complexity. On the whole, most courses demonstrated the features of this key skill, however, only seven (21%) showed evidence of "holistic systems thinking." Given that the majority of the TLO was evidenced in 89%, the researcher decided to report it as such, hence the result excludes the (1.3) holistic thinking and complexity (see Figure 2).

There appears to be a need for stronger "systemic knowledge" and "ethical practice" as TLOs. Systemic knowledge includes transdisciplinary frameworks of knowing as well as value, ethics and interest in Indigenous peoples. This was less apparent in most course profiles. Finally, "ethical practices" which focuses on ethical conduct, reflective learning and decision-making was also seen to a limited extent in less than half of the course profiles (42%). This is surprising given the ethical nature of tourism and sustainability and as "being ethical" is also seen as a key component of managing sustainable tourism. Particular aspects of "ethical practices" such as engaging with Indigenous approaches to overcoming sustainability challenges was not evident. Overall, the analysis shows that the majority of the courses do not appear to be expressing strong sustainability nor are they demonstrating some of the key sustainability skills needed by graduates.

Sustainable development goals under-represented

Finally, content analysis of the courses for evidence of the 17 SDGs revealed that keywords relating to key aspects of the goals are under-represented in the majority of the sustainable tourism courses analysed (Figure 3 below). Over 80% of the course profiles analysed revealed no (0%) keywords relating to the 17 SDGs and cases of the course profiles showing 4+ keywords for any of the SDGs was only recorded twice (Goal 8 and 12). Very few courses provided evidence of at least one keyword per SDG and even less showing 2–3 keywords per SDG. Of the three key SDGs specifically referring to tourism, two of these (Goals 12 and 14) were not evident in 48 of the 60 analysed course profiles (80%). Goal 8 appeared in 82% of course profiles, however, this is due to the economic focus of the goal "decent work and economic growth" which is deemed to be a less-than strong conceptualisation of sustainable tourism. Although sustainable development is not deemed to be a strong form of sustainability, it would still be expected that key concepts relating to the UNs international agenda would be evident in most sustainable tourism courses around the world. This finding must be treated with caution, however, due to the limited nature and content of some university course profiles in relation to the SDGs.

To summarise, few undergraduate sustainable tourism courses appeared to be reaching beyond the traditional triple bottom line/three domains, and therefore represented moderate conceptualisations of sustainability. The course designs also seemed to be under-developing some vital sustainability skills needed in tourism graduates. In order for universities to achieve the pedagogical goal of developing conceptualisations of "strong sustainability" amongst

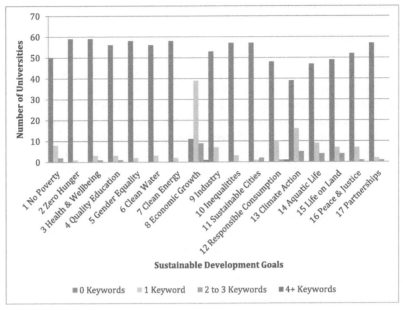

Figure 3. Number of SDG-related keywords evident in international sustainable tourism courses.

graduates of tourism degrees, and in alignment with targets for the 2030 Agenda for Sustainable Development, these issues need to be addressed further.

Discussion

The main objective of this study was to identify the current sustainability conceptualisations being used in university undergraduate sustainable tourism courses internationally including conceptualisations, key sustainability skills and SDGs underpinning the design of course profiles. In answer to the first research question, moderate conceptualisations of sustainability were underpinning international undergraduate tourism courses, as opposed to very strong sustainability. Overall, there was a heavy focus on the concepts of "triple bottom line" that replicates the findings of a similar study conducted by Boyle et al. (2015) in which Australian tourism courses were underpinned by weak conceptualisations of sustainability. Although a small number represented "strong sustainability," the analysed courses in this international study also failed to demonstrate "very strong sustainability." In addition, the suggestion that sustainable tourism course design is possibly influenced by the aforementioned less-than-strong conceptualisations of sustainability replicates the findings of Wilson and von der Heidt (2013) who highlighted barriers to implementing sustainability courses within Australian business schools. This study seems to affirm that the same issues are present around the world and that the less-than-strong conceptualisations of sustainability possibly stem from the business nature of tourism and the fact that most of these courses are situated within university business schools.

The second question examines whether internationally university undergraduate tourism courses are designed to help graduates to be equipped with essential and relevant sustainability skills necessary for more complex ways of thinking about sustainability. The findings of this study indicated that despite skills being a strong focus of most tourism courses, the courses focused on giving students "critical thinking" skills and "transdisciplinary knowledge," whereas "holistic thinking" and "systems thinking" were under-represented. This replicates the findings of a similar study conducted by Thomas and Day (2014) who also found that Australian university graduates were lacking key skills, such as systems/holistic thinking, needed for sustainability. It is also worth noting that "ethical practice" skills, which is evidenced in 33% of courses, one of the key features of this is reflection on learning and practice in the environment and sustainability. This is positive that a third of courses are making attempts to ask students to be reflective of their own sustainability learning. It is unclear from this study, however, whether educators are actually teaching students how to think critically and reflectively about sustainability within the course, or whether it is just a key graduate attribute they must adhere to. The findings of this study suggest that more knowledge is needed about how to build and develop key competencies in sustainability.

The third question addresses whether key SDGs are evident in sustainable tourism curricula and to what extent they can be achieved internationally. SDGs were under-represented in the analysis of course profiles. Although this result is somewhat expected, as many were designed prior to the development of SDGs, it would be assumed that key generic concepts from the preceding MDGs would be included in course design. This paper also raises a critical issue regarding how educators can use the international SDGs to not only support sustainable tourism course design but also to consider the strength of the sustainability conceptualisations underpinning these (Cotterell et al., 2018; Hák et al., 2016). However, it is important for tourism educators to not only teach strong sustainability conceptualisations together with sustainability skills, but also to encourage knowledge of how to implement the SDGs from a stronger perspective. SDG8 was also the goal resulting in the highest keyword search result emphasizing the economic focus of some curriculum. The search also revealed zero results for terms such as "inclusive growth" or "slow growth" with only two course profiles making references to "limits to tourism growth." Overall, limited concepts related to strong sustainability are evidenced in the SDGs and hence the course profiles. Hence, it may be useful for tourism educators to use critically reflective practice (CRP) in order to encourage students to think more deeply about the SDGs and how they can be applied in more holistic and interdisciplinary ways. This paper proposes that educators should be critically reflective to ensure they teach for stronger sustainability and in relation to achieving the SDGs. Critical reflection on a range of strong sustainability concepts will help in this process. Such concepts include: questioning the concepts of economic growth, questioning the centrality of humans, examining the overuse of resources, exploring new models of development and business, incorporating ecological integrity of decision making, involving ethical standards and values in actions, and exploring the transdisciplinary nature of wicked sustainability problems. Being critical of the SDGS may facilitate deeper understandings of sustainability systems.

Evaluation was made of the key sustainability concepts underpinning the SDGs together with ways in which educators can use critical questions related to the SDGs as ways to incorporate them into courses (see Table 2). This highlighted ways in which the tourism industry can work together with multiple stakeholders to achieve the 17 SDGs in a holistic and integrated manner. A questioning strategy is needed to address critical approaches to the concepts underpinning SDGs. We have not provided an exhaustive list of questions but rather offer an example of the types of questions required to develop strong sustainability within the SDGs framework. It is essential that future (and current) tourism industry workers understand that the goals are inter-related and that if managed well have the power to transform the lives of multiple stakeholders along its value chain (World Tourism Organisation and United Nations Development Program, 2017, p. 28).

This study also acknowledges that for some educators, due to the political climate of their department (i.e. overcrowding of curriculum; business/economic focus), it is still "business as usual" (Wilson & von der Heidt, 2013, p. 145) confirming that there is still resistance to conceptualisations of strong sustainability being embedded into tourism curriculum – not only in an Australian context but also internationally. Rather than teaching from a predominantly neo-liberal business viewpoint, where there is an unbalanced focus on the economic outcomes of tourism, this paper argues that globally universities need to teach tourism students about much stronger and varied conceptualisations of sustainability that consider different perspectives including "very strong sustainability." It is imperative that immediate changes are made given

Table 2. Using critical questioning to incorporate the SDGs underpinned by a stronger approach to sustainability.

Sustainable development goals	Key concept(s) underpinning SDGs	Research supporting stronger conceptualisations	Critical questions to incorporate the SDGs
1. No poverty[a]	Pro-poor policies	Phi, Whitford and Reid (2016) Scheyvens (2007)	What international activities can influence pro-poor tourism?
2. Zero hunger[a]	End hunger	Sims (2009)	How can tourism destinations support sustainable food systems and reduce malnutrition?
3. Health/well-being[a]	Reduce deaths, disease and substance abuse	Uysal, Sirgy, Woo, and Kim (2016)	How can tourism help contribute to social capital in the destination?
4. Quality education[a]	Lifelong learning; Inclusive quality education;	Dredge et al. (2012)	How can tourism businesses contribute to achieving eco-literacy amongst locals and tourists? How can systems thinking be used to educate all tourism stakeholders?
5. Gender equality[a]	Gender equality; Female empowerment	Ferguson (2011)	How can tourism be reconstructed to promote gender equality and empower minorities fairly?
6. Clean water and sanitation	Improve water and sanitation for all; Water-use efficiency	Hadjikakou, Miller, Chenoweth, Druckman, and Zoumides (2015)	How can tourism work with local communities to improve water and sanitation for all? How can tourism related businesses improve water use efficiency of tourists?
7. Affordable and clean energy[a]	Increase renewables Reduce greenhouse gases	Becken and Simmons (2002) Gössling (2000)	Can tourism businesses contribute more by using clean energy and non-renewables? Can tourism help to give local communities access to affordable and clean energy?
8. Decent work and economic growth	Sustainable economic growth; Inclusive growth	Bakker and Messerli (2017) Hall (2009)	Can destinations focus more on 'steady-state tourism' and 'slow tourism'? What does the local community want in terms of tourism growth?
9. Industry, innovation and infrastructure	Sustainable infrastructure and industrialization; Information technology for all	Boers and Cottrell (2007)	How can technology and infrastructure be developed that has social and environmental benefits (not externalities)?
10. Reduced inequalities[a]	Income growth for population below poverty line	Kokkranikal and Morrison (2011)	How can tourism give equal opportunity to the local community and empower all through equality?
11. Sustainable cities and communities[a]	Sustainable housing and transport systems	Bakker and Messerli (2017)	How can tourism destinations work with governments to support public transport for all (not only tourists)? How can tourism be used to maximise protection of world cultural and natural heritage?

(*continued*)

Table 2. Continued.

Sustainable development goals	Key concept(s) underpinning SDGs	Research supporting stronger conceptualisations	Critical questions to incorporate the SDGs
12. Responsible consumption and production	Reduce footprint; Efficient use of natural resources; Sustainable consumption;	Higgins-Desbiolles (2010,2017)	Can tourism businesses work towards achieving 'zero waste'? How can tourism help to promote non-material sources of happiness?
13. Climate action	Climate change mitigation	Scott and Becken (2010)	How can destinations work with all stakeholders to return to atmospheric carbon dioxide levels of 350 ppm?
14. Life below water	Conserve oceans for sustainable development	United Nations Environment Programme (UNEP) and World Tourism Organization (WTO) (2012)	Can tourism destinations focus more on being eco-system centric? How can tourism engage the local community and tourists to take active ownership of life below water?
15. Life on land	Conserve, restore and sustainably use ecosystems; End poaching and trafficking of protected species	UNEP and WTO (2012)	Can biodiversity values be integrated into planning? How can tourism engage the local community and tourists to take active ownership of life on land (long-term)?
16. Peace and justice[a]	Reduce victims of violence; End child abuse and trafficking; Justice for all; Reduce corruption	Jamal and Carmago (2014)	How can destinations contribute efficiently to end violence, child abuse, trafficking and corruption? How can tourism businesses incorporate justice for all?
17. Partnerships for the goals[a]	Global macroeconomic stability; Neo-liberalism; Collaborative planning	Waligo, Clarke, and Hawkins (2013)	How can tourism destinations take a more holistic integrated approach to understanding that all actions directly link to multiple stakeholders? Can a systems thinking approach be developed to help achieve the SDGs?

Note: [a]More research is needed on exploring the connections between sustainable tourism and these SDGs (Bramwell, Higham, Lane, & Miller,2017).

the current climate of "overtourism" in the tourism industry worldwide (e.g. Barcelona, Lisbon, Kyoto, Venice, Amsterdam, Boracay in the Philippines, Koh Phi Phi Leh in Thailand). This may also be a reason why a "paradigm shift in thinking" is still required (Boyle, 2015) as globally the tourism industry (and educators) are still a long way off fully understanding how to achieve sustainable tourism (Seraphin et al., 2018). Some teachers are also "yet to respond to the 'paradigm shift in thinking' required for sustainability education" meaning course content is prioritized according to the lecturer's (often less than ecocentric) viewpoint (Boyle, 2015). However, recent issues emerging surrounding "overtourism" around the world show that "very strong sustainability" conceptualisations need to be embedded as a matter of urgency both in education and industry practice. The planet can no longer sustain "moderate" levels of sustainability.

It is also acknowledged that embedding, for example, systems thinking, into a sustainable tourism course is not a straightforward task and may require a competency that even the educator themselves does not possess. This then requires professional development/training workshops for educators of sustainability. The delivery of sustainable tourism courses needs to be challenged by both educators and Deans. Study findings also seem to indicate that universities are still focusing on EaS rather than EfS particularly as systems/holistic thinking is a key factor in EfS (Rieckmann, 2012). More research is needed on developing systems thinking especially given its merits (Sterling, 2003) and current lack of evidence in key tourism programs around the world (Thomas & Day, 2014).

Theoretically, this paper challenges the superficiality of sustainability conceptualisations currently underpinning international tourism courses and adds to the previous discussion surrounding weak to strong sustainability in the tourism industry. Additionally, it has contributed to the tourism literature surrounding sustainability conceptualisations as well learning outcomes for sustainability-related courses.

Practically, the study highlights that sustainable tourism courses, as indicated by course profiles, fail to provide the necessary curriculum to develop tourism graduates who will be capable of making significant contributions to the long-term future of the industry as well as contributing to the achievement of the UN's SDGs by 2030. The suggested framework (Table 2) to strengthen the SDGs in tourism curricula serves as a possible guide for teaching and learning about the SDGs in tourism courses. Overall, the findings of this study support the notion that tourism education needs to take a stronger approach to implementing sustainability education that is more in line with the thinking of key sustainability scholars.

Limitations and further research

Whilst care was taken to select a range of course profiles from high-performing universities for analysis, some countries and continents have been over-represented. Countries within Asia are still represented, however the number is minimal in comparison to the UK, North America and Australia. This is partly due to the limited course profiles made publicly available.

Content analysis is criticized by some as being subjective and subject to bias (Frey et al., 1999). To prevent the analysis being subject to the researchers' own bias and beliefs, the researcher has used the research team to cross-check the results of the analysis. Furthermore, any course profiles that gave a limited insight (e.g. limited information on course inclusions and weekly topics) into the course content were not used for analysis. The researcher also acknowledges that the visible content of the course profiles used for analysis does not necessarily represent the hidden agenda and invisible delivery of the course and it does not in any way confirm the teaching and learning style of the delivery of the course. It also does not guarantee that a course that, for example, has multiple references to "critical thinking" will actually result in critical thinking. The method does, however, give a good indication of the focus of the course and suggests areas where international tourism educators' attention needs to be given.

Overall, the initial results of this study need to be further explored. Future assessment of sustainable tourism courses that include better representation from Asia and Africa would be appropriate. Interviews could also be undertaken to ascertain what actually takes place in the teaching of the course, or of educators' conceptualisations of sustainability. Future research into the level of SDGs being embedded into not only sustainable tourism but broader tourism curricula is also essential to ensure international engagement by teachers with SDG education. Finally, further research is needed on how tourism can connect with more of the SDGs and thus contribute to sustainability (Bramwell, Higham, Lane, & Miller, 2017).

Conclusion

This study supports the views of key sustainability scholars who argue that conceptualisations of sustainability are still strongly grounded in Western ways of thinking, and linked to ideas of growth, progress and economics, which need to be challenged. In order for universities to create future industry workers capable of being sustainability leaders, skill development in areas such as reflective thinking (Howlett et al., 2016), systemic thinking, compassion and empathy, and ethical practices (Wals & Blewitt, 2010) need to be developed. This paper argues that globally universities need to teach tourism students about much stronger and varied conceptualisations of sustainability that consider different perspectives including "very strong sustainability" rather than from a predominantly neo-liberal business viewpoint that can lead to overtourism issues.

Educating students about the variety of sustainability conceptualisations is necessary if students are to be enabled to reflect on varying worldviews and to have transformative learning experiences. Assisting students to understand more eco-centric conceptualisations increases the possibility that they will graduate armed with the critical thinking skills needed to transform business practices (Wilson & von der Heidt, 2013). To achieve this, an increase in CRP and systems thinking training for educators and in tourism workplaces is essential. This is the only way to ensure that the tourism industry becomes deeply eco-literate, with an understanding of very-strong sustainability. If the tourism industry develops stronger approaches to sustainability, then the industry will be able to play an important role in achieving the SDGs rather than the current "growth fetish that is resulting in tourism killing tourism" (Higgins-Desbiolles, 2017, p. 157). As previously mentioned, the planet can no longer sustain "moderate" levels of sustainability.

Disclosure statement

No potential conflict of interest was reported by the authors.

References

Australian Government's Australian Learning and Teaching Council (ALTC). (2010). *Assessing sustainability: Graduate skills—Standards of achievement*. Retrieved from http://www.graduateskills.edu.au/sustainability/.

Bakker, M., & Messerli, H. R. (2017). Inclusive growth versus pro-poor growth: Implications for tourism development. *Tourism & Hospitality Research, 17*(4), 384–391.

Becken, S. (2017). Evidence of a low-carbon tourism paradigm? *Journal of Sustainable Tourism, 25*(6), 832–850.

Becken, S., & Simmons, D. G. (2002). Understanding energy consumption patterns of tourist attractions and activities in New Zealand. *Tourism Management, 23*(4), 343–354.

Boers, B., & Cottrell, S. (2007). Sustainable tourism infrastructure planning: A GIS-supported approach. *Tourism Geographies, 9*(1), 1–21.

Boluk, K., & Carnicelli, S. (2015). Activism and critical reflection through experiential learning. *Journal of Teaching in Travel & Tourism, 15*, 242–251.

Boyle, A. (2015). *Space for sustainability? From curriculum to critical thinking in Australian tourism higher education* (Doctoral dissertation, Southern Cross University). Retrieved from https://epubs.scu.edu.au/cgi/viewcontent.cgi?article=1451&context=theses

Boyle, A., Wilson, E., & Dimmock, K. (2014). *Wrestling with the 's' word: How tourism academics understand 'sustainability (pp. 758–762.)*. CAUTHE 2014: Tourism and Hospitality in the Contemporary World: Trends, Changes and Complexity.

Boyle, A., Wilson, E., & Dimmock, K. (2015). Transformative education and sustainable tourism: The influence of a lecturer's worldview. *Journal of Teaching in Travel & Tourism, 15*(3), 252–263.

Bramwell, B., Higham, J., Lane, B., & Miller, G. (2017). Twenty-five years of sustainable tourism and the. *Journal of Sustainable Tourism: Looking Back & Moving Forward.Journal of Sustainable Tourism, 25*(1), 1–9.

Bryman, A., & Bell, E. (2011). *Business Research Methods* (3rd ed.). New York, NY: Oxford University Press.

Camargo, B. A., & Gretzel, U. (2017). What do tourism students know about sustainability and sustainable tourism? An exploratory study of Latin American students. *Journal of Teaching in Travel & Tourism, 101*(2), 117.

Connell, K., Remington, S., & Armstrong, C. (2012). Assessing systems thinking skills in two undergraduate sustainability courses: a comparison of teaching strategies. *Journal of Sustainability Studies, 3.*. Retrieved from: http://krex.k-state.edu/dspace/bitstream/handle/2097/13783/Assessing%20systems%20-%20publisher%27s%20PDF.pdf?sequence=1&isAllowed=y .

Cotterell, D., Arcodia, C., & Ferreira, J. A. (2015). *Educating tourism students to have a sustainable mindset: A study into how universities can develop students' capabilities to have more complex understandings of sustainability* (p. 436). Paper presented at the CAUTHE 2015 Conference on Rising Tides and Sea Changes: Adaptation and Innovation in Tourism and Hospitality, Gold Coast, QLD.

Cotterell, D., Arcodia, C., & Ferreira, J. (2017). Teaching for strong sustainability in university tourism courses. In P. Benckendorff & A. Zehrer (Eds.), *Handbook of teaching and learning in tourism* (pp. 373–388). Cheltenham, UK: Edward Elgar Publishing.

Cotterell, D., Ferriera, J., Hales, R., & Arcodia, C. (2018). *Cultivating conscientious tourism caretakers: A phenomeno-graphic continuum towards stronger sustainability*. Manuscript submitted for publication.

Cotterell, D., Hales, R., Arcodia, C., & Ferreira, J. (2018, February). *The power of variation theory in educating about the sustainable development goals* (p. 638). Paper presented at the CAUTHE 2018 Conference on Get Smart: Paradoxes and Possibilities in Tourism, Hospitality and Events Education and Research, Newcastle, NSW.

Davies, G. R. (2013). Appraising weak and strong sustainability: Searching for a middle ground. Consilience. *The Journal of Sustainable Development, 10*(1), 111–124.

Dovers, S. (2005). *Environmental and sustainability policy: Creation, implementation, evaluation*. Sydney, AU: Federation Press.

Dredge, D., Beckendorff, P., Day, M., Gross, M. J., Walo, M., Weeks, P., & Whitelaw, P. (2012). The philosophic practitioner and the curriculum space. *Annals of Tourism Research, 39*(4), 2154–2176.

Dunlap, R. E., Van Liere, K. D., Mertig, A. G., & Jones, R. E. (2000). New trends in measuring environmental attitudes: measuring endorsement of the new ecological paradigm: A revised NEP scale. *Journal of Social Issues, 56*(3), 425–442.

Dwyer, L. (2017). Saluting while the ship sinks: the necessity for tourism paradigm change. *Journal of Sustainable Tourism, 1* 20.

Dwyer, L., Forsyth, P., & Dywer, W. (2010). *Tourism economics and policy*. Bristol, UK: Channel View Publications.

Faber Canziani, B. F., Sonmez, S., Hsieh, Y., & Byrd, E. R. (2012). A learning theory framework for sustainability education in tourism. *Journal of Teaching in Travel & Tourism, 12*, 3–20.

Ferguson, L. (2011). Promoting gender equality and empowering women? Tourism and the third millennium development goal. *Current Issues in Tourism, 14*(3), 235–249.

Fisher, B., & McAdams, E. (2015). Gaps in sustainability education. *International Journal of Sustainability in Higher Education, 16*(4), 407–423.

Frey, L., Botan, C., & Kreps, G. (1999). *Investigating communication: An introduction to research methods* (2nd ed.). Boston, NY: Allyn & Bacon.

Fullagar, S., & Wilson, E. (2012). Critical pedagogies: A reflexive approach to knowledge creation in tourism and hospitality studies. *Journal of Hospitality & Tourism Management, 19*, 1–6.

Gössling, S. (2000). Sustainable tourism development in developing countries: Some aspects of energy use. *Journal of Sustainable Tourism, 8*(5), 410–425.

Hadjikakou, M., Miller, G., Chenoweth, J., Druckman, A., & Zoumides, C. (2015). A comprehensive framework for comparing water use intensity across different tourist types. *Journal of Sustainable Tourism, 23*(10), 1445–1467.

Hák, T., Janoušková, S., & Moldan, B. (2016). Sustainable development goals: A need for relevant indicators. *Ecological Indicators, 60*, 565–573.

Hall, C. M. (2009). Degrowing tourism: Decroissance, sustainable consumption and steady-state tourism. *Anatolia. An International Journal of Tourism & Hospitality Research, 20*(1), 46–61.

Higgins-Desbiolles, F. (2010). The elusiveness of sustainability in tourism: The culture-ideology of consumerism and its implications. *Tourism & Hospitality Research, 10*(2), 116–129.

Higgins-Desbiolles, F. (2017). Sustainable tourism: Sustaining tourism or something more? *Tourism Management Perspectives*, Advance online publication. Retrieved from https://doi.org/10.1016/j.tmp.2017.11.017

Howlett, C., Ferreira, J. A., & Blomfield, J. (2016). Teaching sustainable development in higher education: Building critical, reflective thinkers through an interdisciplinary approach. *International Journal of Sustainability in Higher Education, 17*(3), 305–321.

Hunter, C. (1997). Sustainable tourism as an adaptive paradigm. *Annals of Tourism Research, 24*(4), 850–867.

Jamal, T., & Camargo, B. A. (2014). Sustainable tourism, justice and an ethic of care: Toward the just destination. *Journal of Sustainable Tourism, 22*(1), 11–30.

Jones, P., Hillier, D., & Comfort, D. (2017). The sustainable development goals and the tourism and hospitality industry. *Athens Journal of Tourism, 4*(1), 7–17.

Kidd, C. V. (1992). The evolution of sustainability. *Journal of Agricultural & Environmental Ethics, 5*(1), 1–26.

Kokkranikal, J., & Morrison, A. (2011). Community networks and sustainable livelihoods in tourism: The role of entrepreneurial innovation. *Tourism Planning & Development, 8*(2), 137–156.

Kopnina, H. (2012). Evaluating education for sustainable development (ESD): Using ecocentric and anthropocentric attitudes toward the sustainable development (EAATSD) scale. *Environment, Development & Sustainability, 15*(3), 607–623.

Lee, H., Au, N., Li, G., & Law, R. (2014). An insight into research performance through a citation counting analysis. *Journal of Hospitality & Tourism Management, 21*, 54–63.

McCool, S., Butler, R., Buckley, R., Weaver, D., & Wheeller, B. (2013). Is concept of sustainability utopian: Ideally perfect but impracticable? *Tourism Recreation Research, 38*(2), 213–242.

McKercher, B., & Prideaux, B. (2011). Are tourism impacts low on personal environmental agendas? *Journal of Sustainable Tourism, 19*(3), 325–345.

Miller, G. (2001). The development of indicators for sustainable tourism: results of a Delphi survey of tourism researchers. *Tourism Management, 22*(4), 351–362.

Neumayer (2003). *Weak versus strong sustainability: Exploring the limits of two opposing paradigms*. London, UK: Elgar.

Nilsson, M., Griggs, D., & Visbeck, M. (2016). Map the interactions between sustainable development goals: Mans Nilsson, Dave Griggs and Martin Visbeck present a simple way of rating relationships between the targets to highlight priorities for integrated policy. *Nature, 534*(7607), 320–323.

Paul, R. (2005). The state of critical thinking today. *New Directions for Community Colleges, 2005*(130), 27–38.

Pearce, D. (1993). *Blueprint 3: Measuring sustainable development*. London, UK: Earthscan.

Phelan, L., McBain, B., Ferguson, A., Brown, V., Hay, I., Horsfield, R., & Taplin, R. (2015). *Learning and teaching academic standards statement for environment and sustainability*. Sydney: Office for Learning and Teaching. Retrieved from: http://environmentltas.gradschool.edu.au/uploads/content/drafts/ES_LTAS_Statement_Final.pdf

Phi, G. T., Whitford, M., & Reid, S. (2016). What's in the black box? Evaluating anti-poverty tourism interventions utilizing theory of change. *Current Issues in Tourism, 1* 16.

QS (2017). *QS World university rankings by subject 2017*. Retrieved from https://www.topuniversities.com/university-rankings/university-subject-rankings/2017/hospitality-leisure-management

Rieckmann, M. (2012). Future-oriented higher education: which key competencies should be fostered through university teaching and learning? *Futures, 44*(2), 127–135.

Roychoudhury, A., Shepardson, D. P., & Hirsch, A. S. (2017). Systems thinking and teaching in the context of climate system and climate change. In D. P. Shepardson, A. Roychoudhury, & A. S. Hirsch (Eds.), *Teaching and learning about climate change: A framework for educators* (pp. 29–4). New York, NY: Taylor & Francis.

Scheyvens, R. (2007). Exploring the tourism–poverty nexus. *Current Issues in Tourism, 10*(2–3), 231–254.

Scott, D., & Becken, S. (2010). Adapting to climate change and climate policy: Progress, problems and potentials. *Journal of Sustainable Tourism, 18*(3), 283–295.

Senge, P. M. (2006). *The fifth discipline: The art and practice of the learning organisation* (revised ed.). London, UK: Random House.

Seraphin, H., Sheeran, P., & Pilato, M. (2018). Over-tourism and the fall of Venice as a destination. *Journal of Destination Marketing & Management, 9*, 374–376.

Severt, D. E., Tesone, T. J., Bottorff, T. J., & Carpenter, M. L. (2009). A world ranking of the top 100 hospitality and tourism programs. *Journal of Hospitality & Tourism Research, 33*(4), 451–470.

Sheldon, P., Fesenmaier, D., Woeber, K., Cooper, C., & Antonioli, M. (2008). Tourism education futures 2010–2030: Building the capacity to lead. *Journal of Teaching in Tourism & Travel, 7*(3), 61–68.

Sipos, Y., Battisti, B., & Grimm, K. (2008). Achieving transformative sustainability learning: Engaging head, heart and hands. *International Journal of Sustainability in Higher Education, 9*(1), 68–86.

Sims, R. (2009). Food, place and authenticity: Local food and the sustainable tourism experience. *Journal of Sustainable Tourism, 17*(3), 321–336.

Solow, R. (1993). An almost practical step toward sustainability. *Resources Policy, 19*(3), 162–172.

Springett, D. V. (2003). *Corporate conceptions of sustainable tourism in New Zealand: A critical analysis* (Doctoral dissertation). Durham University, UK. Retrieved from http://etheses.dur.ac.uk/3147/1/3147_1172.pdf?UkUDh:CyT

Springett, D. (2010). Education for sustainability in the business studies curriculum: Ideological struggle. In P. Jones, D. Selby & S. Sterling (Eds.), *Sustainability education: Perspectives and practice across higher education* (pp. 75–92). Oxon, UK: Earthscan.

Sterling, S. (2003). *Whole systems thinking as a basis for paradigm change in education: Explorations in the context of sustainability* (Doctoral dissertation). University of Bath, UK. Retrieved from http://www.bath.ac.uk/cree/sterling/sterlingthesis.pdf

Sterling, S., & Thomas, I. (2006). Education for sustainability: The role of capabilities in guiding university curricula. *International Journal of Innovation and Sustainable Development, 1*(4), 349–369.

Sustainable Aotearoa New Zealand (SANZ). (2009). *Strong sustainability for New Zealand: Principles and scenarios.* Retrieved from https://earthcharter.org/invent/images/uploads/Strong sustainability for NZ (2).pdf

Sustainable Development Solutions Network (SDSN). (2017). *Australia/Pacific getting started with the SDGs in Universities: A guide for Universities, Higher Education Institutions, and the Academic Sector. Australia, New Zealand and Pacific edition.* Australia/Pacific, Melbourne: Sustainable Development Solutions Network. Retrieved from http://ap-unsdsn.org/wp-content/uploads/2017/08/University-SDG-Guide_web.pdf

Thomas, I., & Day, T. (2014). Sustainability capabilities, graduate capabilities, and Australian universities. *International Journal of Sustainability in Higher Education, 15*(2), 208–227.

Tilbury, D. (1995). Environmental education for sustainability: Defining the new focus of environmental education in the 1990s. *Environmental Education Research, 1*(2), 195–212.

Tribe, J. (2002). The philosophic practitioner. *Annals of Tourism Research, 29*(2), 338–357.

United Nations (UN). (2017). *Global indicator framework for the sustainable development goals and targets of the 2030 agenda for sustainable development (A/RES/71/313).* Retrieved from https://unstats.un.org/sdgs/indicators/Global Indicator Framework_A.RES.71.313 Annex.pdf

UNESCO. (2014). *Aichi–Nagoya declaration on education for sustainable development. Education for sustainable development 2014. World Conference, Aichi–Nagoya (Japan),* 10–12 November 2014. Retrieved from http://unesdoc.unesco.org/images/0023/002310/231074e.pdf

United Nations World Tourism Organisation (UNWTO). (2017). *Sustainable development of tourism: Definitions.* Retrieved from http://sdt.unwto.org/content/about-us-5

United Nations Environment Programme and World Tourism Organization. (2012). *Tourism in the green economy: Background report.* Retrieved from https://www.cbd.int/financial/doc/tourism-greeneconomy.pdf

University Leaders for a Sustainable Future (ULSF). (2016a). *The talloires declaration.* Retrieved from http://ulsf.org/talloires-declaration/.

University Leaders for a Sustainable Future (ULSF). (2016b). Retrieved from http://ulsf.org/about/.

Uysal, M., Sirgy, M. J., Woo, E., & Kim, H. L. (2016). Quality of life (QOL) and well-being research in tourism. *Tourism Management, 53*, 244–261.

Von der Heidt, T., & Lamberton, G. (2014). How academics in undergraduate business programs at an Australian university view sustainability. *Australian Journal of Environmental Education, 30*(02), 215–238.

Wackernagel, M., & Rees, W. (1998). *Our ecological footprint: Reducing human impact on the earth.* Gabriola Island, BC, Canada: New Society Publishers.

Waligo, V. M., Clarke, J., & Hawkins, R. (2013). Implementing sustainable tourism: A multi-stakeholder involvement management framework. *Tourism Management, 36*, 342–353.

Wals, A. E. J., & Blewitt, J. (2010). Third-wave sustainability in higher education: Some (inter)national trends and developments. In P. Jones, D. Selby, & S. Sterling (Eds.), *Sustainability education: Perspectives and practice across higher education* (pp. 55–74). Oxon, UK: Earthscan.

Wang, J., Ayres, H., & Huyton, J. (2013). Is tourism education meeting the needs of the tourism industry? An Australian case study. *The Journal of Hospitality & Tourism Education, 22*(1), 8–14.

Weaver, D. (2005). *Sustainable tourism: Theory and practice.* Jordan Hill, UK: Routledge.

Weaver, D. (2008). *Ecotourism*. Queensland, AU: Wiley.

Wiek, A., Withycombe, L., & Redman, C. L. (2011). Key competencies in sustainability: A reference framework for academic program development. *Sustainability Science, 6*(2), 203–218.

Wilson, E. (2010). *Practice what you teach: Using critically reflective practice in teaching sustainable tourism planning* (p. 1671). CAUTHE 2010: Tourism and Hospitality: Challenge the Limits.

Wilson, E., & von der Heidt, T. (2013). Business as usual? Barriers to education for sustainability in the tourism curriculum. *Journal of Teaching in Travel & Tourism, 13*, 130–147.

World Commission (1987). *Our common future: World commission on environment and development*. Oxford, UK: Oxford University Press.

World Tourism Organization and United Nations Development Programme. (2017). *Tourism and the sustaianable development goals – Journey to 2030*. http://www.undp.org/content/dam/undp/library/Sustainable%20 Development/ UNWTO_UNDP_Tourism%20and%20the%20SDGs.pdf; Retrieved from UNWTO website.

No sustainability for tourism without gender equality

Daniela Moreno Alarcón and Stroma Cole

ABSTRACT
This paper explores the interconnections between the Sustainable Development Goals (SDGs) and tourism from a gender perspective. It is the first paper to take a critical analysis of how SDG 5 relates to tourism, and how tourism and gender equality interconnects with the other SDGs. First, we analyse the recent gender sensitive sustainable development agenda in order to set out the challenges – both past and present – that any sector involved in sustainable development faces. We then explore the links between the SDGs and tourism development from a gender perspective. In the third part of the paper, based on the field experiences of the authors, we use the examples of SDG 6 ("clean water and sanitation") and SDG 8 ("sustainable economic growth and decent work") to highlight the interconnections between gender equality and the other SDGs. Finally, we suggest some tools to help tourism businesses improve their performance with respect to gender equality thereby enhancing their capacity to contribute towards the achievement of the SDGs. We argue that, without tackling gender equality in a meaningful and substantive way, tourism's potential to contribute to the SDGs will be reduced and sustainable tourism will remain an elusive "pot of gold".

Introduction

Gender and tourism studies have grown considerably over the past 20 years (Burrell, Manfredi, Rollin, Price, & Stead, 1997; Ferguson, 2009; Gibson, 2001; Harvey, Hunt, & Harris, 1995; Kinnaird & Hall, 1994, 1996; Lakovidou & Turner, 1995; Norris, Wall, Cooper, & Lockwood, 1994; Nozawa, 1995; Pritchard, Morgan, Ateljevic, & Harris, 2007; Scheyvens, 2007; Sinclair, 1997; Swain, 1993, 1995, 2007; Swain & Hall, 2007; Wilkinson & Pratiwi, 1995). Gender and tourism studies have opened doors for better understanding the opportunities, and the challenges, confronting tourism stakeholders in terms of poverty reduction (Tucker & Boonabaana, 2012); policy-making and projects (Ferguson, 2010a, 2010b, 2011; Ferguson & Moreno, 2015), and decent working conditions (Carvalho, Costa, Lykke, & Torres, 2014; Gentry, 2007; Huete, Brotons, & Sigüenza, 2016; Iverson, 2000; Jordan, 1997; Ladkin, 2011; Moreno & Cañada, 2018; Muñoz-Bullón, 2009; Purcell, 1996; Skalpe, 2007; Thrane, 2008; Vandegrift, 2008).

As widely recognised in the literature, without gender equality there can be no sustainability (Bidegain Ponte, 2017; Bidegain Ponte & Enríquez, 2016; UN Women, 2018b). The number of academic journal articles exploring gender, tourism and empowerment has grown in recent years (Feng, 2013; Figueroa-Domecq, Pritchard, Segovia-Pérez, Morgan, & Villacé-Molinero, 2015; Knight

& Cottrell, 2016; Moswete & Lacey, 2015; Movono & Dahles, 2017; Panta & Thapa, 2018; Ramos & Prideaux, 2014; Tran & Walter, 2014; Tucker & Boonabaana, 2012). Nonetheless, the implications of these research findings have not been sufficiently understood and translated into policy and practice at all levels of the tourism industry. A great deal of gender and tourism analysis is emerging in tourism (Figueroa-Domecq et al., 2015; Suárez, Barquín, Jiménez, & Alfonso, 2016), but this is not the case in the field where there is a dearth of gender sensitive policies. Thus it is vital to champion gender equality in the context of tourism and the Sustainable Development Goals (SDGs). The global context of sustainability, reflected in the SDGs, makes it imperative to integrate gender equality within the SDGs and tourism development (UNWTO, 2017, 2018). From an academic point of view, little attention has been paid to clarifying the significance of the SDGs for "gender responsible tourism", or consideration given to the broader context of the sustainable development of tourism from a gender perspective. Few academics have considered the broader policy environment or made links to structural barriers (Swain & Swain, 2004), or to intersectionality. The most significant structural barriers to gender equality are: eliminating all forms of violence against women and addressing unpaid care and domestic work (UN Women, 2018b). Intersectionality refers to women's multiple, mutually constructed systems of subordination and thus how multiple demographic factors such as race, ethnicity, age, education and ability mediate experiences of equality and empowerment (Cole, 2017; Mooney, 2018). Thus women are not understood as a homogenous group, and context specific intersectional approaches allow for critical unpacking of social relations, justice and power. The "leave no-one behind" pledge within the SDGs attempts to focus attention on those who have been historically marginalised and hence is committing to an intersectional approach.

The United Nations' declaration of 2017 as the Year of Sustainable Tourism for Development (IY2017) reflected tourism's importance as a sector capable of contributing to sustainable development, including human rights. However, while the importance of gender equality has been widely recognised as integral to sustainability, relatively few tourism structures have embraced gender equality and women's empowerment (Equality in Tourism, 2017; Ferguson, 2018; Ferguson & Moreno, 2015). This is problematic when tourism projects and policy are developed in the field (Ferguson & Moreno, 2015; Moreno, 2018b). Frequently, actions undertaken to improve the conditions of women working in tourism are not to be based on sound gender analysis, which is a prerequisite for meaningfully improving women's positions. For example, in Spain, many hotels' CSR policies include the creation of women's executive networks, but make no reference to the discrimination faced by women workers on a daily basis (Ferguson & Moreno, 2016).

The main objective of this paper is to highlight the importance of SDG 5, gender equality, for the development of tourism and its relationship to the other SDGs. By first examining the place of gender equality in the SDGs and the interconnection between SDG5 and the other SDGs, the paper then explores these interconnections in relation to sustainable tourism. In doing so this paper highlights that SDG 5 is a critical component of sustainable tourism and offers some first steps businesses can take to support SDG 5.

It is our contention that a feminist perspective is required in tourism development (Aitchison, 2005; Swain, 2007) in order to ensure tourism's sustainability. According to Moreno (2018a, p. 25) "Gender equality without feminism is confined to reproducing and making invisible the gaps between men and women. This also draws, for example, on the fact that having more or only women in a specific initiative does not guarantee gender equality if the symbolic and normative codes promoted by patriarchy are not analysed as the main challenges for reducing poverty in developed and developing countries". This may be one of the reasons, as Figueroa-Domecq et al. (2015) have argued, there is a little dialogue between some gender and tourism researchers and "those in the wider social sciences" and the lack of "transformative feminist politics in international development institutions" (Ferguson, 2015, p. 380).

Drawing on the literature in gender mainstreaming that points out the importance of gender equality being a core component not an add-on (Caglar, Prügl, & Zwingel, 2013; Daly, 2005; Hoard, 2015; Mukhopadhyay, 2014; Standing, 2004) this paper argues that sustainable tourism is not possible if gender remains an "additional" element for sustainable tourism development, or if the veneer of gender is used as a way of silencing feminism. The "time's up now" for gender equality in tourism because tourism has sought to champion sustainable development from economic, social and environment standpoints, but gender equality frequently remains completely absent when sustainability is pursued by tourism stakeholders (Hardy, Beeton, & Pearson, 2002; Ruhanen, Weiler, Moyle, & McLennan, 2015).

The methodology of this paper is based on the experiences of participatory, first-hand practical and theoretical research, grounded in fieldwork. It draws upon the authors' extensive experience as academics, as well as gender and tourism consultants, who have worked in diverse countries and contexts over the past decade in international development. The focus on SDG 6 and 8 is based on our most recent and in depth fieldwork (for more details of the fieldwork see Moreno, 2017a and Cole, 2017).

The article will contribute to the growing body of literature on the role of tourism to contribute to the SDGs aiming to improve the lives of both women and men, while encouraging the sustainable development of tourism as a whole. It offers tools to tourism businesses to support their responsibilities to achieve the SDGs and will also provide inputs for policy-makers who are willing to transform tourism by integrating a gender perspective. First, we begin by analysing the recent gender sensitive sustainable development agenda in order to set out the challenges facing all sectors involved in sustainable development. Second, we explore the links between the SDGs and tourism development from a gender perspective. The third part of the paper explores gender and tourism using the context of SDG 6 ("clean water and sanitation") and SDG 8 ("sustainable economic growth and decent work") as two examples, to expose how gender equality plays a pivotal role in achieving all the SDGs. We then suggest some tools tourism businesses can use to support their responsibilities for achieving the SDGs.

The sustainable development agenda underpinned by a feminist lens

In 2000, the United Nations General Assembly, representing 191 governments, adopted the Millennium Declaration. With its eight Millennium Development Goals (MDGs), 18 targets and 48 indicators, the Declaration affirmed global aims to be reached by 2015. The Millennium Declaration outlined mechanisms to guarantee women's and men's equal access to rights and opportunities, as well as to end violence against women through the implementation of the Convention on the Elimination of all Forms of Discrimination Against Women (CEDAW) (United Nations, 2000).

The understanding of gender equality as a human right was affirmed in the framework of MDGs 5, "improve maternal health", and target 3.A "eliminate gender disparity in primary and secondary education … ". The MDGs therefore, were gender-guided in terms of the promotion of maternal health and girls' education. Understood from a feminist perspective, however, the MDGs established distractions from their own aims due to a lack of feminist analysis (Antrobus, 2006; Ariffin, 2004; Kabeer, 2015; Mujeres en Red, 2005). According to De la Cruz (2015), the definition and application of the MDGs generated an important debate at the core of the women's movement. For some, the MDGs were a reduction of the recommendations agreed upon during the 1990s through the Beijing Platform for Action. For others, the MDGs represented an opportunity for promoting action plans and mobilizing resources in line with the feminist agenda, as envisaged at the United Nations Conferences in Cairo in 1994, in Copenhagen in 1995, and during the follow-up meetings of the original Beijing Conference in 1995, known as Beijing +5 and Beijing +10.

The weakness of the MDGs lies in the lack of theoretical and practical connections between poverty, gender equality and women's lives. Whereas the Beijing Platform for Action was "based on a strong body of evidence that spelt out the complex and interdependent causalities underlying women's subordinate status across the world there was no such clear analytical logic to the MDGs" (Kabeer, 2015, p. 389). For example, the MDGs entailed a perception of maternal health or death devoid of causal elements, which suggested that the starting point for achieving improved maternal health, was at the point of pregnancy. The MDGs did not take into consideration important contextual, sexual and reproductive rights (Fernández-Layos & Ruiz, 2011). Another critique was directed at some of the indicators applied in assessing women's access to employment. For example, indicator 3.2 refers to the "share of women in wage employment in the non-agricultural sector", such as, for example, the service sector. However, as pointed out by UNIFEM (2000), access to income and salaries linked to the service industry does not necessarily imply emancipation because this sector is strongly linked with other forms of subordination.

The 2030 Agenda for Sustainable Development, adopted in September 2015 by the United Nations General Assembly, encompasses 17 SDGs and their 169 corresponding targets. These aim "to build on the MDGs and complete what they did not achieve. They seek to realise the human rights of all and to achieve gender equality and the empowerment of all women and girls. They are integrated and indivisible and balance the three dimensions of sustainable development: the economic, social and environmental" (United Nations, 2015b, p. 2). As stated, "the achievement of full human potential and of sustainable development is not possible if one half of humanity continues to be denied its full human rights and opportunities" (Ibid., p. 6).

In order to more successfully identify women's differing needs, the SDGs are grounded upon a process of contextualization and conceptualization with respect to the links between poverty and gender equality (Chant, 2008). According to the Post-2015 Women's Coalition (2015), this process was vital to ensure that sustainable development truly means human development, environmental protection and social development. As a result, and given Agenda 2030s universal approach, it is no longer a North–South aid agenda. Rather, the SDGs offer significant possibilities for a more transformative and broader change agenda (Fukuda-Parr, 2016). The following measures are outlined by the United Nations aimed at integrating gender equality and women's empowerment into the SDGs:

- The improvement of women's capacities and their enjoyment of all human rights.
- The assessment, reduction and redistribution of unpaid care work performed by women and girls.
- The full and equal participation of women in sustainable development as agents and decision-makers in the processes that affect their lives and the futures of their families, communities, countries and the world.
- The experience and leadership of those who defend women's rights and gender equality in parliaments, unions, cooperatives and community associations.
- The elimination of discriminatory laws, policies and practices and the promotion of legislation, policies and measures aimed at enhancing gender equality and women's empowerment (UN Women, 2018b; United Nations, 2015a, 2015b).

The potential of the SDGs to achieve gender equality and women's empowerment is enhanced by the recognition of the need to address violence against women and girls and to recognise their sexual and reproductive rights (Esquivel & Sweetman, 2016). According to Razavi (2016), although SDG 5 on "gender equality" failed to include any reference to "women's rights" or "women's human rights" in its title, it must be considered a step forward because most of the key strategic elements demanded by women's rights organizations were included. However, De la Cruz (2015) stresses that the SDGs indicators and targets still fail to adequately reflect women's priorities in relation to social norms, domestic decision-making, taxation and access to

Table 1. The Sustainable Development Goals and tourism from a gender perspective.

SDGs	Gender perspective inputs
SDG 1 – End poverty in all its forms everywhere	There is a complex link between poverty, and gender equality, which is not based on job creation and income alone. The link between poverty alleviation, tourism and gender equality requires a broad analysis from a gender perspective including exploring the feminization of poverty in tourism i.e. tourism income does not necessarily free women from gender based violence or give them equal power.
SDG 2 – End hunger, achieve food security and nutrition, promote sustainable agriculture	The importance of food sovereignty and safety is complicated when communities are involved with tourism. Women are frequently responsible for food production and maintaining a supply of food for their family while hosting tourists can be a challenge. Producing food for tourists' tastes can compete for land with primary production for local people. Furthermore, women frequently do not have land certificates but are the first to lose out to usufruct rights to tourism developers.
SDG 3 – Ensure healthy lives and promote well-being for all at all ages	Limited reproductive and sexual rights are exacerbated by sex tourism. Increases in sexually transmitted diseases, unwanted pregnancies, rape and sexual exploitation of women, girls and boys, all need to be recognised and addressed. Increased health spending for the benefit of local populations, including gender-based violence, safe sex education and provision, and reduced stigmatization of HIV, could be promoted though tourism.
SDG 4 – Ensure inclusive and equitable quality education and promote lifelong learning for all	Developing a tourism curriculum from a gender perspective is a challenge, and rarely exists, even though more women than men study and teach tourism! Tourist education has lacked an exploration of the roles, experiences and contributions of women within tourism, or a consideration of the barriers that prevent women from reaching their potential (Pritchard, 2018). Cultural factors, reproductive labour roles and basic education deficits frequently limit opportunities for community tourism education for women.
SDG 5 – Achieve gender equality and empower all women and girls	Including a gender perspective in tourism is a clear and concrete action not only to reduce poverty, but also to invest smartly in that reduction. Tourism models, including those that are promoted as less harmful, will not be sufficiently sustainable and accountable if a gender-based approach and the empowerment of women are not incorporated in a real and sustained way. This implies adjusting all declarations, instruments of planning, management and analysis related to tourism.
SDG 6 – Ensure the availability and sustainable management of water and sanitation for all	Women bear the brunt of water scarcity when communities lose out to the tourism industry for water supplies. A human rights approach to water management would ensure a fairer distribution of water. Women's voices in the access, use, control and administration of water is critical.
SDG 7 – Ensure access to affordable, reliable, sustainable and modern energy for all	The tourism industry needs a lot of power. To be sustainable, it must prioritise the use of renewable sources of energy. Besides promoting its own self-interest and sustainability, it can also promote the use of reliable green sources of energy in the communities where it is based. Increased access to electricity will also promote womens education and security, as well as the creation of new jobs.
SDG 8 – Promote sustained, inclusive and sustainable economic growth, employment and decent work for all	A gender perspective in tourism employment policies places emphasis on salary gaps, sexual abuse and harassment by colleagues and tourists, and fosters female workers' participation and decision-making.
SDG 9 – Build resilient infrastructure, promote inclusive and sustainable industrialisation and foster innovation	Awareness of the infrastructure used by women is essential to ensure their safety; without due consideration, tourism development can limit this. Since innovation implies transformation, tourism should embrace the transformational opportunities promoted by gender equality.
SDG 10 – Reduce inequality within and among countries	Better regulation and monitoring of global financial markets and better representation of developing countries in international decision-making will reduce inequality. Therefore, it would be

(continued)

Table 1. Continued.

SDGs	Gender perspective inputs
	very useful to know the gender impact of foreign direct investment in the tourist sector and the fiscal benefits that tourism enjoys in many developing countries.
SDG 11 – Make cities and human settlements inclusive, safe, resilient and sustainable	The guaranteed safety of women, both locals and tourists is required if tourism is to be sustainable. Over-tourism is a significant issue for many cities, as yet there has been no gender analysis of the problems experienced by citizens as a result of this problem.
SDG 12 – Ensure sustainable consumption and production patterns	Ensuring sustainable production requires the integration of a gender analysis in the value chain to consolidate fair trade and ensure women's participation.
SDG 13 – Take urgent action to combat climate change and its impacts	Climate change will have a greater impact on women than men (Denton, 2002). According to UN Women (2018a, 2018b) women and children are 14 times more likely to die in a disaster than men. Women's voice is essential in climate change resilience and tourism related planning, policymaking and implementation.
SDG 14 – Conserve and sustainably use the oceans, seas and marine resources for sustainable development	Forty-seven percent of the 120 million people who work in the capture and post-harvest fisheries sectors are women (FAO, 2015)so their voice in the sustainable use of the oceans must move beyond them as products for tourism.
SDG 15 – Protect, restore and promote sustainable use of terrestrial ecosystems and halt biodiversity loss	Loss of land through tourism is well documented. Land certification for women is critical and must not be compromised by tourism development. Women's role as custodians of biodiversity needs to be nurtured and given greater recognition.
SDG 16 – Promote peaceful and inclusive societies, provide access to justice for all and build inclusive institutions	In order to promote peaceful and inclusive societies, it is vital to understand that structural inequalities are mainly produced by patriarchy, which perpetuates gender-based violence in the form of physical, economic, psychological, sexual and political abuse. Therefore, the identification and implementation of measures to end gender-based violence, embedded in or related to tourism, must be a priority for achieving SDG 16.
SDG 17 – Strengthen the means of implementation and revitalise the global partnership for sustainable development	According to UNWTO (2013), more than half of the poorest countries in the world use tourism as an instrument for poverty reduction. The UNWTO needs to recognise the critical contribution that Civil Society Organisations, particularly women's groups, will make to their policy and agenda. The inclusion of women's voices will give more value to multi-stakeholder partnerships and public-private sector initiatives.

services, nor do they analyse women's poverty with respect to access to income, time and property titles. Thus, whereas the SDGs are definitely an improvement on the MDGs from a feminist perspective, a number of weaknesses still remain to be addressed.

The SDGs and tourism from a gender perspective

In 2015, the United Nations World Tourism Organization (UNWTO) sought to mainstream tourism within all 17 SDGs (UNWTO, 2015, 2017). This was done through the framework of the International Year of Sustainable Tourism for Development (IY2017), however, gender equality was not a key element. As pointed out by the non-governmental organization Equality in Tourism (2017) in response to UNWTO's Discussion Paper on the occasion of the International Year of Sustainable Tourism for Development 2017,[1] the UNWTO failed to grasp the importance of SDG 5 for achieving all of the other SDGs. This is particularly surprising in light of the growing recognition of the importance of gender equality across UN policy and civil society discourse. The UNWTO discussion paper dealt with narrow aspects of gender equality issues in tourism. For instance, while it addressed employment and decent work, it left out discussions of political empowerment and broader questions of structural inequalities. As such, it did not make clear how tourism is meant to contribute to achieving SDG 5, nor did it shed light on the role of institutions in working towards gender equality in tourism. Furthermore, it mixed "women" and "youth" in an unhelpful conflation, thus diluting the importance of gender issues to both the SDGs and the tourism sector. Moreover, achieving gender equality is not possible without dedicating specific resources to addressing the gender dimensions of tourism; specific budgets are required to advance tourism's contribution to SDG 5. As pointed out by Ferguson (2018, p. 20) "While gender issues were mentioned in a number of speeches and core documents, in reality there has been no substantive support from the secretary-general or programme directors for gender equality to be a priority issue for UNWTO". Furthermore, the SDGs, "leave no-one behind agenda" underscores the importance of intersectionality, which the UNWTO have failed to adequately consider.

A gender analysis of how tourism relates to all the SDGs means more than merely including the word gender equality or women's empowerment in every SDG. First, it involves recognizing that gender equality is a human right. As Bakas, Costa, Durão, Carvalho, and Breda (2018) suggest, many of the issues that women face in tourism are not a matter of increased equality, rather they are human rights issues. The outdated "add women and mix" strategy frequently applied to tourism, must be replaced with an analysis of women and gender-based power relations when designing, proposing, creating and implementing new tourism policies and initiatives (Moser, 1993; Rathgeber, 1990; Razavi & Miller, 1995). In other words, gender mainstreaming is a critical concern for implementing tourism development from a gender perspective (Lee-Gosselin, Briere, & Ann, 2013; Lombardo & Mergaert, 2013; Walby, 2005) in tourism. Table 1, based on Moreno (2017b), provides an outline of some valuable avenues to consider when conducting a gender analysis of the SDGs as they relate to tourism. The following section then explores SDGs 6 and 8 in greater detail.

Gender and tourism in SDG 6 and SDG 8 and pushing forward

We now use the examples of SDG 6, "ensure availability and sustainable management of water and sanitation for all", and SDG 8, "promote sustained, inclusive and sustainable economic growth, employment and decent work for all", to explore in greater depth the considerations and analysis required for tourism to become a real engine for gender equality and women's empowerment. These two examples are chosen based on the authors' recent in depth research. Gender inequality in employment is one of the major factors preventing decent work in tourism, as the first author discovered while working for UN Women in Cape Verde on their Action Plan for Gender Mainstreaming in tourism; and in Albania where she reviewed the tourism strategy from a gender perspective. Water is the most important natural resource for the future of tourism, and a global tourism concern (Gössling & Peeters, 2015), although its importance sometimes remains invisible. As the second author discovered in Labuan Bajo, Indonesia, water supply can be a limiting factor for women's participation in tourism.

SDG 6 – ensure availability and sustainable management of water and sanitation for all

There is a close relationship between water justice and gender (Ahlers & Zwarteveen, 2009; O'Reilly, Halvorson, Sultana, & Laurie, 2009; Sultana, 2011; Truelove, 2011) and this has been explored specifically in relation to tourism in a number of destinations (Cole, 2017; Cole & Ferguson, 2015; Cole & Tulis, 2016). The tourism industry exerts an enormous strain on water supplies. This generates a range of social problems, not least because local inhabitants often have to compete with the tourism sector over the access, allocation and use of water for their personal and domestic needs. Globally, women and girls are responsible for water collection in 80% of households (UN Women, 2018a). Women suffer to a greater extent when water resources are mismanaged (Hemmingway, 2004). As caregivers, food providers, and health care suppliers, women in many countries are responsible for domestic water provision and management. Their roles are often "naturalised", unpaid, and unrecognised, which means that women live with issues of water scarcity and contamination on a daily basis. Women's experiences were not monolithic. Nationality, ethnicity, life-stage and occupation all intersected and compounded their experiences of capitalism, patriarchy and water injustice (Cole, 2017).

Women's water work is part of reproductive labour, lacks visibility, and is integral to water supply. Despite this, women are frequently excluded from water distribution policy and decision-making (Cole, 2017) and decisions on "big water issues" such as allocation have been gender blind (UN Women, 2018a). The exclusion of women's voices in the public domain reinforces unequal power dynamics in the household and community. Struggles over water in tourism destinations contribute to gendered processes of empowerment and disempowerment (Cole & Ferguson, 2015) and women's disproportionate responsibility for water impacts on their ability to work (Cole, 2017). Where tourism receives priority over communities, conflict and resentment will grow, and the potential for tourism to contribute to sustainable development will be undermined. Tourism could have a real impact on SDG 6 by promoting a gender-sensitive water agenda. Infrastructure improvements including the supply of improved water and sanitation is a well-documented positive impact of tourism (Wall & Mathieson, 2006). However, this is clearly not always the case, with far reaching consequences for women in many destinations. For tourism to contribute to both SDG 5 and SDG 6 it requires firstly the recognition of unpaid and domestic work so the opportunity costs of women's water work can be accounted for. Secondly, affirmative action in water governance is needed to address the gender imbalances that drive inequitable water allocation and distribution. This requires strengthening women's voice in the access to and control over water supplies, its administration, pricing and use, and thus their participation in water management and decision-making. However, this increased participation needs to be achieved without increasing women's workloads. Research highlights how leadership in destination management can be improved when a human rights based approach is taken (Cole, 2014).

We know that increased tourism will add to climate change (Lenzen et al., 2018) and that it is those who are most vulnerable, will be the worst off. This is particularly the case in relation to water scarcity. Women face greater health and safety risks when water and sanitation systems are compromised by climate-induced drought (UN Women, 2017). As Cole's (2017) research has highlighted it is women that take on increased domestic and care work to compensate, walking further for collection, eking out meagre supplies and worrying about provision for their families.

The interlinkage of SDG 6 with all the other SDGs is, of course, one of the most apparent – after all, water is life. For example, without it we cannot grow food, affecting our food security (SDG 2). When we have to pay for it, it affects our poverty levels (SDG 1) and our health (SDG 3). When there are no piped supplies, we have to collect it – usually girls – affecting opportunities for education (SDG 4). As electricity is required to pump water, SDG 7 is affected through the water-energy nexus. Waiting for water to flow down pipes impacts women's opportunities for employment (SDG 8). As discussed by Cole (2017), gender is implicated in all these impacts. A critical gender analysis of water and tourism has the potential to not only impact SDGs 5 and 6 but may have ramifications across a host of other SDGs.

SDG 8 – promote sustained, inclusive and sustainable economic growth, employment and decent work for all

For tourism stakeholders, the major promise is the creation of employment. In fact, this discourse is at the heart of the trend to promote tourism as a tool for poverty reduction, especially for women (UNWTO & UN Women, 2011). Globally, some 55% of tourism workers are women. In some countries, such as Peru or Lithuania, this percentage is over 70% (Baum, 2013). Women tend to be concentrated in the kinds of occupations that are seen to befit "feminine character-istics" (Bolles, 1997). As Sinclair (1997) argues, when tourism is not gender aware, tourism con-verts women's characteristics – that is, "feminine characteristics" imposed by patriarchy – into merchandise. The "feminisation" of such types of work has also been associated with strong gen-der discrimination that is expressed in lower wages and a lack of professional recognition (Guimarães & Silva, 2016). As such, women workers' capacity to influence the trade union agenda is severely limited (Cañada, 2016). Within this context, any analysis that integrates the dimension of "intersectionality" is very important since the construction of their identities as a group of workers entails complex interactions between their gender, class, race and ethnicity (Adib & Guerrier, 2003; De los Reyes, 2017; McBride, Hebson, & Holgate, 2015). As Dyer, McDowell, and Batnitzky (2010) discuss, gender and other identities are also implicit in relation to manager and customer requirements who expect "particular gendered performances" (2010, p. 641).

At present, tourism largely fails to provide decent work for many women especially those at the lowest levels of the occupational pyramid. For example, according to Cañada (2016), working conditions in hotels' housekeeping departments in Spain, with a high range of migrant women, have given rise to higher rates of accidents and serious injuries than any other jobs in the ser-vice industry. This is the case even though they only constitute 30% of staff. The situation, more-over, has deteriorated because of outsourcing which has led to the loss of professional categories recognised in workers' contracts, leading to a decline in working conditions, status and pay. Thus "hotel maid" is reduced to categories such as "cleaner" or "labourer" (Cañada, 2018).

This situation also promotes what Burrell et al. (1997) call "parking area" training. That is, few opportunities for career progression because of a lack of incentives to invest in more and improved training. However, at the launch of the Spanish version of the Global Report of Women in Tourism in 2012 at Madrid's International Tourism Fair (FITUR), the participants (mainly Spanish women) did not agree with the claim that women in tourism were less well trained than men. On the contrary, several women participants suggested that the main obstacle to decent work for women in tourism is not a lack of training, but a lack of opportunities offered to women and the low social value of a trained woman in the labour market (UNWTO, 2012). Thus, for example, in Portugal, although women work more hours and are better trained than men, they earn less than their male colleagues in the accommodation, travel agencies and tour oper-ation sectors (Carvalho et al., 2014).

Tourism has a great responsibility to ensure gender sensitive decent work. The prevailing dis-course on employment in tourism is that the sector supports 1 in 10 jobs globally, many of these jobs are based on gender occupational segregation. In other words, most women's jobs are con-centrated at the lower end of the ladder and women remain grossly under-represented at the management level and board level (Equality in Tourism, 2018). Therefore, employing women or supporting them to become entrepreneurs does not necessarily change the gendered dynamics in which they are embedded, nor does it necessarily impact their relationships with managers, customers or between co-workers.

Gender sensitive decent work in tourism also means reconciliation between work and family life. This is just as important for men as it is for women workers, enabling men to become equal stakeholders in their families and in care work. When men take their children to school, or finish work early to pick them up as often as women do, then greater flexibility will be offered to all workers and care work will be better shared (Cole, 2018). As Bakas et al. (2018) suggest, when men have care duties, the invisibility of childcare comes to light. Women face challenges when seeking to reach the highest positions in tourism companies not because "women are doing something wrong" or because of a problem inherent to women. The fact is that most women workers in tourism are located within the lowest rungs of companies' occupational pyramids. Therefore, according to Moreno and Cañada (2018), the feminisation in tourism employment in most cases indicates precariousness and women's lack of power. The disempowerment of women working in tourism weakens women's ability to maximise their potential contribution to the sector, thereby undermining the sustainability of the tourism industry.

Pushing forward

The private sector was actively involved in shaping the SDGs (Le Blanc, 2015). As Milne and Gray (2013) suggest, there is an emerging consensus that transnational corporations can, and ought to, contribute to sustainable development by enhancing positive impacts – such as on livelihoods, health and education – and reducing negative impacts – for instance, those related to resource consumption, pollution and human rights violations. However, corporate social responsibility (CSR) practices hardly ever address system-wide sustainability challenges, such as overcoming patriarchy. This is particularly the case in large-scale mass tourism which, as Scheyvens, Banks, and Hughes (2016) suggest, "is dominated by businesses that have built their business models around being short-term operators with high levels of flexibility" (p. 378). While good for profit, this means that these businesses are not invested in destinations and have no interest in their sustainability, in overcoming current inequities, or in advancing gender equality.

In order for businesses to take on responsibility and support the SDGs, either voluntarily or by government regulation, they will require tools to implement, manage and measure their progress. Human rights are the foundation for the SDGs and since the Guiding Principles on Business and Human Rights (United Nations, 2011) some elements of the tourism industry have begun interpreting them (Sandang, 2015). For example, the International Tourism Partnership (2014) has suggested that the key areas of concern for hotel businesses are workers' rights, supply chain related issues, community rights, human trafficking risks, customers' rights and governance related issues. The same organization has highlighted global water concerns and argued that hotels should take action (International Tourism Partnership, 2018). As discussed previously in this journal, Human Rights Impact Assessments (HRIAs) are an essential starting point for companies to conduct the necessary due diligence (Cole, 2014). Human Rights Impact Assessments have not yet been standardised to the same degree as environmental impact assessments but a helpful guide for tourism businesses and destinations on how to conduct an HRIA has been produced (Twentyfifty, 2017). Taking human rights based approach is more than a requirement to do no harm: it requires an active commitment to implement key tenets of the UN Guiding Principles, and therefore the SDGs. There are a few limited examples that already exist in tourism, for example lodges that provide water (Smith, 2018), and gender awareness training (Equality in Tourism, 2015), in the surrounding communities. However, it is unlikely that most companies will comply with the necessary due diligence requirements without governments' active engagement and enforcement.

Human Rights Impact Assessments are an essential tool for businesses to conduct due diligence to comply with the UN Guiding Principles and understand their impact on their stakeholders. However, they are not specifically gender focused. Gender focused tools exist but they are not adapted for tourism. For example, UN Women and UN Global Compact developed the Women Empowerment Principles (WEPs) as a tool for businesses to empower women across the workplace, marketplace and the community. While they aim to help companies around the world to assess their gender equality performance, they will need to be refined to be useful for many tourism businesses.

Other tools, such as participatory gender audits, can help to identify organizational strengths and challenges in terms of mainstreaming gender. Conducting gender audits would help companies and destinations spotlight gender (in)equality and identify systems, policy, processes and organizational culture that require change. Audits are used for certification, which, although not without critics in tourism (Font & Harris, 2004), are considered effective instruments to improve companies' sustainability performance (Ayuso, 2007). Unfortunately, major tourism specific audit and certification schemes, such as Travelife, are yet to include gender equality measures. However, tourism companies that have opted for broader certification schemes, such as B Corp, have shown that it has improved their gender equality (Intrepid Travel, 2018).

Businesses need to ensure that they are vigilant about complying with SDG target 5.2, "eliminate all forms of violence against all women and girls in the public and private spheres, including trafficking and sexual and other types of exploitation", through their company policies and procedures. Immense numbers of tourism workers have experienced sexual harassment, so much so that Pritchard (2018) calls it the topic of the next decade.

Conclusion

The SDGs offer a potentially radical improvement and departure from the MDGs. This is because the SDGs are based on the identification and analysis of the main challenges to gender equality – challenges that the MDGs did not cover. The SDGs include consideration of strategic elements considered essential by women's organisations. Although there has been some debate about the appropriateness of making "gender equality" a standalone goal, this is explained by the need to secure political will and resource mobilization. Yet, this does not mean that gender equality is not integral to all the other SDGs. The importance of SDG 5 for achieving all of the other SDGs is consistently highlighted by UN policy discourse and civil society. However, the UNWTO and other tourism organisations have yet to acknowledge the need for gender to be mainstreamed. Without tackling gender equality in a meaningful and substantive way, tourism's potential to contribute to all 17 SDGs will be substantively reduced.

Although the SDGs "talk the talk" on gender equality, when we critically analyse the interconnection between the SDG 5 and other SDGs in the tourism context we shine a light on the gap between rhetoric and reality. Tourism can support the provision of piped water to remote communities, supporting SDG 6, but tourism induced water mismanagement and scarcity affects women in many destinations on a daily basis. Tourism can create jobs and support SDG 8 but, as we have uncovered, the nature of tourism jobs frequently does not support SDG 5 or gender mainstreaming. Providing jobs for women alone does not change patriarchal structures, nor does it redistribute unpaid care work, reduce the gender pay gap or combat sexual harassment. The same patriarchal structures, frequently reinforced by tourism policy, dictate water work as women's work, which is unpaid and unaccounted for, and prevents some women from taking jobs.

A human rights approach is embedded in the SDGs and our work starts to explore how to make this a reality for women in tourism. We have suggested the use of Human Rights Impact Assessments, Women's Empowerment Principles and Gender Audits by business as initial steps business can take to play their part towards achieving the SDGs. There is no doubt that all this requires critical thinking, political will, a re-evaluation of priorities, and a dedicated budget. There are gaps, both in the theory and practice, of implementing gender equal and, therefore, sustainable tourism. Some of the areas that require far more detailed analysis include the sexual harassment that women, in particular, face and how to squash it; the intersectional issues women face and how to confront them; and the additional burdens tourism places on women.

There is substantial work needed to further our understanding of how tourism intersects with gender equality and the other SDGs. This will require (1) the collection and analysis of gender sensitive tourism data, (2) training and tourism studies' curricula that integrate gender within sustainable development, (3) tourism practice that draws on feminist gender analysis, (4) more use of intersectional approaches to understand tourism relationship with the SDGs, and (5) an evaluation of methods utilised to improve gender equality and the dissemination of best practice. Much remains to be done, but the benefits, both for the tourism sector and for the global community that stands to benefit far exceed the costs involved.

Note

1. Available   here: http://www.tourism4development2017.org/wp-content/uploads/2017/05/070417_iy2017-discussion-paper.pdf

Acknowledgements

The authors very much appreciate to Angela Hadjipateras, Dr. Lucy Ferguson, and Dr. Tricia Barnett for assistance and comments that improved the manuscript and to the British Academy for the funding of the Gender, Tourism and Water research.

Disclosure statement

No potential conflict of interest was reported by the authors.

References

Adib, A., & Guerrier, Y. (2003). The interlocking of gender with nationality, race, ethnicity and class: The narratives of women in hotel work. *Gender, Work & Organization, 10*(4), 413–432. doi:10.1111/1468-0432.00204

Ahlers, R., & Zwarteveen, M. (2009). The water question in feminism: Water control and gender inequities in a neo-liberal era. *Gender, Place and Culture, 16*(4), 409–426. doi:10.1080/09663690903003926

Aitchison, C. (2005). Feminist and gender perspectives in tourism studies: The social-cultural nexus of critical and cultural theories. *Tourist Studies, 5*(3), 207–224. doi:10.1177/1468797605070330

Antrobus, P. (2006). Gender equality in the new millennium: Goal or gimmick? *Caribbean Quarterly, 52*(2/3), 39–50. doi:10.1080/00086495.2006.11829698

Ariffin, J. (2004). Gender critiques of the Millennium Development Goals: An overview and an assessment. Work presented at the International Council on Social Welfare (ICSW), 31st International Conference on Social Progress and Social Justice, 16–20 August 2004, Kuala Lumpur, Malaysia.

Ayuso, S. (2007). Comparing voluntary policy instruments for sustainable tourism: The experience of the Spanish hotel sector. *Journal of Sustainable Tourism, 15*(2), 144–159. doi:10.2167/jost617.0

Bakas, F., Costa, C., Durão, M., Carvalho, I., & Breda, Z. (2018). An uneasy truth: Female tourism managers and organisational gender equality measures in Portugal. In S. Cole (Ed.), *Tourism and gender equality: Beyond empowerment* (pp. 34–43). Wallingford: CABI.

Baum, T. (2013). *International perspectives on women and work in hotels, catering and tourism.* Geneva: ILO. Retrieved from https://www.ilo.org/wcmsp5/groups/public/@dgreports/@gender/documents/publication/wcms_209867.pdf

Bidegain Ponte, N. (2017). La Agenda 2030 y la Agenda Regional de Género: sinergias para la igualdad en América Latina y el Caribe. Retrieved https://repositorio.cepal.org/bitstream/handle/11362/41016/S1700105A_es.pdf?sequence=7&isAllowed=y

Bidegain Ponte, N., & Enríquez, C. R. (2016). Agenda 2030: A bold enough framework towards sustainable, gender-just development? *Gender & Development, 24*(1), 83–98. doi:10.1080/13552074.2016.1142227

Bolles, A. (1997). Women as a category of analysis in scholarship on tourism: Jamaican women and tourism employment. In E. Chambers (Ed.), *Tourism & culture: An applied perspective* (pp. 77–92). Albany: State University of New York.

Burrell, J., Manfredi, S., Rollin, H., Price, L., & Stead, L. (1997). Equal opportunities for women employees in the hospitality industry: A comparison between France, Italy, Spain and the UK. *International Journal of Hospitality Management, 16*(2), 161–179. doi:10.1016/S0278-4319(97)00003-0

Caglar, G., Prügl, E., & Zwingel, S. (Eds.). (2013). *Feminist strategies in international governance*. London and New York: Routledge.

Cañada, E. (2016). Promote sustained, inclusive and sustainable economic growth, full and productive employment and decent work for all. *Transforming Tourism, Goal 8: Decent Work and Economic Growth*. Retrieved from http://www.transforming-tourism.org/goal-8-decent-work-and-economic-growth.html.

Cañada, E. (2018). Too precarious to be inclusive? Employment of hotel maids in Spain. Tourism Geographies, 20(4), 653–674.

Carvalho, I., Costa, C., Lykke, N., & Torres, A. (2014). An analysis of gendered employment in the Portuguese tourism sector. *Journal of Human Resources in Hospitality & Tourism, 13*(4), 405–429. doi:10.1080/15332845.2014.888509

Chant, S. (2008). The 'feminisation of poverty' and the 'feminisation' of anti-poverty programmes: Room for revision? *The Journal of Development Studies, 44*(2), 165–197. doi:10.1080/00220380701789810

Cole, S. (2014). Tourism and water: From stakeholders to rights holders, and what tourism businesses need to do. *Journal of Sustainable Tourism, 22*(1), 89–106. doi:10.1080/09669582.2013.776062

Cole, S. (2017). Water worries: An intersectional feminist political ecology of tourism and water in Labuan Bajo, Indonesia. *Annals of Tourism Research, 67*, 14–24. doi:10.1016/j.annals.2017.07.018

Cole, S. (2018). Introduction to S. Cole (Ed) gender equality and tourism. Beyond empowerment. In S. Cole (Ed.), *Gender, tourism and empowerment: Women's critical voices* (pp. 1–11). Wallingford: CABI.

Cole, S., & Ferguson, L. (2015). Towards a gendered political economy of tourism and water. *Tourism Geographies, 17*(4), 511–528. doi:10.1080/14616688.2015.1065509

Cole, S., & Tulis, I. M. (2016). *For the worry of water: Water, women and tourism in Labuan Bajo. Initial policy paper*. London: Equality in Tourism. Retrieved from http://equalityintourism.org/wp-content/uploads/2015/11/Stroma-For-the-worry-of-water-Final.pdf

Daly, M. (2005). Gender mainstreaming in theory and practice. *Social Politics: International Studies in Gender, State and Society, 12*(3), 433–450. doi:10.1093/sp/jxi023

De la Cruz, C. (2015). Cambio, Poder y Justicia de Género en la Agenda 2030: Reflexiones para no perdernos en el camino [Change, Power and Gender Justice in the 2030 Agenda: Reflections not to get lost along the way] (Working Paper No. 1). Madrid: ICEI.

De los Reyes, P. (2017). Working life inequalities: Do we need intersectionality? *Society, Health & Vulnerability, 8*(sup1), 1332858. doi:10.1080/20021518.2017.1332858

Denton, F. (2002). Climate change vulnerability, impacts, and adaptation: Why does gender matter? *Gender & Development, 10*(2), 10–20. doi:10.1080/13552070215903

Dyer, S., McDowell, L., & Batnitzky, A. (2010). The impact of migration on the gendering of service work: The case of a West London hotel. *Gender, Work & Organization, 17*(6), 635–657. doi:10.1111/j.1468-0432.2009.00480.x

Equality in Tourism. (2015, November). Lessons from Zala Beach Lodge. *Equality in Tourism*. Retrieved from http://equalityin-tourism.org/working-towards-gender-equality-and-empowerment-lessons-from-zalala-beach-lodge-mozambique-2/

Equality in Tourism. (2017, July). UNWTO Discussion Paper on the occasion of the International Year of Sustainable Tourism for Development 2017: Equality in Tourism Comment. *Equality in Tourism*. Retrieved from http://equalityin-tourism.org/equality-in-tourism-responds-to-unwto-discussion-paper-on-the-occasion-of-the-international-year-of-sustainable-tourism-for-development-2017/

Equality in Tourism. (2018). *Sun, sand and ceilings: Women in tourism and hospitality board rooms 2018*. Retrieved http://equalityintourism.org/wp-content/uploads/2018/11/sun-sand-and-ceilings-2018.pdf

Esquivel, V., & Sweetman, C. (2016). Gender and the Sustainable Development Goals. *Gender & Development, 24*(1), 1–8. doi:10.1080/13552074.2016.1153318

FAO. (2015). *Globefish Research Programme: The role of women in the seafood industry*. Rome: FAO. Retrieved from http://www.fao.org/3/a-bc014e.pdf

Feng, X. (2013). Women's work, men's work: Gender and tourism among the Miao in rural China. *Anthropology of Work Review, 34*(1), 2–14. doi:10.1111/awr.12002

Ferguson, L. (2009). *Analysing the gender dimensions of tourism as a development strategy*. Retrieved from https://eprints.ucm.es/10237/1/PP_03-09.pdf

Ferguson, L. (2010a). Interrogating 'gender' in development policy and practice: The World Bank, tourism and microenterprise in Honduras. *International Feminist Journal of Politics, 12*(1), 3–24. doi:10.1080/14616740903429080

Ferguson, L. (2010b). Tourism development and the restructuring of social reproduction in Central America. *Review of International Political Economy, 17*(5), 860–888. doi:10.1080/09692290903507219

Ferguson, L. (2011). Promoting gender equality and empowering women? Tourism and the third Millennium Development Goal. *Current Issues in Tourism, 14*(3), 235–249. doi:10.1080/13683500.2011.555522

Ferguson, L. (2015). "This is our gender person": The messy business of being a gender expert in international development. *International Feminist Journal of Politics, 17*(3), 380–397. doi:10.1080/14616742.2014.918787

Ferguson, L. (2018). Gender equality and tourism: The global policy context. In S. Cole (Ed), *Gender equality and tourism. Beyond empowerment* (pp. 14–22). Wallingford: CABI.

Ferguson, L., & Alarcón D. M. (2015). Gender and sustainable tourism: Reflections on theory and practice. *Journal of Sustainable Tourism, 23*(3), 401–416. doi:10.1080/09669582.2014.957208

Ferguson, L., & Moreno, D. (2016). Gender expertise and the private sector: Navigating the privatization of gender equality funding. In M. Bustelo, L. Ferguson, & M. Forest (Eds.), *The politics of feminist knowledge transfer: Gender training and gender expertise* (pp. 62–79). Basingstoke: Palgrave Macmillan.

Fernández-Layos, A., & Ruiz, M. (2011). *Claves para la incidencia política en derechos sexuales y reproductivos en África [Keys to political advocacy on sexual and reproductive rights in Africa]*. Madrid: Red de MujeresAfricanas y Españolas por un Mundo Mejor.

Figueroa-Domecq, C., Pritchard, A., Segovia-Pérez, M., Morgan, N., & Villacé-Molinero, T. (2015). Tourism gender research: A critical accounting. *Annals of Tourism Research, 52*, 87–103.

Font, X., & Harris, C. (2004). Rethinking standards from green to sustainable. *Annals of Tourism Research, 31*(4), 986–1007. doi:10.1016/j.annals.2004.04.001

Fukuda-Parr, S. (2016). From the Millennium Development Goals to the Sustainable Development Goals: Shifts in purpose, concept, and politics of global goal setting for development. *Gender & Development, 24*(1), 43–52. doi: 10.1080/13552074.2016.1145895

Gentry, K. (2007). Belizean women and tourism work: Opportunity or impediment? *Annals of Tourism Research, 34*(2), 477–496. doi:10.1016/j.annals.2006.11.003

Gibson, H. (2001). Gender in Tourism: Theoretical perspectives. In Y. Apostolopoulos, S. Sonmez, & D. Timothy (Eds.), *Women as producers and consumers of tourism in developing countries* (pp. 19–43). Westport: Praeger.

Gössling, S., & Peeters, P. (2015). Assessing tourism's global environmental impact 1900–2050. *Journal of Sustainable Tourism, 23*(5), 639–659. doi:10.1080/09669582.2015.1008500

Guimarães, C. R. F. F., & Silva, J. R. (2016). Pay gap by gender in the tourism industry of Brazil. *Tourism Management, 52*, 440–450. doi:10.1016/j.tourman.2015.07.003

Hardy, A., Beeton, R. J., & Pearson, L. (2002). Sustainable tourism: An overview of the concept and its position in relation to conceptualisations of tourism. *Journal of Sustainable Tourism, 10*(6), 475–496. doi:10.1080/09669580208667183

Harvey, M. J., Hunt, J., & Harris, C. C. (1995). Gender and community tourism dependence level. *Annals of Tourism Research, 22*(2), 349–366. doi:10.1016/0160-7383(94)00081-6

Hemmingway, S. (2004). The impact of tourism on the human rights of women in South East Asia. *International Journal of Human Rights, 8*(3), 275–304.

Hoard, S. (2015). *Gender expertise in public policy: Towards a theory of policy success*. Abingdon and New York: Palgrave Macmillan.

Huete, R., Brotons, M., & Sigüenza, M. C. (2016). La desigualdad entre mujeres y hombres en el sector hostelero español [Inequality between women and men in the Spanish hospitality sector]. *Estudios y Perspectivas en Turismo, 25*(1), 73–87.

International Tourism Partnership. (2014). *Know how guide: Human rights & the hotel industry*. Retrieved from http://www.greenhotelier.org/wp-content/uploads/2015/01/Know-How-Guide-Human-Rights.pdf

International Tourism Partnership. (2018). *Water stewardship for hotel companies*. Retrieved from https://www.tourismpartnership.org/download/2212/

Intrepid Travel. (2018). *How B Corp certification changes the way we operate*. Retrieved from https://www.intrepidtravel.com/uk/b-corp

Iverson, K. (2000). The paradox of the contented female manager: An empirical investigation of gender differences in pay expectation in the hospitality industry. *Hospital Management, 19*(1), 22–51.

Jordan, F. (1997). An occupational hazard? Sex segregation in tourism employment. *Tourism Management, 18*(8), 525–534. doi:10.1016/S0261-5177(97)00074-5

Kabeer, N. (2015). Tracking the gender politics of the Millennium Development Goals: Struggles for interpretive power in the international development agenda. *Third World Quarterly, 36*(2), 377–395. doi:10.1080/01436597.2015.1016656

Kinnaird, V., & Hall, D. R. (1994). *Tourism: A gender analysis*. Chichester: Wiley.

Kinnaird, V., & Hall, D. R. (1996). Understanding tourism processes: A gender-aware framework. *Tourism Management, 17*(2), 95–102. doi:10.1016/0261-5177(95)00112-3

Knight, D., & Cottrell, S. (2016). Evaluating tourism-linked empowerment in Cuzco, Peru. *Annals of Tourism Research, 56*, 32–47. doi:10.1016/j.annals.2015.11.007

Ladkin, A. (2011). Exploring tourism labor. *Annals of Tourism Research, 38*(3), 1135–1155. doi:10.1016/j.annals.2011.03.010

Lakovidou, O., & Turner, C. (1995). The female gender in Greek agrotourism. *Annals of Tourism Research, 22*(2), 481–484. doi:10.1016/0160-7383(94)00099-9

Le Blanc, D. (2015). Towards integration at last? The Sustainable Development Goals as a network of targets. *Sustainable Development, 23*(3), 176–187. doi:10.1002/sd.1582

Lee-Gosselin, H., Briere, S., & Ann, H. (2013). Resistances to gender mainstreaming in organizations: Toward a new approach. *Gender in Management: An International Journal, 28*(8), 468–485. doi:10.1108/GM-10-2012-0081

Lenzen, M., Sun, Y. Y., Faturay, F., Ting, Y. P., Geschke, A., & Malik, A. (2018). The carbon footprint of global tourism. *Nature Climate Change, 8*(6), 522–531. doi:10.1038/s41558-018-0141-x

Lombardo, E., & Mergaert, L. (2013). Gender mainstreaming and resistance to gender training: A framework for studying implementation. *NORA-Nordic Journal of Feminist and Gender Research, 21*(4), 296–311. doi:10.1080/08038740.2013.851115

McBride, A., Hebson, G., & Holgate, J. (2015). Intersectionality: Are we taking enough notice in the field of work and employment relations? *Work, Employment and Society, 29*(2), 331–341. doi:10.1177/0950017014538337

Milne, M. J., & Gray, R. (2013). Whither ecology? The triple bottom line, the global reporting initiative and corporate sustainability reporting. *Journal of Business Ethics, 118*(1), 13–29. doi:10.1007/s10551-012-1543-8

Mooney, S. (2018). Illuminating intersectionality for tourism researchers. *Annals of Tourism Research, 72 (C)*, 175–176. doi:10.1016/j.annals.2018.03.003

Moreno, D. (2017a). *Turismo y Género: un enfoque esencial en un contexto de desarrollo sostenible y responsable del turismo* (Unpublished doctoral dissertation). Universidad Complutense, Madrid.

Moreno, D. (2017b). *ODS, Turismo y Género: fundamentos y recomendaciones para la educación y sensibilización* [*SDGs, tourism and gender: Foundations and recommendations for education and awareness*]. Córdoba: El Centro de Iniciativas para la Cooperación Batá.

Moreno, D. (2018a). Feminist perspectives in the development of action plans for tourism. In S. Cole (Ed.), *Gender, tourism and empowerment: Women's critical voices* (pp. 14–22). Wallingford: CABI.

Moreno, D. (2018b). *Cómo elaborar un diagnostic de género y turismo en un context rural* [*How to elaborate a diagnostic on gender and tourism in a rural context*]. Retrieved from http://www.albasud.org/publ/docs/84.pdf

Moreno, D., & Cañada, E. (2018). *Gender dimension in tourism work*. Retrieved from http://www.albasud.org/publ/docs/81.en.pdf

Moser, C. O. (1993). *Gender planning and development: Theory, practice and training*. London: Routledge.

Moswete, N., & Lacey, G. (2015). 'Women cannot lead': Empowering women through cultural tourism in Botswana. *Journal of Sustainable Tourism, 23*(4), 600–617. doi:10.1080/09669582.2014.986488

Movono, A., & Dahles, H. (2017). Female empowerment and tourism: A focus on businesses in a Fijian village, Asia Pacific. *Journal of Tourism Research, 22*(6), 681–692. doi:10.1080/10941665.2017.1308397

Mujeres en Red. (2005). Reflexiones desde el feminismo sobre los Objetivos del Milenio. Comité Regional Pekín + 10 – América Latina [Reflections from feminism on the Millennium Development Goals-Rights – Beijing +10]. *Mujeres en Red*. Retrieved from http://www.mujeresenred.net/spip.php?article119

Muñoz-Bullón, F. (2009). The gap between male and female pay in the Spanish tourism industry. *Tourism Management, 30*(5), 638–649. doi:10.1016/j.tourman.2008.11.007

Mukhopadhyay, M. (2014). Mainstreaming gender or reconstituting the mainstream? Gender knowledge in development. *Journal of International Development, 26*(3), 356–367.

Norris, J., Wall, G., Cooper, C., & Lockwood, A. (1994). Gender and tourism. *Progress in Tourism, Recreation and Hospitality Management, 6*, 57–78.

Nozawa, H. (1995). Female professionals in the Japanese tourism industry. *Annals of Tourism Research, 22*(2), 484–487. doi:10.1016/0160-7383(94)00100-6

O'Reilly, K., Halvorson, S., Sultana, F., & Laurie, N. (2009). Introduction: Global perspectives on gender-water geographies. *Gender, Place and Culture, 16*(4), 381–385. doi:10.1080/09663690903003868

Panta, S. K., & Thapa, B. (2018). Entrepreneurship and women's empowerment in gateway communities of Bardia National Park, Nepal. *Journal of Ecotourism, 17*(1), 20–42. doi:10.1080/14724049.2017.1299743

Post-2015 Women's Coalition. (2015). *Feminist sustainable development: A transformative alternative for gender equality, development and peace*. Retrieved from http://www.peacewomen.org/sites/default/files/Post2015WomensCoalitionVisionStatement_FINAL.pdf

Pritchard, A. (2018). Predicting the next decade of tourism gender research. *Tourism Management Perspectives, 25*, 144–146. doi:10.1016/j.tmp.2017.11.014

Pritchard, A., Morgan, N., Ateljevic, I., & Harris, C. (2007). Editors' introduction: Tourism, gender, embodiment and experience. In A. Pritchard, N. Morgan, I. Ateljevic, & C. Harris (Eds.), *Tourism and gender: Embodiment, sensuality and experience* (pp. 1–12). Wallingford: CABI.

Purcell, K. (1996). The relationship between career and job opportunities: Women's employment in the hospitality industry as a microcosm of women's employment. *Women in Management Review, 11*(5), 17–24. doi:10.1108/09649429610122618

Ramos, A., & Prideaux, B. (2014). Indigenous ecotourism in the Mayan rainforest of Palenque: Empowerment issues in sustainable development. *Journal of Sustainable Tourism, 22*(3), 461–479. doi:10.1080/09669582.2013.828730

Rathgeber, E. M. (1990). WID, WAD, GAD: Trends in research and practice. *The Journal of Developing Areas, 24*(4), 489–502.

Razavi, S. (2016). The 2030 Agenda: Challenges of implementation to attain gender equality and women's rights. *Gender & Development, 24*(1), 25–41. doi:10.1080/13552074.2016.1142229

Razavi, S., & Miller, C. (1995). From WID to GAD: Conceptual shifts in the women and development discourse (Vol. 1, No. 3). Geneva: United Nations Research Institute for Social Development.

Ruhanen, L., Weiler, B., Moyle, B. D., & McLennan, C. L. J. (2015). Trends and patterns in sustainable tourism research: A 25- year bibliometric analysis. *Journal of Sustainable Tourism*, 23(4), 517–535.

Sandang, Y. (2015). After UNGPs on human right and business: Study on several follow-up in tourism. In *Developments of the New Tourism Paradigm in the Asia Pasific Region* (pp. 277–280). Asia Pacific Tourism Association (APTA).

Scheyvens, R. (2007). Ecotourism and gender issues. In J. Higham (Ed.), *Critical issues in ecotourism* (pp. 185–213). Burlington, MA: Elsevier.

Scheyvens, R., Banks, G., & Hughes, E. (2016). The private sector and the SDGs: The need to move beyond 'business as usual'. *Sustainable Development*, 24(6), 371–382. doi:10.1002/sd.1623

Sinclair, M. (1997). Gendered work in tourism: Comparative perspectives. In M. Sinclair (Ed.), *Gender, work and tourism* (pp. 220–234). New York: Routledge.

Skalpe, O. (2007). The CEO gender pay gap in the tourism industry – Evidence from Norway. *Tourism Management*, 28(3), 845–853. doi:10.1016/j.tourman.2006.06.005

Smith, J. (2018). *Transforming tourism realising the potential for sustainable tourism*. Wallingford: CABI.

Standing, H. (2004). Gender, myth and fable: The perils of mainstreaming in sector bureaucracies. *IDS Bulletin*, 35(4), 82–88. doi:10.1111/j.1759-5436.2004.tb00159.x

Suárez, P., Barquín, R., Jiménez, G., & Alfonso, M. J. (2016). Teorías y métodos en la investigación sobre turismo, género y mujeres en Iberoamérica: un análisis bibliográfico [Theories and methods in research on tourism gender and women in Ibero-america: A bibliographic analysis]. *Cuadernos de Turismo*, 38, 485–501. doi:10.6018/turismo.38.271531

Sultana, F. (2011). Suffering for water, suffering from water: Emotional geographies of resource access, control and conflict. *Geoforum*, 42(2), 163–172. doi:10.1016/j.geoforum.2010.12.002

Swain, M. (1993). Women producers of ethnic arts. *Annals of Tourism Research*, 20(1), 32–51. doi:10.1016/0160-7383(93)90110-O

Swain, M. (1995). Gender in tourism. *Annals of Tourism Research*, 22(2), 247–266. doi:10.1016/0160-7383(94)00095-6

Swain, M. (2007). On the road to a feminist tourism studies. In D. Nash (Ed.), *The study of tourism: Anthropological and sociological beginnings* (pp. 197–208). Oxford/Amsterdam: Elsevier.

Swain, M., & Hall, M. (2007). Gender analysis in tourism: Personal and global dialectics. In I. Ateljevic, A. Pritchard, & N. Morgan (Eds.), *The critical turn in tourism studies: Innovative research methodologies* (pp. 91–104). Oxford: Elsevier.

Swain, M., & Swain, M. T. B. (2004). An ecofeminist approach to ecotourism development. *Tourism Recreation Research*, 29(3), 1–6. doi:10.1080/02508281.2004.11081451

Thrane, C. (2008). Earnings differentiation in the tourism industry: Gender, human capital and socio-demographic effects. *Tourism Management*, 29(3), 514–524. doi:10.1016/j.tourman.2007.05.017

Tran, L., & Walter, P. (2014). Ecotourism, gender and development in northern Vietnam. *Annals of Tourism Research*, 44, 116–130. doi:10.1016/j.annals.2013.09.005

Truelove, Y. (2011). (Re-) conceptualizing water inequality in Delhi, India through a feminist political ecology framework. *Geoforum*, 42(2), 143–152. doi:10.1016/j.geoforum.2011.01.004

Tucker, H., & Boonabaana, B. (2012). A critical analysis of tourism, gender and poverty reduction. *Journal of Sustainable Tourism*, 20(3), 437–455. doi:10.1080/09669582.2011.622769

TwentyFifty. (2017). *Human rights assessments in the tourism sector: A data collection guide for practitioners*. Retrieved from https://www.twentyfifty.co.uk/en/news-views/publications/2017/human-rights-assessments-in-the-tourism-sector/

United Nations. (2000). *Millennium Declaration. A/RES/55/2. Resolution adopted by the General Assembly on 8 September 2000*. New York: United Nations.

United Nations. (2011). *Guiding principles on business and human rights*.

United Nations. (2015a). *Draft outcome document of the United Nations summit for the adoption of the post-2015 development agenda. A/RES/69/315. Resolution adopted by the General Assembly on 1 September 2015*. New York: United Nations.

United Nations. (2015b). *Transforming our world: The 2030 Agenda for Sustainable Development. A/RES/70/1. Resolution adopted by the General Assembly on 25 September 2015*. New York: United Nations

United Nations Development Fund for Women (UNIFEM). (2000). *Progress of the World's Women 2000*. New York: UNIFEM.

UN Women. (2017). *In focus: Climate action by, and for, women*. Retrieved from http://www.unwomen.org/en/news/in-focus/climate-change.

UN Women. (2018a). *Gender equality in the 2030 Agenda: Gender-responsive water and sanitation systems*. Retrieved from http://www.unwomen.org/en/digital-library/publications/2018/6/issue-brief-gender-responsive-water-and-sanitation-systems

UN Women. (2018b). *Turning promises into action: Gender equality in the 2030 agenda for sustainable development.* Retrieved from http://www.unwomen.org/-/media/headquarters/attachments/sections/library/publications/2018/sdg-report-gender-equality-in-the-2030-agenda-for-sustainable-development-2018-en.pdf?la=en&vs=4332

UNWTO. (2012). *Informe del taller sobre el empoderamiento de las mujeres en el sector turístico como motor de desarrollo.* Madrid: UNWTO.

UNWTO. (2013). *Guidebook: Sustainable tourism for development.* Madrid: UNWTO.

UNWTO. (2015, September 28). UNWTO welcomes the adoption of the Sustainable Development Goals. *UNWTO.* Retrieved from http://media.unwto.org/press-release/2015-09-28/unwto-welcomes-adoption-sustainable-development-goals

UNWTO. (2017). *Tourism and the Sustainable Development Goals – Journey to 2030.* Madrid: UNWTO.

UNWTO. (2018). *Tourism and the Sustainable Development Goals – Good Practices in the Americas.* Madrid: UNWTO.

UNWTO & UN Women. (2011). *Global report on women in tourism 2010.* Madrid: UNWTO.

Vandegrift, D. (2008). This isn't paradise – I work here: Global restructuring, the tourism industry, and women workers in Caribbean Costa Rica. *Gender and Society, 2*(6), 778–798. doi:10.1177/0891243208324999

Walby, S. (2005). Gender mainstreaming: Productive tensions in theory and practice. *Social Politics: International Studies in Gender, State and Society, 12*(3), 321–343. doi:10.1093/sp/jxi018

Wall, G., & Mathieson, A. (2006). *Tourism: Change, impacts and opportunities.* Harlow: Pearson Education Limited.

Wilkinson, P. F., & Pratiwi, W. (1995). Gender and tourism in an Indonesian village. *Annals of Tourism Research, 22*(2), 283–299. doi:10.1016/0160-7383(94)00077-8

Assessing gender representation in knowledge production: A critical analysis of UNWTO's planned events

Catheryn Khoo-Lattimore ⓘD, Elaine Chiao Ling Yang and Jess Sanggyeong Je

ABSTRACT

With critical feminism as its epistemological lens, this study employed a content analysis on the 121 events organised and/or held by the United Nations World Tourism Organization (UNWTO) in 2017. The aim was to investigate where UNWTO stands in terms of knowledge production, and to what extent if any, the invited speakers reinforce stereotypes that undermine women's expertise and intellectual competencies; or meet their goals to achieve gender equality and empowerment of women and girls in tourism. Data on gender was intersected with ethnicity for a more dynamic understanding of how tourism knowledge is produced and disseminated. This paper provides a compelling case study for how the marginalisation of gender and its intersection with ethnicity can be explained by enduring forms of implicit bias, including both unconscious sexism and racism. The study contributes to knowledge by extending the audit of gender representation in tourism knowledge production beyond academe. It identifies the notion of femwashing and proposes a conceptual framework of tourism knowledge production. Actionable recommendations are provided to promote the fifth United Nation's sustainable development goal (i.e. gender equality) at an institutional level.

Introduction

Current studies on gender inequality in tourism knowledge representation and production have centred on academic landscapes (Chambers, Munar, Khoo-Lattimore, & Biran, 2017; Munar et al., 2015; Walters, 2018). These studies have suggested that even the educated population adopts negative gender norms and unconsciously accepts prejudicial social practices (e.g. Morley, 2013; Xu, Wang, & Ye, 2017). In particular, academic conferences have been argued to be the most visible indicator of gender inequality. In 2013 for example, less than 24% of the keynote speakers, invited speakers and expert panel members across 33 tourism academic conferences were women (Munar et al., 2015). An updated review in 2017 indicates a persistent trend with a marginal increase to 30% of women representation of speakers across 53 tourism academic conferences (Walters, 2018). This disparity between male and female speakers is problematic especially when the information of speakers, who represent the knowledge leaders in tourism and its subfields, is publicly available on the conference websites and used as a drawcard to promote the events. Given that business events such as industry meetings and conferences convey the social order and norms of the community to the attendees (George, Roberts, & Pacella, 2015; Walters, 2018), this study aims to investigate the gendered representation of knowledge produced at such tourism events outside academe, and more specifically, by a significant international tourism organization, the United Nations World Tourism Organization (UNWTO).

UNWTO is an agency of the United Nations tasked with the promotion of responsible, sustainable and universally accessible tourism, and is the leading international organization in the field of tourism. In 2010, UNWTO in partnership with UN Women published the *Global Report on Women in Tourism* in which they highlighted pronounced gender gap in international tourism. In 2017, UNWTO claims a commitment to United Nations' fifth Sustainable Development Goals to have its member countries achieve gender equality and empower women. However, a cursory investigation into UNWTO's activities indicate an underrepresentation of women as knowledge leaders at their main business events. While they aim to "mainstream gender issues in their respective tourism policies" (UNWTO, 2017a), current anecdotal evidence implies the possibility of "femwashing". This is to say that their management practices might still be insistently patriarchal and continue to produce and reproduce attitudes, traditions, and norms that privilege the masculine as the authoritative norm. This study stems from an intention to utilise the open qualities of human discourse, as Foucault has called for, by expanding the indicators of gendered tourism leadership and excellence to tourism knowledge produced outside of academe – knowledge that is arguably more pervasive on a daily basis. By doing so, this study will construct a conceptual framework to critically but constructively mediate how knowledge is perceived and produced in sites where a particular power discourse prevails.

Literature review

United Nations' fifth sustainable development goal

Sustainability has been typically associated with "greening" the environment. Against this predominating green discourse, gender equality, which is the fifth goal of the 17 United Nations Sustainable Development Goals (UNSDGs), receives relatively less attention. This goal to "achieve gender equality and empower all women and girls" (United Nations, 2017a) places specific emphasis on women and girls' access to safety, education, employment, health care, and representation in leadership roles. Two of the key targets of Goal 5 that are pertinent to the current study are to "ensure women's full and effective participation and equal opportunities for leadership at all levels" and "adopt and strengthen sound policies and enforceable legislation for the promotion of gender equality" (United Nations, 2017b). These targets have a potential to reconfigure the structures of power at an institutional level so this study aims to assess how these targets have been achieved through the investigation of gender representation at UNWTO's planned events.

Leadership role of UNWTO in knowledge production and promoting gender equality

UNWTO plays an important leadership role in setting the agenda and targets that drive the tourism sector across 158 member countries and over 500 affiliate members representing tourism authorities, education providers, private sector and professional associations. UNWTO is the leader in tourism knowledge production as it shapes the ways of thinking, teaching and practicing tourism that are in accordance with the United Nations' 2030 Agenda for Sustainable Development (UNSD). One of the initiatives to raise awareness of the UNSD within the tourism sector is through the establishment of the year 2017 as the International Year of Sustainable Tourism for Development (#IY2017). Although tourism is widely recognised as an important vehicle to empower women, gender equality was not explicitly featured in the five key areas of #IY2017 (UNWTO, 2017b).

Women make up a majority of tourism workforce and in many less developed countries, tourism has provided women access to economic and entrepreneurship opportunities that would not exist otherwise (UNWTO & UN Women, 2010). However, the concept of gender had been marginalised in UNWTO's agenda until 2007 when it launched World Tourism Day 2007 with the theme, "Tourism Open Doors for Women" (Ferguson, 2011). Since then, UNWTO has been working together with UN Women on projects that focus on training, skill development and employment of women at a grassroots level (Ferguson, 2011; UN Women, 2011). However, it remains that little is known about how gender equality is practised in UNWTO, especially at the leadership level, and how the effect of gender equality trickles down to the paradigm, discourse and policy making of the organization as well as to those of the member countries and affiliate members across the globe.

Gendered knowledge production in tourism

What we do understand about knowledge production within tourism is mainly from academia, which plays a central role in producing cutting-edge research to advance tourism industry practices and inform policy making at the regional and national levels. In theory, tourism has the potential to transform people's lives (Dredge et al., 2012) but in practice, as far as gender is concerned, tourism has a notorious history of being and has continued to be a highly gendered and sexualised industry (Ferguson, 2011; Pritchard & Morgan, 2000; Yang, Khoo-Lattimore, & Arcodia, 2018a). Tourism academia is supposed to be the thought leader that challenges the status quo and promotes gender equality, but the knowledge production of tourism is still profoundly gendered and dominated by hegemonic male perspectives, which means subordinated masculinities (e.g. gay men or black men) are also neglected/silenced (Chambers et al., 2017; Munar et al., 2015; Pritchard & Morgan, 2017).

The gendered knowledge production in tourism is evidently reflected in the publication of tourism gender research – less than 250 gender studies have been published in tourism and hospitality journals since the 1980s (Figueroa-Domecq, Pritchard, Segovia-Pérez, Morgan, & Villacé-Molinero, 2015; Khoo-Lattimore & Yang, 2018). The marginalisation of gender studies in tourism is a direct result of the underrepresentation of women academics at leadership and gatekeeping positions. This is explained in the "While Waiting for the Dawn" project by Munar et al. (2015), which extensively mapped the gender gap in the tourism academia. According to their report, half of the tourism academics were women but only 25% of tourism journal editors, who are the knowledge gatekeepers of the field, were women. Pritchard and Morgan (2017) later revealed that women made up only 11% of professoriate positions in the United Kingdom, 16% in Australia and 12% in New Zealand.

Another channel for the creation of tourism knowledge is through conferences. The intellectual dialogues and thought rhetorics that take place during formal sessions and informal networking events shape the development of tourism knowledge. While according to Walters (2018), the number of women in tourism conference organising committees in 2017 has increased since the 2013 statistics published by Munar et al. (2015), it is important to caution the feminisation or hostessing nature (Veijola & Jokinen, 2008) of conference organising where women take on the 3 Cs (i.e. cleaning, caring, and catering) (Toynbee, 2003) instead of leadership roles. The representation of women speakers at conferences remains marginal with only 30% women representing the total number of keynote speakers, invited speakers and expert panel members. This distribution of conference leadership positions, where more women than men take on organising secretariat roles and more men than women assigned keynote roles, is inherited from a long-held structure of knowledge reproduction that privileges men, and attributed to unconscious sexism and implicit bias (Chambers et al., 2017), which will be explained in the next section.

Statement culture, femwashing, and implicit bias

Three notions have emerged from the review of the handful of literature that has considered gender representation in tourism knowledge leaders. The first notion is *statement culture* where diversity and gender equality are mainly exercised rhetorically through statements and slogans instead of actual practices (Chambers et al., 2017). Statement culture is observed in several tourism academic associations where diversity and/or gender equality are commonly underlined in the value statements and conference themes but the underrepresentation of female speakers at the events hosted by these associations indicates an incongruent between practice and rhetoric (Walters, 2018). Whether statement culture exists in UNWTO's events is unknown, as this has not been mapped until this study.

The second notion is *femwashing*, a term proposed in this study to examine the dubious communication that emphasises gender equality in order to project a favourable public image for an organization, which is UNWTO in this case. The term is derived from greenwashing, a prevalent word in the literature of sustainability that is used to describe "communications that mislead people into adopting overly positive beliefs about an organization's environment performance, practices, or products" (Lyon & Montgomery, 2015, p. 225). The practice of greenwash is evident in both public and corporate sectors to shape desirable images through misleading sustainable rhetorics (Bramwell & Lane, 2002). Femwashing and statement culture are parallel concepts but the former is more fitting in critically auditing the gender gaps (if any) between rhetorics and practices in the green discourse of UNWTO.

The third notion is *implicit bias*, which encompasses unconscious prejudice and attitude towards people with different social identities, such as gender (i.e. unconscious sexism) and ethnicity (i.e. unconscious racism) (Greenwald & Krieger, 2006; Munar, Khoo-Lattimore, Chambers, & Biran, 2017; Pritchard & Morgan, 2017). The implicit bias is so deeply rooted in the social structures, cultures and organizations, that even the educated population adopts negative gender norms and unconsciously accepts prejudicial social practices (e.g. Benschop & Brouns, 2003; Morley, 2013; Xu et al., 2017). Xu et al. (2017) in particular, found a lack of awareness of gender (in)equality among Chinese academics, which results from the varying levels of conscious and unconscious bias in different social and cultural contexts. Regardless of the level of awareness, prior research has provided evidence of the detrimental effect of implicit bias on women's opportunities for leadership roles in general (Hogue & Lord, 2007; Hoyt & Burnette, 2013; Rudman & Kilianski, 2000) as well as in the tourism academia (Munar et al., 2017; Pritchard & Morgan, 2017; Walters, 2018). Implicit bias is therefore, a separate issue from the awareness of gender inequality, the latter being the result of the former.

Tourism knowledge as neo-colonialism

Not only is tourism knowledge gendered in that it is often produced and disseminated by males, it is also often produced by White males (Chambers & Buzinde, 2015). Even in non-English speaking academic systems, Western epistemologies and ontologies tend to be duplicated in attempts to generate new knowledge (Chang, 2015; Mura, Mognard, & Sharif, 2017; Oktadiana & Pearce, 2017). While gender representation in academia has begun to receive a growing attention in the past few years, other diversity dimensions such as ethnicity remain uncharted.

There has been little concerted effort that maps the ethnic composition of tourism academe. One of the few exceptions is Lee, Khoo-Lattimore, and Yang (2017) who examined Asian academics in the Australian tourism academe. The interviewees in their study revealed the gender and racial stereotypes that they experienced in the academia – Asian academics were perceived by others to lack English-language proficiency, their young appearances were associated with the lack of credibility, and Asian females were assumed domestic roles. The study concluded that tourism academia is reproducing the colonial and patriarchal structures of power (Lee et al.,

2017). This is problematic because it firstly reduces the legitimacy of *other* knowledges, and subsequently causes us to miss out on theories and views that might help advance tourism knowledge (Chambers & Buzinde, 2015). This notion of neo-colonisation of tourism knowledge (Wijesinghe, Mura, & Bouchon, 2017) when intersected with gendered tourism knowledge, addresses a central theoretical issue within critical feminist research.

Intersectionality brings together inter and intra connections between ethnicity, class and gender, and fits neatly into the critical feminist perspective of this study to conceptualise the identities of speakers at UNWTO's events. While information on class is not available, an analysis of the speakers' ethnicity and nationality provides a fuller understanding of the focus, perspective and impact of knowledge that UNWTO has produced. Although non-Western speakers may still replicate Western paradigm from education and socialisation, their voices at UNWTO's events are an important step towards decolonising tourism knowledge. The normalisation of their presence at business events can potentially challenge Western structures of power in tourism spaces.

Methodology

Critical feminist content analysis

Thus far, the topics of patriarchy and neo-colonised knowledge production were identified as a concern from two theories: criticality and feminism. As such, events held by UNWTO were analysed using critical feminist content analysis. Content analysis is a broad method that consists of a systematic investigation of written texts and cultural artefacts, including visual, audio and audio-visual materials (Leavy, 2007). Content analysis can be incorporated in studies with different theoretical perspectives and can be conducted using a quantitative, qualitative or mixed-method design, depending on the research questions and the nature of the data. In this particular study, a feminist content analysis with a quantitative design was used to count and map the representation of female and minority speakers at UNWTO events.

Critical feminist content analysis differentiates from general content analysis in its critical perspective and activist agenda. Feminism is "a movement, and a set of beliefs, that problematise gender inequality" (DeVault, 1996, p. 31). The end goal of a research that uses a feminist methodology is to promote equality for women and minorities through conducting research that reveals women's perspectives and that minimises power difference in the research process (DeVault, 1996). Prior research has demonstrated the potential of content analysis in identifying patterns that unveil gender as well as racial bias, and the findings can be used to advance social changes (Leavy, 2000, 2007). Some examples of feminist content analysis studies include investigations of athlete representation in newspapers (Kinnick, 1998), sexualisation of adolescent girls in magazines (Schlenker, Caron, & Halteman, 1998; Trimble-Clarke, 2012), and gender portrayal in popular films (England, Descartes, & Collier-Meek, 2011; Jocelyn, 2005). Content analysis is valuable for critical feminist research because the data (i.e. cultural artefacts) embody and reflect the gender discourse in the society in which the artefacts emerge. Likewise, content analysis usually involves data that exist prior to and independently of the research; the data are not created or co-created by the researcher through surveys or interviews (Leavy, 2000, 2007).

Guiding by a critical feminist lens, the content analysis in the current study connects the research questions and the interpretation of the data to the broader social, cultural and political context. The analysis of the list of keynote speakers hosted by UNWTO serves to audit the dynamics of power and the gender hierarchical structure within the organization, and to assess whose views and whose voices are represented on UNWTO's knowledge production platform. While gender is at the core of the study, the analysis also incorporates an intersectionality perspective to consider the interactions and mutually constitutive relations of gender and other social identities such as ethnicity and nationality, and to examine if voices of *other* women and

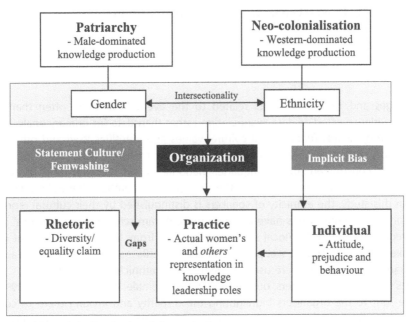

Figure 1. Conceptual framework of tourism knowledge production.

other men are heard. Figure 1 presents the conceptual framework that guided the design of the study.

Procedures

Sample

In 2017, a total of 121 UNWTO events were held (UNWTO, 2017c). Information on these events was featured on their websites, and some of these events were video recorded and translated into multiple languages for wider dissemination. Of the 121 events, one was the *Internationale Tourismus-Börse (ITB) Berlin*, which was a significant international tourism trade fair, consisting of multiple concurrent events. For this reason, *ITB Berlin* was removed from the sample but eight of the associated UNWTO events held at the ITB were included. In addition, there were three parts to the *10th Working Group Meeting of the Convention on the Protection of Tourists and the Rights and Obligations of Tourism Service Providers*, which were portrayed by UNWTO to be three separate events. Although there were web links to parts one and three, no information could be found on part two. The latter event was therefore removed from the sample and in total, 119 events were included in this study for investigation.

Data collection

The aim of this study was to understand where UNWTO stood in terms of knowledge production, and to what extent if any, the invited speakers reinforced stereotypes that undermine women's expertise and intellectual competencies; or met their goals to achieve gender equality and empower women. For each of the 119 events, the researchers followed multiple leads for information on the dates, locations, event aims, event partners, number of speakers, gender of speakers, and distribution of speakers by gender and ethnicity. The primary leads for data were UNWTO's own webpages as well as the websites of their member states, affiliates and partners that document their past events. The researchers also followed links to YouTube recordings,

Table 1. Number of UNWTO's 2017 events with speaker information.

Information	No.	%
Available	64	53.78
Unavailable	55	46.22
Total	119	100.00

Facebook pages and Twitter accounts related to the events, but more often than not, these social media evidence acted as data triangulation rather than data for primary analysis.

An ethnic group shares fundamental cultural values and identifies itself and others by constituting a category distinguishable from other categories of the same type (Barth, 1998). The identity is socially constructed from language, national origin, religion and culture, and is continuously revised and revitalised by the group and member themselves (Nagel, 1994). Therefore, in this study, the ethnicity of speakers is distinguished by their cultural representations and/or nationalities. Some events have included the program schedule and speakers' information that indicated where the invited/local speakers had come from. If there was a lack of information about speakers, the professional webpages and social media pages (i.e. LinkedIn, Facebook and Twitter) of individual speakers were used to identify their ethnicity/nationality.

In events where male speakers outnumbered their female counterparts by 300% or more, emails were sent to the organisers highlighting the disparity and inviting them to comment on their perception and awareness of gender issues with regards to tourism leadership and representation at their own events. Although half of the events (where speakers' information was available) had approximately 200% more males than females, this is considered by many event organisers to be the norm. So, the researchers focused on the 29 events that saw a more discernible imbalance towards male speakers. Not all of these events had contact details of the organising committee, and in cases where they did, the email addresses for the contact person tended to be the same (i.e. x@unwto.org). In total, 10 emails were sent to 29 of the events held in 2017. These comments were not used during primary analysis. Rather, they were utilised to complement and enrich the findings and discussions.

Findings

Table 1 shows that of the 119 events, only 64 had information available on their speakers. One of the reasons for this could be attributed to the closed membership of the delegates who attended the events, and any information would have been disseminated within the small number of delegates – the *Working Lunch with the Central-America Tourism Ministers* event is an example. The *44th Meeting of the UNWTO Board of the Affiliate Members* is another, where its webpage clearly stated that the meeting was convened, "with the provisional agenda established by the Secretary-General in consultation with the Chairman of the Board". Sometimes, the events were promoted in languages besides English. For instance, the only information published for the *Tourist Routes for Community Development* course was in French and Spanish. Occasionally, events in the dataset had no information on speakers – the *UNWTO/THEMIS Capacity Building Workshop on Current Trends in Tourism e-Marketing* was one such example. In such cases, attempts were made to locate this information from other sources on the web, to no avail.

In total, 1656 speakers were identified from UNWTO website, as well as the websites of their member states, affiliates and partners. Of these, there were 1151 or 70% male speaker engagements compared to only 505 or 30% female speaker engagements. Table 2 shows that male speakers outnumbered their female counterparts in 59 of the 64 events, while female outnumbered males in only 4 events, one of which was caused by the odd number of speakers. In this case, there were 7 speakers in total with 3 males and 4 females. In addition, only 1 event saw a balanced representation of male-female speakers.

Table 2. Gender representation of speakers at UNWTO's events in 2017.

Gender representation	No.	%
Males outnumbered females	59 events	92.19
Females outnumbered males	4 events	6.25
Balanced	1 event	1.56
Total	64	100.00

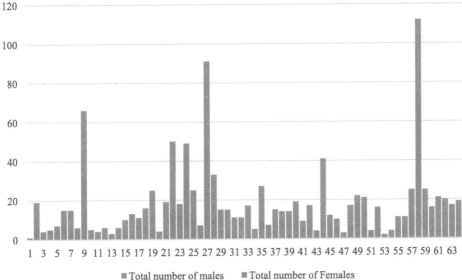

■ Total number of males   ■ Total number of Females

Figure 2. Illustration of male-female speakers at UNWTO's 2017 events.

Figure 2 illustrates the gender representation of speakers at the 64 events. At the 11th *UNWTO Asia Pacific Executive Training Programme on Tourism Policy and Strategy*, held in Papua New Guinea, there was a total of 13 speakers, none of whom were female. The *General Assembly Special Session on Smart Tourism* held in Chengdu, China had 41 male speakers compared to only 3 females. Female speakers outnumbered male speakers at the *32nd meeting of the World Tourism Network on Child Protection* in Berlin, Germany (7 females, 4 males), the *Meeting of the UNWTO Committee of Tourism and Sustainability* in Madrid, Spain (4 females, 3 males), the 2nd International Western Silk Road Workshop in Sofia, Bulgaria (7 females, 3 males), and the *Special Meeting of the Members of the Committee on Statistics and TSA* in Chengdu, China (4 females, 2 males).

No event was found where there were three times more female speakers than male. On the contrary, Table 3 shows that male speakers outnumbered female speakers three-fold or more in almost half the analysed events (29 events). For instance, at the *61st UNWTO Regional Commission for the Americas and International Seminar on New Technologies Applied to Tourism* in Honduras, male speakers (17) outnumbered female speakers (2) almost eight-fold. At the *3rd Euro-Asian Mountain Resorts Conference* in Georgia, there were five times more male speakers (25) compared to female (5).

When event organisers were contacted for their comments on the predominant male line-up of speakers, the responses were not at all encouraging. The majority did not reply, and of those who did, the response was the obligatory one-liner of, "your comment was well-received and appreciated". When probed with a separate email, this response became, "As already mentioned in my earlier e-mail: the comment was well received and appreciated". The most engaging response was received by the organiser of the *61st meeting of the UNWTO Regional Commission for the Americas*, who replied, "...we do not choose the speakers based on gender but on

Table 3. Events where males outnumber females three-fold or more.

Event name	Date (2017)	Location	Male speakers	Female speakers
13th UNWTO Awards Forum	16 Jan	Madrid, Spain	19	6
13th UNWTO Awards Ceremony & Gala Dinner	18 Jan	Madrid, Spain	5	0
UNWTO & Casa Arabe Ministerial Discussion Forum on Strengthening the resilience of Tourism in the Middle East and North Africa and sustaining growth	19 Jan	Madrid, Spain	7	2
17th session of the UNWTO Committee on Statistics and Tourism Satellite Account	24–25 Jan	Madrid, Spain	15	3
UNWTO Regional Statistics Capacity Building Programme	13–15 Feb	Algiers, Algeria	6	2
UNWTO Panel on Indigenous Tourism: Promoting equitable partnerships	9 Mar	Berlin, Germany	6	1
6th UNWTO Silk Road Tour Operators Forum at ITB	9 Mar	Berlin, Germany	3	1
New platform tourism services (or the so-called sharing economy)	9 Mar	Berlin, Germany	6	2
11th UNWTO Asia Pacific Executive Training Programme on Tourism Policy and Strategy	20–23 Mar	Port Moresby, Papua New Guinea	13	0
3rd Euro-Asian Mountain Resorts Conference	4–7 Apr	Tiblisi, Georgia	25	5
2017 MCSTO Training Programme for China Observatories – Tourism Destination Carrying Capacity Management	17–21 Apr	Zhanjiajie, China	4	1
59th meeting of the UNWTO Commission for Africa and High-level Meeting on Chinese Outbound Tourism to Africa	18–21 Apr	Addis Ababa, Ethiopia	5	1
UNWTO & ATM Ministerial Round Table on Tourism's contribution to sustainable and inclusive economic growth and diversification in the MENA region	24 Apr	Dubai, UAE	19	3
WTTC/UNWTO Ministerial Roundtable	25 Apr	Bangkok, Thailand	50	15
3rd UNWTO World Forum on Gastronomy Tourism	8–9 May	San Sebastian, Spain	33	10
Round Table on "Sustainable Urban Tourism"	10 May	Madrid, Spain	15	5
The 29th Joint Meeting of the UNWTO Commission for East Asia and the Pacific and the UNWTO Commission for South Asia (29th CAP-CSA) & UNWTO Regional Forum on Crisis Communication	15–17 May	Chittagong, Bangladesh	15	4
PATA/UNWTO Ministerial Debate	20 May	Negombo, Sri Lanka	11	2
Master Class on Attracting Chinese Tourism to the Mediterranean	24 May	Valletta, Malta	11	1
61st UNWTO Regional Commission for the Americas and International Seminar on New Technologies Applied to Tourism	29 May–2 Jun	Roatán, Honduras	17	2
World Conference on Tourism and Future Energy: Unlocking low-carbon growth opportunities	26–27 Jun	Astana, Kazakhstan	27	9
International Conference on Rural Tourism	16–18 Jul	Huzhou, China	14	2
22nd session of the UNWTO General Assembly	11–16 Sep	Chengdu, China	17	5
	14–15 Sep	Chengdu, China	41	3

(continued)

Table 3. Continued.

Event name	Date (2017)	Location	Male speakers	Female speakers
General Assembly Special Session on Smart Tourism				
World Tourism Day 2017 Official Celebration: Sustainable Tourism – A Tool for Development	27 Sep	Qatar, Doha	3	0
The 11th UNWTO/PATA Forum on Tourism Trends and Outlook	10–12 Oct	Guilin, China	21	7
UNWTO/ILO Joint Conference on Decent Work and Socially Responsible Tourism	20 Oct	Madrid, Spain	16	5
6th Global Summit on Urban Tourism	4–6 Dec	Kuala Lumpur, Malaysia	21	5
2017 International Symposium and Annual Conference of the 10YFP Sustainable Tourism Programme: Empowering Tourism Destinations' Sustainability	7–9 Dec	Kasane, Botswana	20	6

expertise and recommendations from our partners. As the technology industry [new technologies was the topic of the seminar] is predominantly male-dominated, this has in a way reflected on the final selection of the panellists."

Table 4 provides a geographical and intersectional analysis of the speakers' ethnicity and gender in relation to the locations of UNWTO events. As far as ethnicity is concerned, the findings indicate a positive pattern where 879 or 53% of the 1656 speakers identified in this study were Westerners while 777 or 47% were non-Westerners, of which 326 were Asians (20%), 199 were Non-Anglo Americans (12%), 133 were Africans (8%), 103 were Middle Easterners (6%) and 16 (1%) were Pacific Islanders. Non-Western speakers generally outnumbered Western speakers in events held in Africa, Middle East, North America, Oceania, South America and Asia. Where events were held in Europe, the disparity between Western and non-Western speakers was apparent with 2.4 times more Western speakers than their non-Western counterparts. On the contrary, although there were more non-Western speakers at Asian locations, the disparity was relatively smaller with non-Western (275) outnumbering Western (141) speakers by only 1.9 times. The only negative exception was the WTTC/UNWTO Ministerial Roundtable held in Bangkok, Thailand, where there were 36 Western speakers compared to 23 Asian speakers. It is also worthwhile noting that the lack of information, particularly regarding speakers, was compounded in events held in Asian locations, that is, 20 out of the 34 events held in Asia had no information about the speakers.

As presented in Table 4, an intersectional analysis of the speakers' identities indicates an underrepresentation of non-Western female speakers. Among 1656 speakers, Western male speakers were identified as the leading group, accounting for 36% of all speakers, followed by non-Western males at 33% and Western females at 17%. Non-Western women were the least represented group at only 14%. The underrepresentation of non-Western female speakers was especially apparent in events held in the Middle East, Oceania, and Europe. It appears that although the voices of non-Western speakers were well represented in UNWTO events held in non-Western locations, the voices of *other* women remain marginalised.

Discussions

The findings of this study show that even for an organization that has pledged gender equality, there is a significant marginalisation of gender in the majority of their main business events in 2017. More males than females were seen as expert speakers in over 90% of the business events (those that had information available on their speakers) promoted by UNWTO and in 45% of the events, male speakers substantially outnumbered female by 300% or more. This lack of female

Table 4. Distribution of speakers in terms of location, gender, and ethnicity.

Event location	No. of events	No. of speakers	Gender	No.	%	Ethnicity	No.	%	Intersectionality	No.	%
Europe	35	843	M	572	68	W	593	70	WM	395	47
									N-W M	177	21
			F	271	32	N-W	250	30	WF	198	23
									N-W F	73	9
Africa	5	85	M	60	71	W	23	27	WM	17	20
									N-W M	43	51
			F	25	29	N-W	62	73	WF	6	7
									N-W F	19	22
Asia	15	416	M	307	74	W	143	34	WM	104	25
									N-W M	203	49
			F	109	26	N-W	273	66	WF	39	9
									N-W F	70	17
Middle East	3	52	M	39	75	W	17	33	WM	11	21
									N-W M	28	54
			F	13	25	N-W	35	67	WF	6	12
									N-W F	7	13
North America	3	208	M	133	64	W	87	42	WM	59	28
									N-W M	74	36
			F	75	36	N-W	121	58	WF	28	13
									N-W F	47	23
Oceania	1	13	M	13	100	W	1	8	WM	1	8
									N-W M	12	92
			F	0	0	N-W	12	92	WF	0	0
									N-W F	0	0
South America	2	39	M	27	69	W	15	38	WM	11	28
									N-W M	16	41
			F	12	31	N-W	24	62	WF	4	10
									N-W F	8	21
All events	64	1656	M	1151	70	W	879	53	WM	598	36
									N-W M	553	33
			F	505	30	N-W	777	47	WF	281	17
									N-W F	224	14

M, Male; F, Female; W, Western; and N-W, Non-Western.

representation threatens the fifth UNSDG of gender equality and is perceived to have limited equal opportunities and representation in leadership roles for women. It further compounds the current patriarchal management of tourism knowledge production and policy making spaces.

Previous statistics already show that gender inequality in tourism industry persists. For examples, women are underrepresented in the tourism sector, earn 10—15% less than men in both management and nonmanagement levels, and are relegated to lower-paid hospitality jobs because of implicit bias and perceived gendered roles (Twining-Ward & Zhou, 2017). The literature is imbued with empirical evidence that women in tourism whether as travellers (e.g. Harris & Wilson, 2007; Yang, Khoo-Lattimore, & Arcodia, 2018b) or workers (e.g. Kensbock, Bailey, Jennings, & Patiar, 2015; Poulston, 2008), continue to perceive varied forms of risks and constraints in public tourism spaces but it would be logical to anticipate that these gendered challenges would diminish with a higher representation and subsequently, perception of women as equally powerful actors and co-creators of tourism experiences. Unfortunately, the incessant images of men on stage and the unremitting messages that men are the tourism experts thwart the very core of our collective efforts to, "achieve gender equality and empower all women and girls".

When approached for comments on the significant underrepresentation of women speakers at their events, one organiser who demonstrated empathy for the issue justified the overrepresentation of male speakers with meritocracy, and assuming the position that objective evaluations of the speakers were based primarily on expertise and recommendations from their partners, and not gender. However, many studies have already shown that meritocratic practices do not result in objective evaluations (Ekman, Lindgren, & Packendorff, 2016; Nielsen, 2016) because gendered norms would unconsciously bias merit measurements and prejudice who is considered merited or otherwise. While gender bias against female speakers may be "unconscious", the same organiser, in the response to the concern, "consciously" acknowledged that the area of expertise featured in the event was male-dominated. It appears that the organising committee has not made meaningful effort to promote gender equality despite being aware of the gender gap. Other UNTWO event organisers appeared nonchalant about the concern raised and undertook an avoidance response strategy.

To a large extent, these responses exemplify femwashing and statement culture, which might result in the perception of UNWTO embodying organizational hypocrisy, that they exert more energy into appearing to be doing the right thing rather than actually striving to do it. For example, a #UNWTO thread through the Women Academics in Tourism's (WAiT) Facebook group page documented animosity of members towards a plenary session that had a line-up of nine male panel speakers. Accompanied by a photo (Figure 3), the heading of the thread read, "It was supposed to be a conference about "inclusive" growth. But… congrats on another ALL WHITE MALE PANEL [the use of capital letters is reported as is] in Jamaica." (Women Academics in Tourism, 2018).

The findings also show that there is an overall representation and diversity in terms of ethnicity at UNWTO events, so the critique on "Anglo-Western centrism" that many scholars observed in academia is not as noticeable in UNWTO's organised events. However, a detailed analysis highlights a disparity between Western and non-Western speakers at a majority of the events. There is already caution that power is distributed amongst cultural identity groups, and this power distribution will consequently influence how a person behaves in the workplace (Alderfer, 1987). Further, individuals frequently evaluate the power and status of others on the basis of ethnicity (Ridgeway, 1991), and certain groups in Western society tend to be more powerful than others, and that whites are more so than minorities (Ely & Thomas, 2001).

Figure 3. Facebook post on WAiT. Source: Women Academics in Tourism (2018). Photo credit: Mariana Aldrigui.

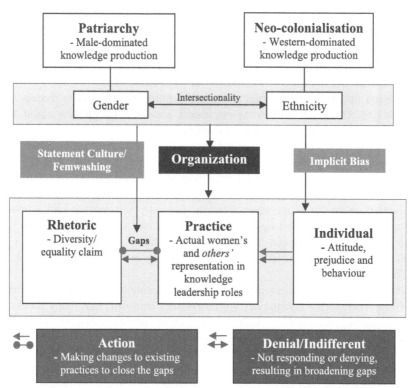

Figure 4. Conceptual framework of tourism knowledge production with the possible effect of different responses.

The confluences of speakers from one ethnic group outnumbering other ethnic groups should not be encouraged because an equal ethnic representation of speakers in all events despite topics, agendas and locations would better result in the "pluralism" of tourism knowledge. Events that promote the intersections of gender and ethnicity would make tourism knowledge less "normative", and encourage a more complex and dynamic understanding of any given tourism topic, provided that UNWTO encourages other forms of knowledge and different ways of representing knowledge. Unfortunately, an intersectional analysis of the speakers' gender and ethnic identities show that non-Western women remained the least represented group at the UNWTO's knowledge production space, even though tourism is widely promoted as a vehicle for women and girls empowerment and employment, especially in non-Western developing countries. A greater representation of *other* women, who have the contextual knowledge at the knowledge leadership level is likely to facilitate a better understanding and empowering tourism solutions to the challenges faced by women at the grassroots level.

Finally, the study reiterates the importance of UNWTO's events in materialising, producing, reproducing and highlighting tourism expertise and knowledge. The findings in this study support Tribe (2006)'s contention that tourism knowledge (in this case, outside academe), is produced and filtered by various power structures (in this study, gender, ethnicity, and ideology) that will shape "the interpretation and representation of tourism as phenomenon" (Wijesinghe et al., 2017, p. 5). As the thought leader, tourism academia has failed to be at the forefront of promoting UNSDG for gender equality and in particular, ensuring women's full and effective participation, and equal opportunities for leadership – this is especially pronounced for women from minority groups. This is hopefully changing as a result of the emergence of "disruptive" forces – for example, While Waiting for the Dawn project, Women Academics in Tourism (WAiT) Facebook group, and the publication of a special issue on Gender and The Tourism Academy in the journal, Anatolia (Munar, Chambers, Khoo-Lattimore, & Biran, 2017) – which have pushed for gender equality discourse and practices in the academia and to challenge the status quo. This study has extended the disruptive force to UNWTO by scrutinising if the leading tourism organization "walks the talk" of promoting the fifth sustainable development goal or it is merely a "femwashing". The findings do not necessarily imply that the organization is femwashing but unfortunately, UNWTO is not yet walking the talk either.

Theoretical implications

As Twining-Ward and Zhou (2017, p. 13) stated, "There remains much to be learned about how to take full advantage of the opportunities tourism can provide for women, but it is clear that tourism project designs that lack a gender lens cannot fully leverage the advantage tourism offers for women." Responding to this call, this study is the first to employ a gender lens to assess the gender representation in tourism knowledge production beyond academe. Scholars have critiqued the gendered knowledge production in tourism (Munar et al., 2015; Walters, 2018), but knowledge created outside of academia has a more pervasive reach and a greater impact to women at the grassroots level and hence, warrants a critical analysis of its own.

Furthermore, existing research on gender representation has mainly focused on gender as the sole unit of analysis and assumed women as a homogenous group. While valuable in identifying the structural gender inequality and providing a united voice for women, such an approach overlooks the intersection of and the mutually constitutive relations between gender and other social identities such as ethnicity. In fact, intersectionality as a theoretical approach has been often cited but rarely applied in tourism literature because of its complexity and ambiguity (Gao & Kerstetter, 2016; Yang et al., 2018b). This study has demonstrated the need for and practicality of intersectionality analysis to unpack the complex patriarchal and neo-colonial power structures in tourism knowledge production. It is clearly evident in this study that the voices of non-Western or *other* women have been double-marginalised on the knowledge production platform of UNWTO, even though the empowering effect of tourism is likely to be felt more strongly by non-Western women in less developed communities. Such implication can be easily overlooked if the analysis focuses on only one social dimension, either gender or ethnicity.

In addition to accounting for different social dimensions, this study employed critical feminism (Leavy, 2000, 2007) as the guiding gender lens. The criticality of the study lies in its feminist agenda to advance social changes through research (DeVault, 1996). To achieve this objective, the researchers undertook four tasks: (1) critically assessed the gender (and ethnic) representation of knowledge leaders at UNWTO events; (2) initiated dialogues with event organisers to express the concerns; (3) proposed a framework based on the findings to facilitate further research in this area; and (4) constructively provided recommendations to promote women's representation and opportunities in tourism knowledge leadership roles – the recommendations will be discussed in further detail in the *Practical Implications* section.

Tasks 1 and 2 constituted the main analysis of the study and were reported in previous sections. In terms of task 3, a conceptual framework (see Figure 4) is proposed to illustrate the interactions of various power structures (i.e. patriarchy and neo-colonialism), notions (i.e. implicit bias, statement culture and femwashing), and processes (i.e. individual, practice, and rhetoric) related to gender representation in tourism knowledge production at an institutional level, as well as the possible effect of different responses (i.e. action and denial/indifferent). Further empirical research is encouraged to substantiate and expand the conceptual framework. Research that collects empirical data from UNWTO and event organisers, and that follows up on the effect of different responses on widening or closing the gaps between rhetoric and practice will be especially valuable.

Practical implications

While mainstream literature has incessantly admonished women travellers to employ techniques for reducing risks and constraints, little has been done by prominent tourism businesses and/or influential organizations who can be instrumental in leading change towards gender-neutral spaces. Much more needs to be done to address the implicit bias and to bridge the official gender equality rhetoric of UNWTO and the management practices of their business events, through multi-level approaches. For one, the people behind the committees tasked with organising these events need to know more about how to increase inclusivity that is visible not only to the delegates who attend them, but also to the populations who work for and with UNWTO, and those whom they aim to impact. An inclusion-scoping checklist should be developed for use during event planning, which incorporates common gender and ethnicity constraints with some recommended suggestions for resolving them. The Tourism Education Futures Initiative (TEFI)'s guidelines for promoting gender equity and balance in tourism conferences could be a starting point but can be further developed and implemented as a compulsory criteria set for any event to run. All UNWTO event organisers should at the very least understand the influence of implicit bias on the notion of meritocracy, and look beyond traditional representations of expertise and recognition. For example, instead of recruiting all male speakers for a seminar on new technologies in tourism only because the technology industry is predominantly male-dominated, females working with innovative technologies in other industries connected to tourism could be engaged.

Event organisers for UNWTO should be trained to incorporate intersectionality issues in events, which eventually means that event management courses globally should include a diversity curriculum. It is recommended that UNWTO's event organisers develop some formal protocols to ensure that their events comprise equal representations of ethnically-diverse speakers even for potentially ethnically-homogenous delegates in ethnically-homogenous locations. This can be implemented through the UNWTO Themis Foundation and their UNWTO TedQual certifications. Technologically, a database of qualified, expert speakers should be developed with an application that is capable of stratifying the number of speakers for any given event based on equal representation of ethnicity and gender and perhaps even age and other forms of inclusivity. Rationally, UNWTO should monitor their future events for diversity representation against the findings of this study as one of the measurements for improving the fifth UNSDG. One immediate way to achieve gender and racial balance is to always have an even number of speakers. In summary, imperative actions are needed because failing to act on the rhetoric-practice gaps, UNWTO would appear to be "femwashing" their gender equality claims.

Conclusions

This study contributes to knowledge in three major ways. The first and most direct contribution is to the literature on tourism knowledge production. Framed by the two pillars of patriarchy and neo-colonisation within critical feminist theory, and underpinned by notions of statement culture, femwashing and implicit bias, this is the first study to empirically show that while there is satisfactory surface-level ethnic diversity among speakers at UNWTO business events, there is also a critical underrepresentation of women speakers, and non-Western women speakers in particular, and an unequal balance of ethnicity in the speakers for individual events.

Second, this study also highlights the inconsistency between what UNWTO wants to achieve and what they are realising. The findings, particularly those that show how male speakers outnumbered female by three-fold and more, and importantly, the responses from the event organisers, do not correspond with the fifth UNSDG to achieve gender equality and empower all women. While many studies have advanced convincing normative arguments for equity and inclusion, very little research has sought to empirically investigate the actual performances of public tourism organizations.

Finally, this study paves the way for a more inclusive space for the tourism industry to embrace diverse tourism identities, cultures, languages, and epistemologies. As Mura and Khoo-Lattimore (2018) have said, "everyone in the research community, institutional structures and corporate publishers of academic work [should] reflect on the current meritocracy discourse that privileges entrenched ways of knowledge production which replicates exclusions of 'other knowledges'" (p. 17).

The study, however, is not without limitations. Importantly, the study referred to gender and ethnicity as social identity markers of the speakers. These social identities are parsimonious in themselves and considerations had not been made for subordinated masculinities and femininities within gender and the intricacies of Western influences (e.g. through education, socialisation, media, and popular culture) within ethnicity. Future research is encouraged to investigate the complexities of implicit gender and racial bias of speakers themselves. Furthermore, the researchers were not able to accurately categorise speakers with mixed ethnicity/nationality and therefore, identified them according to the most obvious social indicator (e.g. the affiliation that is publicly available online). Other social identities such as transgender were also not considered.

Similar to prior studies (Munar et al., 2015; Walters, 2018), the current study only investigated knowledge representation at business events over the course of one year. A longitudinal study would be useful for observing if there is a measurable improvement in the representation of female and non-Western speakers at UNWTO events, and for quantifying the extent to which UNWTO achieves their fifth UNSDG. This study was carried out by employing a critical feminist theory but the issues in this study could be examined by employing other theoretical underpinnings. For example, cultural identity theory could advance the understanding on why the disparity between ethnic groups is but should not be persisting, while multilevel theory, complexity theory and connectionist theory would explain how gender bias occurs (Dinh et al., 2014) within UNWTO itself.

Finally, it is worth situating the researchers in this study. The first two researchers are Malaysian Chinese females, while the third researcher is a South Korean female. All three have research interests that centre on women in tourism and their service work revolve around advocating women's rights and empowerment in the tourism space. Being at the intersection of female and Asian enables a double perspectives but often, the embodiment of this intersectionality feels more like a double-edged sword in the workspace. The researchers' professional biographical events, impacted by their gender and ethnicity have circuitously inspired this study and it is not clear if researchers with different identities examining this topic would discover new findings. The researchers also acknowledge their research training in Anglo-Saxon universities and therefore, would have unconsciously embraced Western paradigms. In this case, their implicit bias is complicated as it is built on the lines of gender, racial and postcolonial structures of power.

Acknowledgement

This work was supported by Griffith Institute for Tourism.

ORCID

Catheryn Khoo-Lattimore (iD) http://orcid.org/0000-0003-2858-870X

References

Alderfer, C. P. (1987). An intergroup perspective on group dynamics. In J. Lorsch (Ed.), *Handbook on organizational behavior* (pp. 190–222). Englewood Cliffs, NJ: Prentice Hall.

Barth, F. (1998). *Ethnic groups and boundaries: The social organization of culture difference.* Illinois, USA: Waveland Press.

Benschop, Y., & Brouns, M. (2003). Crumbling ivory towers: Academic organizing and its gender effects. *Gender, Work and Organization, 10*, 194–212. doi:10.1111/1468-0432.t01-1-00011

Bramwell, B., & Lane, B. (2002). The journal of sustainable tourism: The first ten years. *Journal of Sustainable Tourism, 10*(1), 1–4. doi:10.1080/09669580208667149

Chambers, D., & Buzinde, C. (2015). Tourism and decolonisation: Locating research and self. *Annals of Tourism Research, 51*, 1–16. doi:10.1016/j.annals.2014.12.002

Chambers, D., Munar, A. M., Khoo-Lattimore, C., & Biran, A. (2017). Interrogating gender and the tourism academy through epistemological lens. *Anatolia, 28*(4), 501–513. doi:10.1080/13032917.2017.1370775

Chang, T. C. (2015). The Asian wave and critical tourism scholarship. *International Journal of Asia Pacific Studies, 1*, 83–101.

DeVault, M. L. (1996). Talking back to sociology: Distinctive contributions of feminist methodology. *Annual Review of Sociology, 22*(1), 29–50. doi:10.1146/annurev.soc.22.1.29

Dinh, J. E., Lord, R. G., Gardner, W. L., Meuser, J. D., Liden, R. C., & Hu, J. (2014). Leadership theory and research in the new millennium: Current theoretical trends and changing perspectives. *The Leadership Quarterly, 25*(1), 36–62. doi:10.1016/j.leaqua.2013.11.005

Dredge, D., Benckendorff, P., Day, M., Gross, M. J., Walo, M., Weeks, P., & Whitelaw, P. (2012). The philosophic practitioner and the curriculum space. *Annals of Tourism Research, 39*(4), 2154–2176. doi:10.1016/j.annals.2012.07.017

Ekman, M., Lindgren, M., & Packendorff, J. (2016). Fragmented meritocratisation: On mobilisation and demobilisation of gender in higher education. Manor, NY: Paper Presented at the Academy of Management. doi:10.5465/AMBPP.2016.10460abstract

Ely, R., & Thomas, D. (2001). Cultural diversity at work: The effects of diversity perspectives on work group processes and outcomes. *Administrative Science Quarterly, 46*(2), 229–273. doi:10.2307/2667087

England, D. E., Descartes, L., & Collier-Meek, M. A. (2011). Gender role portrayal and the Disney princesses. *Sex Roles, 64*(7–8), 555–567. doi:10.1007/s11199-011-9930-7

Ferguson, L. (2011). Promoting gender equality and empowering women? Tourism and the third millennium development goal. *Current Issues in Tourism, 14*(3), 235–249. doi:10.1080/13683500.2011.555522

Figueroa-Domecq, C., Pritchard, A., Segovia-Pérez, M., Morgan, N., & Villacé-Molinero, T. (2015). Tourism gender research: A critical accounting. *Annals of Tourism Research, 52*, 87–103. doi:10.1016/j.annals.2015.02.001

Gao, J., & Kerstetter, D. L. (2016). Using an intersectionality perspective to uncover older Chinese female's perceived travel constraints and negotiation strategies. *Tourism Management, 57*, 128–138. doi:10.1016/j.tourman.2016.06.001

George, J., Roberts, R., & Pacella, J. (2015). 'Whose festival?' Examining questions of participation, access and ownership in rural festivals. In A. Jepson & A. Clarke (Eds.), *Exploring community festivals and events* (pp. 79–91). London, UK: Routledge.

Greenwald, A. G., & Krieger, L. (2006). Implicit bias: Scientific foundations. *California Law Review, 94*(4), 945–968. doi: 10.2307/20439056

Harris, C., & Wilson, E. (2007). Travelling beyond the boundaries of constraint: Women, travel and empowerment. In A. Pritchard, N. Morgan, I. Ateljevic, & C. Harris (Eds.), *Tourism & gender: Embodiment, sensuality and experience* (pp. 235–250). Oxfordshire, UK: CABI.

Hogue, M., & Lord, R. G. (2007). A multilevel, complexity theory approach to understanding gender bias in leadership. *The Leadership Quarterly, 18*(4), 370–390. doi:10.1016/j.leaqua.2007.04.006

Hoyt, C. L., & Burnette, J. L. (2013). Gender bias in leader evaluations: Merging implicit theories. *Personality and Social Psychology Bulletin, 39*(10), 1306–1319. doi:10.1177/0146167213493643

Jocelyn, S. (2005). Cultural representations of gender and science: Portrayals of female scientists and engineers in popular films. *Science Communication, 27*(1), 27–63. doi:10.1177/1075547005278610

Kensbock, S., Bailey, J., Jennings, G., & Patiar, A. (2015). Sexual harassment of women working as room attendants within 5-star hotels. *Gender, Work & Organization, 22*(1), 36–50. doi:10.1111/gwao.12064

Khoo-Lattimore, C., & Yang, E. C. L. (2018). Tourism gender studies. In C. Cooper, S. Volo, W. Gartner & N. Scott (Eds.), *The SAGE handbook of tourism management* (pp. 38–48). London: SAGE.

Kinnick, K. N. (1998). Gender bias in newspaper profiles of 1996 Olympic athletes: A content analysis of five major dailies. *Women's Studies in Communication, 21*(2), 212–237. doi:10.1080/07491409.1998.10162557

Leavy, P. L. (2000). Feminist content analysis and representative characters. *The Qualitative Report, 5*(1), 1–16. Retrieved from http://nsuworks.nova.edu/tqr/vol5/iss1/3

Leavy, P. L. (2007). The feminist practice of content analysis. In S. N. Hesse-Biber & P. L. Leavy (Eds.), *Feminist research practice* (pp. 222–248). Thousand Oaks, CA: SAGE.

Lee, H., Khoo-Lattimore, C., & Yang, E. C. L. (2017). Minority academics in the tourism academy: An exploration of meta-stereotype amongst Asian female and male academics in Australian tourism academia. *Paper presented at the Travel and Tourism Research Association Asia-Pacific Chapter Conference*, Hong Kong.

Lyon, T. P., Montgomery, A. W. (2015). The means and end of greenwash. *Organization & Environment, 28*(2), 223–249. doi:10.1177/1086026615575332

Morley, L. (2013). The rules of the game: Women and the leaderist turn in higher education. *Gender and Education, 25*(1), 116–131. doi:10.1080/09540253.2012.740888

Munar, A. M., Biran, A., Budeanu, A., Caton, K., Chambers, D., Dredge, D., … Ram, Y. (2015). The gender gap in the tourism academy: Statistics and indicators of gender equality. Copenhagen, Denmark: While Waiting for the Dawn.

Munar, A. M., Chambers, D., Khoo-Lattimore, C., & Biran, A. (2017). Gender and the tourism academy [Special Issue]. *Anatolia, 28*(4), 501–591.

Munar, A. M., Khoo-Lattimore, C., Chambers, D., & Biran, A. (2017). The academia we have and the one we want: On the centrality of gender equality. *Anatolia, 28*(4), 582–591. doi:10.1080/13032917.2017.1370786

Mura, P., & Khoo-Lattimore, C. (2018). Locating Asian research and selves in qualitative tourism research. In *Asian Qualitative Research in Tourism*. Singapore: Springer.

Mura, P., Mognard, E., & Sharif, S. P. (2017). Tourism research in non-English-speaking academic systems. *Tourism Recreation Research, 42*(4), 436–445. doi:10.1080/02508281.2017.1283472

Nagel, J. (1994). Constructing ethnicity: Creating and recreating ethnic identity and culture. *Social Problems, 41*(1), 152–176. doi:10.2307/3096847

Nielsen, M. W. (2016). Limits to meritocracy? Gender in academic recruitment and promotion processes. *Science and Public Policy, 43*(3), 386–399. doi:10.1093/scipol/scv052

Oktadiana, H., & Pearce, P. L. (2017). The "bule" paradox in Indonesian tourism research: issues and prospects. *Asia Pacific Journal of Tourism Research, 22*(11), 1099–1109. doi:10.1080/10941665.2017.1374987

Poulston, J. (2008). Metamorphosis in hospitality: A tradition of sexual harassment. *International Journal of Hospitality Management, 27*(2), 232–240. doi:10.1016/j.ijhm.2007.07.013

Pritchard, A., & Morgan, N. (2017). Tourism's lost leaders: Analysing gender and performance. *Annals of Tourism Research, 63*, 34–47. doi:10.1016/j.annals.2016.12.011

Pritchard, A., & Morgan, N. J. (2000). Privileging the male gaze: Gendered. *Tourism Landscapes. Annals of Tourism Research, 27*(4), 884–905. doi:10.1016/S0160-7383(99)00113-9

Ridgeway, C. (1991). The social construction of status value: Gender and other nominal characteristics. *Social Forces, 70*(2), 367–386. doi:10.1093/sf/70.2.367

Rudman, L. A., & Kilianski, S. E. (2000). Implicit and explicit attitudes toward female authority. *Personality and Social Psychology Bulletin, 26*(11), 1315–1328. doi:10.1177/0146167200263001

Schlenker, J. A., Caron, S. L., & Halteman, W. A. (1998). A feminist analysis of seventeen magazine: Content analysis from 1945 to 1995. *Sex Roles, 38*(1/2), 135–149. doi:10.1023/a:1018720813673

Toynbee, P. (2003). *Hard work: Life in low-pay Britain.* London, UK: Bloomsbury Publishing, UK.

Tribe, J. (2006). The truth about tourism. *Annals of Tourism Research, 33*(2), 360–381. doi:10.1016/j.annals.2005.11.001

Trimble-Clarke, B. (2012). A feminist content analysis of "Seventeen" magazine (Master's Degree), Minnesota State University. Retrieved from http://search.proquest.com.libraryproxy.griffith.edu.au/docview/1022503263?accountid=14543. ProQuest Dissertations & Theses Global database.

Twining-Ward, L., & Zhou, V. (2017). *Women and tourism: Designing for inclusion.* Retrieved from Washington, DC, USA.

UN Women. (2011). Gender equality in the tourism industry. Retrieved from http://www.unwomen.org/en/news/stories/2011/9/gender-equality-in-the-tourism-industry

United Nations. (2017a). Goal 5: Achieve gender equality and empower all women and girls. Retrieved from http://www.un.org/sustainabledevelopment/gender-equality/

United Nations. (2017b). Sustainable development goal 5. Retrieved from https://sustainabledevelopment.un.org/sdg5

UNWTO. (2017a). Gender and Tourism. Retrieved from http://ethics.unwto.org/content/gender-and-tourism

UNWTO. (2017b). International Year of Sustainable Tourism for Development. Retrieved from http://www.tourism4-development2017.org/

UNWTO. (2017c). UNWTO Calendar of Events 2017. Retrieved from http://calendar.unwto.org/

UNWTO & UN Women. (2010). Global report on women in tourism 2010. Madrid, Spain: UNWTO and UN Women.

Veijola, S., & Jokinen, E. (2008). Towards a hostessing society? Mobile arrangements of gender and labour. *NORA—Nordic Journal of Feminist and Gender Research, 16*(3), 166–181. doi:10.1080/08038740802279901

Walters, T. (2018). Gender equality in academic tourism, hospitality, leisure and events conferences. *Journal of Policy Research in Tourism, Leisure and Events, 10*(1), 17–32. doi:10.1080/19407963.2018.1403165

Wijesinghe, S. N., Mura, P., & Bouchon, F. (2017). Tourism knowledge and neocolonialism–A systematic critical review of the literature. *Current Issues in Tourism*, 1–17. doi:10.1080/13683500.2017.1402871

Women Academics in Tourism. (2018). In Facebook [Group page]. Retrieved from https://www.facebook.com/groups/1602606203299747/

Xu, H., Wang, K., & Ye, T. (2017). Women's awareness of gender issues in Chinese tourism academia. *Anatolia, 28*(4), 553–566. doi:10.1080/13032917.2017.1370780

Yang, E. C. L., Khoo-Lattimore, C., & Arcodia, C. (2018a). Constructing space and self through risk taking: A case of asian solo female travelers. *Journal of Travel Research, 57*(2), 260–272. doi:10.1177/0047287517692447

Yang, E. C. L., Khoo-Lattimore, C., & Arcodia, C. (2018b). Power and empowerment: How Asian solo female travellers perceive and negotiate risks. *Tourism Management, 68*, 32–45. doi:10.1016/j.tourman.2018.02.017

Gender and sustainability – exploring ways of knowing – an ecohumanities perspective

Kumi Kato

ABSTRACT

This article takes up the challenge to apply critical enquiry to the interface between tourism and the United Nations' Sustainable Development Goals (SDGs). Applying a political ecology perspective, it examines the intersectionality of gender and (ocean) sustainability through a study of traditional women divers in Japan. Recognizing the SDGs as an agenda setting platform, this work engages with Goal 5: *Gender Equality*, and proposes that engaging with multiple and diverse ways of knowing is critical to promoting a sustainability agenda with gender perspectives an essential component. Employing ecohumanities as a methodological foundation, a qualitative study of women divers in Japan (*ama*) is reported with a focus on their particular relationship with the ocean. The study identifies the power of women's knowledge in its inclusiveness, reciprocity and intuitive way of knowing. The example also shows that while tourism can be an important social and economic force, it can also devalue these core qualities as a result of the negative impacts caused by gender stereotypes. These findings indicate that the sustainability agenda can be advanced by challenging hierarchical systems of knowledge and valuing alternative ways of knowing, in this case, women's knowledges.

Introduction

This article examines the intersectionality of gender and (ocean) sustainability from a political ecology perspective (Mostafanezhad, Norum, Shelton, & Thompson-Carr, 2016; Mosedale, 2015; Peterson, 2005). The Sustainable Development Goals (SDGs, UN, 2017) is used as an agenda setting platform for critical thinking and inquiry in its implementation in tourism systems. With particular reference to Goal 5: *Gender Equality: Achieve gender equality and empower all women and girls*, the article proposes that acknowledging the characteristic of multiplicity in knowledge and ways of knowing is critical in promoting sustainability agenda, for which gender equality is one fundamental cornerstone.

Taking ecohumanities (Rose & Robin, 2004; Weir, 2008) as a methodological foundation, a qualitative inquiry is conducted into the example of women divers in Japan (*ama*), focusing on their particular relationship with the ocean. Ama free-dive in coastal seas to harvest shellfish, seaweed, and other food resources. This traditional practice has existed since the country's early history, and is even depicted in some of the early literature, including the oldest chronicles, *Kojiki* (711–712) and *Nihonshoki* (720). The practice is believed to have originated in the Ise-Shima region, the central east coast of Japan, and has a mythological connection with the Sun Goddess Amaterasu, who is regarded as Japan's origin. In recent years, this traditional practice has become a popular tourism resource through regional promotion and attention from various media sources. While tourism can be an important social and economic force, as recognized in academia (Higgins-Desbiolles, 2006, 2009; Jamal & Camargo, 2014; McCabe & Johnson, 2013), it can also generate gender stereotypes, which devalue the core qualities of the practice. The paper proposes that the women's power lies in their knowledge and ways of knowing, and acknowledgement of this would allow a true advancement of the sustainability agenda, and tourism as a "system of knowledge production" (Figueroa-Domecq, Pritchard, Segovia-Pérez, Morgan, & Villacé-Molinero, 2015, p. 89). This approach would also initiate an alternative discourse on gender and sustainability, and present an opportunity for a critical and creative research direction.

To begin this exploration into women, knowledge, and sustainability, the SDGs are used as an agenda-setting platform, which is then discussed from a political ecology perspective to locate power (or the lack thereof) within the knowledge hierarchy. This topic is then further explored through the example of women working with the ocean, interpreting the stories regarding their particular relationship with it. This is a qualitative and interpretive inquiry grounded by ecohumanities as its methodological foundation, which also directed the style of writing employed in this paper.

Sustainable development goals – *knowledge* as a missing agenda

Among the 17 interrelated SDGs (UN, 2015), Goal 5: *Gender Equality: Achieve gender equality and empower all women and girls* promises to put an end to barriers that prevent women and girls from realizing their full potential. This has been an ongoing focus following the UN Millennium Development Goals (MDGs) 3: *to promote gender equality and empower women).* Promoting gender equality is, in fact, critical to the achievement of all 17 SDGs, as asserted in the UN Women report, *Turning promises into Action: gender equality in the 2030 agenda for sustainable development* (UN Women, 2018, p. 4).

Clearly, sustainable development is not possible if the female population, which comprises half of humanity "continues to be denied its full human rights and opportunities, including equal access to quality education, economic resources and political participation, employment, leadership, and decision-making at all levels" (UN, 2015, para 20). Empowering all women and girls is therefore crucial for "improving all parts of society"(Jahnsen, 2018, p. 22). Tackling gender issues would also improve other policy-related issues included in the 2030 Agenda's focus on sustainability, equality, peace, and human progress, which aims to provide "a powerful counter-narrative to current practices of extraction, exclusion and division" (UN Women, 2018, p. 2). This implies *inclusiveness*, as stated in Goal 16, which calls for efforts to "promote peaceful and inclusive societies for sustainable development, provide access to justice for all and build effective, accountable and inclusive institutions at all levels" (UN, 2015). However, as Goetz and Jenkins (2016) assert in their critique, the concept of inclusiveness is not clearly defined. This also raises a question regarding the true meaning of the phrase *"Leaving no one behind"* (Stuart & Woodroffe, 2016).

Inclusiveness has been discussed as a means of removing social barriers and obstacles from diverse perspectives, including those of multiculturalism (Fleras, 2009; Rivera, 2017), disability, and other social equity viewpoints (Ravneberg & Soderstrom, 2017; Zhao & Zhang, 2018) as well as development (Agola & Hunter, 2016), environmental vulnerability (Leal Filho, 2018; Fankhauser & McDermott, 2014) and resilience (Ruiz-Ballesteros, 2011; Shaw, Rahman, Surjan, & Parvin, 2016; West & Haug, 2017). In a social-environmental context, inclusiveness is related to sustainability, as indicated by the following statement: "If our ecological relationships are unsustainable, so are the social relations that produce them" (Norum, Mostafanezhad, Shelton, & Thompson-Carr, 2016, p. 305); conversely, "to remedy this lack of a suitable ethics, we must seek out sustainability in relationships, not just between all humans, nonhuman species, and our material setting, but also relations among various humans based on respect and tolerance, freedom of thought, equality, and equity" (Norum et al., 2016, p. 305). This understanding of inclusiveness connects sustainability and gender equality, for which it is critical to value different qualities of knowledge and ways of knowing.

While gender equality is a major global challenge, for tourism, it presents an opportunity to advance the sector as a "knowledge-generating system" (Figueroa-Domecq et al., 2015, p. 89), especially in the context of sustainability (Ferguson & Moreno Alarcón, 2015). The research opportunity for tourism is clear, as suggested by Ferguson's call for more research on "grassroots feminist tourism projects across the world" to "offer alternative ways of understanding the relationship between gender and tourism development, and provide inspiration for creative and progressive ways of harnessing tourism to meet this goal" (Ferguson, 2011, p. 246).

This implies that the gender equality discourse has the power to open up possibilities for non-divisive thinking; tourism has a role to fulfil in the advancement of knowledge production. One such possibility is explored in the discussion on political ecology in the next section, which attempts to specifically connect women, knowledge, and sustainability.

Women's knowledge and sustainability: a political ecology perspective

Political ecology of knowing

Political ecology is defined as "a branch that considers the environment as critical to our understanding of the relationship between the social and environmental disparities that are experienced unequally". It aims "to understand the complex relations between nature and society through a careful analysis of access and control over resources and their implications for the environment" (Cole, 2016, p. 31). Among the range of political ecology debates that have been conducted (Mosedale, 2015; Norum et al, 2016; Peterson, 2005), gender perspective is one critical variable "in shaping resource access and control, interacting with class, caste, race, culture, and ethnicity to shape processes of ecological change" (Rocheleau et al., in Cole, 2016, p. 33).

Women as a community can be "a group of individuals who share characteristics such as ethnicity, heritage, religious, spiritual, cultural beliefs and values as well as geographical spaces" (Thompson-Carr, 2016, p. 25). They can be seen as a community that holds a specific power of knowledge – ecology of the environment, and resource management (Cole, 2016, Cole & Ferguson, 2015; Hanson & Buechler, 2015; Williams & Golovnev, 2015). Goebel suggests that "Given this shared position of oppression between women and the earth, and women's association with life-giving and conserving work, women are conceived as having a "privileged epistemological approach to nature, a better understanding of both what is wrong with human/environment relations and how to promote positive change"(Goebel, 2004, p. 3). In the context of ecotourism, Scheyvens (2000) also argues that women who tend to be placed in close connection with the natural environment develop specialist knowledge of that environment, and therefore also have an interest in protecting it. Thus, an effective tourism knowledge production system should "encourage the active involvement of women, even if their primary concern is not gender equity" (Scheyvens, 2000, p. 235).

Women's ecological knowledge as power

In the promotion of sustainability, women's ecological knowledge is referenced by Goebel (2004), who claims that the role of women in subsistence activities makes them "crucial actors in contexts of environmental degradation, reclamation and sustainable use" (Goebel, 2004, p. 3). At the same time, systems of gender inequality prevent women's attempts to "meet subsistence needs or manage resources sustainably" (Goebel, 2004, p. 4). In reference to women's knowledge about the ocean environment and its changes, Hanson states that women's stories and narrative oral histories are "critical forms of knowledge for confronting garbage-induced water, health, and development challenges in tropical coastal areas …. Women's oral histories of socio environmental change express their embodied knowledge and the lived experiences navigating and confronting global patterns of consumption and conservation" (Hanson, 2015, p. 166).

Understanding environmental degradation and resource access requires an understanding of "social relations (such as class, gender, and culture) to see the multiple roles they play. Doing so allows for changes that are not just technical in nature, but social as well" (Norum et al., 2016, p. 304). Here, the relationship between people and the land becomes "the template for society and social relations" (Graham, 2008, p. 182) and shifts "our stories to the earth [or sea] others on the moral principle that we live by enabling others to live" (Matthews, 2015, p. 73). Such views pay particular attention to "the mutual embeddedness of hierarchies of power based on gender, class, ethnicity, and race in the politics of control and access to environmental resources" (Hanson, 2015, p. 167). The articulation of women's knowledge is a form of empowerment that establishes their position in the society.

As an overarching goal, empowerment will help individuals to "develop their capabilities, have a sense of control over their wellbeing and lead dignified lives" (Knight & Cottrell, 2016, p. 34); it is also connected to people's sense of cultural and social integrity (Scheyvens & Russell, 2012). Achieving the goal of empowerment will unlock stereotypes and shift the focus to more fundamental values, in addition to counteracting perpetuated inequalities (Wearing, 2002). In this sense, empowerment not only entails addressing economic status; it also requires the assertion and assignment of the fundamental power that exists in knowledge and knowledge production. This fact is asserted by Tucker and Boonabaana (2012), who challenge an instrumentalist approach and a Eurocentric ideal by suggesting that we need "to move beyond simplistic and fixed ideas of women's economic empowerment, particularly in non-western contexts, and consider more fully the cultural complexity and the shifting dynamics of how gender norms, roles and inequalities affect, and are affected by, development and poverty reduction outcomes" (Tucker & Boonabaana, 2012, p. 438). Similarly, Swain and Wallentin argue that in tourism, women's empowerment can only take place when "the existing norms and cultures of a society" are challenged (Swain & Wallentin, 2008, p. 24). Higgins-Desbiolles also suggests that tourism is a powerful social force that can "achieve many important ends when its capacities are unfettered from the market fundamentalism of neoliberalism and instead are harnessed to meet human development imperatives and the wider public good" (Higgins-Desbiolles, 2006, p. 1192). Tourism's achievement may include "fostering cross-cultural understanding, facilitating learning, contributing to cultural protection supplementing development, fostering environmental protection, promoting peace" (Higgins-Desbiolles, 2006, p. 1197) towards a globally conscious society. Harris also suggests that alternative and pluriversal knowledge is necessary to foster alternatives to the "hegemonic ways of doing things" (Harris, 2015, p. xxii). In the following section, such multiplicity of knowledge and knowing is explored through the specific example of women divers in Japan, drawing on the ecohumanities perspective as a methodology for this qualitative inquiry, which is briefly described below.

Methodological foundation – ecohumanities of knowing

The qualitative approach, Ecological humanities or ecohumanities (Rose & Robin, 2004; Weir, 2008), is defined by its founding scholar, Deborah Bird Rose, as "a new inter-discipline that has emerged specifically to address the fact that current ecological problems, including extinctions, climate change, toxic death zones, water degradation, and many others, are anthropogenic events originating from the nature/culture divide, reflected also in the academic division between arts and sciences" (Rose, 2015a, p. 1). Another ecohumanities thinker, the late environmental philosopher, Val Plumwood, also wrote, "The real threat is not so much global warming itself … as our own inability to see past the post-enlightenment energy, control and consumption extravaganza we so naively identify with the good, civilized life to a sustainable form of human culture. The time of *Homo Reflectus*, the self-critical and self-revising one, has surely come.… We will go onwards in a different mode of humanity, or not at all" (Plumwood, 2007, p. 1).

The ecohumanities approach is positive, striving to "engage in life and the living world in an unconstrained and expansive way" (Gibson, Rose, & Finch, 2015, p. ii), which is further detailed in the manifesto issued by the group formed by Gibson, Rose and other scholars.

> Our thinking needs to be in the service of life—and so does our language. This means giving up preconceptions, and instead listening to the world. This means giving up delusions of mastery and control, and instead, to see the world as uncertain and yet unfolding. So our thinking needs to be - *Curious; Experimental; Open; Adaptive; Imaginative; Responsive; and Responsible. We are committed to* think with the community of life and contributing to healing. (Gibson et al., 2015, p. ii)

The approach includes feminist political ecology perspectives, where methodological and theoretical perspectives from the feminist discipline are linked with an analysis comprising multiple layers of ecological, economic, and political power relations (Ateljevic, Pritchard, & Morgan, 2012; Carney, 1993; Cole, 2016; Cole & Ferguson, 2015; Jarosz, 2011; Truelove, 2011).

The primary guiding theme of ecohumanities is: *connectivity, connectedness* or *being connected* (Weir, 2008). Rose and Robin (2004) argue that "the imperative of learning to think about and with connectivity can be operationalized as an imperative to enlarging the boundaries of thought and thinking itself – to enhance our ability to think in dialogue and, perhaps, in empathy with others". The Ecohumanities perspective also challenges the boundaries and divides that are prevalent in academia, and the ranking of knowledge systems that places western science at the top of an epistemological ladder. This impedes "our capacity for knowledge sharing within fields of plural and diverse knowledges" (Rose and Robin, 2004). Such ways of knowing relate to Indigenous knowledge, which is a "complex and intimate knowledge of how to live sustainably in some very harsh and forbidding environments" (Higgins-Desbiolles, 2009, p. 147).

In the context of sustainability, the concept of connectivity may be expressed as reciprocity, which Abram defines as "the ceaseless give and take, the flow that moves in two directions" and is "the foundation of any real ethics" (Abram, 2004, p. 81). A reciprocal human-nature relationship is characterized by dialogical, sensory/experiential, and place-specific qualities. Such qualities signify "a capacity that recognizes the elements that supports our lives … in the essentially narrative terms of naming and interpreting the land, of telling its story in ways that show a deep and loving acquaintance with it and history of dialogical interaction" (Plumwood, 2002, pp. 229–230). This is rephrased by Rose (2018) as life that is flowing out of the earth, and contains not only biodiversity and ecosystems but also "the languages, senses, emotions, and timeless connections with the earth other". The place-specific quality of reciprocity is an orientation towards *genius loci* (spirit of place)—the authenticity of place and integrity sustained over time (Norberg-Schulz, 1980), which may be expressed by care, sentiment, concern, warmth, love, and sacredness. Reciprocity may be expressed as a dialogue (Rose, 2015b) or an offering (care, gratitude, prayer) that is physical, conceptual, or spiritual in nature. Rose (2018) defines such exchange in her lecture, "Gift of life in the shadow of death", where she asserts the importance of celebrating the power of life – not only human life but all kinds of life, and its will to give.

Inclusiveness, connectivity, and reciprocity can be situated as fundamental qualities for sustainability, a positioning which challenges the hierarchical division of knowledge. This also applies to women's knowledge and the ways of knowing presented in the next section.

Qualitative inquiry of the women and the ocean

Ama divers

Ama (海女, literally *sea women*) dive primarily for shellfish such as abalone (*awabi*), sea snails (*sazae*), seaweeds, and other small shore creatures. The term ama generally refers to female divers. In certain regions, men (ama, 海士) also take part in diving, which is a more recent phenomenon since the introduction of wetsuits and mechanized boats from the 1950s onwards. A similar diving practice exists in Jeju province, South Korea, where the divers are called *Haenyo* or sea women. According to a national survey, 2,174 ama existed in Japan in 2011, nearly one-sixth of the figure established in 1931: 12,426 (Tōyō suisan kagaku kyōkai, 2011). The average age of the ama continues to rise, putting pressure on the local areas to recruit from younger generations to continue the tradition.

Previous research on ama focused on anthropological, historic, or religious aspects (Martinez, 2004; Maraini, 1962, Tanabe, 1993; Kawaguchi, 2013). Certain works gave specific attention to the women's traditional ecological knowledge through their observation of the environmental changes and ethical orientation towards the ocean environment (Kato, 2007a, 2017). This was developed into a radio documentary, *Waiting for the tide* (Kato, 2007b), using environmental sound to articulate this practice beyond words. It has been shown that this simple harvesting practice is equipped with traditional ecological knowledge, being sensitive to environmental changes, safety and wellbeing of the divers themselves, and the ocean environment (Kato, 2007a; Martinez, 2004). Their embodied knowledge and life experiences, often expressed in stories, rituals, and cultural practices as well as various kinds of self-imposed regulations, form an important foundation for living as part of the environment, similar to Indigenous perspectives discussed in tourism, environmental management, and ecosophy literatures (Booth & Harvey, 2001; Higgins-Desbiollos, 2009; Kirksey & Helmreich, 2010; Liao, Relle, & Kassam, 2016; Low, 1999; Rose, 1996).

Qualitative inquiry of ama practice

Building on these works, the current study is a qualitative and interpretive inquiry (Atkinson & Delamont, 2011; Willis, 2007), specifically attempting to draw out the multiplicity and complexity of the voices on the ground (Fine, 2011; Jackson & Mazzei, 2009). Ethnographic fieldworks, using methods such as direct participant observation and semi-structured interviews, were conducted between 2015 and 2017 at various coastal regions in Japan to elicit oral histories of the women. Regions visited include Toba in Mie Prefecture, Minami-chō (Abu, Izari) in Tokushima Prefecture, Iki Island in Nagasaki, Kuji in Iwate, and Chikura in Chiba Prefecture. At these locations, visits were made to the local fishery unions, fish markets, community halls, museums, history rooms, local restaurants, shops, guesthouses, as well as shrines, temples, and monuments. To gain an insider perspective, on one occasion, the researcher participated in a harvest, swimming with the women off the boat.

In each site, the local fishery union office was the first contact. This enabled introduction to one or two women leaders in the area, who then contacted other women willing to participate in the study. Seniority and cultural protocol were important considerations in selecting participants. A consent form, clarifying the ethical condition of the study, was signed by each participant, and after the analysis, a summary of the comments was returned to the fishery union and each participant for verification and approval. All communication took place in Japanese, and excerpts of the women's comments, presented in this paper, were translated into English by the author.

Twenty women, who were currently working or had worked as ama divers, aged 30 to 86, participated in this study. A certain number of women were involved in tourism to various degrees, formally or informally. Each interview lasted about 60 minutes, with questions focused on such issues as: what are some of the environmental changes observed; what are the rules followed; and what are the fears and concerns confronted. Although a set of questions were used as guidelines for the interview, it is more appropriate to define these sessions as story-telling. Storytelling is an established form of qualitative enquiry (Charmaz, 2005; Ozyıldırım, 2009; Rooney, Lawlor, & Rohan, 2016; Stapleton & Wilson, 2017; Willis, 2007), which is "a social process that constructs meaning through interaction". The approach does not attempt to present "the truth of the matter as objective description does, but instead to represent, in detail, the perspectives of participants in the process or setting being studied" (Willis, 2007, p. 10). Considering Charmaz's view, a story, as one narrative type, in this case, is much more than a fable, imagination or metaphor and is "concrete reality, rather than a construction that we place on these data" (Charmaz, 2005, p. 526). Accordingly, its interpretation is hermeneutic, holistic, and exploratory, seeking to clarify the collective reality of the world the women share.

Ama and tourism development

An earlier study on ama included visits to a few remaining ama huts, where the value of women's stories was acknowledged (Kato, 2007a). Subsequently, one of these ama women developed an ama hut tourism experience called *Hachiman Kamado* (open fire kitchen). This became a prototype of tourism activity, in which guests sample ama cuisine and participate in cultural experiences. This was adopted in many other regions.

> I never thought I'd start a tourism business myself, but it's a good way to use my knowledge and stories from my experience – the 70 year worth of stories from the sea (R, 86 years old)

> We now all have jobs other than diving, and don't spend time anymore hanging around the ama hut. So this tourism kamado is a place we meet. It's our new ama-hut (K, 72 years old)

The ama hut, housing a *kamado*, was traditionally the place where ama practiced and related culture evolved. It is a place to rest between dives, warming up the body, eating, chatting, and sharing stories. Recently, however, majority of ama dive between other jobs, coming and going by motorbike or car. As a result, the original cultural traditions associated with the ama hut are disappearing. Instead, tourism experiences centring around the *kamado* and hut have proved to be popular among families, groups of women, and student groups, and even visitors coming from overseas. A popular tour activity is story telling by an ama while cooking the ama's harvest, dressed in traditional ama costume and taking photos with the tourists. Certain huts provide *ama* merchandise, including talismans (*o-mamori*) from the shrine worshiped by ama, and talismans featuring their lucky charms. In this region, a pentagram-and-lattice motif (*sei-man dō-man*), drawn with purple shell dye, was traditionally used. They are believed to bring good luck and the strength of the ama women, who work in the ocean, to the holder. These souvenirs are popular, particularly with young women seeking to "gain power from the strong ama women" (Pers. Com., 14 August 2017).

Recently, collecting *shuin* (red seal stamp) has become popular among visitors of Shinto shrines and Buddhist temples. Shuin is stamped alongside a calligraphy denoting the main deity at the shrine and temple, also marking the date of the visit. Visitors take their own books (shuin-cho) to receive shuin on one of the pages, for which a small fee is charged. The shuin at one ama shrine (Ishigami in Shinmei Shrine) is popular among the women, as its female deity is believed to allow one wish to come true for all women. The shrine's shuin features the *sei-man dō-man* symbols (Figure 1).

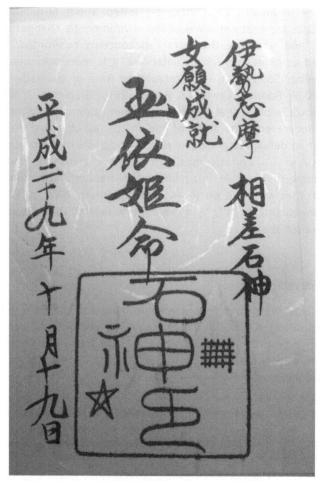

Figure 1. Shuin from Ishigami shrine with sei-man dō-man symbols (Author's photograph).

In another region, Izari community of Minami-chō, Tokushima Prefecture, the ama *hut* is now a restaurant, Izari Café, with an accommodation facility. The café is open for lunch, and two or three ama women take turns to manage the café.

> At the beginning we all thought, what is a café? No one drinks coffee in this remote village. But our lunch special (tiger prawn donburi) became famous through a magazine article, and people come from quite far. It's good to know we (ama) can do work other than diving, and it's also fun to work with other ama women (M, 65 years old).

> I started diving quite late so I'm still not really good at it. Working here, as we talk while we cook in the kitchen, I get to hear the stories of other women who are much more experienced than me. I like that aspect. (S, 50 years old).

Alongside the café, the community also runs an ama experience course. It is a one-day program introducing ama work, including diving and harvesting shells, targeting women aged 20 to 40. Three courses were held in 2016, and two in 2017, each offering ten places, which filled up quickly. The two courses in 2017 were held on the third and fourth Saturdays of August, and a total of 20 women from across Japan participated. The women running the course told me that part of their motivation is to recruit new ama women who may settle in the area. So far, they have managed to recruit one such person, who "brought new vibrance to the village" (Pers. Comm, 20 June 2017).

Media and publicity in tourism development

The recent tourism developments by ama and their expanding range of activities are reshaping the image, identity, as well as the practice itself internally and externally, both positively and negatively. Tourism, on one hand, has enabled the ama to continue the seasonal practice, while supplementing their income from diving. It is interesting to observe that tourism ventures, collaboratively managed by women, provide opportunities for women to maintain their inner community network, once developed in their huts. Women now engage in various kinds of work other than diving – farming and working in shops as well as domestic duties and community work. The tourist facility continues to provide a meeting place for exchanging information and stories, which helps the women maintain their diving practice.

Tourism also provides opportunities for a new generation of young men and women to choose a different lifestyle, seeking freedom and a sustainable lifestyle in rural communities, often escaping from a highly stressful city life, searching for a sea change. These "lifestyle migrants" unwittingly inherit the critical ecological knowledge and skills, empowering themselves and maintaining the practice of diving once considered outdated. A young novice ama (O, 27 years old) on Iki Island now runs a guesthouse with her husband, while being one of the young members advancing the tradition. O grew up in a coastal section of the Tohoku region, which was devastated by the East Japan Earthquake in 2011. The family relocated to the region to work in a business owned by a relative.

> I was working in a shop in the city, but as I grew up with the ocean, I always wanted to do a job related to the ocean. When I saw an advertisement about an ama position to help revive the local economy, I jumped at the opportunity. I've never regretted it. (O, 27 years old)

The guesthouse, owned by this ama woman, is becoming a community hub, popular for both local youth and tourists. Various events, concerts, and small festivals are regularly organized at the guesthouse, and are favourably received by local community members (Pers. Comm., 17 Aug. 2017).

> Young people bring new ideas to the island. We have to value them, otherwise we won't survive ourselves. We older ama can only do what we can do, but young people have to live differently, and they can bring in new ideas to ama work too. (T, 69 years old)

Inevitably, tourism can assist in overcoming inherent gender division and inequality and provide leadership opportunities for women. When women especially utilize their ecological knowledge, senses, and holistic communication approach, new insights and values can be brought into traditional primary industries of fishing, farming, and forestry, as creative forces. Tourism can provide these women opportunities to articulate their connection, power and knowledge. At the same time, however, tourism promotion often reinforces stereotypical images of women, misrepresenting the reality, as seen in the example below. This works to dismiss and devalue the essence of the women's power, ecological knowledge and connection with the ocean.

Stereotypical images in tourism

Recent depictions of ama, including Toba City tourism promotion (Toba City, 2018, Figure 2) and one in All Nippon Airlines magazine *Innovative Voice* (ANA, 2018), feature women divers dressed in traditional white robes, which they no longer wear. Nor is the sea they dive in so blue or clean. Women are often depicted as mystic "mermaids," usually highly sexualized. Traditionally, the women dived semi-naked. This complete natural exposure with the elements, placed the women in a position to sense everything from tidal movements to currents or temperature changes. Despite this, headlines persist as demonstrated in this web-based article, "Japan's tough, topless free-diving mermaid" (Shubach, 2015). Another example is an anime character,

Aoshima Megu (Maribon, 2015) (Figure 3), who is a young girl aspiring to become a skillful ama. The long-haired girl is a "moe" character, which implies a somewhat erotic attractiveness in anime, manga, and game sub-culture. Another popular image of ama originated from a TV

Figure 2. Toba City Tourism Promotion Brochure (Reproduced with permission).

Figure 3. Aoshima Megu, MARIBON (Reproduced with permission).

drama series, *Ama-chan* or "Little Darling Ama" broadcasted from 1st April to 28th September 2013 (NHK, 2013). The 15-minute morning series, popularly referred to as Asa-dora (morning drama), is shown daily for six months. Each series generally features the life of a woman, her family and community, her personal and career development, and is mostly based on a true story. Among the 98 series aired so far since 1961, *Oshin* (1983) gained international fame. The series Ama-chan was based on a radio drama "Hokugen-no Ama" (northernmost ama, written by Mizuki Yoko, aired in 1959) (Hokugen-no Ama, 2013). The series told the story of a young city girl going to live in her mother's home village, where her grandmother was one of the last remaining ama. There, *chan* is a diminutive suffix attached to personal names or family roles, and the word Ama also reads as a verb "amaeru," which implies the sweet, dependent, pampered or spoiled nature of a young girl who grows into an independent woman.

The practicing ama women laugh at the images of young ama.

> You have to be so careful so that you don't get tangled in ropes and other things. No one has long hair for that reason. (T, 69 year old)

> You get sweaty, dirty and sun, wind and salt burnt – you cannot be pretty doing this job. We are nothing like them! (S, 50 years old)

In Japan, the ama women are idealized and celebrated as they are believed to be connected to Japan's origin, the Sun Goddess Amaterasu (Kawaguchi, 2013; Tanabe, 1993). Such idealized depiction was included in the G7 Summit report, which referred to ama as the "heart of Japan" when the spouses of the heads of states met 85 ama women (Mainichi Shimbun, 2016; Sankei West, 2016). Interestingly, little was mentioned about the nine *okami*, or female managing directors of traditional Japanese hotels (ryokan) who were also present, nor the first female Executive Chef at the Summit venue, Shima Kanko Hotel, who hosted the Summit dinner (Shima Kanko Hotel, 2014).

While ama women are understood to be free, strong, and capable, stereotypical images place them in a fixed tourist scape of romanticized heritage. This was observed in the previous example of a new young ama in Oki island, where the focus of attention was only given to her appearance and novelty, not the importance of her being a new bearer of ecological knowledge. In this context, tourism does not "improve well-being, but in fact reinforces traditional gender roles and unequal divisions of labour" (Jiménez-Esquinas, 2017, p. 311), making the people "national objects of attention" (Venkatesan, 2009, p. 92) and transforming people into "picturesque bearers of an obsolescent tradition" (Herzfeld in Jiménez-Esquinas, 2017, p. 316). This trivializes the women's power and identity and denies the essence of their practice and knowledge, which are observational and experiential, articulating their intuitive understanding of sustainability.

Changes in the ocean and women's ecological knowledge

Since the ama practice free-diving without any special equipment, the harvest is controlled by the physical limits of each breath. There is little risk of overfishing, nonetheless, all ama communities visited developed their own regulations to prevent such an eventuality. Apart from harvest size (no less than 10.5 cm for abalone), many of the rules are unwritten, existing in their beliefs, taboos, and mythologies, which practically serve as self-regulation.

> We want to come back every year … if the shell is too small, we'll put them back in the ocean … so that we can come back next year. (T, 69 years old).

> We don't go into the ocean if there are bad things in family (eg death, illness) so that we don't bring bad luck into the ocean. (R, 86 years old).

At the same time, the inevitable changes in the environment over the past decades have seriously affected the ocean and its resources. Women describe the dramatic change in their catch over the last 30 years both in number and size, despite the fact that their practice remains mostly unchanged. Women believe, based on their observation, that these changes are the result of infrastructural developments (sand erosion, building of walls, barriers, roads, bridges, and riverside developments), contamination (sewage, chemicals such as detergents), and the (global) warming as well as unregulated overfishing by others.

> We used to get the shells this big (30 cm), but they have become so much smaller now. We used to get them this big, almost half a kilo, but now, they are so small. (H, 89 year old)

> Since the new road was built, the ocean has changed – lots more rubbish, and dirty. So less fish, seaweed and everything. The sea used to be so rich. (M, 70 years old)

> The sea is now dirty – rubbish at the bottom, less seaweed, and different kinds of fish. (T, 69 years old)

> We were told to leave one if there were three, when we were young, but now we may not find any. (E, 55 years old)

Maintaining ama practice and knowledge

Each ama community has debated on whether to introduce goggles (introduced from around 1890), wetsuits (from the 1960s), and other clothing. Although none of the communities restrict the use of goggles, wetsuits were introduced along with certain control measures, such as a time restriction, allowing only one or two hours per day to dive, and a catch rotation system, or a one-wetsuit per family policy. Various other restrictions apply, such as allowing only the upper or lower part of the suit or short pants. One group who did not introduce wetsuits is the Yahata community, Ashibe-chō in Iki Island, where only the wetsuit hoods are allowed. Instead, women wear dance "leotards" on top of layers of clothes – tracksuits, cotton shirts or woollen tops and bottoms. The colourful dance costumes are, according to women, for safety as well as expressing their fashion identity (Figure 4). Here, the author's observation is included, as the women invited her to join them on the boat trip on a calm sunny day. The women explained how they decided against the use of wetsuits (Pers. Comm., 12 Aug, 2017).

> If we wear them, we have to limit diving time. We didn't want to be controlled by the Union. We want to be free. (T, 69 years old)

This desire for freedom is framed by a self-confidence in their own form of intuitive self-regulation.

> Not wearing wetsuits, it is actually easier to swim. Wetsuits make you tired, as you have to swim harder. (N, 57 years old)

> Not wearing wetsuits… It's good so we won't be greedy, although we cannot get that many now. (T, 69 years old)

There were five boats on the bay, including one occupied by sisters, aged 80 and 82, the oldest in the community.

> It is something we look forward to. Feeling the ocean is good for you. (F, 80 years old)

> We never wear any wetsuits – we didn't fit into them. They are so tight. (laughing) (Y, 82 years old)

As the boat came back into the port, all women stood on the boat, put their hands together and bowed towards the shrine gate facing the sea. The gate leading to the local shrine was built on the edge of the shore by the group of ama women, so that they could pray when they left and came back into the port.

> That is the local sea gods we worship every day, before we go, and as we come home. We thank them that we came home safe. (N, 57 years old)

Prayer is an essential part of ama culture, praying for and being grateful for safety and a good harvest. Praying, a woman explained, is also a way to remind them that the "Sea can be dangerous. It can change anytime. So we pray, always pray." One such reminder is a group of six small Jizo (earth deities *Ksitigarbha*) statues standing on the Yahata shore, Ashibe-town, Iki Island (Figure 5).

Figure 4. Ama diver (Author's photograph).

Figure 5. Six Jizo Statues in the sea (Author's photograph).

At low tide, the tide washes gently at their feet, and on high tide, the water rises up to their chest. These Jizo are called *Harahoge (chest hole)-jizo*, as these stone statues have a small dip in the chest level. The dip was apparently made so that offerings given to these statues, such as sweets, fruits, or coins, would not get washed away in high tides. There is no record of who made them or why; however, the local women believe that they were made to commemorate the lives lost in the sea, including those of women divers in the region. Consequently, they "always give offerings to these statues, so that they look after the ocean, and us of course," a woman said as she placed a small rice cake on each of the six statues. For these women, prayer is an articulation of knowledge, and is a way of knowing the world.

Conclusion

The women's stories, observations, and senses illustrate the nature of knowledge and knowing based on their particular relationship with the ocean environment. Their power lies in their connectivity with their ocean environment, which guides them in maintaining their strict self-regulation despite their clear understanding that the ocean is changing because of many external forces. Their ways of knowing rely on their senses of connectivity, inclusiveness, and reciprocity, which are also expressed through their stories as care, gratitude, fear, ethics, offerings, and prayer. The recognition of these qualities as one socio-environmental foundation allows a move towards sustainability, in which gender equality presents a strong narrative to counter discourse that is divisive, exclusive, or hierarchical. As the cornerstone of sustainability, gender equality, and thus the promotion of all SDGs, encourages inclusiveness at all levels, propelling the oft-discussed aspirations, *"leave no-one behind"* and *"turning promises into action"* (United Nations, 2015).

The year 2017 was designated as The United Nations *International Year of Sustainable Tourism for Development* based on the Sustainable Development Goals towards 2030 (UN, 2017). The colourful banner comprising the 17 goals now appears in a wide range of activities, such as peace education, welfare, and conservation, as well as business marketing strategies. While the popularization of the term *sustainability* is a positive development, its fundamental values should be constantly reiterated, which will, according to Plumwood (2008), "restore place honesty". She suggested that we follow the path that allows us "to recognize the reality of multiple relationships to place but insist that they be reshaped as meaningful and responsible". Such multiplicity of relationships characterized by sensitivity and respect comprise women's contribution to the system of knowledge generation.

Regarding knowledge systems, Rose states that we are "called to build dialogical bridges between knowledge systems: between ecological sciences and the humanities, between Western and other knowledge systems" (Rose, 2015a, p. 1). The basic axioms that underlay these socio-environmental systems are: *land is the law*; and *you are not alone in the world*, which she refers to as a "practice of connectivity" (Rose, 2015a, p. 4). This implies that all living things, including humanity as a participant in a larger living system, must recognize and submit to the laws of the living world. Here, "respect is a matter of knowledge—of knowing the connections so that one knows the many contexts in which respect is due, and knowing how to look after things so that one can fulfil one's role in life … Web of life is a web of mutual inter-dependencies, which is in essence the earth" (Rose, 2015a, p. 5). The ama women's perspectives demonstrate an inclusive way of knowing through their sense of connectivity and reciprocity, which is critical to our understanding of sustainability. Maintaining such inter-dependencies through stories, prayers, senses, gratitude, and care may be what sustainability looks like. Women's capacities to foster such uniting practices supports weaving together the diverse elements addressed through SDGs, ensuring that we *"leave no-one behind."*

As suggested earlier by Ferguson (2011), grassroots feminism has the ability to inject a creative and progressive energy into tourism. Higgins-Desbiolles articulates that tourism can be a social force through its "ability to foster contact between peoples who increasingly need to understand each other and cooperate harmoniously in a world where space, resources and options are shrinking quickly" (Higgins-Desbiolles, 2006, p. 1205). Women, such as the ama in this article, clearly play an important role as holders of knowledge whose ability to live with both the land and the seas is critical today. At the same time, the imposition of stereotypes, quite separate from the reality, devalues the women's knowledge and their ways of knowing.

Finally, it is suggested that tourism's potential is only limited by "our imaginations to harness its powers for the public good" (Higgins-Desbiolles, 2006, p. 1205). From the ecohumanities perspective, it is imperative for academia to promote such imagination by incorporating more creativity into thinking and writing, and being unafraid to use the words of spirituality, hope, and love. The example of the ama of Japan reveals another system of knowledge concerning living sustainably. These findings have shown that the sustainability agenda can be advanced by challenging hierarchical systems of knowledge and valuing alternative ways of knowing. The ama women's knowledge presented here reveals a way of knowing ocean ecology and a way of being with nature and others that is valuable in our quest to build a more sustainable, inclusive and reciprocal future.

Acknowledgement

This article is dedicated to late Deborah Bird Rose, who led us to the new world of ecohumanities, and whose words of beauty and love keep us inspired.

References

Abram, D. (2004). Reciprocity. In B. Foltz & R. Frodeman (Eds.), *Rethinking nature: Essays in environmental philosophy*. Bloomington: Indiana University Press.

Agola, N., & Hunter, A. (Eds.). (2016). *Inclusive innovation for sustainable development theory and practice*. Palgrave Macmillan.

ANA (2018). Ama culture, *Innovative Voices No. 78*, https://www.ana.co.jp/dom/promotion/iv/1802/.

Ateljevic, I., Pritchard, A., & Morgan, N. (2012). *The critical turn in tourism studies: Promoting an academy of hope*. Oxford: Elsevier.

Atkinson, P., & Delamont, S. (Eds). (2011). *Sage qualitative research methods*. Thousand Oaks.

Booth, A., & Harvey, J. (2001). Ties that Bind: Native American Beliefs as a Foundation for Environmental Consciousness. In M. Boylan (Ed.). *Environmental ethics*. New Jersey: Prentice Hall.

Carney, J. (1993). Converting the wetlands, engendering the environment – the intersection of gender with agrarian change in the Gambia. *Economic Geography*, 69(4), 329–348. doi:10.2307/143593

Charmaz, K. (2005). Grounded theory in the 21st century. In Denzin, Y., & Lincoln, Y. *The SAGE handbook of qualitative enquiry* (3rd ed.). Thousand Oaks: SAGE.

Cole, S. (2016). A gendered political ecology of tourism and water. In M. Mostafanezhad, R. Norum, E. Shelton & A. Thompson-Carr (Eds.), *Political ecology of tourism. Community, power and the environment*. New York: Routledge, Chapter 1, 31–49.

Cole, S., & Ferguson, L. (2015). Towards a gendered political economy of water and tourism. *Tourism Geographies*, 17(4), 511–528. doi:10.1080/14616688.2015.1065509

Fankhauser, S., & McDermott, T. (2014). Understanding the adaptation deficit: Why are poor countries more vulnerable to climate events than rich countries? *Global Environmental Change*, 27, 9–18. doi:10.1016/j.gloenvcha.2014.04.014

Ferguson, L. (2011). Promoting gender equality and empowering women? Tourism and the third millennium development goal. *Current Issues in Tourism*, 14(3), 235–249. doi:10.1080/13683500.2011.555522

Ferguson, L., & Moreno Alarcón, D. (2015). Gender and sustainable tourism: Reflections on theory and practice. *Journal of Sustainable Tourism*, 23(3), 401–416. doi:10.1080/09669582.2014.957208

Figueroa-Domecq, C., Pritchard, A., Segovia-Pérez, M., Morgan, N., & Villacé-Molinero, T. (2015). Tourism gender research: A critical accounting. *Annals of Tourism Research*, 52, 87–103.

Fleras, A. (2009). *The politics of multiculturalism. Multicultural governance in comparative perspective*. New York: Palgrave Macmillan.

Fine, G. (2011). Towards a peopled ethnography. Developing theory from group life. In Atkinson, P., & Delamont, S. (Eds). *Sage qualitative research methods.* Thousand Oaks: Sage, 42–60.

Gibson, K., Rose, D.B., & Finch, R. (Eds.). (2015). *Manifesto for living in the Anthropocene.* Sydney: Puncton Books.

Goebel, A. (2004). Women and sustainability: What kind of theory do we need? *Canadian Woman Studies,* 23(1), 77–84.

Goetz, A., & Jenkins, R. (2016). Gender, security, and governance: The case of Sustainable development goal 16. *Gender & Development,* 24(1), 127–137. doi:10.1080/13552074.2016.1144412

Graham, M. (2008). Some thoughts on the philosophical underpinnings of aboriginal worldviews. *Australian Humanities Review,* 45, 181–194.

Hanson, A. (2015). Shoes in the seaweed and bottles on the beach Global garbage and women's oral histories of socio-environmental change in coastal Yucatán. In S. Buechler & A. Hanson (Eds.), *A political ecology of women, water and global environmental change.* New York: Routledge, Chapter 9, 165–184.

Hanson, A., & Buechler, S. (2015). Introduction. Towards a feminist political ecology of women, global change, and vulnerable waterscapes. In S. Buechler & A. Hanson (Eds.), *A political ecology of women, water and global environmental change.* New York: Routledge, 1–16.

Harris, L. (2015). A quarter century of knowledge and change: pushing feminism, politics, and ecology in new directions with feminist political ecology. In S. Buechler & A. Hanson (Eds.), *A political ecology of women, water and global environmental change.* New York: Routledge, xix–xxiii.

Higgins-Desbiolles, F. (2006). More than an industry: The forgotten power of tourism as a social force. *Tourism Management,* 27(6), 1192–1208. doi:10.1016/j.tourman.2005.05.020

Higgins-Desbiolles, F. (2009). Indigenous ecotourism's role in transforming ecological consciousness. *Journal of Ecotourism,* 8 (2), 144–160. doi:10.1080/14724040802696031

Hokugen-no-ama Promotional Committee (2013). *Hokugen-no-ama (The northernmost ama).* Morioka: Hokugen-no-ama Promotional Committee.

Jackson, A., & Mazzei, L. (Eds.). (2009). *Voice in qualitative inquiry: Challenging conventional, interpretive, and critical conceptions in qualitative research.* New York: Routledge.

Jahnsen, C. (2018). Women are key to achieving the sustainable development goals. *International Trade Forum,* 1, 22–23.

Jamal, T., & Camargo, B. A. (2014). Sustainable tourism, justice and an ethic of care: Toward the Just Destination. *Journal of Sustainable Tourism,* 22(1), 11–30. doi:10.1080/09669582.2013.786084

Jarosz, L. (2011). Nourishing women: Toward a feminist political ecology of community supported agriculture in the United States. *Gender, Place & Culture,* 18(3), 307–326. doi:10.1080/0966369X.2011.565871

Jiménez-Esquinas, G. (2017). "This is not only about culture": On tourism, gender stereotypes and other affective fluxes. *Journal of Sustainable Tourism,* 25(3), 311–326. doi:10.1080/09669582.2016.1206109

Kato, K. (2007a). Waiting for the tide, tuning in the world. Traditional knowledge, environmental ethics and community. In R. Bandt, M. Duffy & D. MacKinnon (Eds.), *Hearing places: Sound place time culture.* Newcastle: Cambridge Scholars Publishing.

Kato, K. (2007b). Waiting for the tide. ABC Radio National Radio Eye (now Earshot, first broadcasted on 21 July, 2007, http://www.abc.net.au/radionational/programs/earshot/waiting-for-the-tide/6660984

Kato, K. (2017). Traditional industry and sustainable tourism. Traditional ecological knowledge of ama women divers. *Tourism Culture,* 23–24.

Kawaguchi, Y. (2013). *Ama.* Tokyo: Hokuto Books.

Kirksey, S. E., & Helmreich, S. (2010). The emergency of multispecies ethnography. *Cultural Anthropology,* 25(4), 545–576. Vollssuedoi:10.1111/j.1548-1360.2010.01069.x

Knight, D., & Cottrell, S. (2016). Evaluating tourism-linked empowerment in Cuzco, Peru. *Annals of Tourism Research,* 56, 32–47. doi:10.1016/j.annals.2015.11.007

Leal Filho, W. (Ed.). (2018). *Climate change impacts and adaptation strategies for coastal communities.* Cham: Springer.

Liao, C., Ruelle, M. L., & Kassam, K.-A. S. (2016). Indigenous ecological knowledge as the basis for adaptive environmental management: Evidence from pastoralist communities in the Horn of Africa. *Journal of Environmental Management,* 182, 70–79. doi:10.1016/j.jenvman.2016.07.032

(1999). Low, N. (Ed.). *Global Ethics and Environment.* London: Routledge.

McCabe, S., & Johnson, S. (2013). The happiness factor in tourism: Subjective wellbeing and social tourism. *Annals of Tourism Research,* 41, 42–65. Vol. doi:10.1016/j.annals.2012.12.001

Mainichi Shimbun (2016). Spouses meet Ama. Encountering the heart of Japan (26 May, 2018. https://mainichi.jp/articles/20160527/k00/00m/040/084000c.

Maribon (2015). Aoshima Megu. http://ama-megu.com

Maraini, F. (1962). *The island of the fisherwomen.* San Diego: Harcourt, Brace & World.

Martinez, D. P. (2004). *Identity and Ritual in a Japanese Diving Village. The Making and Becoming of Person and Place.* Honolulu: University of Hawai'i Press.

Matthews, F. (2015). Earth as ethic. In K. Gibson, D. B. Rose & R. Fincher (Eds.), *Manifesto for living in the Anthropocene*. New York: Punctum books, 72–74

Mosedale, J. (2015). Critical engagements with nature: Tourism, political economy of nature and political ecology. *Tourism Geographies, 17*(4), 505–510. doi:10.1080/14616688.2015.1074270

Mostafanezhad, M., Norum, R., Shelton, E., & Thompson-Carr, A. (2016). Introduction, In M. Mostafanezhad, R. Norum, E. Shelton & A. Thompson-Carr (Eds.), *Political ecology of tourism. Community, power and the environment*. New York: Routledge, 1–21.

NHK (2013). *Amachan*. http://www6.nhk.or.jp/drama/pastprog/detail.html?i=asadora88.

Norberg-Schulz, C. (1980). *Genius loci: Towards a phenomenology of architecture*. New York: Rizzoli.

Norum, R., Mostafanezhad, M., Shelton, E., & Thompson-Carr, A. (2016). Conclusion. Towards future intersections of tourism studies and political ecology. In M. Mostafanezhad, R. Norum, E. Shelton & A. Thompson-Carr (Eds.), *Political ecology of tourism: Community, power and the environment*. New York; Routledge, 302–308.

Ozyıldırım, I. (2009). Narrative analysis: An analysis of oral and written strategies in personal experience narratives. *Journal of Pragmatics, 41*, 1209–1222.

Peterson, V. (2005). How (the meaning of) gender matters in political economy. *New Political Economy, 10*(4), 499–521. doi:10.1080/13563460500344468

Plumwood, V. (2002). *Environmental culture. The ecological crisis of reason*. London: Routledge.

Plumwood, V. (2007). A review of Deborah Bird Rose's 'Reports from a Wild Country: Ethics for Decolonisation'. *Australian Humanities Review* (22). http://australianhumanitiesreview.org/2007/08/01/a-review-of-deborah-bird-roses-reports-from-a-wild-country-ethics-for-decolonisation/

Plumwood, V. (2008). Shadow places and politics of dwelling. *Australian Humanities Review, 44* http://australianhumanitiesreview.org/2008/03/01/shadow-places-and-the-politics-of-dwelling/ accessed 16 April, 2018.

Ravneberg, B., & Soderstrom, S. (2017). *Disability, society and assistive technology*. New York: Routledge.

Rivera, V. (2017). A path to social inclusion in multicultural Australia. https://www.internationalaffairs.org.au/news-item/a-path-to-social-inclusion-in-a-multicultural-australia/.

Rooney, T., Lawlor, K., & Rohan, E. (2016). Telling Tales: Storytelling as a methodological approach in research. *The Electronic Journal of Business Research Methods, 14*(2), 147–156.

Rose, D. (1996). *Nourishing Terrains*. Canberra: Commonwealth of Australia.

Rose, D. B. (2015a). The ecological humanities. In K. Gibson, D. B. Deborah & R. Fincher (Eds.), *Manifesto for living in the Anthropocene*. New York: Punctum books, Chapter 1, 1–6.

Rose, D. B. (2015b). Dialogue. In K. Gibson, D. B. Deborah & R. Fincher (Eds.), *Manifesto for living in the Anthropocene*. New York: Punctum books, Chapter 20, 127–132.

Rose, D. B. (2018). *Gift of life in the shadow of death*. Human Nature Lecture Series, Australian Museum (8 March, 2018). https://soundcloud.com/australianmuseum/live-at-the-am-humannature-lecture-series-deborah-bird-rose.

Rose, D., & Robin, L. (2004). The ecological humanities in action: An invitation. *Ecological Humanities* (31–32). http://australianhumanitiesreview.org/category/issue/issue-31-32-april-2004/.

Ruiz-Ballesteros, E. (2011). Social-ecological resilience and community-based tourism: An approach from Agua Blanca, Ecuador. *Tourism Management, 32*(3), 655–666. doi:10.1016/j.tourman.2010.05.021

Sankei West. (2016). Foreign media impressed with Ama and Hospitality, *Sankei West* (May 28, 2018. https://www.sankei.com/west/news/160528/wst1605280045-n1.html.

Scheyvens, R. (2000). Promoting Women's Empowerment Through Involvement in Ecotourism: Experiences from the Third World. *Journal of Sustainable Tourism, 8*(3), 232–249. doi:10.1080/09669580008667360

Scheyvens, R., & Russell, M. (2012). Tourism, land tenure and poverty alleviation in Fiji. *Tourism Geographies, 14*(1), 1–25. doi:10.1080/14616688.2011.593188

Shaw, R., Rahman, A., Surjan, A., & Parvin, G. (Eds.). (2016). *Urban disasters and resilience in Asia*. Amsterdam: Butterworth-Heinemann.

Shima Kanko Hotel (2014). *Press release: The first female executive chef*. https://www.miyakohotels.ne.jp/file.jsp?id=97854.

Shubach, A. (2015). *The disappearing Ama: Japan's tough, topless free-diving mermaids*. https://jezebel.com/the-disappearing-ama-japans-tough-topless-free-divin-1679290183

Stapleton, K., & Wilson, J. (2017). Telling the story: Meaning making in a community narrative. *Journal of Pragmatics, 108*, 60–80. doi:10.1016/j.pragma.2016.11.003

Stuart, E., & Woodroffe, J. (2016). Leaving no-one behind: Can the Sustainable Development Goals succeed where the Millennium Development Goals lacked? *Gender & Development, 24*(1), 69–81. doi:10.1080/13552074.2016.1142206

Swain, R. B., & Wallentin, F. Y. (2008). Economic or non-economic factors: What empowers women? (No. 2008: 11). *Working Paper*. Sweden: Department of Economics, Uppsala University.

Tanabe, S. (1993). *Ama*. Tokyo: Hosei University Publishing.

Thompson-Carr, A. (2016). Introduction to community and power. In M. Mostafanezhad, R. Norum, E. Shelton & A. Thompson-Carr (Eds.), *Political ecology of tourism: Community, Power and the environment*. New York: Routledge, 25–30.

Toba City (Tourism Promotion) (2018). *Toba walking handbook (Toba Osanpo techo)*, http://tobakanko.jp/modules/pamphlet/detail.php?dtid=30.

Tōyō suisan kagaku kyōkai (2011). *Report on the current state of ama in Japan.* Toba Sea Folk Museum.

Truelove, Y. (2011). (Re-)conceptualizing water inequality in Delhi, India through a feminist political ecology framework. *Geoforum, 42*(2), 143–152. doi:10.1016/j.geoforum.2011.01.004

Tucker, H., & Boonabaana, B. (2012). A critical analysis of tourism, gender and poverty reduction. *Journal of Sustainable Tourism, 20*(3), 437–455. doi:10.1080/09669582.2011.622769

United Nations (2015). *Transforming our world: The 2030 agenda for sustainable development.* New York: UN, https://sustainabledevelopment.un.org/content/documents/21252030%20Agenda%20for%20Sustainable%20Development%20web.pdf.

United Nations (2017). UN *Sustainable development goals 17 goals to transform our world.* http://www.un.org/sustainabledevelopment/sustainable-development-goals/.

UN Women (2018). *Turning promises into action: Gender equality in 2030 agenda for sustainable development.* http://www.unwomen.org/en/digital-library/publications/2018/2/gender-equality-in-the-2030-agenda-for-sustainable-development-2018#view

Venkatesan, S. (2009). Rethinking agency: Persons and things in the heterotopia of "traditional Indian craft". *Journal of the Royal Anthropological Institute, 15*(1), 78–95. doi:10.1111/j.1467-9655.2008.01531.x

Wearing, S. (2002). Re-centering the self in volunteer tourism. In G. Dann (Ed.), *The tourist as a metaphor of the social world.* New York: CABI, 237–262.

Weir, J. (2008). Connectivity. *Australian Humanities Review, 45*, 153–164.

West, J., & Haug, R. (2017). The vulnerability and resilience of smallholder-inclusive agricultural investments in Tanzania. *Journal of Eastern African Studies, 11*(4), 670–691. doi:10.1080/17531055.2017.1367994

Williams, C., & Golovnev, I. (2015). Pamiri women and the melting glaciers of Tajikistan. A visual knowledge exchange for improved environmental governance. In Buechler, S., & Hanson, A. (Eds.). *A political ecology of women, water and global environmental change.* New York: Routledge, Chapter 11, 207–225.

Willis, J. (2007). *Foundations of qualitative research: Interpretive and critical approaches.* Thousand Oaks, CA: Sage Publications.

Zhao, W., & Zhang, C. (2018). From isolated fence to inclusive society: The transformational disability policy in China. *Disability & Society, 33*(1), 132–137. Vol. doi:10.1080/09687599.2017.1375246

The land has voice: understanding the land tenure – sustainable tourism development nexus in Micronesia

T. S. Stumpf and C. L. Cheshire

ABSTRACT

Externally-generated prescriptions for development continue to be imposed on Pacific Island societies. Frequently lost in this process is provision for the idiosyncratic localized realities of the people actually living in these places. Using an interpretivist critical discourse analysis, this study examines Indigenous perspectives on land, and how these perspectives interface with such standardized development ideals. More specifically, this study explores how issues related to Indigenous land holding rights in Micronesia are at the core of the 17 Sustainable Development Goals (SDGs) set forth by the United Nations in the 2030 Agenda for Sustainable Development. The results elucidate how the current SDG targets lack sufficient provision for how Micronesian societies function, what is valued by the people that comprise these societies, and how Indigenous land holding rights form the bedrock of the sustainability of Micronesian livelihoods.

Introduction

In the vast swath of earth dominated by water, there has been nothing of more importance and consequence to its human civilizations than land. For the people and islands of Oceania, issues of land holding have defined their histories, current circumstances, and future trajectories in ways that are difficult to overstate. Indeed, those islands with governing bodies which have retained Indigenous land holding rights stand in stark contrast to those characterized by liberalized land laws which have opened the floodgate of foreign ownership, and the subsequent sociocultural and economic implications that inevitably follow. (Banner, 2007) Today, the remaining Indigenous land holding systems in Pacific Island countries (PICs) that prohibit foreign land ownership by law have been cited by external financial institutions, multinational organizations, and governments of aid-providing nations as a roadblock to development. (Asian Development Bank, 2015; Cheshire, 2010; Connell, 2007; Duncan, Codippily, Duituturaga, & Bulatale, 2014) According to the purview of some of the more influential of these entities operating in the Asia-Pacific region (see Abbott & Pollard, 2004; Asian Development Bank, 2015; Holden, Bale, & Holden, 2004), such PICs cannot attract the resources (i.e. foreign investment) required for development (and all the promised aspects of improved health, prosperity and livelihoods supposedly therein) via industries like tourism without substantial institutional reforms, including liberalized land holding laws.

However, it is imperative to recognize Indigenous perspectives on the role and value of land in Pacific Island societies, and how they interface with standardized development prescriptions imposed externally. To what extent the idiosyncrasies of localized realities are reflected in blanket development criteria is an issue that has been raised previously and referred to as "representativeness." (Bäckstrand, 2006) Reed, Fraser, and Dougill (2006, p. 407) state that such approaches "may miss critical sustainable development issues at the local level and may fail to measure what is important to local communities." For example, Taylor (2008) raises questions about the relevance of the United Nation's Millennium Development Goals to Indigenous people in Australia. While Rametsteiner, Pülz, Alkan-Olsson, and Frederiksen (2011) suggest the need for provisions of local norms in sustainable development indicators, there is a dearth of critical analyses on such issues in Pacific Islands.

The aim of this paper is to elucidate how issues related to Indigenous land holding rights in PICs are at the core of the 17 Sustainable Development Goals (SDGs) set forth by the United Nations in the 2030 Agenda for Sustainable Development. To this end, an interpretivist methodological approach is used to critically analyze discourse from 19 Indigenous residents regarding land holding and sustainable development via tourism across four island states in the Federated States of Micronesia (FSM). The findings suggest a need for more contextualized understandings of the SDGs and the land holding – sustainable tourism development nexus in the FSM and PICs like it. More specifically, the analysis highlights the disconnect between the content of the SDGs and how land holding rights are central to localized interpretations of the issues embedded within them.

This paper proceeds as follows. First, a historical and conceptual foundation of land and land holding systems in PICs is presented, with particular focus on Micronesia. This includes a discussion of the decolonization process and subsequent evolution of tourism as a driver of economic development in the islands. Next, the methodology for the data collection and analysis of the present research is detailed. This is followed by a critical analysis of how the findings elucidate a need for localized conceptualizations of how an illustrative sample of the 17 SDGs relate to Indigenous land holding systems and sustainable development via tourism in the FSM. Finally, some implications of the findings and analysis of this research are offered.

Literature review

Land and land holding in pacific islands

Various arrangements can exist between land and humans. The parameters of such arrangements can range from ownership to stewardship, individual to communal, private to public, fee hold to free hold, and traditional to modern. The present study focuses on Indigenous land holding systems in Micronesia. In this paper, "Micronesia" is the term applied to the regional sea of islands, communities, and social networks found in western Oceania (Hanlon, 1994; Hau'ofa, 2008), and in addition to the FSM includes the Republic of Palau, the Republic of the Marshall Islands, the Republic of Kiribati, the Republic of Nauru, the Commonwealth of the Northern Marianas Islands. (Ballendorf, 1988) It is recognized that the term "Micronesia" is itself a qualitative symbol designating a history of geopolitical imperialism characterized by artificial demarcation of islands into groups of states and nations by hegemonic Western powers. (Hanlon, 1994) Next, the term "land holding systems" (as opposed to alternatives such as "land tenure" or "ownership") is used in this paper to acknowledge the idea that people do not technically own the land. Rather, they own holding rights to a specified piece of land, and such holding rights occur within formal and informal systems developed by respective island societies. (Crocombe, 1971)

Finally, the term "Indigenous" in regards to land holding is used in lieu of alternatives such as "traditional" or "customary". There have been various invented traditions across Oceania in regards to the relationship between past and present day land holding systems. (Ward & Kingdon, 1995, p. 14) The current Indigenous land holding systems in Micronesia (and across

Oceania) often bear little resemblance to the traditional systems that were used prior to European contact. For instance, traditional land systems across Micronesia were often characterized by an autocratic ruling body which held all the land, and dispersed land use/cultivation rights and/or obligations among the people at its discretion. (Banner, 2007; Hanlon, 1994) This power could be consolidated in a single chief as in Kosrae, to an alliance of chiefs as in Palau, or to a network of decentralized chiefs as in Pohnpei. (Haglegam, 1998) In response to the socioeconomic and geopolitical changes brought by various external catalysts of change (i.e. colonization and de-colonization processes, missionary activity, introduction of capitalist economic systems) (Farrell, 1972), these traditional systems were replaced by individual and familial holding systems backed by local government laws. As such, "Indigenous land holding" refers here to specified parcels of land in which Indigenous (non-foreign) individuals retain holding rights which are permanent, inheritable, and transferable to other Indigenous individuals only. (Ward & Kingdon, 1995)

For Micronesians, and other Indigenous Pacific Islanders, attachment to land and place is a central component of personal/familial identity and genealogy. (Diaz & Haulani Kauanui, 2001; Hanlon, 2004) As Diaz and Haulani Kauanui (2001, p. 318) state the sense of place rooted in Indigenous land holding rights is nothing less than "paramount to the continued existence and viability of Pacific Islanders." While the connection between Pacific Islanders and their land was evident in pre-colonial times through the Indigenous names for people and places that illustrate the depth of land-human identity connections, the focus on such connections has subsequently become even more heightened in colonial and post-colonial contexts. (Diaz & Haulani Kauanui, 2001) Specifically, in those Pacific Islands where Indigenous land holding systems were modified (involuntarily or voluntarily) to permit ownership by foreign parties, the sociocultural upheaval that followed was inevitable and substantial. (Banner, 2007) As all the associated adverse effects on islanders' identities, sociocultural institutions, and socioeconomic plights played out over time, issues relating to the imposition of foreign land holding rights became the basis for Indigenous sovereignty movements in places like Hawaii, New Zealand, and Guam. (Diaz & Haulani Kauanui, 2001) Today, in those PICs where Indigenous land holding rights were retained and foreign ownership prohibited by local law, the retention of such rights have been subjected to reform pressures from some influential external entities and the standardized blueprints for development they advocate. This is discussed in greater detail next.

Development ideology in Micronesia

Oceania is a critical region for examining (sustainable) development on account of its unique geographical, historical, sociocultural, and environmental characteristics. (Overton, 1999) In the eighteenth-century, the economic ventures of the Western world began to encroach upon Pacific Island societies in earnest. (Kiste, 1994) From beche-de-mer to whale oil to copra to sugar, these islands served as a breeding ground for centuries of international trade and colonial imposition. (Cheshire, 2010; Kiste, 1994) In the post-World War II period, the colonial superpowers of the Pacific began to instill the development ideologies considered essential to the future of the newly formed PICs, including an emphasis on productive economic activity. (Hanlon, 1998) In Micronesia, this included the use of a "very institutionalized, highly standardized view of what economic development should be" (Hanlon 1998, p. 104) by organizations like the UN Development Program in conjunction with the United States government. As Purdie (1999, p. 64) points out, there has been a "tendency to employ development blueprints constructed in and for contexts differing markedly from those in the Pacific Islands."

These colonial histories combined with the current paradigm of external development assistance from entities that seek to "enforce similar policies across diverse countries" (Dolowitz & Marsh, 2000, p.7) continue to create both implicit and explicit pressure on recently established governments to pursue standardized development ideals as a panacea for improved livelihoods. As Stumpf and Reynolds (2016) show such conformity pressures are also present in development planning around tourism. While thought by their purveyors to "occupy the moral high ground", a critical interpretation reveals "somewhat ill-defined objectives, clouded in good intentions and selectively or inadequately applied." (Connell, 2007, p. 121) As McMillan (2002, p. 225) suggests, notions of development "that are based more on preconceptions than on the specifics of the situation are still regrettably common."

Institutional reform, tourism development, and land

One result of this external influence on local governance across Micronesia is an imbalanced, if not totally misguided, focus on a top-down approach to realizing the tenets of development. (Cheshire, 2010; Stumpf & Swanger, 2017) This top-down approach emphasizes formal institutional reform, including liberalized land holding laws, to pave the way for increased levels of foreign investment in potential drivers of development such as tourism. The bottom-up, informal institutions stemming from sociocultural norms and values are not only ignored, but actually regarded as an "irrational influence" (Connell, 2007, p. 116) that stands in direct contrast to external notions of what constitutes good governance toward development. In the 1960s, a report commissioned by the UN Trusteeship Council referred to traditional land tenure systems in Micronesia as a "lingering anachronism" that must be reformed to achieve economic development, while "ignoring any consideration of what land tenure systems might mean to the different peoples of Micronesia." (Hanlon, 1998, p. 97)

The Asian Development Bank (ADB) continues to be active in advocating for the top-down approach to development across Oceania. (Cheshire, 2010) Headquartered in the Philippines, the ADB espouses the alleviation of poverty through economic development, and provides loans, grants, strategic development advice, and technical assistance to this end across Oceania. (Asian Development Bank, 2016) Since 1990, the FSM has received over $112 million in assistance from the ADB, much of which has centered on governance around private-sector business development through "strengthening of institutional capacity for land administration and management." (Asian Development Bank, 2017) The ADB has a number of formalized relations with the UN, including working arrangements on the UN Economic and Social Commission for Asia and the Pacific (ESCAP), UN Human Settlements Programme (HABITAT), UN International Labour Organization (ILO), UN Development Programme (UNDP), and UN Industrial Development Organization (UNIDO). (Asian Development Bank, 2017a) The ADB is listed as a partner organization for the UN's SDGs on various projects in Oceania including the Poverty-Environment Partnership, the Pacific Region Infrastructure Facility, the Global Platform for Sustainable Cities, and the Coral Triangle Initiative. (United Nations, 2016)

As Scheyvens and Momsen (2008, p. 495) point out, such external entities have discussed Indigenous land holding rights backed by local law as a "curse rather than a blessing", and thus posit the reform and clarification of laws which stymie foreign access to land as requisite to development. While land may be regarded as a relatively less important factor of production in the development of product-based ventures (Parker, 2006), quite the opposite is true for tourism due to the premium placed on ideal location. However, land in Pacific places like Micronesia is "managed under a complex mix of modern and traditional systems" (Federated States of Micronesia Economic Summit, 2004, p. 35), which are "not easily amenable to translation into western codes and conventions." (Connell, 2007a, p. 126) The complexities of Indigenous land holding systems has been documented in case studies across Micronesia and other PICs. (Bascom, 1965; Labby, 1976; Lingenfelter, 1975; Peoples, 1985) Consider the following passage which explains one aspect of the intricacies of land ownership in the FSM state of Yap (Labby, 1976, p. 35–36):

The estate itself was seen to consist not only of the domestic group living on specific land, but also an entire extended network of relations of people and land ... Since the man's claim on his land began with his mother, who had worked to earn it for her children, the land was not simply his alone. It also belonged to his siblings ... Brothers, of course, would have been given pieces of their father's land, but sisters had to marry out ... Although the [sister] could not use the land she left at her natal estate, she and the children she bore stood as guardians to it, watching over those who had taken their place, the woman's brother's wife and her children ... It was only after four generations had passed that the claim of the people established on the land by an in-marrying woman finally expired, that the clan group was fully repaid for its investment in the land.

External organizations pushing for Indigenous land holding reform to facilitate development via tourism often cite such nuanced systems (seemingly inscrutable to Western sensibilities) as evidence of the difficulties outside investors face when trying to acquire land for developing commercial tourism ventures. Such organizations thus promote a form of economic dualism, whereby the ideals from their economic system are superimposed upon what they perceive to be less advanced systems. (McKee & Tisdell, 1990) New depths of understanding regarding the Indigenous land holding – tourism development nexus are needed to develop more holistic, if not accurate, understandings of the development ideals promoted by the UN and its partner entities. Paramount to this is juxtaposing the localized realities of the Indigenous people which actually comprise these societies with such externally-generated ideals.

Methodology

Indigenous voices and perspectives are an under-represented, yet essential component of scholarship on topics related to hegemony, history, identity, culture, economic and geopolitical issues in Pacific Islands. (Diaz & Haulani Kauanui, 2001; Stumpf, 2016) As Hanlon (2004, p. 200) states, "even the most liberal, empathetic, and avowedly radical studies can remain colonialist in their methodologies and colonizing in their inadvertent silencing or displacement of more local voices and histories." To avoid the problem of privileging non-Indigenous thought regarding localized Indigenous issues (Hanlon, 2004), this study uses qualitative interview data combined with an interpretivist critical discourse analysis (CDA) to elucidate a contextualized understanding of Indigenous perspectives regarding the intersection of land, tourism, and the 17 SDGs set forth by the United Nations across four island states in the Federated States of Micronesia (FSM).

The Federated States of Micronesia: an overview

Situated slightly above the equator, the FSM is a sovereign nation of roughly 708 islands (65 inhabited) in the Micronesia sub-region of western Oceania. (see Figure 1) The FSM is a fairly recent geopolitical construction that has been grouped into four states (west to east): Yap, Chuuk, Pohnpei, and Kosrae. Each state is comprised of many islands, with the exception of Kosrae, which is a single island state. The total combined land area of the four states is approximately 271 square miles. (Federated States of Micronesia, 2008) Previously part of the Trust Territory of the Pacific Islands formed by the UN and administered by the U.S. after World War II, the FSM formally gained its political independence in 1986. (Hanlon, 1998) Today, the FSM remains a self-governing nation in free association with the U.S. under the Compact of Free Association arrangement between the countries. The most recent Compact stipulates the U.S. provide roughly $3 billion in development aid to the FSM through 2023 in exchange for certain national defense and security-related provisions. (Federated States of Micronesia Development Partners Forum, 2012) For the FSM, the Compact funds have ostensibly been designed to support increased levels of development and economic self-reliance.

In its national strategic development plan created with technical assistance from external organizations (i.e. the ADB and U.S. Department of Interior) which consider themselves "conduits

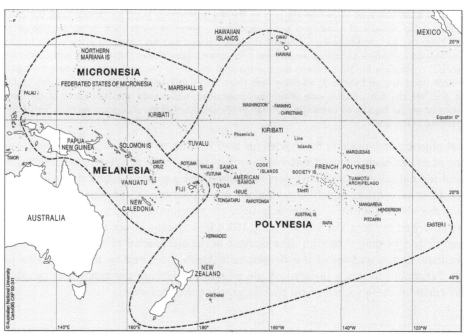

Figure 1. Map of Oceania (courtesy of CartoGIS Services, College of Asia and the Pacific, and The Australian National University).

for policies of good governance" (Larmour, 2005, p. 117) across Oceania, the FSM has singled-out tourism as the industry with the greatest potential to drive such self-reliance. (Federated States of Micronesia Economic Summit, 2004; Federated States of Micronesia Development Partners Forum, 2012) While reliable tourism statistics for the FSM are elusive, annual arrivals between the years 2000 to 2016 ranged from 15,300 to 47,500. (UNWTO, 2018) However, available data do not differentiate between international tourists and FSM citizens visiting friends and relatives, so the actual number of bona fide tourists is unclear.

The FSM faces a number of barriers to developing tourism into a viable industry. For instance, the lack of well-coordinated policies linking air transportation and tourism have been a roadblock to tourism development for island nations around the world (Abeyratne, 1999), and the FSM is no exception. In the 1960s, Continental Airlines led the formation of the United Micronesia Development Association (UMDA). The goals of the UMDA (in which Continental took a 32% interest) were centered on using tourism to spur economic development in the region. Continental concurrently launched Air Micronesia, an air service of which UMDA (49%) and Continental (31%) became the largest shareholders. As part of the proposal, Continental pledged that Air Micronesia would devote itself to the economic development of the islands by creating a tourism industry anchored by resort hotels built and managed by Continental. (Davies, 1984) Continental gained exclusive and permanent rights to service Micronesia in 1971. The company subsequently formed a wholly-owned subsidiary called Continental Hotels, Inc. to build a chain hotels across Micronesia (including the FSM states of Chuuk and Pohnpei) to integrate its tourism operations. (Carlile, 2000; Kelley & Penseyres, 1976) The Continental Hotel in Chuuk was built in 1970 at a size almost twice the original plan and $250,000 over budget. (Kelley & Penseyres, 1976) The proposed hotel in Pohnpei was blocked by the local government and never built. (Hanlon, 1998)

Thus, despite having a monopoly on the region, Continental's efforts to develop tourism into a viable industry in the FSM through an integrated supply chain did not prove successful. In 2011, Continental Airlines was bought by United Airlines, which at the time of this study remains the sole provider of regular air transportation service to the FSM. The FSM states of Kosrae,

Pohnpei, and Chuuk are serviced by United Airlines' "island hopper" route originating out of both Hawaii and Guam, and Yap is serviced separately by United Airlines out of Guam. Given the access challenges for potential tourist markets in the U.S., Japan, Australia, China, Russia, and Korea, the FSM is "unlikely ever to become a high volume destination for leisure tourists." (Federated States of Micronesia Economic Summit, 2004, p. 228)

Tourism in the Federated States of Micronesia: Yap, Chuuk, Pohnpei, and Kosrae

Each FSM state offers a distinct tourism product, and each has its own tourism bureau. The FSM Visitors Board is the national tourism body located in the capital of Palikir on Pohnpei, and ostensibly coordinates tourism activities between the states. Yap State is comprised of 139 islets which amount to about 46 total square miles of land. Approximately 98% of all dry land in Yap is privately owned, with the remaining 2% being public and commercial land. (Federated States of Micronesia, 2008) Yap is also generally thought to have the most intact traditional culture of all four FSM states, and Yapese society is still characterized by a complex sociopolitical organization of castes, councils, and chiefs. Some of the main attractions in Yap are its ancient stone money, cultural tours, deep-sea fishing, and manta ray diving. Some 900 miles to the east of Yap, Chuuk State is comprised of 542 islets amounting to 49 total square miles of land. Similar to Yap, approximately 98% of all dry land in Chuuk is privately owned, with the remaining 2% split evenly between public and commercial land. (Federated States of Micronesia, 2008) Tourism in Chuuk is almost entirely centered on historical resources from World War II. The centerpiece for this is Chuuk Lagoon, which is home to the largest fleet of downed World War II Japanese air and water craft in the world, and is thus considered the world's premiere site for wreck diving.

Four hundred fifty miles to the east of Chuuk is Pohnpei State. Pohnpei is comprised of 26 islets, which together amount to 133 total square miles of land. As opposed to Yap and Chuuk, only about 63% of all dry land in Pohnpei is privately owned, with 36% classified as public land and the remaining 1% as commercial land. (Federated States of Micronesia, 2008) Pohnpei typically ranks the highest among the FSM states in terms of total arrivals due to it being both home to the nation's capital and the nation's largest single island of Pohnpei proper (129 square miles). Pohnpei also offers the most diverse tourism experience of the FSM states, which includes deep-sea fishing, surfing, diving, hiking, World War II historical sites, and Nan Madol, the world's only ancient city built atop a coral reef.

Finally, Kosrae State is the easternmost FSM state, situated 340 miles from Pohnpei. Kosrae is the only FSM state comprised of a single island (42 square miles). Kosrae is unique among the FSM states in that only about 35% of all dry land is privately owned, with 64% classified as public land, and the remaining 1% as commercial land. (Federated States of Micronesia, 2008) Kosrae attracts mainly nature and adventure tourists looking for uncrowded diving, jungle hiking, and mangrove kayaking. Kosrae is also home to the Lelu Ruins, an ancient compound which once served as the ruling center for the high chiefs of the island.

Data collection and analysis

This study uses interpretivist CDA to account for Indigenous voices and perspectives on land, tourism, and the 17 SDGs set forth by the United Nations. CDA, sometimes referred to as "critical language awareness" or "critical language studies" (Billig, 2003), connects human discourse with varying underlying sociological structures and institutions. In particular, CDA examines the discursive linkages between qualitative text, influencing power structures, and localized social situations and cultural identities. (Weiss & Wodak, 2003) In the present study, semi-structured interviews were used to generate qualitative data from Indigenous residents of the FSM associated with the tourism industry. These individuals included hotel owners ($n = 7$), tourism bureau staff ($n = 1$), government officials ($n = 2$), college faculty of hotel and tourism management ($n = 1$), local land owners ($n = 6$), and staff of small business development agencies ($n = 2$). In these small islands, most local residents have at least some tangential association with tourism. While the interview participants in this study had a relatively higher direct association with tourism than most, all interview participants were first and foremost Indigenous Pacific Islanders and members of their respective communities.

These perspectives were then analyzed and interpreted from an ontology and epistemology of cultural (or anthropological) relativism which assumes that an individual's sociocultural context plays a major role in inscribing the contours of their reality, and that a trained researcher can elucidate these localized realities by interpreting the discursive perspectives within the sociocultural context in which they were stated. (Spiro, 1986; Van Dijk, 2003) The authors of this research had a total of approximately 30 years of combined experience living and/or working in the business and economic development, education, community development, and media sectors in the FSM prior to the data collection and analysis.

A total of 22 interviews with 19 different individuals (5 females, 14 males) were conducted for this research, and all interviews were completed face-to-face on site across all four FSM states. Three participants were interviewed twice to follow-up on information provided in their previous comments. The researchers leveraged their personal and professional networks in the FSM to identify potential interview participants, and these individuals were contacted via e-mail roughly 6 months prior to the data collection. Ten individuals provided initial consent to participate in the research as a result, and the other nine participants were located in-country during the field work through reference from other interview participants. Three of the 19 individuals were from Yap State, two from Chuuk State, nine from Pohnpei State, and five from Kosrae State. The interviews totaled 1605 min in length (26.75 h), and the average interview length was 72.95 min. A digital-voice recorder was used to capture the interview data with consent. Each interview was first transcribed word-for-word by the lead author immediately subsequent to completion. The text was then broken down into data incidents and coded.

When coding in CDA, the researcher can adopt various analytical approaches ranging from coding an entire qualitative text corpus in broad terms, coding topical areas of perceived importance, and/or more micro-analytical coding. (Fairclough, 1992) The present study adopted the latter approach whereby groups of 13 sentences (data incidents) were analyzed and assigned a code. Following Fairclough (1992), a three dimensional framework was used to move from text to analysis to code to interpretation. First, the *text analysis* dimension was used in the language analysis of the interview text, with focus on wording, metaphor, and grammar modality. Next, the *discursive practice dimension* was used to begin contextualizing the production and consumption of the discourse of the interview text with its sociocultural context.

Finally, the *discourse as social practice* dimension was used to situate the discourse from the interview text into "the institutional and organizational circumstances of the discursive event and how that shapes the nature of the discursive practice." (Fairclough, 1992, p. 4) The circumstances here were defined by the researchers as the juxtaposition of the individual interview participants in his/her sociocultural context, his/her involvement in tourism, and the 17 SDGs set forth by the United Nations in the 2030 Agenda for Sustainable Development. As part of the critical interpretive process, special attention was given to the interactions between Indigenous ideology and practice regarding land, and the contrasts between the external ideology of the SDGs and the UN's goal of tourism as a vehicle for achieving them. In most cases, the interview participants' knowledge of the SDGs was more a general sense of externally-imposed development criteria as opposed to intimate knowledge of each SDG. The job of the researchers then was to interpret, analyze, and situate the ideological contrasts elucidated via the context of the discourse. The resulting findings of this analytical process is discussed next.

Findings and discussion

Indigenous land holding systems have been targeted as a constraint to development in the FSM and the other island nations in Micronesia. The ADB, a UN partner organization, has played a particularly prominent role in advocating for land holding system reforms to local governments using the rhetoric and promise of development. These reforms are posited as an essential component for realizing the myriad advances (i.e. social, physical and economic well-being) that will supposedly result via increased foreign investments in the keystone industry of tourism. In the tradition of the nineteenth-century colonists and traders which actively sought to influence islands' ruling bodies into alienating Indigenous land rights through land holding reforms (Banner, 2007), such organizations view land through a prism of Western interests, norms, and values. However, conceptualizations of land are highly localized and both culturally and historically determined. As such, it is imperative to understand local perspectives on land from Indigenous individuals who are also involved in the tourism industry, and how they interface with the UN's SDGs.

Indigenous perspectives: land, tourism, and the sustainable development goals

In juxtaposing Indigenous and external ideologies through the CDA, three main thematic pathways emerged that illustrated salient contrasts between specific SDGs and the localized understandings of issues embedded within them. Thus, three of the UN's 17 SDGs are focused on here to illustrate the importance of understanding Indigenous perspectives on the land holding – sustainable tourism nexus in the FSM, and the implications for externally-generated development goals. These include *SDG 1: No poverty*, *SDG 3: Good health and well-being*, and *SDG 16: Peace, justice, and strong institutions*. The thematic insights from this select group of SDGs can be used for further critical analyses of those not included here at readers' discretion.

Sustainable development goal 1: No poverty

A critical interpretation of the discourse from the interview participants points toward the need for a more nuanced understanding of poverty, land, and tourism in the FSM. For instance, while securing land control and ownership rights are listed as targets of *SDG 1* (United Nations, 2017), the present findings indicate that much of the conceptual underpinnings of the *SDG 1: No poverty* goal are nonetheless couched in Western notions of the economics of wealth. Through his discussion of land, the following statement by an interview participant illustrates a variation on how wealth and poverty are conceptualized in the FSM:

> Many outsiders come [to the FSM], see a piece of land that would work for their business, and attach only money value to it. But land here has not only financial value, land here has voice. It is land that determines your role in society, not your financial wealth. So locals would rather be land rich and cash poor than vice versa.

As this statement illuminates, a substantial component of what constitutes wealth for Indigenous Micronesians is rooted in the sociocultural capital accrued through individual and familial land holding rights. Familial pedigree is tracked closely in FSM societies, and plays an important role in forging social identity and status, as well as regulating interpersonal relationships and communication practices. Much of this pedigree and identity is still connected to the ties to land established by one's bloodline. (Hezel, 2012) The sociocultural capital that can be accumulated via bloodline and land is often used in lieu of the financial capital and material symbols that constitute wealth (and therefore economic and social livelihood) in the West.

Land is also parlayed into wealth for Micronesians via its utility in facilitating communal activities that sustain sociocultural norms and values. For instance, in traditional Micronesian society "accumulated wealth meant nothing" and conversely "it was the surrender of this wealth to build up or strengthen interpersonal relationships that counted for everything." (Hezel, 2012, p. 52) While financial wealth has an increased role in FSM society today, engaging in activities like land cultivation in order to participate in ceremonial gift giving and community activities is still a primary means for maintaining and/or accumulating sociocultural capital as a localized form of wealth. (Hezel, 2012) Whereas Western metrics of poverty and livelihood are centered on economic indicators, issues of quality of life, identity, and personhood are hinged upon the social relationships fostered through gift exchange in many Indigenous societies. (Curry, 2003) As such, it is possible for a Micronesian to have almost no accumulated financial wealth, but have considerable sociocultural wealth accumulated through land and its use to maintain a desired community status. As one interview participant stated:

> [In the FSM] it's not money that motivates everybody, because they know they can survive without money ... It is relationships. That's a really strong thing. Relationships and collective interests are often more important than $1 million dollars based on individual interests.

As the FSM has progressed through various planning stages of using tourism as the baseline for sustainable development, such sociocultural norms have been generally regarded by external organizations as the "foremost impediment to general commercial development." (Hanlon, 1998, p. 120) For those entities that desire homogeneity and thus seek to superimpose preordained standards regarding development and improved livelihoods, islands offer "distinct identities and spaces, an apparent combination of isolation and community. (Connell, 2003, p. 573) This combination has created an environment viewed as antithetical to development organizations and the standards they use which assume "that the capitalist business model works everywhere regardless of the cultural environment." (Cheshire, 2001, p. 3) As Hezel (2012, p. 23) states:

> Ironically, the very quality that makes Micronesians so charming in the eyes of the western world also hinders them from achieving the development and governance goals that are being held up for them. This personalization may go a long way in melting the hearts of tourists, but it is perceived as a stumbling block for good government and earns the new island societies a poor rating on the international index.

Thus, provision for localized understandings of what does and does not constitute wealth and poverty in the FSM is important. In a report for the ADB, Abbott and Pollard (2004, p. 90) cite the importance of "enabling land's dead capital value" as part of the poverty reduction plan for Pacific Islands. Contrary to the ADB, the results of this study highlight the reality that Indigenous land holding is paramount to poverty alleviation in the FSM and other places where sociocultural wealth is of equal, or greater, importance than financial wealth. Land in Oceania is far from a detached, perfunctory arena for commodity exchange, but rather deeply embedded in important sociocultural systems. (Swedberg, 1994) For many Pacific Island communities, the "maintenance of social and cultural practices is central to participatory development and just as important as income gains and poverty reduction." (Connell, 2007, p. 130) Land becomes the stage for sociocultural practices, and when islanders come together to work the land, "they are forming social relations of identity, communal labor practices, individual and group exchanges" that are all about community building. (Curry, 2003, p. 417) As one interview participant stated:

> You are who you are because of your land and where you come from. That's what makes it hard for both investors and locals. Because if I give you a land with voice, and afterwards will I still be the same person with the same role and respect? Land here determines who you are and what you are.

Sustainable development goal 3: Good health and well-being

Similar to the one-dimensional perspective on what constitutes wealth and poverty adopted by the UN in *SDG 1: No poverty*, the analysis also elucidated a relatedly narrow view on other issues relating to livelihood promoted by the UN in *SDG 3: Good health and well-being*. Specifically, *SDG*

3 is entirely focused on targeting aspects of physical wellness such as disease eradication and reduction, reproductive health, and child mortality. (United Nations, 2017) While unquestionably important, this is merely one piece of the multidimensional puzzle of what comprises good health and well-being in PICs like the FSM. As the results of this study underscore, a substantial emphasis is placed on community and social relationships as aspects of mental, emotional, and spiritual health and well-being in Pacific societies, for which land plays "a fundamental role in determining livelihood strategies." (Purdie, 1999, p. 77) As opposed to Western notions of land as arenas for various forms of economic exchange (Swedberg, 1994), land becomes the stage for aspects of health and well-being ranging from identity affirmation, communal activity, social interactions, and maintenance of the sociocultural order in Pacific Island societies. As such, land is regarded as that which feeds health and well-being both through agricultural cultivation, as well as through the cultivation of Indigenous personhood. (Diaz & Haulani Kauanui, 2001)

External organizations which advocate for tourism as the vehicle for sustainable development in places like the FSM must understand the impact on islanders' health and well-being when land is objectively treated like an emotionally-neutral commodity that should be optimized for productive capacity through liberalized land laws. An illustrative example of this revealed through the interviews of this study was the recent failed attempt to develop a resort hotel complex in the FSM state of Yap by a large, foreign investment company. According to interview participants with direct knowledge of this project, the foreign investment group vastly underestimated the central role of land and land ownership in the sociocultural landscape of Yap. For instance, the foreign investment group presented Yapese officials with detailed resort development plans on land currently owned by local individuals and families. However, the investors neglected to consult with these parties beforehand, instead choosing to view the land through a lens which assumed that it would undoubtedly be available for a long-term lease at a fair market rate. As one interview participant stated:

> [The foreign investors] took a map of Yap and made a proposal for where the hotel would be and so forth without considering that was actually people's land! Then the local landowners saw the proposal and said, "Wait is that my banana farm? Is that my beach? Is that my taro patch? No way!"

As is often the case with foreign entities operating in PICs, land was improperly treated like an arena for commodity exchange rather than a stage for myriad sources of health and well-being for islanders, and the project unsurprisingly fell apart as a result. Another illustrative example of the complications of developing land for commercial use can be found in the so-called "Battle of Map." This case involved a proposed resort complex called Yap Nature Life Garden, Inc. to be built in the district of Map in Yap State, FSM, and was to be funded by a Japanese investment company. (Hanlon, 1998) In response to the plans for the proposed resort, the district chiefs of Map successfully circulated a petition against what they felt was unlawful use of land inherited in trust to the villagers of Map. Their efforts to protect against what they considered to be foreign exploitation of Yapese land culminated in a government directive requiring Yap Nature Life Garden, Inc. to discontinue the project and withdraw from Yap entirely. (Hanlon, 1998) As one interview participant of this research summarized:

> When outsiders come in here to make deals about land for a hotel, they don't appreciate the value of land to the people that own it. They might see a small parcel of land and attach money value to it, but to those people it means more than that.

As external organizations advocate for sustainable tourism as a means for achieving SDGs, provision for how local conceptualizations of issues like health and well-being are tied to land is of primary importance. This is especially true given the UN's partnerships with the ADB, which has a history of advocating for Indigenous land holding system reform to stimulate foreign investment activity in tourism. Pacific places with less understood sociocultural norms like the FSM differ substantially from the context on which conventional business and economic knowledge is based, and thus work in these areas "must go beyond general schemata, and develop more detailed models of the specific situations and problems." (Dixit, 2004, p. 21) This study suggests that a more detailed model of health and well-being in PICs like the FSM must go beyond mere physical wellness, and include aspects of the mental, emotional, and spiritual health that is tied directly to the retention of Indigenous land holding systems.

Sustainable development goal 16: Peace, justice, and strong institutions

As with *SDG 1: No poverty* and *SDG 3: Good health and well-being*, the results of this research also illuminate how *SDG 16: Peace, justice, and strong institutions* (United Nations, 2017) is rooted in the standardized ideologies which both overlook and undervalue localized realities in the FSM. Specifically, the UN is promoting a one-dimensional view of institutions in *SDG 16* that seemingly does not recognize, understand, and/or value both sides of the institutional coin. This view of institutions places the emphasis solely on the formal institutions (i.e. banks, courts, and government), while ignoring the informal institutions supported by sociocultural norms and values which take precedence in many Pacific Island contexts. (Cheshire, 2010; Stumpf & Swanger, 2017) In the FSM, it is these all-important informal institutions which have a disproportionate influence on myriad aspects of social and economic life. One interview participant described Indigenous views on this relative importance of formal versus informal institutions using the following analogy:

> You know laws don't mean much to us, people here don't really pay a lot of attention to legal rules. So doing business here for locals is like fishing for sea turtles. There are laws about it, but nobody pays attention. If we see someone take a turtle out of season, we pay more attention to who the person is and their standing in the community to determine the consequences much more than anything related to the actual law.

Despite the prominence of informal institutions in the FSM, many external organizations only account for formal institutions, which they argue must be reformed for effectiveness in order to facilitate development. This is particularly true regarding reform around Indigenous land holding rights in order to support foreign investments in tourism as a driver of development. For instance, an ADB report on the FSM entitled "Understanding Land Issues and their Impact on Tourism Development" (2015, p. 5–6) laments that the FSM "has not fully liberalized foreign investment, including investment in tourism" which can deter "the kind of investment that is interested in establishing a long-term presence, expanding that presence, employing local people, contracting local services, and adding local economic value." The report goes on to state that while the current land holding system "remains in favor of domestic business interests … - land and institutional reforms may be considered to advance the productive use of land and to address the remaining weaknesses of land use and management system." (Asian Development Bank, 2015, p. 6) Another ADB report states that in order to develop the kinds of land markets that can effectively parlay into economic development, PICs need "mortgages, property deeds, land surveys, property valuation, and other institutional services that form part of a land management system." (Holden et al., 2004, p. 89)

The assumption is that without clear land holding laws which cater to foreign investment and are backed by Western-standard formal institutions, places like the FSM will not be able to meet preordained development standards. (Cheshire, 2010; Purdie, 1999) However, it is important to point out that successful investments in tourism and associated land use arrangements are being made by leveraging the *informal institutions* that have historically worked in PICs like the FSM. (Cheshire, 2010, Stumpf & Swanger, 2017) The rules supported by sociocultural norms and values may be in direct contrast to those supported by the courts. (Ostrom, 2005) This suggests a need to look beyond a standardized institutional ways and means considered requisite to sustainable development, and instead focus on leveraging the kinds of deeply-embedded informal institutions which actually produce effective outcomes around land use. (see Stumpf & Swanger, 2017)

Further, the one-dimensional emphasis placed on strengthening formal institutions around land holding systems ignores the substantial resistance and barriers to actually achieving this. As Duncan et al. (2014, p. 16) state, external organizations providing development assistance to PICs "have not understood the lack of interest in open markets, secure property rights, and impartial enforcement of contracts and have not given sufficient attention to how to progress economic reform in such circumstances." In the FSM, sociocultural norms and values often act as barriers to the kinds of formal institutional reforms advocated for by organizations which assume that externally-legitimated prescriptions for development should be used irrespective of the sociocultural reality. As Cheshire (2001, p. 3) states, this failure to account for the role of informal institutions of culture in FSM economic life (including land use and holding) is akin to attempting to "run through a river as if it were dry land." As one interview participant commented:

> When you talk about foreign investment in tourism and institutional reform, it's a sensitive issue because most people think this means you want to start looking at changing land laws. That's something people don't want to get into here. [Local] people don't like things that have a great impact on the culture. That's what happened with previous hotel projects that didn't work. Culture is the way to keep the peace here on the island. Too much Western way and that peace won't be there.

This interview participant went on to state that:

> In general, many [outsiders] come in with an "I know better than you" frame of mind, and use an "I'm smarter than you" mentality. It's pretty demeaning and it creates resistance right away. One has to listen to what locals want and need. When outsiders come in and say "Here's what you need", it won't work. It's a difference between what you think local people need and what they actually want.

An uncritical view of the UN's focus on strengthening institutions to promote a more peaceful and just society in Pacific Islands assumes that formal institutions are of primary importance in these contexts, that the barriers to institutional reform are surmountable, and that local institutions should adapt to external standards rather than vice versa. (Stumpf & Swanger, 2017) However, a critical discourse interpretation of Indigenous perspectives reveals the narrow view of institutions these ideas are predicated on. While the formal institutions may be assessed by external metrics as weak (World Bank, 2016), the informal institutions in the FSM are strong. It is these informal institutions that have been used successfully to develop a variety of economic ventures within Indigenous land holding systems across industries, including tourism. (Cheshire, 2010; Stumpf & Swanger, 2017)

While many of these successful ventures and their associated land dealings take substantial time, focus, and effort by Western standards, they nonetheless adhere to the rules-in-use (Ostrom, 2005) utilized by islanders and island societies, and should be recognized and valued as such. A recent study by Milne, Deuchar, Berno, Taumoepeau, Pusinelli, and Raymond (2017, p. 119) of the New Zealand Institute for Pacific Research on how private-sector investment can help PICs achieve sustainable development goals states that "there are no easy solutions to the challenges that surround land and investment." The report also suggests the complexities around land and investment be accepted while ensuring that Indigenous land holding rights are not compromised in the development process. (Milne et al., 2017) Insomuch as land has been, and continues to be tied to personal livelihood and identity in Oceania, diverting focus from strengthening institutions to valuing and building upon existing institutions may indeed represent a more conscientious and productive approach for external organizations to consider.

Conclusion: life on land

This study has used a critical discourse analysis and interpretive approach to juxtapose Indigenous perspectives of land with the UN's SDGs and the use of tourism as a principle driver of development in the FSM. Specifically, *SDG 1: No poverty, SDG 3: Good health and well-being, SDG 16: Peace, justice, and strong institutions* were used to illustrate practical and conceptual disconnects between such externally-validated notions of sustainable development, and how retention of Indigenous land holding systems underscores localized realities of these issues in the FSM and PICs like it.

Organizations which often assume it is their duty to impose development blueprints on the developing world often couch them in frameworks which do not align with local realities. Another, less euphemistic way of stating this is that "the local perspective is frequently seen as subordinate to the global." (Overton, 1999, p. 1) In particular, "rational development experts" often hold views and thus develop plans which treat land as commodified physical spaces detached from "cultural idiosyncrasies." (Connell, 2007, p. 125) These individuals and their associated organizations view land as sites for latent development activity which could potentially lead to improved livelihoods if only local people and governments would get their acts together and treat it as such.

However, Micronesian societies are characterized by localized ideologies that do not always sync with Western conventions. (Connell, 2007; Hanlon, 1998) In these societies where land is much more than a latent economic asset and where society is "written in the ground" (Connell, 2007, p. 126), standardized development prescriptions miss the mark at best, and indeed may threaten the potential for prosperous Indigenous livelihoods at worst. As the results of this study help illustrate, *Life on Land (SDG 15)* is predicated not on liberalized regulations that may facilitate sustainable development via tourism in Pacific Islands, but on retention of Indigenous land holding systems as the lifeblood of the Indigenous livelihoods tied directly to it. For islanders, what is "paramount to the continued existence and viability" of society is the sense of place rooted in land ownership. (Diaz & Haulani Kauanui, 2001)

As such, PICs represent special cases which require alternative theoretical and practical development frameworks. This begins with seeking to understand what is actually valued in local societies, and the functional rules of the game which infuse life and meaning into Indigenous realities. This cannot be accomplished through detached analyses and interpretations of such realities by external consultants and their laptop ruminations from the hotel lobby in places like the FSM. Rather, this can only be accomplished through an engaged, bottom-up approach which understands land for what it is, what it does, and what it says in Pacific societies. Land does not have suppressed economic productive value that must be translated into financial capital as an economic development imperative; Land has culturally and historically created value which is translated into social (and sometimes financial) capital as a sociocultural imperative. Land does not represent an administrative stumbling block and bottleneck to development; Land enables Indigenous personhood and livelihood. Land is not a passive commodity; The land has voice.

What does this bottom-up approach look like in which local norms and values regarding Indigenous land holding rights retain priority? In the FSM, this has required formal institutions which reflect and maintain the respective, and often very different, informal institutions of the various islands. Stated differently, this has required officials and decision-makers in local courts and governments who selectively accept external development aid, technical assistance, and governance prescriptions as members of the global community, while simultaneously prioritizing and adhering to core the sociocultural norms and values that govern everyday life in the islands. Hezel (2012, p. vii) uses the term "dilemmas of development" to refer to this administrative high wire act required to balance "the points of conflict between traditional island culture and the demands of the modern world" in the FSM. There are inevitably give-and-takes throughout these processes of reconciling such dilemmas. However, the past three centuries of Pacific history have illustrated that giving up land holding rights is perhaps above all others, the one concession that is most detrimental to Indigenous livelihoods, and that is least likely to lay a foundation for the sustainable development of Indigenous communities.

Disclosure statement

No potential conflict of interests was reported by the author(s).

References

Abbott, D., & Pollard, S. (2004). *Hardship and poverty in the Pacific*. Manila, Philippines: Asian Development Bank.
Abeyratne, R. (1999). Management of the environmental impact of tourism and air transport on small island developing states. *Journal of Air Transport Management, 5*(1), 1–37.
Asian Development Bank. (2015). *Understanding land issues and their impact on tourism development*. Mandaluyong City: Asian Development Bank.
Asian Development Bank. (2016). *Key indicators for Asia and the Pacific 2016*. Mandaluyong City: Asian Development Bank.
Asian Development Bank. (2017). *Fact sheet*. Retrieved from <https://www.adb.org/publications/federated-states-micronesia-fact-sheet>.
Asian Development Bank. (2017a). Retrieved from <https://www.adb.org/about/united-nations>.
Bäckstrand, K. (2006). Multi-stakeholder partnerships for sustainable development: Rethinking legitimacy, accountability and effectiveness. *European Environment, 16*(5), 290–306.
Ballendorf, D. A. (1988). The new freely-associated states of Micronesia: Their natural and social environmental challenges. *GeoJournal, 16*(2), 137–142.
Banner, S. (2007). *Possessing the Pacific: Land, settlers, and indigenous people from Australia to Alaska*. Cambridge, MA: Harvard University Press.
Bascom, W. (1965). Ponape: A Pacific economy in transition. *Anthropological Records, 22*, 1–156.
Billig, M. (2003). Critical discourse analysis and the rhetoric of critique. In G. Weiss & R. Wodak (Eds.), *Critical discourse analysis: Theory and interdisciplinary* (pp. 35–46). New York, NY: Palgrave Macmillan.
Carlile, L. (2000). Niche or mass market? The regional context of tourism in Palau. *The Contemporary Pacific, 12*(2), 415–436.
Cheshire, C. L. (2001). Family and business in Micronesia. *Micronesian Counselor, 37*, 1–19.
Cheshire, C. L. (2010). Swimming with the tide. *Micronesian Counselor, 81*, 1–10.
Connell, J. (2003). Island dreaming: The contemplation of Polynesian paradise. *Journal of Historical Geography, 29*(4), 554–581.
Connell, J. (2007). Islands, idylls and the detours of development. *Singapore Journal of Tropical Geography, 28*(2), 116–135.
Crocombe, R. G. (1971). *Land tenure in the South Pacific*. Oxford: Oxford University Press.
Curry, G. N. (2003). Moving beyond postdevelopment: Facilitating indigenous alternative for "development". *Economic Geography, 79*(4), 405–423.
Davies, R. E. (1984). *Continental airlines: The first fifty years, 1934–1984*. Woodlands, TX: Pioneer.
Diaz, V. M., & Haulani Kauanui, J. K. (2001). Native Pacific cultural studies on the edge. *The Contemporary Pacific, 13*(2), 315–341.
Dolowitz, D., & Marsh, D. (2000). Learning from abroad: The role of policy transfer in contemporary policy-making. *Governance, 13*(1), 5–24.
Dixit, A. K. (2004). *Lawlessness and economics*. Princeton, NJ: Princeton University Press.
Duncan, R., Codippily, H., Duituturaga, E., & Bulatale, R. (2014). *Identifying binding constraints in Pacific Island economies*. Honolulu, Hawaii: East-West Center.
Fairclough, N. (1992). *Discourse and social change*. Cambridge: Polity Press.
Farrell, B. H. (1972). The alien and the land of Oceania. In R. G. Ward (Ed.), *Man in the Pacific Islands: Essays on geographical change in the Pacific Islands* (pp. 34–73). Oxford: Oxford University Press.

Federated States of Micronesia. (2008). *Federated States of Micronesia Statistical Yearbook*. Palikir, Micronesia: FSM National Government.

Federated States of Micronesia Development Partners Forum. (2012). *Federated States of Micronesia development framework: Looking to the future*. Palikir, Micronesia: FSM Department of Economic Affairs.

Federated States of Micronesia Economic Summit. (2004). *Federated States of Micronesia's strategic development plan (2004-2023): The next 20 years: Achieving economic growth and self-reliance*. Palikir, Micronesia: FSM Department of Economic Affairs.

Haglegam, J. (1998). *Traditional leaders and governance in Micronesia. State, society and governance in Melanesia (Discussion Paper 98/1)*. Canberra: Australia National University.

Hanlon, D. (1994). Patterns of colonial rule in Micronesia. In K. R. Howe, R. C. Kiste, & B. V. Lal (Eds.), *Tides of history: The Pacific Islands in the twentieth century* (pp. 93–118). Honolulu: University of Hawaii Press.

Hanlon, D. (1998). *Remaking Micronesia: Discourses over development in a Pacific territory, 1944 –1982*. Honolulu: University of Hawaii Press.

Hanlon, D. (2004). Wone sohte lohdi; History and place on Pohnpei. In B. V. Lal (Ed.), *Pacific places, Pacific histories* (pp. 195–215). Honolulu: University of Hawaii Press.

Hau'ofa, E. (2008). *We are the ocean: Selected works*. Honolulu: University of Hawaii Press.

Hezel, F. (2012). *Making sense of Micronesia: The logic of Pacific Island culture*. Honolulu: University of Hawaii Press.

Holden, P., Bale, M., & Holden, S. (2004). *Swimming against the tide? An assessment of the private sector in the Pacific*. Manila, Philippines: Asian Development Bank.

Kelley, L., & Penseyres, M. (1976). *Continental Airlines and the development of tourism in the Marianas: TTPI*. Manoa: University of Hawaii.

Kiste, R. C. (1994). Pre-colonial times. In K. R. Howe, R. C. Kiste, & B. V. Lal (Eds.), *Tides of history: The Pacific Islands in the twentieth century* (pp. 3–28). Honolulu: University of Hawaii Press.

Labby, D. (1976). *The demystification of Yap*. Chicago, IL: University of Chicago Press.

Larmour, P. (2005). *Foreign flowers: Institutional transfer and good governance in the Pacific Islands*. Honolulu: University of Hawai'i Press.

Lingenfelter, S. G. (1975). *Yap: Political leadership and culture change in an island society*. Honolulu: University of Hawaii Press.

McKee, D. L., & Tisdell, C. A. (1990). *Developmental issues in small island economies*. New York, NY: Praeger.

McMillan, J. (2002). *Reinventing the bazaar: A natural history of markets*. New York, NY: W.W. Norton & Company.

Milne, S., Deuchar, C., Berno, T., Taumoepeau, S., Pusinelli, M., & Raymond, J. (2017). *Private sector investment in the Pacific*. Auckland: New Zealand Institute for Pacific Research.

Ostrom, E. (2005). Doing institutional analysis: Digging deeper than markets and hierarchies, In C. Menard & M. M. Shirley (Eds.), *Handbook of new institutional economics* (pp. 819–848). Dordrecht, Netherlands: Springer.

Overton, J. (1999). Sustainable development and the Pacific Islands. In J. Overton & R. Scheyvens (Eds.), *Strategies for sustainable development: Experiences from the Pacific* (pp. 1–18). London: Zed Books.

Parker, S. C. (2006). Entrepreneurs as producers. In S. C. Parker (Ed.), *The life cycle of entrepreneurial ventures* (pp. 337–360). New York, NY: Springer Science.

Peoples, J. G. (1985). *Island in trust: Culture change and dependence in a Micronesia economy*. London: Westview Press.

Purdie, N. (1999). Pacific Islands livelihoods. In J. Overton & R. Scheyvens (Eds.), *Strategies for sustainable development: Experiences from the Pacific* (pp. 64–79). London: Zed Books.

Rametsteiner, E., Pülzl, H., Alkan-Olsson, J., & Frederiksen, P. (2011). Sustainability indicator development - science or political negotiation? *Ecological Indicators, 11*(1), 61–70.

Reed, M. S., Fraser, E., & Dougill, A. J. (2006). An adaptive learning process for developing and applying sustainability indicators with local communities. *Ecological Economics, 59*(4), 406–418.

Scheyvens, R., & Momsen, J. (2008). Tourism in small island states: From vulnerabilities to strengths. *Journal of Sustainable Tourism, 16*(5), 491–510.

Spiro, M. E. (1986). Cultural relativism and the future of anthropology. *Cultural Anthropology, 1*(3), 259–286.

Stumpf, T. S. (2016). Navigations: Enhancing qualitative hospitality and tourism research outcomes in Pacific Island Countries. *Asia-Pacific Journal of Innovation in Hospitality and Tourism, 5*(2), 71–87.

Stumpf, T. S., & Reynolds, D. (2016). Institutional conformance and tourism performance: An efficiency analysis in developing Pacific Island countries. *Tourism Planning & Development, 13*(4), 449–468.

Stumpf, T. S., & Swanger, N. (2017). Institutions and transaction costs in foreign-local hotel ventures: A grounded investigation in the developing Pacific. *Tourism Management, 61*, 368–379.

Swedberg, R. (1994). Markets as social structures. In N. J. Smelser & R. Swedberg (Eds.), *The handbook of economic sociology* (pp. 255–282). Princeton, NJ: Princeton University Press.

Taylor, J. (2008). Indigenous peoples and indicators of well-being: Australian perspectives on United Nations global frameworks. *Social Indicators Research, 87*(1), 111–126.

United Nations. (2016). Retrieved from <https://sustainabledevelopment.un.org/partnership/partners/?id=658>.

United Nations. (2017). Sustainable development goals 17 goals to transform our world. Retrieved from <http://www.un.org/sustainabledevelopment/sustainable-development-goals/#prettyPhoto>

UNWTO. (2018). *Yearbook of Tourism Statistics, Data 2012 – 2016, 2018 Edition*. Madrid, Spain: WorldTourism Organization.

Van Dijk, T. A. (2003). The discourse-knowledge interface. In G. Weiss & R. Wodak (Eds.), *Critical discourse analysis: Theory and interdisciplinarity* (pp. 85–109). New York, NY: Palgrave Macmillan.

Ward, R. G., & Kingdon, E. (1995). Land use and tenure: Some comparisons. In R. G. Ward & E. Kingdon (Eds.), *Land, custom, and practice in the South Pacific* (pp. 6–35). Cambridge: Cambridge University Press.

Weiss, G., & Wodak, R. (2003). Introduction: Theory, interdisciplinarity, and critical discourse analysis. In G. Weiss & R. Wodak (Eds.), *Critical discourse analysis: Theory and interdisciplinarity* (pp. 1–34). New York, NY: Palgrave Macmillan.

World Bank. (2016). *Doing business 2016: Economy profile: Federated States of Micronesia*. Washington, DC: The World Bank and the International Finance Corporation.

Critical discourse analysis and the questioning of dominant, hegemonic discourses of sustainable tourism in the Waterberg Biosphere Reserve, South Africa

Andrew Lyon and Philippa Hunter-Jones

ABSTRACT

The aim of this paper is to demonstrate how critical discourse analysis (CDA), an under-utilised methodological approach, can be used to critically question the dominant, hegemonic discourses surrounding sustainable development and sustainable tourism development. The Waterberg Biosphere Reserve in South Africa provides the study context. The United Nations Sustainable Development Goals (SDGs) provide the framework for review, sustainable development is an integral part of this framework. This research study examines three SDGs in particular: discourses surrounding SDG 4 (quality education), SDG 8 (decent work and economic growth) and SDG 15 (life on land). Interviews ($n = 35$) were conducted, in South Africa, with multiple stakeholder groups. CDA techniques were applied to data analysis to examine the sustainable development/sustainable tourism discourses attached to the SDGs under review. Neoliberal discourses linked to the economy, the environment, and a sustaining of the tourism industry through top-down planning and unequal power distributions emerged. Conclusions reflect both upon the opportunities utilising a tool such as CDA presents, along with the limitations to take account of when applying it. CDA applications which explore SDGs by listening to the voices of the poor are suggested as one avenue for further research.

Introduction

The aim of this paper is to demonstrate how critical discourse analysis (CDA), an under-utilised methodological approach founded in critical thinking (Wodak & Meyer, 2009), can be used to critically question the dominant, hegemonic discourses surrounding sustainable development (SD), and, in turn, sustainable tourism development (STD). The Waterberg Biosphere Reserve (WBR), South Africa (SA), provides the study context (see Table 1 for a full list of abbreviations).

SD, an integral part of the United Nations (UN) agenda, is currently underpinned by 17 Sustainable Development Goals (SDGs) which collectively seek an end to poverty, protection of the planet along with peace and prosperity by 2030 (UN, 2017). Partnership and pragmatism are positioned as central tenets (UNDP, 2017). A case study of the UN WBR, SA, provides a working application of SD and allows us to interrogate stakeholder perceptions of three SDGs at a destination level: SDG 4 (quality education), SDG 8 (decent work and economic growth) and SDG 15

Table 1. Key abbreviations.

Abbreviation	In Full
AC	Accommodation Provider
BS	Business Stakeholders
CDA	Critical Discourse Analysis
CS	Civil Society
IYE	International Year of Ecotourism
LC	Land Claimants
MaB	Man and the Biosphere Programme
MAP	The Madrid Action Plan
NGO	Non-Governmental Organisation
PS	Public Sector
SA	South Africa
SD	Sustainable Development
SDG	Sustainable Development Goals
ST	Sustainable Tourism
STD	Sustainable Tourism Development
UN	United Nations
UNDP	United Nations Development Programme
UNESCO	The United Nations Educational, Scientific and Cultural Organization
WBR	Waterberg Biosphere Reserve
WCED	World Commission on Environment and Development
WSSD	World Summit for Sustainable Development

(life on land). Biospheres, with a conservation, development and logistical support remit, are one way of putting SD into practice. Tourism is one of the main economic and land-use sectors within the WBR. How tourism is developed, or seen to be developed, has implications for SD.

Case studies are carried out within the boundaries of one social system, monitoring a phenomenon over a specific time period (Swanborn, 2010). This case study is located within a polarised society, SA, which remains one of the most unequal societies in the world (World Bank, 2018). SA still bears the scars of apartheid and, while socio-economic change is occurring, it is often done in the context of colonialism and white privilege experienced during apartheid (Boluk, 2011a). This, in turn, inhibits African entrepreneurship, credit and infrastructural development, contributing also to information and skills deficits (Booysen, 2007). Access to employment, education, land, housing and health services are still predominantly divided along the lines of race (Neves & Du Toit, 2013).

Formed in 2001, the WBR sits in the Waterberg District in Limpopo Province in SA. It cuts across six predominantly rural settlements and small villages, Mogalakwena, Modimolle, Lephalale, Bela-Bela, Mookgopong, and Thabazimbi, all marked by enduring racial and spatial legacies of poverty. Vaalwater is the only town in the area, itself connected to the adjoining township (i.e. an urban area designated during apartheid and predominantly occupied by the black population) of Leseding. There are other rural settlements and small villages, but the area is predominantly a wilderness, with a very low population density. The main economic activities are tourism and agriculture (Taylor, Holt-Biddle, & Walker, 2003). The rural poor's livelihoods since the apartheid days have been characterised by oscillatory migration to distant urban cities. Informal labour in rural areas is a key source of income as formal labour is limited (Neves & Du Toit, 2013).

The concept of biosphere reserves was initiated by the UNESCO Man and the Biosphere (MaB) programme in 1974. The first biospheres were inaugurated in 1976 and by 2017 there were 669 reserves in 120 countries (UNESCO, 2018). In 1995, the Seville Strategy was adopted by UNESCO. This was a statutory framework which paved the way for future biosphere reserve developments (UNESCO, 2002). Biospheres are one way of the UN putting SD into practice. The Madrid Action Plan (MAP) of 2008 builds on the Seville Strategy, examining how biospheres can effectively respond to, and help to, address global issues and problems which have emerged or intensified since 1995. According to UNESCO (2008), these major challenges further exacerbate poverty and inequality and include: accelerated climate change; accelerated loss of biological and cultural diversity and rapid urbanization, which has major effects on environmental change.

The case study at the heart of this paper adopts what Swanborn (2010) describes as a holistic approach, whereby the discourses of people and social phenomenon within the boundaries of the WBR system are examined. By analysing the discourses of a number of active stakeholders in tourism in the WBR, the paper offers a number of contributions to knowledge. As tourism is one of the main economic sectors in the Waterberg, how this industry develops will have implications for the environment, society and the economy of the region. The WBR is a relatively recent phenomenon. Research on tourism development in the biosphere is similarly in its infancy.

The WBR also represents a microcosm of the larger debate on SD, involving issues about what to develop, where, how, from whose perspective and under which contexts. It is well placed to interrogate the UNs current round of development goals, SDGs, providing insights into the efficacy of such at a local level. Consequently, a study such as this not only adds to the body of knowledge on SD/STD within the case study area, but is of importance to the wider research community too. In line with the work of Kuhn (2007), this paper is not about how we "ought" to manage tourism, rather it is an attempt to comprehend wider perspectives of "what is" and to treat sustainability and tourism as an evolving, dynamic discourse.

The paper is developed as follows. First, the meaning of discourse, CDA, and discourses associated with SD, ST and STD in SA are reviewed in order to provide a theoretical backdrop to the study. Reference to the current SDG agenda is included in this review. Next, the WBR case study is introduced with contextual material necessary for CDA provided. The methods follow which explain more fully the approach adopted in executing CDA. Case study findings illustrate the challenges some of the SDGs, linked to quality education (SDG 4), decent work and economic growth (SDG 8) and life on land (SDG 15) face. Conclusions are drawn regarding the implications of the case study for the SDGs. Limitations acknowledge the shortfalls of CDA suggesting also associated opportunities for future research.

Discourse, power, ideology and knowledge

The term "discourse" has a variety of meanings and interpretations. It involves the use of language, and it is also a form of social practice (Mayr, 2008). A discourse or a communicative interaction can be a policy, a political strategy, a speech, conversations or a historical monument (Wodak & Meyer, 2009). It involves language-in-action, but also thoughts, words, objects, events, actions and interaction (Gee, 2011). In this paper discourse refers to: "all the phenomena of symbolic interaction and communication between people, usually through spoken or written language or visual representation" (Bloor & Bloor, 2007, p. 6).

Discourse comprises all forms of meaningful semiotic human activity which is connected to social, cultural and historical patterns and developments (Blommaert, 2005). In development, those with knowledge of how systems operate, the rules of those systems and how to utilise knowledge, will have influence and power over decision-making. This is evidenced in the work of Grimwood, Yudin, Muldoon, and Qiu (2015). Drawing upon discursive and postcolonial perspectives, Grimwood et al. (2015, p. 22) explore critiques associated with responsibility in Artic tourism. Exemplifying the power of responsibility to "normalize particular versions of truth", these authors go on to illustrate how not all knowledge is equal with some discourses having the capacity to supersede, disenfranchise or even silence others (for insights into Indigenous knowledge, see, for instance, Semali & Kincheloe, 1999; Sillitoe, Dixon, & Barr, 2005).

Discourse reproduces both power and knowledge and affects what is put into practice. In terms of development, organisations such as the multi-lateral agencies, the World Bank and UN, for instance, created post Second World War, are symbolic of the "development and realisation of a discourse as a legitimate reality in a bounded network of action" (Emirbayer & Goodwin,

1994, p. 1438). They are illustrative of the capacity of discourses to result in material realities such as institutions, policies and development projects.

Discourse also mediates ideology and there are various historical and social reasons how and why discourses gain prominence (Wodak & Meyer, 2009). Societal discourses are ideologically based (Bakhtin, 1986). Ideology refers to "a set of beliefs or attitudes shared by members of a particular social group" (Bloor & Bloor, 2007, p. 10). Ideologies are strongly linked to language (Fairclough, 1989). An ideology can be carried by a word such as "development" or "sustainability" and appropriated by stakeholder groups to achieve their ends. Thus, understanding notions of power are essential in the development process with the main arguments summarized by Crush (1995, p. 7): "Power in the context of development is power exercised, power over. It has origins, objects, purposes, consequences, agents and contra Foucault, much of this seems to be quite patently within the realm of the economic and the political". The UN and its SDGs have emanated out of a legitimisation of a particular version of SD, one associated with a particular ideology.

Critical discourse analysis

Multiple approaches to analysing discourse exist (see, for instance, the review by Titscher, Meyer, Wodak, & Vetter, 2002). CDA, selected in this study as the preferred method of textual analysis, is a linguistic method examining both the coherence and cohesion of the text. Coherence is linked to semantic meaning. Cohesion is linked to the textual-syntactic connectedness and the recognisable relationship between words. It involves ideologies associated with power (Wodak & Meyer, 2009). Not only does CDA examine what people say, it also examines why they say these things. Non-linguistic methods such as grounded theory and content analysis only examine coherence. It is through incorporating and analysing syntactic, semantic and pragmatic levels (cohesion) that a deeper understanding of the language used can be gained. CDA recognises that all discourse is not value-free and is part of, and influenced by, social structure and produced in social interaction (van Dijk, 2001).

CDA stems from the work of Habermas (1971) and seeks to understand social problems that are mediated by mainstream ideology and power relationships, which are perpetuated by discourse. Its objective is to uncover the ideological assumptions that are hidden in discourse in order to resist and overcome various forms of "power over" or to gain an appreciation of how power is exercised, which may not always be apparent (Fairclough, 1989). CDA seeks to describe, interpret, analyse, and critique social life reflected in discourse. It is concerned with studying and analysing discourses to reveal the discursive sources of power, dominance, inequality, and bias.

Context is critical in CDA as it examines how these sources are initiated, maintained, reproduced, and transformed within various political social, economic and historical contexts (van Dijk, 1988). Fairclough and Wodak (1997) summarise the foremost principles of CDA to be: CDA addresses social problems; power relations are discursive; discourse constitutes both society and culture; discourse does ideological work; discourse is historical; discourse is knowledge based; the link between text and society is mediated; discourse analysis is interpretative and explanatory; and discourse is a form of social action. These principles position CDA as an appropriate tool to study issues associated with development. Indeed, the recent work by Cummings, Reeger, de Hann, Zweehhorst, and Bunders (2018) adopts this approach specifically within the context of examining SDGs. CDA has also been previously successfully applied within the context of SA to explore the tensions between consumer virtue and the hedonistic behaviours of ethical consumers (Boluk, 2011b). This research study provides a fresh application, using CDA to drill into SDGs within the context of tourism development.

There are numerous approaches to CDA, from inductive to deductive (see Wodak & Meyer, 2009 for a useful analysis of a number of different approaches). This research study links critical

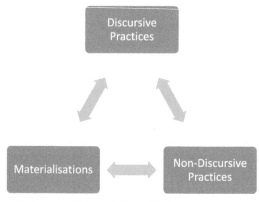

Figure 1. WBR Dispositif. Source: adapted from Wodak and Meyer (2009).

theory and CDA. It uses an inductive critical theory approach, cognisant that discourse is socially consequential and involves issues of power, ideology and epistemological considerations relating to knowledge (van Dijk, 2001). Such thinking correlates with the Derridean and Foucauldian approaches to CDA. Derrida is credited with introducing "deconstruction", a mechanism for critiquing the complex interplay between language and meaning (see Derrida, Butler, & Spivak, 2016). Complexity is central to Foucault (1972) too, whereby a discourse is not a communicative exchange, but an interchange of ideology, strategy, language and practice. This assumes a co-existence of discourse, objects and material realities. The relationship between these three can be labelled a dispositif (see Figure 1). In this paper, it is discourses linked to sustainable development and sustainable tourism development which contribute to the WBR dispositif.

Sustainable development discourse

The background to SD is well-documented with SD discourse historically embedded in literature linked to population growth, resource use, economic development and environmental concerns (Hopwood, Mellor, & O'Brien, 2005). Multiple publications and events have been influential in the evolution of this discourse including the World Commission on Environment and Development (WCED) publication, the "Brundltand Report" (1987) along with two major events in 2002, the International Year of Ecotourism (IYE) and the World Summit for Sustainable Development (WSSD). The IYE and WSSD included tourism in the implementation agenda placing it firmly on the international development map. Along with priorities shifting from "eco" to "social" (Tepelus, 2008), the value-laden development of sustainability (see Hall, 2000), continues to evolve.

The current SD discourse is encapsulated in the new sustainable development agenda adopted in 2015, which seeks to pragmatically move towards SD by 2030 (UN, 2017). Five themes dominate this agenda: people; planet; prosperity; peace; and partnerships. The agenda is articulated via 17 individually identified SDGs and 169 targets (UN, 2017). Themes, goals and targets are all inter-related and integrated. Achieving progress with SDG 10, "Reduce inequality within and among countries" for instance, will also move society closer to realizing SDG 1, "End poverty in all its forms everywhere". Achieving progress with SDG 8, "Promote sustained, inclusive and sustainable economic growth, full and productive employment and decent work for all", can only be realized if SDG 5, "Achieve gender equality and empower all women and girls" is advanced too. Collectively SDGs have much in common with the earlier SD literature. Both chart concerns that the dominant, mainly economic development paradigms of modernization and neoliberalism are having damaging effects on environments and people (Higgins-Desbiolles, 2018).

Sustainable development discourse in South Africa

SA's approach to SD during the apartheid era was based on maintaining pristine environments through biodiversity and conservation for whites' only game parks. Thousands of black Africans were forcibly removed from these elitist enclaves (McDonald, 2002). Scant regard was given to the well-being of the majority of the population or to other aspects of the environment. According to the International Institute for Sustainable Development (IISD, 2004), the Reconstruction and Development programme (RDP), with a strong focus on addressing the inequalities of apartheid, was the first stage in attempting to redress this imbalance. The SA government encouraged integration of sustainable development principles into the government planning cycle. Examples of these varied policies, programmes and laws include: land tenure reform; industrial strategies; regional peace and security; poverty reduction strategies; and integrated sustainable rural development strategies (IISD, 2004).

However, implementation has been variable with economic developments generally prevailing over environmental concerns (Lyon, Hunter-Jones, & Warnaby, 2017). Planning is based around neoliberal aspects of development and trickle-down economics. The environment is seen as an economic resource and economic development is seen as a priority for government (Patel & Graham, 2012). Moving towards environmental sustainability is therefore problematic when economic issues are given precedence. Despite constitutional commitments to environmental sustainability in SA, evidence indicates that the poor and the natural environment continue to be marginalised in decision-making. A gap therefore exists between policy rhetoric embracing SD and uneven implementation in practice (Patel, 2009). The result has been that while social deprivation has reduced since 1994, inequality has worsened since the end of apartheid (World Bank, 2018). Environmental stress is increasing and numerous challenges exist in meeting the SDGs (Cole, Bailey, & New, 2014; Lyon et al., 2017).

The case study context: The Waterberg Biosphere Reserve

The WBR is one of the six biosphere reserves in SA and is only one of the two savanna biospheres in the world, the other being in Tanzania (UNESCO, 2013). It was officially designated by UNESCO in March 2001. The designation is underpinned by a number of unique features. The WBR is a large, contiguous environment of around 10,000 sq. km. with a wilderness quality, in close proximity to SA's economic heartland of Gauteng. The lack of any significant mining, industries or forestry has allowed the natural environment of the area to remain largely intact. Historically, there has been a low population density, but one rich in cultural assets. There is only one town in the area – Vaalwater, one hamlet (Alma) and some 30 rural settlements on the periphery. It has a rich and diverse archaeological heritage. It is home to a critically important water catchment area in a largely water scarce province.

For many in rural SA, life has not changed significantly since apartheid ended. Numerous problems still exist in rural areas. In Limpopo Province, for instance, this includes high unemployment rates, poor education, lack of opportunity, poor infrastructure and service provision, and regional and local governments which have capacity, funding and management problems (LEDET, 2009). Corruption and maladministration issues are also documented (see Auditor General of South Africa, 2011), with money diverted away from socio-economic and environmental projects.

The diverse flora (two thousand plant species), fauna (bird, butterflies, insects and reptiles) and the topography are the main drivers for tourism in the district. Estimates suggest game farms account for nearly 80% of current land use with agriculture around 17% (Boonzaaier & Baber, 2011, p. 155). Major landowners in the WBR, Game Reserve 1 and 2, own 35,000 and 36,000 hectares, respectively. The majority of game farms, however, are relatively small, with over 60% being under 5000 ha. Employment levels in agriculture and tourism are estimated to be at similar levels, employing just over 2000 people. Tourism-related jobs are generally more highly skilled and remunerated. The population is around 100,000 in the WBR. Employment in both these sectors, combined with the limited number of service sector jobs in Vaalwater, are inadequate to support the workforce of the Leseding Township, let alone the other rural settlements in the Waterberg (Boonzaaier & Baber, 2011).

Formal recognition as a biosphere brings with it a number of advantages to the country and local area. These include: significant increases in land value; increased job creation; local involvement in planning and management of biodiversity and private sector involvement in conservation, health, research and education (Live Diverse, 2007). However, there are also a number of particular challenges in the WBR including: the control of development in residential estates; getting government to move past the rhetoric of sustainability to concrete spatial development frameworks; development planning; and the land claims process (Lyon et al., 2017). Land claimants particularly present a challenge in terms of how they use their newly acquired land. Land claimants are groups of individuals/families who had land restored to them through the 1994 Restitution of Land Rights Act. This Act sought to rectify the land conquest of the white population. This started after European colonization in 1652 and was institutionalized by apartheid, resulting in 3.5 million people being forcibly removed from their homes to the Bantustan homelands (Walker, 2008). Land claimants now control large areas of conservation land, although often without land management experience (Waterberg Biosphere Reserve, 2013).

Methods

Research design

The aim of this paper is to demonstrate how CDA, an under-utilised methodological approach, can be used to critically question the dominant, hegemonic discourses surrounding SD and STD in the WBR, SA. This paper examines how tourism development has an effect on three SDGs which have specific relevance to tourism development in the WBR. The UN SDGs play a major part in the SD agenda. Specifically, discourses surrounding SDG 4 (quality education), SDG 8 (decent work and economic growth) and SDG 15 (life on land) are examined.

Despite the criticisms levelled at case studies, particularly the issues of bias, rigour and objectivity (Yin, 2003), adoption of this approach can be justified when an in-depth understanding of a unique phenomenon is required (Ellinger, Watkins, & Marsick, 2005). The WBR has been recognised by UNESCO as a unique area. The case study was built by multiple researchers, in three phases, over a four year period. One researcher led the development of the work, making site visits to collect data. Another acted in a secondary role. The process was also cross-checked by peer researchers who independently reviewed the data collected and emergent themes.

Phase one included thematic analysis of an in-depth literature review followed by a scoping visit to WBR to undertake pilot interviews. Reference to three SDGs (4, 8 and 15) emerge from this initial dataset and are integral to the phase two dataset too. Phase two, the main data collection stage, involved an extended stay in the WBR with data collected via 35 semi-structured interviews and participant observation. Phase three involved a final return to the WBR to complete the remaining interviews designed to follow-up any emerging themes dominant within stages one and two.

Sample

Case studies incorporate the idea that the researcher deals with several stakeholders each with perceptions, interpretations, arguments, explanations and prejudices (Ellinger et al., 2005). Consequently, sample selection was complex. The work of Grimble and Wellard (1997, p. 176) added direction: "the most fundamental division between stakeholders is likely to be between those who *affect* (determine) a decision or action, and those *affected* by this decision or action (whether positively or negatively); these groups may be termed *active* and *passive* stakeholders".

Active stakeholders within the WBR area were targeted on the premise that if they can actively affect sustainability concerns in the WBR, then gaining an understanding of how they see development can help to gain an understanding of the tourism development process. Semi-structured interviews were completed with representatives of multiple stakeholder groups including: public sector (PS) ($n = 7$), accommodation providers (AC) ($n = 13$), other tourism-related businesses (BS) ($n = 5$), civil society individuals or representatives (CS) ($n = 8$) and land claimants (LC) ($n = 2$). The criteria for inclusion in the study was linked to their ability to influence economic, social and environmental issues within the WBR. This implies some position of power either through business ownership, land ownership, ability to affect planning decisions and/or influence over community development. Of the 35 people interviewed, 9 were black SA and 26 were white SA (17 SA nationals and 9 from overseas). Tourists were not interviewed as they cannot directly affect tourism development in the region.

The interviews were semi-structured, designed to take account of the guidance by King and Horrocks (2010). They were what Alvesson (2003) calls "localist" in nature, whereby the interview produces a situated account, drawing upon cultural resources in order to produce morally adequate descriptions. All were face-to-face, the most convenient location as selected by the respondent. To settle respondents into the study, initial contextual questions were addressed. These included: can you tell me a little bit about yourself and what you do here in the Waterberg? What does the Waterberg mean to you? What adjectives would you use to describe the Waterberg? When you hear the words sustainable development or sustainability, do they mean anything to you? Once settled, questions probed three core themes; development and sustainable development, tourism development and the WBR. These themes correlate with the three SDGs identified previously. Example questions include: What do you see as the main development concerns in the area? What do you understand about the biosphere (links to SDG 4)? How has tourism development affected the economy for different groups in the WBR (links to SDG 8)? How do you perceive the biosphere (links to SDG 15)?

Ethical clearance for the research was given after scrutiny at a university research ethics committee and ethical protocols were followed throughout the research process. Interviews lasted between 30 and 75 minutes and were all digitally recorded, transcribed verbatim and analysed using CDA.

Data analysis

As CDA involves an analysis of the coherence and cohesion of text (discourses), producing verbatim transcripts is a necessary first step in the analytical process. Data were subsequently transferred to the NVivo software package. In excess of 100,000 words of data were generated. In order to examine the discourses of STD in the WBR, a post-structural Foucauldian analysis, consistent with the staged approach explained by Wodak and Meyer (2009) was used. The first stage involved stakeholder mapping and profiling by status, stakeholder group, socio-cultural, racial and other relevant information. Next, an analysis of whether the stakeholders are seen as active or passive in STD in the WBR was undertaken and finally, the discourses of the stakeholders were examined. As Foucault argues, it is who controls not only the discourse of development, but also the associated actions that determine outcomes (Foucault, 1980). Complementing Foucauldian thinking, for post-structuralists, there is a relationship between knowledge, power and discourse (Fletcher, 2000). This leads to outcomes or material realities, in this case the biosphere reserve.

In CDA the text needs to be examined as a whole and the discourse strands and sub-strands identified. This examination was undertaken, independently, by three researchers. Two of these researchers were directly attached to the project. The third was an independent peer researcher. Discourse strands are "flows of discourse that centre on a common topic (…) and are conceived of at the level of concrete utterances" (Wodak & Meyer, 2009, p. 46). Within NVivo, and using a thematic analysis, the discourses were grouped into a number of broad thematic areas linked to the macro and micro contexts and consequently coded (e.g. development paradigms, SD, tourism and development, power and STD). The sub-strands under each strand were then identified and coded using the same technique, i.e. a more granular thematic analysis occurred to identify a greater level of depth (e.g. identity, culture and development, appropriate/inappropriate tourism, individuals and power).

The entanglements of discourse strands were also identified. This is where one strand refers to a number of inter-related topics. For example, when discussing the Waterberg as a place, notions of development including politics, economics or the environment may also be referred to. Still looking at the text as a whole, Huckin (1997) recommends, examining the perspective that is being presented. This involves angles, slants, or points of view and is called "framing." For example, how one section of society sees other sections can be seen as a "frame". Discourse positions are also examined. These describe the ideological position from which subjects participate in and encompass their worldviews (Wodak & Meyer, 2009). This involves discourse positions on the environment, economics and development. For example, the neoliberal view of economics is a discourse position, as is a radical view of environmentalism.

Having examined discourse strands, frames and discourse positions, the next stage is to examine the more minute levels of analysis: sentence, phrases, and words. There are numerous CDA techniques to facilitate this level of analysis (see Gee, 2011) including: topicalization; connotation; modality; intertextuality; lexical analysis; semantic contrast and identity and ideology construction through pronoun use.

Topicalization refers to the framing of a sentence and is essentially what the discourse is referring to. It can also involve omission and what is not being said. Insinuations can carry double meanings and again can lead to power in discourse as it involves the ability to deny any intention to mislead. Connotations can be assigned on the basis of the cultural knowledge of the respondents and can be associated with one word, or through metaphors and figures of speech.

Modality refers to what should or ought to be done and again involves connotations of power, ideology and knowledge. The tone of the text is set with the use of specific words to convey the degree of certainty and authority (called modality). Intertextuality refers to the way a text relies on previous texts for its form and reference points (Bloor & Bloor, 2007). For example, discourse on biospheres may refer to texts from the UN or the WCED as they involve SD. A lexical analysis refers to the actual words used and uncovers not only the subject of the discourse, but also the intended meaning. Related to this is semantic contrast. When analysing discourses, speakers use semantic contrast to distinguish between different propositions or concepts, for example, rich/poor, black/white, etc. (van Dijk, 1985). The use of pronouns involves the construction of identity and ideology (Bloor & Bloor, 2007). How individuals refer to themselves, and to others, through pronouns can identify social groupings and distinct views of "the Other".

Context is also an essential component of CDA as it helps to uncover not just what is said, but how and why discourses emerge. This is where the background of not only those being researched is important, but that of the researcher. For example, when analysing the discourses, who is speaking is relevant, their background, race, education, etc. This was taken into account in the analysis and is relevant to the results outlined below. Discourses always involves power and ideologies, and are connected to the past and the current context. They can be interpreted differently because they have different backgrounds and thus positionality and reflexivity of the researcher are important (Thomas, 2009).

As Visser (2000) notes, western academics, when undertaking research in SA, need to do so with respect to cultural, economic, social, racial and gender sensibilities. This was pivotal to

Table 2. Profile of respondents.

Category	Black SA National	White SA National	White SA Overseas
Public Sector (PS)	1, 2, 3, 5, 6	4	7
Accommodation Provider (AC)	N/A	2, 4, 6, 7, 8, 10, 11, 12, 13	1, 3, 5, 9
Tourism Related Business (BS)	N/A	2, 3, 4, 5	1
Civil Society (CS)	4, 8	2, 3, 7	1, 5, 6
Land Claimants (LC)	1, 2	N/A	N/A
Total	9	17	9

Source: Primary data.

framing the reflexive approach applied in this study. Careful consideration of the researcher' biases and values was explored at all stages of the research process. In turn, this influenced how the project was designed, which questions were asked to whom and why. As with all social constructionist approaches, it was recognised that the "correct" interpretation does not exist, whereas a more, or less, plausible or adequate interpretation is likely (Fairclough, 1989).

Validity is also imperative in qualitative research. Whittemore, Chase, and Mandle (2001) identify numerous cross-checking techniques for demonstrating validity. The ones which are relevant to this study include: developing a self-conscious research design sampling decisions (i.e. sampling adequacy); articulating data collection decisions; demonstrating prolonged engagement; providing verbatim transcription; exploring rival explanations; performing a literature review; reflexive journaling; providing evidence that support interpretations; acknowledging the researcher perspective; and providing thick descriptions. Decisions and actions linked to each technique were embedded throughout the research process. Validity was "crystallized" through the inclusion of multiple data sources and the input of an independent peer researcher who assisted in validating the emergent discourse themes.

Results

The primary focus of this section is to exemplify the application of CDA techniques, by using the context of SD and STD discourses associated with the WBR as a means of illustration. Consequently, the material and quotations included in this section are selected on the grounds that they are illustrative of the dominant discourses emerging. For ease of reference, they are linked to a primary SDG in each instance. Seldom in reality do they relate to only one SDG. Table 2 provides the key to respondents

SDG 15: Life on land

SDG 15 is intent upon protecting natural habitats and biodiversity. This is particularly important to the WBR as it is the flora, fauna and topography which are the main drivers for tourism in the region. In interpreting responses linked to this SDG, it is important to acknowledge that land is particularly contested in this region, both in terms of ownership and also meanings associated with it. According to Koch (1997), during apartheid, conservation and land use systems significantly favoured the white ruling minority, with the protectionist attitudes to wildlife reflecting the country's political economy. Black Africans associated conservation with loss of land, forced labour and poll taxes. Seldom were any of the benefits derived from tourism in the area, be it linked to game reserves or casino developments, enjoyed within the wider community (Boonzaaier, 2012).

Interviewees were all asked as to how they perceived the WBR. Their responses have a strong environmental discourse and sense of place, habitat protection an integral part of emergent discourses:

> I've seen some really pretty places, and more pretty than the Waterberg, but there's a rugged beauty about here, there's a kind of a, superficially you know, you get this sense of time having, I don't know, being here, it's been a hell of a process of evolution to get it to where it is, and it's got that written into its stone if you like.
> (AC9)

While framing is one useful CDA tool, modality is another. On examining the language of the respondents, it can be seen that modality is more prevalent in the discourses of those who have direct influence in STD in the WBR. This emphasises the relationship between language and power, which is also an aspect of modality (Winter & Gärdenfors, 1995). For example, the public sector respondents use modality in their discourses:

> As well as being a planner, I am also an environmentalist. As an environmentalist **we must** preserve the natural environment and we **must** protect flora and fauna. If we lose those things as a district then we will not attract tourists to the region. We **must** protect the environment within this district.
> (PS2)

From a CDA perspective, the use of the pronoun "we" in the quote above is insightful. It is not clear from the context of who the "we" refers to. It could be the wider community, environmentalists or the municipal government for who he works, but there is a sense of community and a recognition of the link between the environment and tourism which has long been recognised in the wider literature (Hall & Page, 2000). As Kerstetter and Bricker (2009) argue, sustainability concerns are embedded in a sense of place when the natural environment plays a central part in how the residents identify with a destination. This identity emerges over time:

> Especially after the World Summit on Sustainable Development, I think this sustainability word it somehow became a buzzword (...), there might be conservation, but also conservation of natural resources **must not be closed off** from the fact that there are people who **must benefit** from the same resources (...). Of course when we do that we **must take note of** the fact **we need to be very responsible** in our behaviour in terms of utilising what we have now, so that which remains can still be utilised by the people after us.
> (PS3)

There is a distinct framing at the start of his dialogue, relating the concept of sustainability to the Rio summit on SD (WCED, 1987). This denotes a level of knowledge relating to sustainable development, the origins of the concept and a link to poverty reduction and greater social equity. This knowledge is also evidenced from modality in the discourse (in bold). While not stating specifically the subject in this discourse, there is an inference that it is the black, majority who have not had (economic) benefit from resource access. The "natural resources" is an all-encompassing term, however, it has land-ownership connotations and that it is those with the land who have received the "benefits" at the expense of those who have not. There are economic undertones to the discourse, dictating the nature of life on land.

SDG 8: Decent work and economic growth

The aspirations of SDG 8 are to achieve full and productive employment, and decent work, for all women and men by 2030. As a growth industry, widely acknowledged as labour intensive and entrepreneurial, on the surface, tourism has the capacity to realise this goal. Game reserves, hotels, food and beverage outlets and transport operators all require managers, operational staff, staff with expertise in people, money and communications to succeed. The spectrum of job opportunities, at different career levels, suitable for women and men is considerable. However, the legacy of apartheid has left numerous challenges to overcome in achieving this. These include a poorly skilled labour force, a lack of training and development opportunities, a lack of small-medium sized business opportunities and a lack of community involvement in the value chain (LEDET, 2009).

CDA corroborates this in unravelling discourses which question whether this SDG is even aspirational in the WBR. There is little evidence of participatory planning, called for within the Brundtland Report (WCED, 1987), involving those from disadvantaged communities. The poor are seen as being the recipients of development and not part of the process, a shortfall common to various development approaches, particularly modernisation and neo-colonialism (Long, 2001). While the biosphere is one aspect of participation within the region, the discourses of the active stakeholders point to there being a number of community-related problems that affect more active community participation. Cooperation is seen as problematic with the contextual issues relating to the divisions across SA society a cause of this:

> There is a **divide** between the Afrikaans community, the African community and the English community. Apartheid is still very much in existence, obviously not a legislation any more, but certainly there is a **massive divide**. This is something that one notices and there is **no integration** as such.
> (CS3)

In a lexical analysis of the above text, the words relating to societal divisions are highlighted in bold, showing that obtaining cooperation is problematic due to the historical, political and societal legacies of apartheid. The vestiges of apartheid, have not only left predominantly divided communities, but entrenched views of "the Other" that are difficult to break down, and evident in other discourses too (see for instance AC3; AC7).

If SA and its various regions are to move down a SD pathway, then the legacy of apartheid needs to be addressed. In relation to one aspect of equity, without empowerment, tourism development at the community level has little hope of moving down a sustainable pathway (Sofield, 2003). Empowerment emerges as a particular discourse for a number of respondents (BS4; CS3; CS4; LC1). This resonates with the findings of Berkes (2004) that empowerment is seen by the rural poor as part of equitable development. For example, the owner of one NGO states:

> I see an **impotence**, an **impotent group of people** and I look at apartheid and I see what they have created is that one is **used to hand-outs,** one is **used to being disempowered** and one is used to saying because I need to do this. And one has to say no, because, you have to teach these people how, not to give them hand-outs … that's what sustainability is about.
> (CS3)

The discourse frames the negative aspects associated with a lack of empowerment and for this NGO owner, changing attitudes is part of the empowerment process. There is also a power element to this as empowerment only comes from being taught and it is a white, wealthy, educated NGO owner who is doing this.

Community divisions are accentuated by land ownership problems. Even though some land has gone back to black Africans through the land reclamations process, access to land is not enough to generate decent work and economic benefits as the land claimants testify:

> We cannot do anything, because even now when they give the land to people they don't give the development grant or the skills to develop the land. How are the investors going to invest in the land while we don't have the skills to develop?
> (LC2)

Other resources such as knowledge, business skills and access to capital are required to make a living from the land, particularly in the Waterberg region where there are limited land-use options. The above reaffirms earlier research regarding the land reclamation process, particularly a lack of support for claimants and exclusion and marginality of the poor not being addressed in rural areas (Walker, 2008). This illustrates the need to inter-connect SDGs too. Even where environmental resources are in place, this does not lead to an automatic solution to sustainable development. If anything, returning land to communities has led to a more disenfranchised community as they realise the extent to which marginalisation, and a lack of voice, power and influence exists.

SDG 4: Quality education

SDG 4 seeks to enhance quality of life through a more inclusive educational offering which better equips local communities to contribute to developmental solutions. Considering experiences elsewhere, there are multiple ways Tourism might reasonably facilitate a more inclusive educational offering in the WBR. Formal training and development programmes attached to working in the Tourism Industry can enable a local population to enhance their education and skillsets. This might be achieved through studying in an educational setting, completing qualifications, or engaging in company development programmes, for instance. Informal interaction with tourists can broaden the mind and horizons of the local population, not just vice versa as more commonly appreciated. Yet equally, simply developing a Tourism Industry does not automatically mean that a more inclusive educational offering will emerge. Exclusivity is often an unpalatable consequence of Tourism which must not be overlooked. The discourses of the accommodation providers show that while there are some enlightened employers who do develop staff, and recognise formal and informal training, the extent to which this is available to large numbers of the population in the area who are in need of education is limited.

Interestingly, exploring the multiple discourses linked to SDG 4 exposes the theme of skills deficits eluded to in SDG 8 discourses too. Such again echoes the earlier work of Bond (2004) who argues that new land owners in SA do not have the knowledge, skills or finance to develop the land. Both sets of land claimants recognised this (LC1; L2). The land claimants are in sharp contrast to those who could express much greater understanding of the biosphere. For example, two of the interviewees who communicated a high level of understanding had PhDs (AC3, CS6), at least another three were educated to Masters Level (AC2, AC12, CS7) and the rest either to degree level or they had many years of experience in their relative careers (PS3, AC8, CS1, CS2). Those with previous opportunities often expressed an embarrassment in not knowing more as they are either business owners, landowners, long-term residents, in the accommodation industry or a combination of all of these (negative lexical terms in bold):

> Unfortunately, it [the biosphere] **doesn't mean enough to me**. I **don't truly understand** what the biosphere is doing and I should, I am one of those people who really should know what's going on. (AC1)

As active stakeholders in STD, these individuals have the ability to affect decisions regarding the sustainability of the tourism industry in the WBR. The biosphere is meant to be one way of implementing SD/STD, however, a lack of knowledge of the concept challenges the likely realisation of SDGs. As knowledge levels of the biosphere are often limited from those not directly involved in the biosphere, the concept can evoke emotive discourses:

> There's still quite a jaundiced opinion about what is this biosphere actually doing?
>
> *Is that a common opinion?*
>
> Certainly in the white community. Certainly in the white community it is and probably in the black community there is a lot of ignorance about it, a lot of people won't even know that there is a biosphere. (AC2)

The power position is that the black community are ignorant and the whites have an opinion, albeit a negative one. The concerns over the power regarding the biosphere relates to how individuals buy into the concept of the biosphere:

> This community has **never worked well together** and I don't know why that is but it will happen, it will come eventually but I think people in this, they're also very **wary to stick their necks out** to be the one that **caused the change** because it's a small community, people talk, it's a very small town so you don't want to upset people too much but then again **people are getting upset** so *(laughs)*. (AC11)

The discourse highlights the issues or concerns with trying to affect change (negative lexical aspects of discourse in bold) and how buy-in is problematic. There is a connotation that all is not well with the management of the biosphere. Here, the notion of buying into the biosphere concept is a prominent discourse as it is from a number of those interviewed (PS3; CS2; CS4; CS6; CS7; AC2; AC5; AC8; AC11; AC12; AC13). Without knowledge, information, communication, and communities and individuals working together, the problems of buying into the concept will continue to be jeopardized and any appetite for SD will inevitably remain compromised. Building relationships across a racially divided community is pivotal to moving forward. Inclusivity through information dissemination and learning processes offers mechanisms for realizing this.

Conclusions

This paper has taken a critical approach to examining discourses of SD and STD in the WBR, SA. Adopting CDA, an under-utilized methodological approach, has helped to unravel the dominant, hegemonic discourses in the region.

CDA involves not only what is said, but what is not stated in discourses (Wetherall, Taylor & Yates, 2001). Discourses emergent in this study resonate with the dominant modernisation and neoliberal paradigms, however, dependency and post-colonial discourses are also evident. The poor are positioned as in need of development and empowerment through a post-colonial, apartheid influenced discourse of contrast between whites and blacks. Those in power use mechanisms to perpetuate the socio-economic status quo. Seemingly altruistic motives of powerful stakeholders are more about preserving a way of life and protecting/enhancing land values than wider SD concerns. The poor are positioned as not being involved in determining their own future, and discourses pertaining to communicating with them to find out their needs were absent from the stakeholder discourses. Their discourses are silenced and this invokes the notion put forward by Spivak (1985), that the subaltern has no voice.

Discourses are underpinned by ideological beliefs and affect how "the Other" is positioned. The dominant, Western, neoliberal view of development predominates in the WBR and this has effects on the discourses of SD. Emergent discourses point to a very weak position of sustainability with an approach that has much to do with mild reform, business as usual. Environmental concerns and a conservation discourse do emerge, but they are couched in neoliberal terms. Participation in development and SD is limited which invokes both issues of group and individual power. Social objectives are couched more in economic terms and, although upliftment, empowerment and social mobility are present in the discourses, they are not prominent. Social cohesion as an objective is mentioned. But, conflicts, racial positioning, ideological beliefs and the historical context of apartheid all mitigate against this in either the short or medium terms.

This illustrates the power of discourse and what discourse can do. It can create material realities such as biospheres which have distinct (and in this case) neoliberal approaches to development. Yet, discourses are not value-free and this is where applying CDA to the data offers a contribution to the literature. Exploring not only what people say is important, but where discourses emanate from and the ideological background behind them is important to consider too. For example, the discourses of SD stem from a specific version of the concept as espoused by the UN and the increasing neoliberalization of the concept. This work therefore has implications for how SD/STD is conceptualised. That SD/STD are contestable concepts are prevalent in the literature (Bek, Binns, & Nel, 2004; Butler, 1999; Higgins-Desbiolles, 2018; Liu, 2003). The literature also points to very weak positions of sustainability being adopted and with the dominant neoliberal economic paradigm dictating development concerns. These findings are consistent with those in this case study, where despite the emergence of a strong conservation discourse from all sectors, the environment is couched mainly as an economic resource. Alternative discourses are therefore overshadowed and there is a perpetuation of business as usual for those holding the power and knowledge.

There are a number of policy implications which result from this work. If tourism in SA is to move down a more sustainable pathway, then tourism needs to be not only an economic driver, but a social and environmental one. Arguments have long been presented to substantiate the value of such an orientation (see for instance Higgins-Desbiolles, 2006). The wider aspects of SD, aligned to SDGs relating to basic needs, poverty reduction and new social paradigms for sustainable living, need to be incorporated into development planning. Business as usual will yield limited results. Instead, more radical change is needed if SDGs are to be realised and the wider elements of SD are to occur.

Tourism has the capacity to realise more radical change, but there remains some way to go here. For instance, whilst the study has shown SDG 15, protecting natural habitats and biodiversity, to be integral to the development of a tourism offering, work is needed to tackle the legacy of apartheid which will inevitably raise community questions over whether all will benefit from this protective activity when historically only the white minority did. Similarly, pursuing a tourism strategy has the capacity to realise SDG 8, decent work and economic security, but only if planned activity is able to accommodate deficiencies in the skillset and training of the existing workforce, whilst also opening doors to new enterprises and giving communities a voice in developments. What is particularly interesting in the WBR is that even where quality education has been realised (SDG 4), and educational attainment has been achieved, this has not necessarily resulted in anything meaningful from a Tourism Industry, economic development, or individual perspective. Tracking whether widening educational opportunities to a previously excluded black population changes this presents an important opportunity for further research. Such would add to our understanding of the contribution of educational attainment to tourism economic development along with the capacity of tourism economic development to facilitate educational attainment.

SA has come a long way since Mandela was released in 1990, however, the tourism industry is still predominantly a white-controlled industry from both demand and supply perspectives. This work has shown that greater attention to involve the black population in tourism is required and that they need to be positioned as equals in the development discourse. In the short-term, this is problematic due to issues with land reform and distinct racial positioning, however, other economic sectors have achieved this to some extent and policy-makers need to recognise this and build on what has been achieved in other areas. Framing strategies around the pursuit of SDGs offers a clear route forward.

Biospheres are ways of attempting to move places down a pathway of SD. Consequently, this case study, and the approach adopted is of relevance in other parts of the world, particularly in developing countries where many of the poor have unsustainable lives and poverty reduction is inextricably linked to environmental sustainability (WCED, 1987). Tourism is used as an economic development option in many protected areas, but as knowledge grows on how to manage tourism from both social and environmental perspectives, then how to move down a more sustainable pathway can be better understood. This work has shown that in one biosphere reserve in SA, there are strong environmental discourses and these have resulted in material realities such as biosphere reserves, management plans and spatial development frameworks. Understanding how discourses function in society can be used by policy makers or other interested parties who wish to create or develop biosphere reserves or other protected areas. Making greater use of methodological approaches such as CDA, will enable a wider appreciation of how tourism can contribute to SD to be realised.

Kuhn (2007) states that sustainable tourism should be treated more as an aspiring, evolving discourse, rather than something which is static and achievable. CDA has enabled this paper to take a Kuhn's approach, examining not only the actual discourses, but from where they emanate, the ideologies that support them and the knowledge that underpins them. Consistent with the earlier work of Boluk (2011a, p. 204), it has allowed an in-depth analysis of sustainable discourses in a complex community, and helped to " ... elucidate some contradictions inherent in informants' discourses" in the process. It is a methodology which has its critics (see, for instance Widdowson, 1995). Common concerns include that it is a methodology which is framed and filtered within the researcher's purview. It does not attempt objectivity, but rather is dependent upon the transparency and reflexivity of the researcher applying it. Consequently, researcher bias and positioning needs to be a central consideration in any associated research design process.

Nevertheless, this approach is transferable to a variety of development contexts and has implications for how SD/STD are put into practice. It could be applied to better understand discourses attached to different kinds of stakeholders. The voices of the poor were not part of this study, except for how they were viewed by those interviewed. The poor are therefore framed in certain ways and further research could seek to directly uncover the discourses of this group regarding development concerns and tourism in the WBR. Applying CDA to such data would be important in better understanding not only the WBR, but also in widening our appreciation of SD/STD discourses, whilst giving a voice to those so often overlooked in research.

Disclosure statement

No potential conflict of interest was reported by the authors.

References

Alvesson, M. (2003). Beyond neopositivists, romantics and localists: A reflexive approach to interviews in organizational research. *Academy of Management Review, 28*,13–33.

Auditor General of South Africa. (2011). *General report on national audit outcomes 2010–2011*. Pretoria, South Africa: South African Government.

Bakhtin, B. (1986). *Scientific realism and human emancipation*. London: Verso.

Bek, D., Binns, T., & Nel, E. (2004). 'Catching the development train': Perspectives on 'top-down' and 'bottom-up' development in post-apartheid South Africa. *Progress in Development Studies, 4*,22–46. doi:10.1191/1464993404ps047oa

Berkes, F. (2004). Rethinking community-based conservation. *Conservation Biology, 18*,621–630. doi:10.1111/j.1523-1739.2004.00077.x

Blommaert, J. (2005). *Discourse: A critical introduction*. Cambridge: Cambridge University Press.

Bloor, M., & Bloor, T. (2007). *The practice of critical discourse analysis*. London: Hodder Arnold.

Boluk, K. (2011a). Revealing the discourses: White entrepreneurial motivation in black South Africa. *Tourism Planning and Development, 8*,199–213. doi:10.1080/21568316.2011.573922

Boluk, K. (2011b). Fair Trade Tourism South Africa: Consumer virtue or moral selving? *Journal of Ecotourism, 10*,235–249. doi:10.1080/14724049.2011.617451

Bond, I. (2004). Private land contribution to conservation in South Africa. In Child, B. (Ed.), *Parks in transition: Biodiversity, rural development and the bottom line* (pp.29–62). London: Earthscan.

Boonzaaier, W., & Baber, R. (2011). *Waterberg Biosphere Reserve: Management plan report*. Rustenberg, South Africa: Contour Project Managers CC.

Boonzaaier, C. (2012). Towards a community-based integrated institutional framework for ecotourism management: The case of the Masebe nature reserve, Limpopo province of South Africa. *Journal of Anthropology, 2012*,1. 2012, 20/10/2012

Booysen, S. (2007). With the ballot paper and the brick: The politics of attaining service delivery. *Progress in Development Studies, 7,*21–32. doi:10.1177/146499340600700103

Butler, R. (1999). Sustainable tourism: A state of the art review. *Tourism Geographies, 1,*7–25. doi:10.1080/14616689908721291

Cole, M. J., Bailey, R. M., & New, M. G. (2014). Tracking sustainable development with a national barometer for South Africa using a downscaled "safe and just space" framework. *Proceedings of the National Academy of Sciences, 111,*E4399–E4408. doi:10.1073/pnas.1400985111

Crush, J. (1995). *The power of development.* London: Routledge.

Cummings, S., Regeer, B., de Haan, L., Zweekhorst, M., & Bunders, J. (2018). Critical discourse analysis of perspectives on knowledge and the knowledge society within the Sustainable Development Goals. *Development Policy Review,* Accepted Author Manuscript. 36, 727–742. doi:10.1111/dpr.12296

Derrida, J., Butler, J., & Spivak, G. C. (2016). *Of grammatology.* Baltimore, Maryland: John Hopkins University Press.

Ellinger, A., Watkins, K., & Marsick, V. (2005). *Case study research methods.* San Francisco, CA: Berrett-Koehler Publishing.

Emirbayer, M., & Goodwin, J. (1994). Network analysis, culture, and the problem of agency. *American Journal of Sociology, 99,*1411–1454. doi:10.1086/230450

Fairclough, N. (1989). *Language and power.* Harlow: Pearson.

Fairclough, N., & Wodak, R. (1997). Critical discourse analysis. In van Dijk, T. (Ed.), *Discourse as social interaction* (pp.258–285). London: Sage.

Fletcher, J. (2000). *Disappearing act: Gender, power and relational practice at work.* Boston, MA: MIT Press.

Foucault, M. (1972). *The archaeology of knowledge.* London: Routledge.

Foucault, M. (1980). *Power/knowledge: Selected interviews and other writings 1972–1977.* London: Harvester Press.

Gee, P. (2011). *How to do discourse analysis: A toolkit.* Abingdon: Routledge.

Grimble, R., & Wellard, K. (1997). Stakeholder methodologies in natural resource management: A review of principles, contexts, experiences and opportunities. *Agricultural Systems, 55,*173–193. doi:10.1016/S0308-521X(97)00006-1

Grimwood, B. S. R., Yudin, O., Muldoon, M., & Qiu, J. (2015). Responsibility in Tourism: A discursive analysis. *Annals of Tourism Research, 50,*22–38. doi:10.1016/j.annals.2014.10.006

Habermas, J. (1971). Knowledge and human interests: A general perspective. In Shapiro, J. (Ed.), *Knowledge and human interests* (pp.301–317). Boston, MA: Beacon Press.

Hall, C. M. (2000). *Tourism planning: Policies, processes and relationships.* Harlow: Prentice Hall

Hall, C. M., & Page, S. (2000). *The geography of tourism and recreation.* London: Routledge.

Higgins-Desbiolles, F. (2006). More than an 'industry'. The forgotten capacities of tourism as a social force. *Tourism Management, 27,*1192–1208. doi:10.1016/j.tourman.2005.05.020

Higgins-Desbiolles, F. (2018). Sustainable tourism: Sustaining tourism or something more? *Tourism Management Perspectives, 5,* 157–160. https://doi.org/10.1016/j.tmp.2017.11.017

Hopwood, B., Mellor, M., & O'Brien, G. (2005). Sustainable development: mapping different approaches. *Sustainable Development, 13*(1),38–52. doi:10.1002/sd.244

Huckin, T. (1997). Critical discourse analysis. In T. Miller (Ed.), *Functional approaches to written text* (pp.79–92). Washington DC: US Department of State.

IISD (International Institute for Sustainable Development) (2004). *Analysis of national strategies for sustainable development: South Africa.* Ottawa, Canada: International Institute for Sustainable Development.

Kerstetter, D., & Bricker, K. (2009). Exploring Fijian's sense of place after exposure to tourism development. *Journal of Sustainable Tourism, 17,*691–708. doi:10.1080/09669580902999196

King, C., & Horrocks, N. (2010). *Interviews in qualitative research.* London: Sage.

Koch, E. (1997). Ecotourism and rural reconstruction in South Africa: Reality or rhetoric? In Ghimire, K., Ghimire, K., & Pimbert, M. (Eds.), *Social change and conservation* (pp.214–238). London: Earthscan.

Kuhn, L. (2007). Sustainable tourism as emergent discourse. *World Futures, 63,*286–297. doi:10.1080/02604020601174950

LEDET (Limpopo Department of Economic Development, Environment and Tourism). (2009). *Annual report 2008/2009.* Polokwane, South Africa: Limpopo Department of Economic Development, Environment and Tourism. Retreived from http://www.ledet.gov.za/docs/reports/Annual%20Report%2008-09.pdf:

Liu, Z. (2003). Sustainable tourism development: A critique. *Journal of Sustainable Tourism, 11,*459–476. doi:10.1080/09669580308667216

Live Diverse. (2007). *Sustainable livelihoods and biodiversity in developing countries.* South Africa: Live Diverse.

Long, C. (2001). *Participation of the poor in development initiatives: Taking their rightful place.* London: Earthscan.

Lyon, A., Hunter-Jones, P., & Warnaby, G. (2017). Are we any closer to sustainable development? Listening to active stakeholder discourses of tourism development in the Waterberg Biosphere Reserve, South Africa. *Tourism Management, 61,*234–247. doi:10.1016/j.tourman.2017.01.010

Mayr, A. (2008). *Language and power: an introduction to institutional discourse.* London: Continuum.

McDonald, D. (2002). What is environmental justice? In. McDonald, D. (Ed.), *Environmental justice in South Africa* (pp.1–48). Cape Town, South Africa: University of Cape Town Press.

Neves, D., & Du Toit, A. (2013). Rural livelihoods in South Africa: Complexity, vulnerability and differentiation. *Journal of Agrarian Change, 13,*93–115. doi:10.1111/joac.12009

Patel, Z. (2009). Environmental justice in South Africa: Tools and trade-offs. *Social Dynamics, 35,*94–110. doi:10.1080/02533950802666956

Patel, L., & Graham, L. (2012). How broad-based is broad-based black economic empowerment?. *Development Southern Africa, 9),*193–207. doi:10.1080/0376835X.2012.675692

Semali, L., & Kincheloe, J. (1999). *What is indigenous knowledge? Voices from the academy.* New York: Falmer Press.

Sillitoe, P., Dixon, P., & Barr, J. (2005). *Indigenous knowledge inquiries: A methodologies manual for development.* London: ITDG.

Sofield, T. (2003). *Empowerment for sustainable tourism development.* Oxford: Elsevier.

Spivak, G. (1985). Can the subaltern speak? Speculations on widow-sacrifice. *Wedge, 7/8,*120–130.

Swanborn, P. (2010). *Case study research: What, why and how?* London: Sage.

Taylor, W., Holt-Biddle, D., & Walker, C. (2003). *The Waterberg: The natural splendours and the people.* Cape Town, South Africa: Struik.

Tepelus, C. (2008). Reviewing the IYE and WSSD processes and impacts on the tourism sustainability agenda. *Journal of Ecotourism, 7,*77–86. doi:10.2167/joe176.0

Thomas, G. (2009). *How to do your research project.* London: Sage.

Titscher, S., Meyer, M., Wodak, R., & Vetter, E. (2002). *Methods of text and discourse analysis.* London: Sage.

UNDP (United Nations Development Program). (2017). *International human development indicators, South Africa.* New York. Retrieved from http://hdrstats.undp.org/en/countries/profiles/ZAF.html

UN (United Nations). (2017). *Sustainable developments goals 17 goals to transform our world.* New York. Retrieved from http://www.un.org/sustainabledevelopment/sustainable-development-goals/

UNESCO (United Nations Educational, Scientific and Cultural Organisation). (2011). *UNESCO MaB biosphere reserve directory, South Africa.* Waterberg. Retrieved from http://www.unesco.org/mabdb/br/brdir/directory/biores.asp?mode=all&code=SAF + 03

UNESCO (United Nations Educational, Scientific and Cultural Organisation). (2008). *Madrid action plan for biosphere reserves (2008–2013).* Madrid, Spain: UNESCO.

UNESCO (United Nations Educational, Scientific and Cultural Organisation). (2018). *Man and biosphere program.* Retrieved from http://www.unesco.org/new/en/natural-sciences/environment/ecological-sciences/

van Dijk, T. (1985). *Handbook of discourse analysis.* London: Academic Press.

van Dijk, T. (1988). *News as discourse.* Hillside, NJ: Erlbaum.

van Dijk, T. (2001). Critical discourse analysis. In Tannen, D., Schiffrin, D., & Hamilton, D. (Eds.), *Handbook of discourse analysis* (pp.352–371). Oxford: Blackwell.

Visser, G. (2000). In other worlds. On the politics of research in a transforming South Africa. *Area, 32,*231–235. doi:10.1111/j.1475-4762.2000.tb00134.x

Walker, C. (2008). *Landmarked: Land claims and land restitution in South Africa.* Athens, OH: Ohio University Press.

Waterberg Biosphere Reserve. (2013). *Waterberg biosphere reserve.* Retrieved from http://www.Waterbergbiosphere.org/

WCED (World Commission on Environment and Development). (1987). *Our common future.* Oxford: Oxford University Press.

Wetherall, M., Taylor, S., & Yates, S. (2001). Discourse, theory and practice. London: Sage.

Whittemore, R., Chase, S., & Mandle, C. (2001). Pearls, pith and provocation: validity in qualitative research. *Qualitative Health Research, 11*(4),522–537. doi:10.1177/104973201129119299

Widdowson, H. (1995). Discourse analysis: A critical view. *Language and Literature, 4,*157–172. doi:10.1177/096394709500400301

Winter, S., & Gärdenfors, P. (1995). Linguistic modality as expressions of social power. *Nordic Journal of Linguistics, 18,*137–165. doi:10.1017/S0332586500000147

Wodak, R., & Meyer, M. (2009). Critical discourse analysis: History, agenda, theory and methodology. In R. Wodak , & M. Meyer (Eds.), *Methods of critical discourse analysis* (2nd ed., pp.1–33). London: Sage.

World Bank. (2018). *The World Bank in South Africa.* Retrieved from http://www.worldbank.org/en/country/southafrica/overview

Yin, R. (2003). *Case study research: Design and methods.* London: Sage.

Rethinking the ideology of responsible tourism

Elisa Burrai, Dorina-Maria Buda and Davina Stanford

ABSTRACT
Drawing on the critique of ideology elaborated by the Slovenian philosopher Slavoj Žižek, in this conceptual paper we rethink responsible
tourism. More specifically, in line with Žižek's argument that ideology is
closely linked to reality and not a dreamlike illusion, we reconceptualise
the ideological character of responsible tourism. This ideological character, we propose, is fundamentally rooted in real global issues, and often
inadvertently and implicitly sustains the mechanism of modern global
capitalism. Although responsible tourism has been a powerful unifier
among tourism stakeholders, we argue that its critical conceptual considerations have not yet been given sufficient robust reflection. Hence,
in this conceptual paper, we rethink responsible tourism through the
lens of ideology contributing to further knowledge about this topic. In
doing so, we analyse two key policy documents: the Cape Town (2002)
and Kerala (2008) Declarations from which the term of responsible tourism originated. Following Žižek's critique of ideology, we aspire to
shape more inclusive and effective sustainable and responsible development as advocated by the *Sustainable Development Goals* and responsible tourism stakeholders. Furthermore, the novel interjection of the
Žižekian concept of ideology to the context of responsible tourism
opens up new theoretical possibilities for critical tourism studies.

Introduction

It is easy to understand the appeal of responsible tourism which should "create better places for
people to live in and for people to visit" (Goodwin, 2011, p. x), both for the simplicity of this definition and for its valuable aspirations. Such aspirations refer to responsible tourism as a way of
improving livelihoods and maintaining, protecting, and enhancing the places within which these
livelihoods occur. As such, responsible tourism, addresses several of the United Nations
Sustainable Development Goals (SDGs), with the overall aim of ending poverty, protecting the
planet, and ensuring prosperity for all (United Nations, 2017).

In this paper, we explore, analyse, and reconceptualise responsible tourism via the lens of
ideology, more specifically via the Slovenian philosopher Slavoj Žižek's interpretation of ideology
as closely linked to reality (1989, 2010) rather than to dreamlike illusions as previously proposed
by the German philosophers Karl Marx and Friedrich Engels (1970). We draw, predominantly, on
Žižek's seminal work regarding the critique of ideology elaborated in "The Subliminal Object of
Ideology" (1989) and "Living in the End Times" (2010) because these texts represent his core and
most consistent writings on the subject which have evolved over two decades. Additionally, the
focus on Žižek's most prominent work on ideology resonates with us as authors as it enables us

to develop an in-depth conceptual discussion of responsible tourism by offering novel under-standing of this complex phenomenon.

Not surprisingly, responsible tourism has caught the attention of many of those involved in the field of tourism, including academics in tourism research (Leslie, 2015; Spenceley, 2008; Weeden, 2014) and tourism practitioners (Mihalic, 2016), as well as tourists and society at large (Leslie, 2012). This inclusion of multiple stakeholders in the delivery of responsible tourism is reflected in the 2002 *Cape Town Declaration* which emphasises that sustainability in tourism can only be achieved if various tourism stakeholders (governments, communities, businesses, and consumers) take "responsibility" (Goodwin & Font, 2012).

The term responsible tourism has been a powerful unifier, with many of the stakeholders in tourism acting as its proponents. However, these committed responsible tourism stakehold-ers, although well-meaning, are not a homogenous group. While responsible tourism stake-holders may identify with the term responsible tourism, their/our conceptual interpretations and practice-based engagements with the phenomenon vary. This ambiguity of what is actu-ally meant by responsible tourism in practice is exacerbated by a lack of ontological debates limiting meaningful theoretical and practice-based approaches to responsible tourism (Fennell, 2008).

Critical conceptual considerations of responsible tourism have not been given enough robust reflection and, as such, further knowledge about this concept ought to be informed and sup-ported by vigorous theoretical underpinnings. As the authors of this conceptual paper, we count ourselves amongst the community of responsible tourism stakeholders. Our paper is a concep-tual one that offers a constructive critique of responsible tourism via theoretical underpinnings which rethink the ideology of this concept. This paper has emerged from our desire to continue to research, promote, deliver and experience responsible tourism while also working to enhance and develop the theoretical credibility of the term.

Drawing on the critique of ideology elaborated by Slavoj Žižek (1989, 2010) we address these aspects by proposing critical reconsiderations of responsible tourism as an ideology which often, inadvertently and implicitly, sustain the mechanism of modern global capitalism. In doing so, we map existing terms and debates related to responsible tourism both in academic literature and in tourism policy documents.

Ideology is considered to be a set of ideas and beliefs that characterise groups of people who share similar views and values on social and political issues and as such have become more vocal and visible (Van Dijk, 2006). What Žižek's critique of ideology brings afresh to re-thinking responsible tourism is a re/consideration of the ideological character of responsible tourism far from being an abstract illusion and, instead, being fundamentally rooted in real global issues. Following Žižek's critique of ideology, we unfold the links between responsible tourism on the one hand and neoliberal, capitalist modes of production and consumption on the other. We do so while acknowledging the challenges for responsible tourism stakeholders within this seem-ingly pervasive neoliberal system. Our critique shows, that the ideological nature of responsible tourism takes shape within the needs of capitalism to reinvent itself through more attention to moral production and consumption.

The structure of our paper is as follows. First, we discuss the ideology of responsible tourism via Zizek's critique. Second, we examine the state of the art of responsible tourism in relevant academic literature providing a critique of current research, including its theoretical limitations. Third, we illustrate how the ideological character of responsible tourism is pervasive in two key policy documents: the *Cape Town Declaration* (2002) and Kerala Declaration (2008). We do so by focusing on the Declarations' relevant principles such as moral production and sustainability, localism and host communities, and human rights in responsible tourism. Our discussion of the ideological nature of responsible tourism principles aims to constructively re-build its meaning and to make its aspirations more worthwhile and achievable.

The ideology of responsible tourism

As we propose to re/conceptualise the ideological character of responsible tourism we draw on Žižek's critique of ideology (1989, 2010). In the "Subliminal Object of Ideology" (1989) Žižek offers a novel understanding of ideology based on the Lacanian psychoanalytical concepts of fantasy, the Real and *jouissance [enjoyment]*. In this book, Žižek's conceptualisation of ideology challenges the classical Marxist critique of ideology and the poststructuralist reduction of ideology to discourse (Vighi & Feldner, 2007). In "Living in the End Times" (2010) Žižek further develops his critique of ideology through the discussion of the current capitalist crisis which, as he argues, unfolds through four main 'catastrophes': "the ecological crisis; the consequences of the biogenetic revolution; imbalances within the system itself (problems with intellectual property; forthcoming struggles over raw material, food and water), and the explosive growth of social division and exclusion" (2010, p. x). The collective response to this late capitalist crisis has to go through the stages of grief which are those of ideological denial, anger, attempts at bargaining followed by depression and denial in order for a new beginning to be possible.

Žižek's understandings of ideology as expounded in his two works (1989, 2010) differs from the more traditional considerations of this term proposed by Marx and Engels in *The German Ideology* (1970) who place ideology between illusionary world and objective reality. Theories of ideology enable us to understand the reasons that influence people to hold certain views and, in this sense, these theories attempt to provide explanations on the relation between thought and social reality (Eagleton, 1994). As Eagleton argues, ideology refers to fantasies, illusions and abstractions which are separate from reality (Eagleton, 1994).

In Žižekian terms ideology is placed in closer proximity to reality rather than to dreamlike illusions. More specifically, in the context of this paper we employ such Žižekian engagements with ideology to explain that responsible tourism stakeholders may "hold on to beliefs about capitalism that foreclose a more radical engagement with this destructive social and economic system" (Carrington, Zwick, & Neville, 2015, p. 24).

What is more, as one of the key vehicles for the delivery of responsible tourism, the SDGs can be viewed in terms of a dominant ideology of neo-liberalism. Indeed, it is argued that an explicit goal of the framework for the SDGs is the implementation of contested neoliberal policies (Fletcher & Rammelt, 2017; Weber, 2017). Further critique of the SDGs refer to the 'decoupling' of sustained economic growth from its environmental impact and make the point that decoupling the goals is unlikely to be achieved (Fletcher & Rammelt, 2017). Analysing the situation from the perspective of Lacanian psychoanalysis we argue that "decoupling may constitute a central 'fantasy' of the SDG agenda that 'disavows' the agenda's infeasibility, and thus defers the fundamental question of whether it is in fact possible to achieve the type of 'sustained, inclusive and sustainable economic growth' that the SDGs promise within the framework of a neoliberal capitalist economy" (Fletcher & Rammelt, 2017, p. 451).

Although tourism may have the potential to contribute to all the goals, in particular, it has been included as targets in goals 8, 12 and 14: SDG 8—*Decent work and economic growth*, SDG 12—*Responsible consumption and production*, and SDG 14—*Life below water* (Goodwin, 2016). Goodwin (2016) claims that the SDGs are about more than growth, however if we critically unpack these we can ascertain that they are articulated in a neoliberal idiom of growth. For example, the SDG which at face value has the greatest focus on environmental protection SDG 14—*Life below water* discusses the implementation of this in the language of economic growth with Target 14.7 stating to "by 2030 increase the economic benefits of SIDS [Small Island Developing States] and LDCs [Less Developed Countries] from the sustainable use of marine resources" (Goodwin, 2016, p. 205). This seems to reflect what Weber (2017) identifies as the 'market episteme' where market-based policy solutions are at the heart of development initiatives.

As ideology represents a belief, value or socio-culturally constructed system, responsible tourism, we argue, is an ideological socio-cultural and geopolitical construct. In Marxist terms, ideology legitimates certain social practices to become pervasive or mainstream and to conceal the real difficult socio-economic conditions experienced by the working middle class. Ideology forms within industrial, capitalist and authoritarian societies where individual freedom is constrained by new modes of control. These modes anchor individuals into desires that the society has created "to increase and spread comforts, to turn waste into need, and destruction into construction".

In our economically developed societies, individual freedom is, largely, constrained by new modes of production and consumption where productivity and commodity are often linked to moral values (Carrington et al., 2015). Similarly, tourism operations on a global scale expose both supply and demand to be confronted with issues that require ethical judgements (Fennell, 2002). Furthermore, current political agendas seem largely to take into account neoliberal views of individual empowerment to engage in voluntary actions for the 'good' of societies where people live or that people visit (Burrai & Hannam, 2017). Contemporary lifestyles in economically developed countries and political agendas, therefore, silently impose modes of thinking which are aligned with individual, often egotistic, rather than collective more altruistic interests and which find justification in ideological approaches (Carrington et al., 2015; Kapoor, 2012).

The way we employ Žižek's critique of ideology is by exploring responsible tourism in relation to attempts to reconcile societal concerns in economically developed countries with neoliberal, socio-political and economic developments. This apparent reconciliation, however, could be regarded as problematic because neoliberal development modes internalise and reproduce societal challenges (i.e. loss of values, alienation, individualism and disproportionate distribution of resources). Responsible tourism aims to address these societal challenges.

In rethinking responsible tourism via the ideological conceptualisation of Žižek through Lacanian psychoanalytical theory, we take further inspiration from the discipline of geography which has experienced a psychoanalytic turn (Philo & Parr, 2003; Pile, 1996) and developed the sub-field of psychoanalytic geographies with Žižek at the forefront of such developments (see Kingsbury, 2005). We take heed of Pile's warning that: "[p]sychoanalysis is a controversial account of mental life and a troublesome form of knowledge. Unsurprisingly, therefore, there are no accepted psychoanalytic concepts which can be easily transposed into, superimposed onto, or mapped alongside, geography—regardless of the kind of geography" (Pile, 1996, p. 81).

We agree that psychoanalysis in general, and ideology in particular, provide a productive yet contentious lens to tackle neoliberal global realities (Pile, 1996). Ideology is not the result of seemingly opposing concepts of 'illusion' and 'reality', instead, reality is the "deeper level beyond ideological distortions' (Vighi & Feldner, 2007, p. 147). Therefore, contemplating challenges experienced by current societies lead individuals to construct illusory webs of fantasies to escape reality (Freeden, 2003).

Critiquing the 'reality' of responsible tourism

In his critique of ideology Žižek draws on the Lacanian psychoanalytical explanation of reality as a form of fantasy (1989). In popular views fantasy refers to a wishful scenario as an illusory product of imagination, which contrasts reality. In tourism studies, fantasy conjures up tourist imagination of exotic holiday places and activities, but which are nonetheless symptomatic of more complex unconscious processes (Kingsbury & Brunn, 2003, 2004). In psychoanalysis, fantasy is usually viewed in relation to other-than-conscious psychological activities as reality is not just 'out there' presenting itself in an 'objective' way, but is discursively re/constructed (Buda, 2015; Buda, d'Hauteserre, & Johnston, 2014).

Such explanations are useful in our argument that we, as responsible tourism stakeholders, act within a frame of a discursively constituted and re/constructed reality which is understood "as a fantasy that draws upon ideological mediation, prejudice and unconscious desire" (Carrington et al., 2015, p. 29). Desire is a complex concept beyond the scope of this paper, and which has been discussed by others elsewhere (Buda & Shim, 2015; Kingsbury & Brunn, 2003, 2004). Here, we want to acknowledge the connection between unconscious desire and fantasy. The relation between fantasy and desire on the one hand and responsible tourism on the other hand is via Žižekian ideological explanations. Responsible tourism, we argue, is symptomatic of capitalism, liberal democracy, individualism and a societal sense of alienation, because it generates desires and fantasies pushing subjective identities to relate to specific political ideologies, social roles or patterns of consumption.

To Žižek, capitalism, liberal democracy and alienation belong to the register of *the Real*. The French psychoanalyst Jacques Lacan has put forth *the Real* as a psychoanalytic concept in relation to *the Symbolic* and *the Imaginary*, three registers that are interlaced and govern human life (Lacan, 1977). *The Real* drives us, yet *the Real* is the terrain of that which cannot be expressed, it is intangible and inexpressible. *The Real*, however, cannot exist without the barrier of *the Symbolic*, the second Lacanian order, which is characterised by presence or absence of our desires and feelings, whereas *the Real* is whole, as it is the repository of authenticity, of authentic selves. When such desires and feelings can be expressed through language and forms images in our consciousness and memory, whether individual or collective, we deal with the third order, *the Imaginary*.

Žižek reinterprets Lacanian psychoanalysis to explain and critique neoliberalism, global capitalism, alienation and such like (Žižek, 1989). In light of these Žižekian explanations we aim to (re)define responsible tourism which is framed within the values and the logic of global neoliberalism. We recognise that while responsible tourism stakeholders may well wish to challenge many of the assumptions and practices of neoliberalism, we are required to work within that system in order to do so. Ideology, hence, forms in the attempt to obscure societal insufficiencies and imperfections (Kapoor, 2012).

Tourism, therefore, is understood within these same structures, registers and orders which characterise global societies and responsible tourism is the ideological response to them.

This, in accordance to Žižek and the order of *the Real* means that responsible tourism, if understood in its purest essence and practised with care and compassion, can offer "the social reality itself … an escape from some traumatic, real kernel' (Žižek, 1989, p. 45). Hence, in our attempt to constructively rethink responsible tourism, we need to critically engage with the challenges linked to its ideological character to understand its limitations. This facilitates a more positive way forward for a more meaningful use of the concept.

The *Symbolic register*—based on the opposition between 'absence' and 'presence' of desires, fantasies, feelings—explains how and in what ways individuals may accept the presence of societal rules and dictates believing, somewhat unconditionally, as a ripple effect, mostly because on a collective level others do the same (Lacan, 1977; Žižek, 1989). Here lies the core of neoliberal undifferentiated acceptance of responsible tourism upon an illusionary image or belief 'to do good to people and places'.

We argue that responsible tourism discourses create social fantasy. This collective social fantasy points to the fact that well-meaning interventions of responsible tourism stakeholders might induce a harmonious and altruistic alternative to the more egoistic neoliberal capitalist ventures. Yet, such collective social fantasies rarely subvert neoliberal capitalist activities and, in effect, they interrupt the harmonious and altruistic desires necessary for responsible tourism. When 'doing' responsible tourism as tourists, or even when analysing in an academic context the tenets of responsible tourism, there seems to be a failure to recognise that 'abnormalities' and 'deviances' are integral to our neoliberal system, these deviances are not excluded as we might want an attitude of feeling good about doing responsible tourism (Kapoor, 2012; Žižek, 1989).

In psychoanalysis, *the Real* is a register of which we are aware, but due to its nature of being intangible and absolute we cannot totally address it. Thus, according to Žižek, we are also not totally able to address and resolve these abnormalities, deviances, anxieties about poverty, inequalities, environmental degradations and injustices. In spite of the awareness of *the Real* with its fundamental and absolute anxieties, some responsible tourism stakeholders may still 'buy into the fantasy' of a potentially illusory activity or product such as responsible tourism by engaging in seemingly feel-good responsible practices (Kapoor, 2012, p. 117). These practices entail that money and power are invested and used within the field of responsible tourism to assess local contexts, recommend solutions to local problems, or establish winners of best practice.

This suggests that some responsible tourism stakeholders, not always knowingly, may fail to challenge and subvert neoliberal capitalist development of global economic and socio-political systems and, while partaking in responsible tourism and being active in finding solutions for the world's problems, nurture desires and fantasies. These desires and fantasies are unlikely to be satisfied as they reside at the junction between the two Lacanian registers *Symbolic* and the intangible *Real*.

The ideology of responsible tourism, hence, is unavoidably linked to deeper psychoanalytical processes both at individual and collective levels about the acceptance and even the enjoyment of illusory ethical travelling that makes us 'feel good'. In liberal 'western' societies with economically developed economies, "we blindly submit ourselves to the merciless superegoic command (Enjoy!) of the logic of the market" (Vighi & Feldner, 2007, p. 146).

In what follows we turn our more detailed attention towards existing literature of responsible tourism in academic debates and ascertain the progress undertaken so far in the research of responsible tourism. We subsequently move onto the discussion of some relevant principles of the *Cape Town* and *Kerala* Declarations such as moral production and sustainability, localism and host communities, and human rights in responsible tourism.

Conceptualisations of responsible tourism in academic debates

Research debates in responsible tourism have addressed several aspects such as links between tourist behaviour and responsible tourism (Dodds, Graci, & Holmes, 2010; Juvan & Dolnicar, 2014; Lee, Bonn, Reid, & Kim, 2017; Stanford, 2008); stakeholders and ethical responsibility (Hudson & Miller, 2005); business perspectives such as marketing and corporate social responsibility initiatives (Mosselaer, Duim, & Wijk, 2012); tour operators and sense of responsibility (Miller, 2001); and local perspectives in responsible tourism (Burrai, Font, & Cochrane, 2014; Sin, 2010). However, the focus of much of this research is on the role of stakeholders in delivering responsible tourism rather than an engaging critique of the term responsible tourism itself. In the following we review this literature and present three key limitations around responsible tourism: (i) limited conceptualisations; (ii) ambiguous separation between responsible tourism and sustainable tourism; and (iii) identification of responsible tourism with a social movement.

Limited conceptualisations of responsible tourism

There are some key academic texts[1] in responsible tourism which have, by and large, tackled definitions of responsible tourism. The widely circulated definition of responsible tourism as making better places for people to live in and better places for people to visit (Goodwin, 2011) has rarely been revisited. Leslie (2015), however, discusses specifically what the term means and what it encompasses with emphasis on stakeholders and management of responsible tourism.

---

[1]See Goodwin (2011, 201669) and Leslie (2015).

There is still limited critical consideration on the existence of a unifying term, which would deepen knowledge on the concept of responsible tourism to meaningfully progress studies and practices in the field.

Perhaps, in part, this lack of conceptualisation is the tangible frustration of many of those writing in this field with some of the literature suggesting that developing labels can stall the process of developing a solution and that there is a danger of "being caught in the quagmire of jargon and debate" (Romeril, 1994; Wheeler, 2012, p. 9). With reference to the terms that describe new forms of tourism (alternative, green and such like), we are asked "what does it matter if the definition is not strictly appropriate? … Surely it is the philosophy, and not the semantics, that is important" (Romeril, 1994, p. 25). There is also the recommendation to worry less about terminology, the label and more about the philosophy, because "the way ahead is surely to view responsible tourism as a 'way of thinking' to ensure tourism is responsible to host environments and societies". Capturing this mood of 'getting on with the job', some authors state that responsible tourism is not a niche tourism product or brand, but a "way of doing tourism"—any kind of tourism (Husbands & Harrison, 1996, p. 2).

Blurred conceptual separations between sustainable and responsible tourism

What has prompted the emergence of responsible tourism are changes in consumer demand, the identified negative impacts of mass tourism, as well as criticism on the vagueness and non-operational character of sustainable tourism. Harold Goodwin (2011, p. 31), regarded as one of the key proponents of responsible tourism, also points to the shortcomings of sustainable tourism claiming that:

> sustainable development lacks definition and measurable indicators to determine whether or not tourism is being successfully managed towards sustainability by government. Lip service is paid to the concept: it is used to generate work for consultants and NGOs, to bolster the reputation of companies and governments, but rarely are the outcomes measured or reported. The concept appears to be operative and is often used to secure resources and support, but in practice the principles are not applied, the concept is inoperative, the objectives are not achieved. It is left to someone else. Responsibility is not taken.

He argues that responsible tourism is conceptually different from sustainable tourism highlighting the *practical* virtues of responsible tourism (Goodwin, 2016). Responsible tourism, therefore, can be considered a response to the limitations of sustainable tourism and is often regarded as the practice-based application of the concept of sustainability. However, we suggest here that a conceptual separation of the term from its practice-based use makes its meaning hard to understand. It further remains unclear what makes responsible tourism conceptually different from sustainable tourism. In addition to this, some weakly defined concepts, such as the triple bottom line of sustainability and tourism impacts, are adopted as key principles for (the practice of) responsible tourism.

The interpretation of the term responsibility, which often remains unquestioned, contributes to the problematic nature and application of the concept. The issue is further complicated as terms which relate to alternative business as usual tourism scenarios are often used interchangeably. For example, it has been noted by Stanford (2008) that ethics and responsibility are terms that often converge within the tourism literature and have been used interchangeably by some (Goodwin & Francis, 2003).

Identification of responsible tourism as a social movement

The third limitation concerns the identification of responsible tourism as a social movement. Some academics writing in the field have challenged the concept of responsible tourism arguing that it is a way of allowing relatively affluent tourists a guilt free holiday without having to do much to curb their behaviour or enjoyment:

> responsible tourism is a pleasant, agreeable, but dangerously superficial, ephemeral and inadequate escape route for the educated middle classes unable, or unwilling, to appreciate or accept their/our own destructive contribution to the international tourism maelstrom (Wheeler, 2012, p. 96).

Social movements are characterised by the participation of excluded marginalised local communities to tackle human rights and, thus, attempt to bring about social change in order to improve their limited power and access to resources (Tilly, 1978). Yet, some theorists of social movements add that "addressing collective problems or support of moral values or principles does not correspond to social movements" (Della Porta & Diani, 2006, p. 21). Social movements and changes via tackling human rights cannot be defined as such in responsible tourism when they are representatives of distinct coalitions of interests such as: public, private and third sectors, local communities, tourists, and academics. Additionally, "no single organised actor, no matter how powerful, can claim to represent a movement as a whole" (ibid.), not even academics or consultants at the *Responsible Tourism Day* at the *World Travel Market* in London. Goodwin (2016, p. 258) defines responsible tourism as a social movement, describing it as "a purposive effort by groups of people, who share some common principles and approaches, resulting in a shared sense of direction". However, this shared direction and common principles of addressing human rights in responsible tourism remain somewhat ill-defined. In the light of these considerations, in this paper we refer to responsible tourism stakeholders as a *social group* rather than a *movement*.

Illustrating the ideology of responsible tourism in key policy documents Cape Town Declaration and Kerala Declaration

In this part we exemplify the ideological character of responsible tourism through the discussion of some of the principles of the Cape Town (2002) and Kerala (2008) Declarations. Responsible tourism was first presented as a unified 'movement' in policy documents such as the *Cape Town Declaration* (2002). Subsequently, it became a topic of academic interest in particular associated to ethics, consumers and industry providers.

In 2002 the first conference on responsible tourism was held in Cape Town, South Africa, and this led to the *Cape Town Declaration*. The conference preceded the World Summit on Sustainable Development in Johannesburg and it was organised by the responsible tourism partnership and the public institution Western Cape Tourism. It involved 208 delegates from 20 different countries. More specifically, the conference was represented by tour operators, entrepreneurs and authorities from the public sector as well as members from the third sector, such as charities and NGOs. It also included the World Tourism Organisation and United Nations Environment Programme. The founder of the group Harold Goodwin, compiled the first draft of the Declaration (2016).

A second *International Conference on Responsible Tourism in Destinations* with 500 delegates from 29 countries took place in Kerala, India in March 2008. This led to a second important declaration of responsible tourism, namely the *Kerala Declaration* which developed from the desire to turn the rhetoric of responsible tourism elaborated in the *Cape Town Declaration* into practice. The conference consisted of "four days of discussions about the movement's progress in achieving the aspirations of Responsible Tourism—delegates shared their experience, renewed friendships and made new ones—leaving the conference reinvigorated and determined to increase the pace of change" (Goodwin, online). As highlighted in the policy document, this Declaration focuses on process and approaches to implementation (Kerala Declaration, 2008). However, the conceptual limitations of the first policy document developed in Cape Town expose this second Declaration to similar challenges.

Both the *Cape Town Declaration* (2002) and Kerala Declaration (2008) represent the two key moments for the establishment and development of responsible tourism in theory and practice. Both Declarations have received considerable attention in particular from tourism organisations and businesses which have focused on the implementation of specific and practical guidelines for the industry (Jamal, Camargo, & Wilson, 2013). The documents have also been implemented in practice by, for example, the South African government which embedded the promotion of practising responsible tourism in their Tourism Act of 2014. The Kerala Declaration is implemented, for example, in the form of the *World Travel Market's World Responsible Tourism Day* and *Associated World Responsible Tourism Awards* which typically attracts around 2000 international participants at the World Travel Market in London (Goodwin, 2016).

We argue that the principles that guide the two Declarations are fundamentally ideological and, as such, are driven by the authentic *Real*. The over-simplification of complex contexts and social interactions contribute to making the principles difficult to achieve. The ideology of responsible tourism becomes evident if we focus, among others, on the principles of moral production and sustainability, localism and host communities, human rights.

Critiquing "moral production" and "sustainability" in responsible tourism

The ethical dimension and moral intentions of the principles included in the Declarations are embedded into the corporative logic of seemingly 'moral production'. Although characterised by moral intentions, responsible tourism products are, by and large, focused on the operations of the business or trading mechanism to maximise capital (Burrai & Hannam, 2017; Butcher & Smith, 2015). For example, large tour operators such as Thomas Cook seem to pay lip service to reducing environmental impacts. Thomas Cook do so by partnering with the Carbon Trust, an independent UK company promoting a low carbon economy, "to help turn opportunities for energy saving into real world reductions in energy consumption, carbon emissions and operating costs" (Thomas Cook, 2018, para. 9). This partnership, however laudable, could financially benefit the overall business of Thomas Cook.

Yet, Thomas Cook, and other such large tour operators are still committed to flying millions of customers by air (Smith, Rees, & Murray, 2016). Hence, it appears that flying a large number of tourists to destinations remains the primary concern regardless of the environmental implications (Smith et al., 2016). This particular tour operator is present in 21 countries and "has annual sales of around £9bn, carrying 22.3 million customers, operating a fleet of 93 aircraft, a network of over 3400 owned and franchised travel stores, interests in 86 hotels and resort properties, and employing 31,000 employees" (Smith et al., 2016, p. 192). This shows that these large tour operators enable tourists to feel (morally) better consumers being part of a "fairy tale complete with the promise of a happy ending of a kind, green, and equitable capitalism" (Carrington et al., 2015, p. 30). In Zizekian terms, this 'fairy tale' is a fantasy as it constitutes a discursively re/constructed reality and it is deeply ideological as it attempts to obscure global societal challenges.

The focus on the industry to "take responsibility for minimising its negative and maximising its positive impacts" (Cape Town Declaration, 2002) highlights the complex and often paradoxical association of morals and ethics with business. A vast literature on the moral turn of consumption and consumerism (Carrington et al., 2015) raises the important issue of the perpetuation of inequality and unfairness disguised under the positive values of responsibility, sustainability and meaningful experiences.

The Declarations also refer to commercial, environmental and social sustainability. Sustainability according to some has become the accepted model of the global tourism industry (Bianchi, 2004) arguably fraught with theoretical and practical limitations. Some authors claim responsible tourism to be the operational side of sustainability and such claims further weaken the credibility of the concept of responsible tourism (Higgins-Desbiolles, 2010; Mihalic, 2016).

Tourism is characterised by complex socio-economic dynamics, movements of people, goods and technologies and encounters among different actors. Often these complexities are not captured in analyses of sustainable tourism which offer much more fragmented and localised accounts (Saarinen, 2006). Critical insights into sustainability in tourism address its ideological nature which links to the concept of sustainable development presented in the Brundtland Report (1980) moving it away from a more operational dimension.

Since 2004, at the *World Travel Market* in London, responsible tourism gained an important space to share values of fairness and justice among tourism practitioners and academics. In 2017, the awards given to tourism stakeholders for 'best practice' in responsible tourism were based on the SDGs. Yet, the SDGs have not been situated within contemporary tourism studies and debates. Their nature and effectiveness have not been a field of critical enquiry exposing responsible tourism to further weaknesses.

Limited engagements with host communities and localism in responsible tourism

The philosophy of responsible tourism builds around the concepts of localism and host communities. These concepts are central in developing forms of tourism that can be beneficial for local people. In spite of the laudable aspirations related to these, critical assessment and empirical evidence show the numerous limitations associated with representations of local communities (Sin & Minca, 2014). Local communities are prevalent in responsible tourism discourses as places where actions of empowerment happen (Williams, 2005). Yet, there is often a lack of a deeper engagement and familiarisation of responsible tourism stakeholders with complex socio-political local structures. This is what Žižek refers to as depoliticisation whereby issues of social development, poverty reduction and social inclusion are, seemingly, resolved by managers or 'experts' (Kapoor, 2012, p. 3).

The mistaken homogeneous character of communities opens the problematic situation of progressive actions and participatory development in the 'local'. This view acknowledges the importance of personal reform over political struggle at a micro level and moves away the attention from wider political power structures which dominate local contexts (ibid.). We argue that the focus on local communities in the practice of responsible tourism in general, and as presented in the *Cape Town Declaration,* in particular, is fraught with difficulties. This is because of the inability of some responsible tourism stakeholders to relate the concept to the wider more critical and in-depth discourses of development. To mitigate these difficulties we argue that the local socio-political contexts should be understood via the lens of the heterogeneity of local communities whereby local members have different roles and levels of access to involvement in tourism.

The concept of community is often associated with their well-being and economic benefits deriving from local involvement. This association raises important issues on participation and on imposed values of conventional development which is understood as increased income and unilateral 'westernised' conceptualisations of well-being. Similar to the involvement of international agencies in development, the ideology of responsible tourism reinforces "economically centred development agendas" (Buzinde, Kalavar, & Melubo, 2014, p. 21) which have been criticised for their "exclusionary and imperialistic" (ibid., p. 21) identification of developmental criteria (e.g. Millennium Development Goals, Sustainable Development Goals).

The ideology of responsible tourism as a tool for development reflects diverse, ethical and hierarchical positions within host communities and tourism stakeholders more in general. These diverse positions influence the (lack of) formation of policy and constrain individual agency. As Chock et al. argue, this limits a meaningful engagement with the theory and practice of responsibility. Therefore, it would be beneficial if responsible tourism stakeholders critically reflect on the global geopolitical scenario where responsible tourism operates. In addition, within the field of responsible tourism, we must acknowledge the lack of robust empirical evidence showing the potential of tourism to be used as a tool for development. Critical reflections on the broader context of international development, its weaknesses and structural limitations represent a useful avenue to meaningfully rethink responsible tourism.

In relation to local people, the *Cape Town Declaration*, for example, highlights the importance of involving them in decisions that affect their lives. Participation and equal access are two fundamental elements of responsible tourism discourses. In previous studies, tourism has been criticised for lacking distributive justice which would ensure a more equal spread of its benefits (Reid, 2003). Instead," tourism is characterized by uneven development, ensuring erratic returns and unequal incomes" (Reid, 2003, p. 4). This is more evident in the context of less economically developed countries or forms of tourism which claim to be 'pro-poor'. The responsible tourism rhetoric emphasises the importance of the participation of local people in decision-making processes but it is not clear to what extent this happens and how meaningful this can be (Chock et al., 2007). The concept of participation goes hand in hand with power and specific socio-political structures. As Bebbington suggests (2005, p. 281), participatory development has to engage with questions on attitudes and behaviours necessary to keep "sight of the wider picture—a picture in which questions of capitalist development, state formation, the constitution of civil society and social differentiation all loom large".

Oversimplification of human rights in responsible tourism

In the Declarations commonly shared human rights are discussed and understood as if they share a homogeneous character of universally accepted human rights. This oversimplification of human rights, emphasising their rhetorical rather than practice-based aspects, makes their meaning unclear. For example, human rights such as education, empowerment and inclusion are discussed within the boundaries of tourism which follows neoliberal logics of capitalist societies (Duffy, 2008). Therefore, a critical reflection of these three principles calls to question how responsible tourism can enable these human rights in countries where such rights stand on different foundations. This rhetoric alienates responsible tourism from its proposed actions and brings the discussion to a more ideological level. The reality on the ground is abstract and the 'complex universal context' makes it concrete (Žižek, 1999, p. 90).

Žižek, in Parallax View (2006), problematizes the concept of human rights in the context of '*western*' interventions within 'humanitarian' cases, such as the conflict in Sarajevo. Although of a different nature because of its political military context, this case is emblematic in illustrating, in more generic terms, "the very depoliticised humanitarian politics of 'Human Rights' as the ideology of military interventionism serving specific economic-political purposes" (Žižek, 2006, p. 339). Therefore, transposing Žižek's ideology of human rights within the context of responsible tourism as elaborated in the *Kerala Declaration* illuminates the fact that responsible tourism is legitimised by prevailing geopolitical conditions and economic interests such as the influence and power of consultants in this field. Hence, for example, when some consultants are commissioned to carry out responsible tourism projects while insufficiently informed by conceptual debates, their work is not always anchored in relevant geopolitical contexts (Kothari, 2005; Laurie, Andolina, & Radcliffe, 2005). These consultancies, often, instead of contributing to ameliorating local conditions seem to limit the possibility of meaningful local "collective projects of socio-political transformation" (Žižek, 2006, p. 339).

Taking responsibility in tourism entails the safeguard of social and cultural human rights. As stated in the *Kerala Declaration*: "[r]esponsible tourism should be included in the primary curriculum to foster inclusion, discourage dependency and enable people to engage in the management of tourism impacts" (2008, p. 5). We ponder whether this vision might be problematic and unachievable because of the unconvincing self-reflections on what responsible tourism is and/or should be. These unconvincing self-reflections relate to ways in which some responsible tourism stakeholders prioritise action over reflection "unquestioningly accepting the status quo, for instance, a situation of gender or social inequality" (Kapoor, 2012, p. 99). In line with Žižek's critique of ideology, responsible tourism stakeholders act within a frame of a discursively re/constructed reality which is understood as a fantasy. Fantasy and desire push well-intentioned individuals to identify with specific ideologies or social roles (i.e. those predicated by the responsible tourism Declarations). Yet, in an attempt to conceal societal imperfections (e.g. power imbalances), ideologies form and are strongly anchored to the same neoliberal, imperfect systems which have prompted their development.

The subject of human rights is complex, not least because they are dependent on the culture and geopolitical environments of places. Natural and human rights were first theorised in the modern 'west' and "north Americans and French Revolutionists first used such ideas to construct new political orders" (Donnely, 2007, p. 7). However, current debates show that human rights, as conceptualised and understood in the 'west', are difficult to implement in different contexts (Donnely, 2007). As Žižek (2006) explains, there is a depoliticised humanitarian politics of human rights. Human rights of victims in the 'third world' represent the rights of 'western' powers to politically, economically and culturally intervene to defend 'third world' rights (2006, p. 341). This calls for self-reflection on the concept and practice of responsible tourism in destinations where human rights, such as freedom, equality, gender, education and health are problematic and conceptualised differently.

To conclude, examining the Declarations it becomes apparent that 'moral production', sustainability, engagements of local communities and human rights can be meaningfully tackled by responsible tourism stakeholders. Hence, responsible tourism discourses follow the ideology that doing something is better than doing nothing, regardless of the outcomes (Simpson, 2005). Development, for example, becomes achievable through the actions of well-intentioned volunteer tourists and Eurocentric models of knowledge are central in responsible actions. In the specific case of volunteer tourism, the rhetoric of responsible tourism reinforces, often, images of power and colonialism through the representation of the Other as a distant subject to be explored, educated or helped (Burrai & Hannam, 2017; Reas, 2013). The *Responsible Tourism Awards Day* at the London *World Travel Market* shows limited reflection on these 'responsible' practices, praising 'best practice' (in volunteer tourism, for example) instead of engaging with the root causes of global inequality.

Conclusion

This paper offers a conceptual reconsideration of responsible tourism rethinking its ideological character. We argue that responsible tourism is ideological because, although real "[ideology] is precisely such a reduction to the simplified 'essence' that conveniently forgets the 'background noise' which provides the density of its actual meaning" (Žižek, 2010, p. 4). Actions seem to prevail instead of self-reflection leading to the 'invisible mystification' of ideology rooted in unquestioned and dogmatic beliefs (Žižek, 2010, p. xv). The principles of the *Cape Town* (2002) and *Kerala* (2008) Declarations illustrate how such oversimplification of issues which characterise current global crises (i.e. sustainability; localism; human rights) reduce the meaning of responsible tourism to mere rhetoric. Instead, in this paper we provide a critical reconsideration of responsible tourism to overcome its theoretical and practical limitations and to enable structural and societal changes.

In this paper we explore, analyse and reconceptualise responsible tourism. In doing so, we draw on Žižek's interpretation of ideology which has enabled us to examine the ideological character of responsible tourism. In the paper, we argue that the ideology of responsible tourism is rooted in real global issues such as exclusion, uneven distribution of resources and wealth, loss of values and alienation. However, the attempt to reconcile, through responsible tourism, societal concerns in economically developed countries with modern global capitalism is problematic. This reconciliation is difficult because responsible tourism is framed and develops within the values of global capitalism failing to identify the 'abnormalities' (i.e. global issues) that characterise our neoliberal systems.

To date, research debates in responsible tourism show a limited critical consideration of the term responsible tourism. In reviewing the literature on responsible tourism, we identify three key limitations which constrain meaningful development of studies and practices in the field. These limitations are: the lack of conceptualisation of the term; the ambiguous conceptual separation between responsible and sustainable tourism; and the identification of responsible tourism as a social movement.

To illustrate the ideological character of responsible tourism, we critique some key principles of the *Cape Town* (2002) *and Kerala* (2008) Declarations such as moral production and sustainability; the limited engagements with host communities and localism; and the oversimplification of human rights in responsible tourism. These Declarations represent the most significant moments for the establishment and development of responsible tourism.

This critical approach to the meaning of responsible tourism has enabled us to reconsider the theoretical and practice-based limitations of responsible tourism. These limitations have constrained wider and more meaningful structural and societal changes. We argue that sustainability and responsibility in tourism require a critical reconsideration and acknowledgment of their links to localised geopolitical structures framed within the neoliberal straitjacket.

There is much potential for future research on the interpretation of Žižek's work in responsible tourism and in tourism studies in general. In this conceptual paper we have elaborated mainly on Žižek's early seminal work on ideology as expounded in *The Sublime Object of Ideology* (1989) and in *Living in the End Times* (2010) because of his in-depth critique of ideology. His other relevant work *First as Tragedy, Then as Farce* (2009) on the crises of global capitalist systems presents interesting research avenues if interjected into the field of tourism. Furthermore, other research avenues include building on the concept of the ideology of responsible tourism taking inspiration from the work of Eagleton in relation to Marxism (1994).

Drawing further on psychoanalytic theories and more specifically on psychoanalytic geographies, responsible tourism can be researched via concepts such as voyeurism, or desire. We propose that the focus lies on understanding the link between the realm of ethics as interpreted by responsible tourism stakeholders and Freud and Lacan accounts of desire and morality. Hence, the nexus between thought, action and desire can be examined within the boundaries of psychoanalytic ethics.

In line with the turn to emotions and affects recently advocated in tourism literature (Buda, 2015; Buda et al., 2014), a potential further avenue for research is to examine both the concept and practice of responsible tourism via emotions, feelings and affects. Such examinations would contribute understandings of the emotional engagements with places, or affective dynamics of responsibility between tourists and locals. This can be undertaken by analysing individual and collective emotions such as guilt, happiness, anger, for example.

The ideology of responsible tourism can also be examined in relation to topical subjects and challenges that societies are currently facing, such as overtourism. Overtourism is the term used to describe destinations, such as Barcelona, Prague or Venice that are affected by large numbers of tourists damaging the social, natural and built environments of destinations. Responsible tourism has been flagged as a solution to the problem of overtourism in some mass media accounts (Burrai, 2018, online).

However, as we argued in this paper, it might be helpful to engage, first, in the task of thinking about the concept of responsible tourism rather than its practice. Furthermore, as researchers we could reflect more critically on the problems raised by society at large, especially those causing overtourism. Such critical self/reflections could offer solutions more meaningful to our societies and cultures in line with a reformed concept of responsible tourism. Unchallenged neoliberal assumptions regarding growth, need radical rethinking and the implications for how alternatives to a growth and a *'business as usual'* approach affect tourism and the communities that rely on this activity need further consideration. Further empirical and methodological research, with a focus on ethnography, especially in these destinations affected by overtourism, could shed light on the ideological character of responsible tourism and potential innovative reinterpretations of the concept, as well as how the term is translated into practice.

Our paper has challenged some of the comforting assumptions of working *with* and *within* the concept of responsible tourism. We, therefore, hope that this will generate further debate and scrutiny of the concept and the practice to ensure that tourism develops in a truly responsible manner.

Disclosure statement

No potential conflict of interest was reported by the authors.

References

Bebbington, A. (2005). Theorising participation and institutional change: Ethnography and political economy. In S. Hickey & G. Mohan (Eds.), *Participation: From tyranny to transformation? Exploring new approaches to participation in development.* London: Zed Books.

Bianchi, R. (2004). Tourism restructuring and the politics of sustainability: A critical view from the European Periphery (The Canary Islands). *Journal of Sustainable Tourism, 12*(6), 495–529. doi:10.1080/09669580408667251

Buda, D. M. (2015). The death of drive in tourism studies. *Annals of Tourism Research, 50*, 39–51. doi:10.1016/j.annals.2014.10.008

Buda, D. M., d'Hauteserre, A.-M., & Johnston, L. (2014). Feeling and tourism studies. *Annals of Tourism Research, 46*, 102–114. doi:10.1016/j.annals.2014.03.005

Buda, D. M., & Shim, D. (2015). Desiring the dark: 'A taste for the unusual' in North Korean tourism? *Current Issues in Tourism, 18*(1), 1–6. doi:10.1080/13683500.2014.948813

Burrai, E. (2018). Tourists not welcome: How to tackle the issue of overtourism. *The Conversation.* http://theconversation.com/tourists-not-welcome-how-to-tackle-the-issue-of-overtourism-101766. Accessed 18/11/2018.

Burrai, E., Font, X., & Cochrane, J. (2015). Destinations stakeholders' perceptions of volunteer tourism: An equity theory approach. *International Journal of Tourism Research, 17*(5), 451–459. doi:10.1002/jtr.2012

Burrai, E., & Hannam, K. (2017). Challenging the responsibility of 'responsible volunteer tourism'. *Journal of Policy Research in Tourism, Leisure and Events, 9*(3), 1–6.

Butcher, J., & Smith, P. (2015). *Volunteer tourism: The lifestyle politics of international development.* London: Routledge.

Buzinde, C. N., Kalavar, J. M., & Melubo, K. (2014). Tourism and community wellbeing: The case of the Maasai in Tanzania. *Annals of Tourism Research, 44*, 20–35. doi:10.1016/j.annals.2013.08.010

Cape Town Declaration. (2002). *Cape Town Conference on responsible tourism in destinations.* Retrieved from http://www.capetown.gov.za/en/tourism/Documents/Responsible%20Tourism/Toruism_RT_2002_Cape_Town_Declaration.pdf. Accessed 05/04/2018.

Carrington, M., Zwick, D., & Neville, B. (2015). The ideology of the ethical consumption gap. *Marketing Theory*, 1–18.

Della Porta, D., & Diani, M. (2006). *Social movements: An introduction.* London: Blackwell.

Dodds, R., Graci, S. R., & Holmes, M. (2010). Does the tourist care? A comparison of tourists in Koh Phi Phi, Thailand and Gili Trawangan, Indonesia. *Journal of Sustainable Tourism, 18*(2), 207–222. doi:10.1080/09669580903215162

Donnely, J. (2007). The relative universality of human rights. *Human Rights Quarterly*, *29* (2), 281–306.

Duffy, R. (2008). Neoliberalising nature: Global networks and ecotourism development in Madagascar. *Journal of Sustainable Tourism*, *16*(3), 327–344. doi:10.2167/jost748.0

Eagleton, T. (1994). *Ideology*. London: Verso.

Fennell, D. A. (2002). *Ecotourism programme planning*. Wallingford, UK: CABI Publishing.

Fennell, D. (2008). Responsible tourism: A Kierkegaardian interpretation. *Tourism Recreation Research*, *33*(1), 3–12. doi:10.1080/02508281.2008.11081285

Fletcher, R., & Rammelt, C. (2017). Decoupling: A key fantasy of the post-2015 sustainable development agenda. *Globalizations*, *14* (3), 450–467. doi:10.1080/14747731.2016.1263077

Freeden, M. (2003). *Ideology: A very short introduction*. Oxford: Oxford University Press.

Goodwin, H. (2011). *Taking responsibility for tourism*. Oxford: Goodfellow.

Goodwin, H. (2016). *Responsible tourism: Using tourism for sustainable development* (2nd ed.). Oxford: Goodfellow.

Goodwin, H., & Font, X. (2012). *Progress in responsible tourism*, Vol. 2(1). Oxford: Goodfellow.

Goodwin, H., & Francis, J. (2003). Ethical and responsible tourism: Consumer trends in the UK. *Journal of Vacation Marketing*, *9*(3), 271–284. doi:10.1177/135676670300900306

Higgins-Desbiolles, F. (2010). The elusiveness of sustainability in tourism: The culture-ideology of consumerism and its implications. *Tourism and Hospitality Research*, *10* (2), 116–129. doi:10.1057/thr.2009.31

Hudson, S., & Miller, G. (2005). The responsible marketing of tourism: The case of Canadian mountain holidays. *Tourism Management*, *26*(2), 133–142. doi:10.1016/j.tourman.2003.06.005

Husbands, W., & Harrison, L. C. (1996). Practicing responsible tourism: Understanding tourism today to prepare for tomorrow. In L. C. Harrison and W. Husbands (Eds.), *Practicing responsible tourism: International case studies in tourism planning, policy and development*. New York: John Wiley.

Jamal, T., Camargo, B. A., & Wilson, E. (2013). Critical omissions and new directions for sustainable tourism: A situated macro-micro approach. *Sustainability*, *5*(11), 4594–4613. doi:10.3390/su5114594

Juvan, E., & Dolnicar, S. (2014). The attitude-behaviour gap in sustainable tourism. *Annals of Tourism Research*, *48*, 76–95. doi:10.1016/j.annals.2014.05.012

Kapoor, I. (2012). *Celebrity humanitarianism: The ideology of global charity*. London and New York: Routledge.

Kerala Declaration, 2008. http://www.haroldgoodwin.info/documents/KeralaDeclaration.pdf. Accessed 05/04/2018.

Kingsbury, P. T. (2005). Jamaican tourism and the politics of enjoyment. *Geoforum*, *36*(1), 113–132. doi:10.1016/j.geoforum.2004.03.012

Kingsbury, P. T., & Brunn, S. D. (2003). Traversing the fantasies of post-September 11 travel magazines. In C. M. Hall, D. J. Timothy & D. T. Duval (Eds.), *Safety and security in tourism: Relationships, management, and marketing* (pp. 39–61). Binghamton, NY: Haworth Press.

Kingsbury, P. T., & Brunn, S. D. (2004). Freud, tourism, and terror: Traversing the fantasies of post-September 11 travel magazines. *Journal of Travel and Tourism Marketing*, *15*(2–3), 39–61. doi:10.1300/J073v15n02_03

Kothari, U. (2005). Authority and expertise: The professionalisation of international development and the ordering of dissent. *Antipode*, *37*(3), 425–446. doi:10.1111/j.0066-4812.2005.00505.x

Lacan, J. (1977). *Écrits: A selection* (A. Sheridan, Trans.). New York, NY: Norton.

Laurie, N., Andolina, R., & Radcliffe, S. (2005). Ethnodevelopment: Social movements, creating experts, and professionalising Indigenous knowledge in Ecuador. *Antipode*, *37*(3), 470–496. doi:10.1111/j.0066-4812.2005.00507.x

Lee, H. Y., Bonn, M. A., Reid, E. L., & Kim, W. G. (2017). Differences in tourist ethical judgment and responsible tourism intention: An ethical scenario approach. *Tourism Management*, *60*, 298–307. doi:10.1016/j.tourman.2016.12.003

Leslie, D. (2015). *Responsible tourism. Concepts, theory and practice*. Wallington: CABI.

Marx, K., & Engels, F. (1970). *The German ideology*. London: Lawrence & Wishart.

Mihalic, T. (2016). Sustainable-responsible tourism discourse e towards 'responsustable' tourism. *Journal of Cleaner Production*, *111*, 461–470. doi:10.1016/j.jclepro.2014.12.062

Miller, G. (2001). Corporate responsibility in the UK tourism industry. *Tourism Management*, *22*(6), 589–598. doi:10.1016/S0261-5177(01)00034-6

Mosselaer, F. V. D., Duim, R. V. D., & Wijk, J. V. (2012). Corporate social responsibility in the tour operating industry: The case of Dutch outbound tour operators. In D. Leslie (Ed.), *Tourism enterprises and the sustainability agenda across Europe* (pp. 71–92). Farnhan, UK: Ashgate.

Philo, C., & Parr, H. (2003). Introducing psychoanalytic geographies. *Social & Cultural Geography*, *4*(3), 283–293. doi:10.1080/14649360309074

Pile, S. (1996). *The body and the city: Psychoanalysis, space, and subjectivity*. London, England: Routledge.

Reas, P. J. (2013). 'Boy, have we got a vacation for you': Orphanage tourism in Cambodia and the commodification and objectification of the orphaned child. *Thammasat Review*, *16*(1), 121–139.

Reid, D. G. (2003). *Tourism, globalization and development: Responsible tourism planning*. London: Pluto Press.

Romeril, M. (1994). Alternative tourism: The real tourism alternative? In C. P. Cooper & A. Lockwood (Eds.), *Progress in tourism, recreation and hospitality management*. Chichester: John Wiley & Sons Ltd.

Saarinen, J. (2006). Traditions of sustainability in tourism studies. *Annals of Tourism Research, 33*(4), 1121–1140. doi: 10.1016/j.annals.2006.06.007

Simpson, K. (2005). Dropping out or signing up? The professionalisation of youth travel. *Antipode.* 447–469.

Sin, H. L. (2010). Who are we responsible to? Locals' tales of volunteer tourism. *Geoforum, 41*(6), 983–992. doi: 10.1016/j.geoforum.2010.08.007

Sin, H. L., & Minca, C. (2014). Touring responsibility: The trouble with 'going local' in community-based tourism in Thailand. *Geoforum, 51*, 96–106. doi:10.1016/j.geoforum.2013.10.004

Smith, L., Rees, P., & Murray, N. (2016). Turning entrepreneurs into intrapreneurs: Thomas Cook, a case-study. *Tourism Management, 56*, 191–204. doi:10.1016/j.tourman.2016.04.005

Spenceley, A. (2008). *Responsible tourism: Critical issues for conservation and development.* London: Earthscan.

Stanford, D. (2008). Exceptional visitors: Dimensions of tourist responsibility in the context of New Zealand. *Journal of Sustainable Tourism, 16*(3), 258–275. doi:10.2167/jost788.0

Thomas Cook. (2018). *Sustainable tourism partners.* Retrieved from https://www.thomascook.com/sustainable-tourism/sustainable-tourism-partners/

Tilly, C. (1978). *From mobilization to revolution.* Reading, MA: Addison-Wesley. doi:10.1086/ahr/84.1.114

UN. (2017). *Sustainable development goals 17 goals to transform our world.* Retrieved from http://www.un.org/sustainabledevelopment/sustainable-development-goals/. Accessed 04/04/2018.

Van Dijk, T. (2006). Ideology and discourse analysis. *Journal of Political Ideologies, 11*(2), 115–140. doi:10.1080/13569310600687908

Vighi, F., & Feldner, H. (2007). Ideology critique or discourse analysis? Žižek against Foucault. *European Journal of Political Theory, 6*(2), 141–159. doi:10.1177/1474885107074347

Weber, H. (2017). Politics of 'Leaving No One Behind': Contesting the 2030 Sustainable Development Goals Agenda. *Globalizations, 14*(3), 399–414.

Weeden, C. (2014). *Responsible tourist behaviour, [electronic resource].* n.p.: London: Routledge.

Wheeler, B. (2012). Heritage tourists: Responsible (f)or what?. In T. V. Singh (Ed.), *Critical debates in tourism.* Bristol: Channel View Publications.

Williams, G. (2005). Towards a repoliticization of participatory development: Political capabilities and spaces of empowerment. In S. Hickey & G. Mohan (Eds.), *Participation: From tyranny to transformation? Exploring new approaches to participation in development.* London: Zed Books.

Žižek, S. (1989). *The sublime object of ideology.* London: Verso.

Žižek, S. (1999). *The ticklish subject: The absent centre of political ontology.* London: Verso.

Žižek, S. (2006). *The parallax view.* Cambridge, MA: MIT Press.

Žižek, S. (2010). *Living in the end of times.* London: Verso.

Sustaining precarity: critically examining tourism and employment

Richard N.S. Robinson ⓘ, Antje Martins, David Solnet and Tom Baum

ABSTRACT
There is consensus that both the social, or people, dimension of sustainability and the workforce are neglected in the tourism literature and policy. Premised on the understanding that sustainability is inherently set in neo-liberal discourses of progress, development and growth we set about to investigate tourism's performance principally relative to Sustainable Development Goal (SDG), no. 8 (UN, 2015), which calls for 'decent work'. Adopting critical approaches, and presenting a review of 14 industry reports from global, regional and national levels, we demonstrate that tourism sustains precarity vis-à-vis its employment practices. Precarity, an emerging sociological concept applied in the workforce context, speaks to the insecurities of work in capitalist economies. Our findings suggest that, contrary to academic and practitioner narratives championing humanist and sustainable tourism futures, tourism (employment) sustains precarious employment but also contributes to deep social cleavages and economic inequalities. Our paper concludes by mapping precarity into other SDGs which mark out precarious lives and propose a recalibration of the three sustainability pillars.

Introduction

Shared understandings of sustainability are inherently set in neo-liberal discourses of progress, development, and growth. As part of the market economy, tourism (whether branded as sustainable or not) is entangled in "an aggressive economic liberalism" (Bianchi, 2009, p.493). This notion is exemplified and amplified by Sustainable Development Goal, no. 8 (United Nations, 2015), which calls for 'decent work and [simultaneously] economic growth', and whose targets call for 'economic growth', 'higher levels of economic productivity', 'development-orientated policies', 'improve progressively', 'expand access to banking'—in other words a developmental process (Melissen, 2013). Yet literal definitions of sustain(ability), capture less assumptive, assertive and/or developmentally ambitious objectives; *inter alia* 'to hold', 'to strengthen', 'continue', and to 'maintain'. As Melissen (2013) suggests, sustainability in itself is a stasis, or stage— possibly the end product of sustainable development. Regardless, this article assumes these less fully laden designations in a critical investigation of the inter-relationships between sustainability, tourism and workforce, with the contention that the tourism industry holds, strengthens, continues and maintains, or sustains, precarity via its employment policies and practices (a thesis finding sympathy in Lee, Hampton, & Jeyacheya, 2015). Precarity, in a work context, is characterised be a lack of security and predictability and which manifests as material and psycho-social depravation (cf. Alberti, Bessa, Hardy, Trappmann, & Umney, 2018).

Tourism contributes to employment for 275 million persons globally (WTTC, 2017), yet the academy has largely neglected the complexities and contributions of (working) people to tourism (Baum, Kralj, Robinson, & Solnet, 2016b). We demonstrate how tourism (historically and currently) sustains precarity *vis-à-vis* its employment practices. Precarity, an emerging sociological concept applied in the workforce context, speaks to the insecurities of work in capitalist economies. Precarity exposes implicit effects on the marginalisation and mobility, and exclusion and exploitation, of vulnerable populations (Alberti, Holgate, & Tapia, 2013). Our contention is that tourism (employment) sustains deep social cleavages and economic inequalities thereby extending the precarious nature of work itself. We argue that not only is this unsustainable but, to disrupt this precarious cycle, the tourism academy and the tourism industry need to recalibrate the primacy of 'people', or the 'social' dimension of sustainability, in particular tourism workers, relative to the other dimensions of sustainability.

Ontologically, the all-pervasive neo-liberal paradigm that governs contemporary political, economic and social discourses, particularly in tourism, inhibits the ideals of sustainability (Gibson, 2009; Gössling, Ring, Dwyer, Andersson, & Hall, 2016; Tribe, Dann, & Jamal, 2015). As others have argued, capitalist and political agendas and applied business and managerial standpoints, drive tourism discourses without being recognised and challenged by conceptual, theoretical, and empirical work in the field (Bianchi, 2017). This is no more so evident than in employment practices in tourism, which are generally characterised by such factors as low entry barriers, poor working conditions, loose regulation and mostly absent union representation (Baum, 2015). It is also worth reflecting, in our consideration of this theme, that a key mantra within the neo-liberal agenda is that of the flexible labour market (Arnold & Bongiovi, 2013). Flexibility, in this context, is rarely reciprocal (Bolton & Houlihan, 2007), with industry benefitting far more than workers in the long term, providing (as we will show) a fertile breeding ground for precarious work. Consequently, there is a pressing need to critically evaluate the values that underpin sustainability discourses in the context of employment. No other sector is as diverse as tourism especially with regards to its sub-sectors and its differences within local socio-politico-economic conditions. We embrace this diversity within this paper as do most of the data sources that we use. However, we also caution against an overgeneralisation of our findings across the entire sector and hence include alternative interpretations of our arguments to remind the reader of the inherent complexities.

Employment in tourism

Tourism employment is diverse in the range of job types and skills it encompasses and is located across very different sub-sectors (such as travel facilitation, transport, accommodation, food services, attractions, heritage, events) at multiple levels within micro, medium, and large organisations, both local and multinational. It is geographically dispersed and can be found in remote areas where a local skilled workforce is not readily available (Robinson, Ritchie, Kralj, Solnet, Baum, & Ford, 2014). It is also work that can be greatly influenced by the impacts of seasonality on precariousness, can be antisocial in the demands it makes on the working day and is frequently perceived to be of low status and limited desirability from a career perspective (Mooney, 2018). Tourism employees are highly mobile (Duncan, Scott, & Baum, 2013), frequently in the form of the exploitative employment of migrant labour (Janta, Ladkin, Brown, & Lugosi, 2011). Finally, tourism is at the forefront of the emergent collaborative or gig economy, within which the long-term employment consequences are unclear (Bertoli, Fernández-Huertas Moraga, & Keita, 2017; Dredge & Gyimóthy, 2015). Therefore, it is difficult to generalise about work and the workforce in tourism. Writing some 20 years ago, eerily echoing much earlier Orwellian themes (1933), Wood (1997, p. 198), provided a challenging perspective on work in one of tourism's largest sub-sectors, hospitality, when he declared that "hospitality work is largely exploitative, degrading, poorly paid, unpleasant, insecure and taken as a last resort or because it can be tolerated in the light of wider social and economic commitments and constraints".

As Baum (2015, 2018a) serves, the fundamental characteristics of tourism employment do not seem to have reformed with the passage of time. Employment in tourism continues to be associated with a lack of respect, esteem, and standing relative to employment in other sectors, and poor remuneration is a perennial complaint (cf. De Beer, Rogerson, & Rogerson, 2014). The industry is largely hostile towards the endeavours of the trade union movement (Bergene, Boluk, & Buckley, 2015) and workplace contexts remain persistently obstinate regarding the expectations of legislation and broader industrial and community ethical requirements and expectations respectively (Poulston, 2008; The Guardian, 2018). Tourism work is almost synonymously associated with "low skills" (Ladkin, 2011) although it is acknowledged that this is partially a western-centric perspective (Nickson, Warhurst, Cullen, & Watt, 2003). In its broadest interpretation, tourism work can include engagement with exploitative employment, bordering on modern slavery that includes child labour, child sex work, child trafficking but also the exploitation of vulnerable adults through forced labour (Armstrong, 2016). Robinson (2013, p. 94) highlighted modern slavery, in the tourism and hospitality context, as a "profound violation of human rights".

However, there is also recognition of a lack of clarity with respect to interpretations of job quality in the sector (Knox, 2016; Knox, Warhurst, Nickson, & Dutton, 2015). Granted, what for a critical and agenda-driven outside observer the descriptor of 'bad job' may be apt, from the perspective of the job custodian it may represent an entirely different set of propositions. Perceptions of the quality of tourism jobs is contingent on the macro-context (economic and socio-cultural) in terms of, for example, gender and ethnicity (Adler & Adler, 2004; McDowell, Batnitzky & Dyer, 2009) as well as that of the attitude and aspirations of the individual in assessing the relative job opportunities available within the sector and the wider economy (Gursoy, Chi, & Karadag, 2013). It is also clear that there are many examples of tourism companies that commit to broad-based corporate social responsibility (CSR) and exhibit the highest standards in terms of ethical employment, offering work and careers on par with some of the best employers worldwide (Hughes & Scheyvens, 2016).

Complex value chains that support the 'front-line' businesses are part of the tourism sector and provide additional challenges in terms of responsibility for working conditions and employment (Becker, Carbo, & Langella, 2010). As Methven O'Brien and Dhanarajan (2016, p. 551) note, "companies' failures to remediate more general supply chain responsibility issues probably remain the biggest problem of all" and, in tourism, these links extend across a wide range of sectors, both local and international. Consideration of employment in the industry is further complicated because of the fast-changing nature of the business structures that are evident in the form of partnerships, alliances, franchising, and off-shored ownership models coupled with multi-employer sites, outsourcing, temporary forms of employment and self-employment. Compared to other sectors of the economy, tourism operates within two parallel and largely interdependent worlds in organisational terms. These worlds represent, on the one hand, businesses within the formal, recognised and often registered (with tourism authorities) industry alongside, on the other, a grey or informal and unregulated tourism economy which can include a significant proportion of the total sector in many countries (Bertoli et al., 2017; Jones, Ram, & Edwards, 2004; MacDonald, 1994). This is frequently in the form of self-employment or family-based work. Furthermore, with the emergence of a growing collaborative, platform or gig economy in tourism onto the international stage, the distinction between the formal and the informal is becoming increasingly blurred and, arguably, problematic from an employment perspective (Bertoli et al., 2017). These conditions only heighten the precarious nature of much tourism employment.

Precarity, precarious work and the 'precariat'

Precariousness, or precarity, in the broadest sense relates to a state defined by a lack of security and predictability, which when applied to the human condition manifests as material and psycho-social depravation (Alberti et al., 2018). Returning to our neo-liberal capitalist precepts (Bianchi, 2009, 2017; Gibson, 2009; Tribe et al., 2015), social scientists almost exclusively associate precarity with un/under and/or unstable employment (Wacquant, 2014). Standing's (2011) evocation of the Marxian proletariat (working class) in his portmanteau designation, 'the precariat', underscores the immutable entanglement of social and economic precarity with degrees of participation in the workforce. Precarious work is characterised by employment that is irregular and insecure; part-time/casual, quasi-self-employment, project or fixed-term work, temporary work (often via agencies), work on commission, on-call work, and increasingly a rise in home-based employment, and so-called 'telecommuting'. Unpaid training and development and volunteering have somehow been ascribed as 'work' furthering the link between precarity and (un)employment (Smith, 2010). Vallas and Prener (2012, p. 332) observe that these non-standard forms of employment, work that lacks continuation over time and pay as well as social protection, have become increasingly prevalent since "large corporations have moved to dismantle the centralised or Fordist bureaucratic models on which they once relied". While labour history and industrial relations have always been prone to change, the past three decades have seen an acceleration of deregulation and privatisation (Ross, 2009) resultant in downsizing, even outsourcing, of labour within organisations changing standard working arrangement to increasing temporary, contract, and part-time arrangements, often against the volition of employees. The effects of insecure and unstable employment, or precarious work, include a higher exposure to declining health (mental as well as physical), increased financial instability, and widening societal gaps (Quan, 2017), thus creating precarious lives.

However, other narratives have developed framing the emergence of contingent work as a positive evolution for organisations and workers alike. The numerical and functional flexibility (Timo, 1999) afforded to employers, and the ability to reduce their payroll at a moments' notice contributes to nimble firms not constrained by the permanency of a standing workforce. Moreover, contingent workers rarely receive the entitlements of their permanent counterparts; leave and sickness benefits, superannuation, insurances and the like (Ross, 2009) thus further reducing payroll responsibilities to the benefit of organisations. From a worker's perspective, commentators have hinted at the emancipatory qualities of the new work order for employees to express 'free agency' (Vallas & Prener, 2012) despite lessening financial stability. Among these are breaking the shackles of despotic and irrational workplace routines, with the introduction of flexible and project-based work, being able to take personal control and to charge fees commensurate with skills (Barley & Kunda, 2006). Bearing the 'creative class' trademark (Florida, 2014), the concept of the creative city has been born as a vision for the future, whereby workers in the knowledge economy thrive in fluid, highly connected, digitalised and vibrant, entrepreneurial and tech-edgy spaces that define the fourth industrial revolution (World Economic Forum, 2016). However, this also represents exclusion for those whose skills do not match the demands of the creative economy (Baum, 2018b). Yet critiques of casual, or contingent, work have also been commiserative.

The espoused benefits of contingent work, and that of the creative class, have been applied to highly remunerated and skilled professionals and managers of one description or another (Vallas & Prener, 2012). Indeed, Gill and Pratt (2008, p. 3) consider creative workers to be "the poster boys and girls of the new 'precariat'". Freelancers, consultants, entrepreneurs and start-up owners almost exclusively apply to those that work with their 'heads rather than their hands'— members of the knowledge economy (cf. Barley & Kunda, 2006; Osnowitz, 2010). Manual jobs that provided stable and secure employment for a developed world middle-working class have disappeared due to a combination of automation and outsourcing, suggesting a polarisation of the workforce (Kalleberg, 2011).

Returning to the creative class, and illustrating this labour market dualism, Baum (2018b) has highlighted how an under-class of service workers, who are largely concealed and neglected in the 'creative cities' discourse, largely provision for the needs of those employed in the knowledge economy. Many provide services in the 'gig economy' (Horney, 2016)—rides with Uber, the raft of home delivery services for takeaway food and groceries, house cleaning, gardening services and so on. Ironically, many of these platforms disrupt poorly paid and unstable occupations, such as restaurant, transport and cleaning work, which incidentally are key services in tourism destinations. Baum (2018b) also posits that the inherently precarious nature of much creative (knowledge) work places many 'creatives' in direct labour market competition with 'traditional' service workers and that, for aesthetic rather than technical reasons, they are likely to displace them in many jobs. The rise of exploitative, unpaid internships within the creative sector is another example of precarious working (Siebert & Wilson, 2013).

Other transient and mobile workers also compete for the service work in the new economy. As Anderson (2010, p. 300) asserts, "migrants are often portrayed as working in sectors such as hospitality, construction, sex, agriculture and private households at the sharp end of de-regulated labour markets in jobs characterised by low wages, insecurity and obfuscated employment relations". Migrants, asylum seekers and refugees are particularly vulnerable to not only precarious work, but also to various forms of harassment and discrimination (McDowell et al., 2009). Two other specific labour markets are marked out by their transience and mobility, even if this is defined by temporality as much as it is by space and place. Women's and youth workforce participation has been steadily increasing for decades, yet each cohort has encountered issues of equality and wage parity. This is notwithstanding the willingness to engage in mobile and temporary labour, given the affordances of geographic mobility, for backpackers for instance (Cohen, 2011). Indeed, youth "acknowledge insecurity as a condition of youthful working life" (Morgan, Wood, & Nelligan, 2013, p. 410). Research consistently shows the intersectionality of migrants, women, ethnicity, race, youth, class and other marginal social groups (cf. Alberti, 2016; Alberti et al., 2013; Browne & Misra, 2003; McDowell et al., 2009; Morgan et al., 2013). This is often a potent combination that culminates in two vulnerable, insecure, untenable and often inescapable conditions; precarious work and precarious lives.

Precariousness, sustainability and the social dimension and work

Precarious work and lives fall right within the ambit of social sustainability as they concern the people working within the tourism industry. Considering the emergence of sustainable tourism several decades ago following the seminal work of the Brundtland et al., report (1987) precariousness should technically be addressed and eliminated as part of the three-sphere model. However, Boström (2012) highlights the neglect of the social pillar by policy makers and, indeed, researchers—the social dimension garners less attention or is dismissed altogether (Cuthill, 2010; Dillard, Dujon, & King, 2008). Similarly, within the tourism domain, several authors have pointed out the neglect of the social sustainability sphere (Coles, Fenclova, & Dinan, 2013; Ruhanen, Weiler, Moyle, & McLennan, 2015) alongside that of bio-physical aspects (Vallance, Perkins & Dixon, 2011).

The social, or people, domain is still poorly defined relative to its environmental and economic cousins (Dillard et al., 2008), yet elements such as community, education, health, housing, human rights and liveability are generally included within this domain. Equity, inclusivity, equality, diversity, representation and wellbeing, among others, are issues frequently lobbied for in the context of workplace, industrial relations and human resource development (Garavan, Heraty, & Morley, 1998). All elements that are in stark contrast to the concepts of precarity, precarious work and precarious lives. Baum (2018a) highlights the neglect of employment considerations in

Table 1. Key sensitising constructs.

SDG	Constructs		
	Demographics	Individual attributes	Industry characteristics
Goal 1: To end poverty in all its forms and everywhere.	• Gender • Age • Level of education • Race/religion/ethnicity • Sexuality • Class	• Accommodation/housing status	• Wages • Benefits (i.e. leave, medical benefits, retirement funds/super) • Grey/informal economy • Black economy (slavery, sex tourism, trafficking)
Goal 3: To ensure healthy lives and well-being for all at all ages.		• Flexibility in regards to career obligations • Flexibility overall • Substance abuse • Mental health • Accommodation/housing status	• Hours of work • Working conditions • Benefits (i.e. leave, medical benefits, retirement funds/super) • Black economy (slavery, sex tourism, trafficking)
Goal 4: To ensure inclusive and equitable quality education and promote lifelong learning opportunities for all.		• Flexibility in regards to career obligations • Flexibility overall	• Level of skills • Promotional opportunities/ career progression/career pathways • Grey/informal economy
Goal 5: To achieve gender equality and empower all women and girls.		• Flexibility in regards to careers obligations • Flexibility overall • Parental status	• Wages • Benefits (i.e. leave, medical benefits, retirement funds/super) • Promotional opportunities/ career progression/career pathways • Grey/informal economy • Black economy (slavery, sex tourism, trafficking)
Goal 8: To promote sustained, inclusive and sustainable economic growth, full and productive employment and decent work.		• Flexibility in regards to careers obligations • Flexibility overall • Tenure/mobility	• Wages • Hours of work • Working conditions • Benefits (i.e. leave, medical benefits, retirement funds/super) • Grey/informal economy • Black economy (slavery, sex tourism, trafficking)
Goal 10: To reduce inequality within and among countries.		• Mental health	• Mobility/portability of skills • Black economy (slavery, sex tourism, trafficking)
Goal 16: To promote peaceful and inclusive societies for sustainable development, provide access to justice for all and build effective, accountable and inclusive institutions at all levels.		• Substance abuse • Mental health	• Mobility/portability of skills • Black economy (slavery, sex tourism, trafficking)

discussion, even in contemporary accounts of sustainable tourism (cf. Miller, Rathouse, Scarles, Holmes, & Tribe, 2010). He notes the absence of employment or workforce-related themes within the dominant sustainability narrative. This is somewhat surprising considering sustainability agendas are invariably carried out by the tourism workforce, whether of a strategic nature in the design of policy, administrative or operational procedures, or indeed actually delivering them, for example effective recycling or reducing towel and sheet wash loads. No doubt, the design of organisational training and development programs prepare employees for their roles as agents of sustainable practices.

Yet sustainability, as a concept, has pervaded the employment literature, even if tourism has yet to take note of this development. Sustainable human resource management (SHRM) relates to practices that contribute to the development of human and social capital within the organisation. "Sustainable HRM represents a new approach to managing people, by identifying broader purposes for HRM, through its recognition of the complexities of workplace dynamics and the explicit recognition of the need to avoid negative impacts of HRM practices" (Kramar, 2014, p. 1085). Congruent with the sustainability concept overall, sustainable human resource management has seen several offshoots (Ehnert, Harry, & Zink, 2013), such as socially responsible HRM, which is closely linked CSR. CSR is arguably a philanthropic and voluntary function, often designed to enhance market perceptions of an organisation (Coles et al., 2013) and so its sustainability priorities are less directed at the wellbeing of employees as such, but rather on economic sustainability.

However, as Longoni and Cagliano (2015, p. 218) assert, "social sustainability refers to actively supporting the preservation and creation of skills as well as the capabilities of future generations, promoting health and supporting equal and democratic treatments that allow for good quality of life both inside and outside of the company context". In this sense, there is a broader vision for sustainability extending beyond the workplace with the potential to address precariousness across all domains. Indeed, while Sustainable Development Goal no. 8 (UN, 2015), which calls for the promotion of 'sustained, inclusive and sustainable economic growth, full and productive employment and decent work', acts as a starting point for our work, a more lateral and nuanced approach to interpreting the SDGs via a workforce lens suggests the social, or people, dimension of sustainability, is spoken to by several of the SDGs (Baum et al., 2016a) (Table 1).

The remainder of this paper will critically examine a sample of contemporary reports and documents, which directly or indirectly speak to the precarious work and precarious lives of those employed in tourism and its allied industry sectors; *inter alia* hospitality, events, services and leisure. In so doing we aim to challenge current notions of sustainability more broadly, but particularly as applied to tourism, which we have already demonstrated in academic and policy endeavours marginalises both the sustainability social, or people, dimension—and its workforce.

Data and methods

To investigate the proposition that the tourism industry sustains precarity in its employment policies and practices, we sought to identify suitable industry literature within which we could conduct a critical content analysis. Precarity is conceptualised here as lack of security and predictability resulting in some form of depravation. Applying this concept to the realities of the (neo-liberal) tourism industry as outlined here, but also in other work (cf. Ladkin, 2011) a range of sensitising constructs (King, 2004) emerge. These constructs (as identified in Table 1) range from demographics (i.e. women or youth as marginalised groups in tourism work), to individual worker attributes (i.e. the increasing mobility of tourism employing frequently resulting in exploitative migrant labour) to industry characteristics (i.e. low wages, low skills, and black/grey economy). To allow the analysis of the sustainability dimension of our argument below, the constructs are mapped against the SDGs in the left column, providing a basis for our industry data review below.

Industry data search and analysis

To explore our contention that the precarious nature of tourism employment is at odds with sustainability, we sought secondary industry data to investigate whether tourism employment represents precariousness. The industry data was identified and analysed in a two-step process, which was informed by the methodologies of similar document analyses (Homeshaw, 1995;

Table 2. Data sources per level of analysis.

Level	Reports
Global data	• The World Tourism and Travel Council's Global talent trends and issues for the travel and tourism sector (2015), • The World Bank's Worldbank Indicators data platform (2018), • The ILO's Developments and challenges in the hospitality and tourism sector (2010), • The ILO's Key indicators of the labour market (2016) and • ILOSTAT data (2018).
Regional data	• OECD's Supporting Quality Jobs in Tourism (Stacey,2015), • The EU's Skills Panorama (2018) platform, • The EU's Eurostat: Tourism industries employment (2018) and • APEC's Developing the Tourism Workforce of the Future in the APEC Region (2017).
National data	• Deloitte's Australian Tourism Labour Force Report: 2015–2020 (2015), • Biehl and Kaske's report on Tourism in Austria (2011, where required translated from German by one of the authors), • Berg & Farbenlum's (2017) Wage theft in Australia, • ANZ's Servicing Australia's future (2016) and • Australia Parliament's Current vacancies: Workforce challenges facing the Australian tourism sector (2007).

Solnet, Nickson, Robinson, Kralj, & Baum, 2014). Initially, a purposive tiered sample of industry reports and data was sought according to the following selection criteria:

a. In sampling preference was given to the most comprehensive primary data reports, from reputable and recognisable organisations, although secondary data (reports that had already processed data to generate some argument, narrative or advocacy position) were included;
b. A quantitatively balanced sample for three tiers was established: global data, regional data and national data relating to the tourism and hospitality industry/sector. Several of the resources did not necessarily have sector-specific data but rather contained economy-specific data (e.g., International Labour Organisation [ILO]). Where feasible this was cross-referenced with highly tourism dependent economies (e.g. the Maldives, where tourism comprises 28% of GDP and over 60% of their foreign exchange earnings). The assumption was that the ILO data for highly tourism dependent countries would more closely approximate industry conditions.
c. A qualitatively balanced data set reflecting the global labour market and workforce in tourism (e.g. developed and developing economies).

Our final sample included 14 reports. Table 2 outlines the reports by level of analysis (global, regional or national). We searched these documents for the constructs listed in Table 1. Some topics, for example wages and gender, were overrepresented and others, such as substance abuse and mental health, did not yield any results despite these appearing in tourism occupational literature (cf. Giousmpasoglou, Brown, & Cooper, 2018; Kotera, Adhikari, & Van Gordon, 2018).

In analysing the reports using the constructs identified, two separate but linked themes were evident. First, evidence of precarious employment within the tourism industry, including employment that lacks security or predictability, either temporarily, spatially or monetarily. Second, and as a result of the first theme, evidence emerged of how employment in tourism, and its allied sectors, contributes to precarious lives. Both themes form the basis of the analysis which follows.

Precarious employment

Focusing initially on working conditions, globally tourism workers consistently earn less than the all-industries average. In Canada tourism workers earn 47% of the average, in Chile, 91%,

New Zealand, 49%, Philippines, 42% and Indonesia 17%. (APEC, 2017). Specifically, according to OECD reports, in hotels and restaurants earnings were about 37% lower than average earnings in the economy as a whole, and up to 60% lower in some countries (Stacey, 2015). Similarly, EuroSTAT (2015) reported that average hourly earnings were €14.10 in 2010 and average tourism hourly earnings amounted to €12.10, adding that for the same year accommodation sector gross hourly earnings were €9.50, evidence corroborated by the literature *vis-à-vis* hotel workers (Alberti, 2016). In a survey of APEC economies, (2017), foodservice roles were particularly poorly remunerated, and predominated as the lowest paid job regardless of nationality, across four of the six top countries (China, South Korea, Brazil and India). According to Biehl and Kaske (2011), the median monthly income in tourism in Austria was a third below the overall median, trailing only the home services and agriculture industries.

Evidence supported the expectation that tourism had a high share part-time, casual and seasonal employment profile (WTTC, 2015). Within the EU and other Western contexts, the United Kingdom (50%) and the Netherlands (68%) reported high rates of part-time tourism employment (ILO, 2010), in the Czech Republic and Sweden the proportion of part-time workers in tourism is almost twice as high as it is in the economy as a whole (EuroSTAT, 2015). In Australia 41% of tourism employees are employed part-time compared to all-industries average of 32.5% (Australian Parliament, 2007). In Spain only 64% of the workforce is employed throughout the whole year—a consequence of the sun, sea and sand driven seasonality (ILO, 2010).

Subcontracting and outsourcing accounted for 4.6% of tourism employees in Spain. Moreover, tourism dominated marginal employment contracts, 18% compared with 8% in the overall economy (Biehl & Kaske, 2011). Enterprise bargaining agreements have gradually been replacing award-based systems in Australia (Australian Parliament, 2007) whittling away penalty rates, traditionally geared at rewarding non-standard working hours (Knox, 2006). While the hospitality and tourism sector is characterised by high fragmentation, approximately 20% of the workforce is located within multinational corporations (MNC). MNCs have a high propensity for both casualised and outsourced labour (McDowell et al., 2009). Workers in (contingent) non-standard employment, highly prevalent in tourism (Baum, 2015), faced substantial wage penalties in the US and Europe, relative to comparable standard workers, reaching 30% (ILO, 2016). Across the reports there was consistent evidence of longer hours than in other sectors (Berg & Farbenblum, 2017).

Tourism is a significant employer of women globally (56% females to 46% males) (The World Bank, 2018), and much higher in many economies, for example in Poland and Slovakia 67% are employed in tourism versus 36% in the economy as a whole (EuroSTAT, 2015). Tourism has been a driver of women's workforce participation, although assumptions regarding whether this is positive are being questioned (Duffy, Kline, Mowatt, & Chancellor, 2015). Regardless, in Australia women's participation in the tourism labour force increased from 51% in 1978 to 70% in 2016 (ANZ, 2016). Typically, women in developed nations comprise 50–60% of the workforce, while in developing countries the figure can be much higher, with Thailand (65%), Vietnam (70%) and Peru (76%) being illustrative examples, although rates of self-employment in these nations are higher (APEC, 2017)—in itself a marker of precarity (Bertoli et al., 2017; Jones et al, 2004). Interestingly, however, the data consistently show women's earnings, across all jurisdictions, lagging behind that of men (Berg & Farbenblum, 2017; Biehl & Kaske, 2011; EuroSTAT, 2015), by an average of 25% less for comparable skills (ILO, 2010), according to accounts of gender precarity in tourism and hospitality employment (Santero-Sanchez, Segovia-Pérez, Castro-Nuñez, Figueroa-Domecq, & Talón-Ballestero, 2015).

Tourism is an important employer of youth (WTTC, 2015). For example, in Spain 43% of workers in the sector are aged 25–34 (ILO, 2010), in Denmark, Malta and the Netherlands the figure exceeds 20% (EuroSTAT, 2015). Across European OECD countries 47% of the 15–34 years cohort are employed in tourism, compared to 32.4% in the economy as a whole (Stacey, 2015). This compares to 26% in Australia (Australian Parliament, 2007). The US Bureau of Statistics reports that in food preparation and service roles there are more workers aged between 16 and 20 than those aged 20 and over (ILO, 2010). The prevalence of youth in the workforce perhaps speaks to the low skilled occupations that comprise its sectors.

Yet still, skill gaps persist especially in developed countries (ILOSTAT, 2018; WTTC, 2015). A majorative 69% of Australian businesses identified skills deficiencies in their tourism workforce (APEC, 2017), yet the industry is notorious for being training avoiders (Lashley, 2009). Our data show that few companies in most economies seriously consider skills investment, Iceland being an anomaly (Stacey, 2015). However, when marginal groups are considered the picture changes complexion. High proportions of skilled and educated women and migrants are under-employed, relevant to their qualifications (Biehl & Kaske, 2011), and given that worldwide educational levels of the labour force are improving, there is evidence that un/under employment is a higher risk to the uneducated than the educated migrant (ILO, 2016) further making vulnerable populations susceptible to exploitative conditions (Browne & Misra, 2003; McDowell, et al., 2009). Our study shows that tourism is decreasingly becoming a 'catch all' for those with lower levels of education (EuroSTAT, 2015; Stacey, 2015) although the reasons are contextual and varied. Nonetheless, from EuroSTAT (2015) data 30 from 40 regions with the highest tourism intensity have an unemployment rate below the national average.

Regardless, tourism and mobility are synonymous, affording benefits to those who are prepared to move for employment. However, the data show that workers in tourism demonstrated a higher proclivity for seeking exit strategies from their work. The Biehl and Kaske (2011) report found that a third of tourism workers wanted to leave their organisation or sector, compared to 16% of those in other sectors. The OECD reports that 45% of tourism employees stayed in the same job for less than two years, as compared to the 25% all-industries average (Stacey, 2015) with EuroSTAT (2015) reporting similar statistics. Australian data show that employees, especially in regional areas, consider tourism employment as only short-term (Deloitte Access Economics, 2015).

Mobility into tourism is eased by low entry barriers (WTTC, 2015). Biehl and Kaske (2011) report that seasonality is the catalyst for much mobility, with only 54% of tourism workers employed year-round. Moreover, 71% of workers took extended breaks out of tourism, with women far more likely to interrupt than men. Interestingly, economies with higher rates of temporary employment were more likely to see workers transiting between contingent labour and unemployment. The likelihood of transitioning to better jobs was less probable (ILO, 2016).

In relation to mobility, the industry is more likely to attract foreign workers compared to the economy average precipitating high rates of cross-border migration (WTTC, 2015), as evident in much recent literature (cf. Janta et al., 2011; McDowell, 2009; Robinson et al., 2014). In Biehl and Kaske's (2011) Austrian report social security data reveals that 36% of the tourism workforce (compared with 13.8% in the whole economy) have foreign citizenship. Foreign workers comprise 8% of the air transport sector, in travel agencies and/or tour operators, yet 17% of the accommodation labour market (EuroSTAT, 2015). Unsurprisingly, international students, working holiday makers and temporary migrants all intersect with the lowest wages (Berg & Farbenblum, 2017). These populations are vulnerable to the grey and black economies (ILO, 2010) as noted in the literature (Armstrong, 2016). Berg and Farbenblum (2017), in the Australian context, reveal that unauthorised workers on tourist visas and temporary migrants work for well-below award wages, and are often paid in cash with no payment record. Their recourse to challenge their working conditions is seriously comprised, as is their ability to live stable and dignified lives beyond work. We now turn to themes in the data that speak to precarious lives.

Precarious lives

The Biehl and Kaske (2011) data from an Austrian survey found that 46% of respondents stated that their wage is just enough to make ends meet, and 15% reported that it was not sufficient.

Table 3. Sustainable development goals and tourism employment.

SDG	Implications of precarious employment in tourism
Goal 1: To end poverty in all its forms and everywhere.	We have seen the extent to which part-time, seasonal and other forms of precarious work feature in tourism. Such work can frequently perpetuate in-work poverty, creating the working poor
Goal 3: To ensure healthy lives and well-being for all at all ages.	The nature of much tourism work runs counter to work-life balance objectives and runs counter to this goal in relation to workers, their families and their communities.
Goal 4: To ensure inclusive and equitable quality education and promote lifelong learning opportunities for all.	Those in precarious work are disproportionately disadvantaged in terms of accessing education and opportunities for lifelong learning, compounded by a sector, tourism, where investment in training and development is significantly lower than economy averages in most countries.
Goal 5: To achieve gender equality and empower all women and girls.	Women are over-represented in the global tourism industry, especially in terms of self-employment within the informal economy but they are markedly under-represented in positions of authority and leadership. Tourism, therefore, contributes little to gender equality
Goal 8: To promote sustained, inclusive and sustainable economic growth, full and productive employment and decent work.	Tourism, as noted in this paper, faces systemic and structural challenges with respect to the delivery of decent work opportunities and perpetuates exploitative work that, at times, merges with modern slavery.
Goal 10: To reduce inequality within and among countries.	The precarious nature of tourism work leaves many employees in a marginal relationship with the wider society in which they live, unable to participate fully in economic, social or cultural terms. Tourism work, by and large, does not provide opportunities for social mobility or the reduction in inequalities in most countries
Goal 16: To promote peaceful and inclusive societies for sustainable development, provide access to justice for all and build effective, accountable and inclusive institutions at all levels.	Peace and inclusivity require communities in harmony with themselves, based in an equitable distribution of opportunity for key stakeholders (e.g. youth and women) and fair access to collective wealth. The nature of much precarious tourism work runs diametrically counter to this SDG.

In addition, 25% of the Austrian respondents suspected that their wages would not be enough to earn them a pension on which they would be able to live (Biehl & Kaske, 2011). In Australia, a steady decline in real wages contributed to rising income inequality such that household spending dropped and concurrently income to buy capital assets, such as housing, reduced further (ANZ, 2016). A report on employees of Disneyworld (although caution must be exercised in the interpretation of its findings) revealed that 56% of workers responding to their survey reported concerns regarding eviction, that one in 10 had been homeless in the past two years, and that over half resided in overcrowded accommodation (Drier & Flaming, 2018), a clear illustration of the working poor, the precariat, in tourism.

While our earlier discussion focused on wage inequality, in the Maldives, on average 2% of all employed females' earnings left them below the poverty line, compared to about 1.7% of males (ILOSTAT, 2018; see also Horemans, Marx, & Nolan, 2016). Cultural and structural reasons, for instance the aforementioned Maldivian Muslim observances (Jafari & Scott, 2014) and child-caring responsibilities (Browne & Misra, 2003) respectively, underpin why women make up less than 40% of total wage employment, yet represent 57% of part-time employees. Many women work part-time as it allows them to combine paid work with domestic and care responsibilities (ILO, 2016). Similarly, either formal labour market exclusion, or flexibility to fulfil career duties (McMillan, O'Gorman, & MacLaren, 2011), conspire to make self-employment attractive. OECD data reports that 24% of women seek self-employment in tourism compared to 19% in the overall economy (Stacey, 2015). Similarly, contingent workers in the gig economy, in data obtained from Uber, Airbnb, and a report on Crowd workers indicates that it is not millennials who dominate the sector, but rather workers in their notional 'prime' (25–55 years old) (APEC, 2017). Women, in particular seem to show more willingness to 'dip their toes in the water' of traditional male-dominated industries, via the gig economy (APEC, 2017). The immense flexibility, demands and precarity characterizing the gig economy (Baum, 2018b) can be a mixed blessing. In some economies, for example Singapore and the Philippines, Uber is promoted as a life-style choice, allowing flexibility in choices in some economies (Lim, 2017; Moragra, 2017) yet the low rates of pay, and pressure to 'put food on the table' may be incompatible with the parenthood duties that invariably fall on middle-aged women, in developed and developing economies alike.

On a more sombre note, predominantly in developing countries, it is estimated that two million children are commercially and sexually exploited (ILO, 2010), with Robinson (2013) arguing that the sex, tourism and hospitality industries are inherently intertwined. By any definition these children are being deprived their childhood and dignity (Black, 1995). Needless to say, that these workers in the grey and/or black economies are excluded from their employment benefits, but the evidence is that so too are many non-standard, or contingent workers in tourism (ILO, 2016). These contingent tourism worker entitlements, which include *inter alia* sick leave, medical care, recreation leave and retirement funds lag behind all-industry comparisons (APEC, 2017), and are significant in that they impact quality of life beyond the workplace, spatially and temporally.

Triangulating the evidence from our study there is also evidence of the intersectionality of some aspects of precarity beyond that of the commonly presented socio-economic: that is the intersection of the demographics and characteristics of workers, for example gender, age, race, class, and migrant or refugee status (e.g., Alberti, 2016; Browne & Misra, 2003; Morgan et al., 2013). We have found evidence of precariousness *at work*, compounding the insecurity *of work* itself and the precariousness *of life*. This triumvirate of precarity compounds the existing double-jeopardy of precarious work and precarious lives, and further marks out Standing's (2011) notion of the precariat.

Sustaining precarious tourism employment

Summarising key findings relative to sustainability, precarious work and precarious lives several key themes emerge that connect these topics. Intersectionality (Alberti, 2016), mobility (Duncan et al., 2013), exploitation (Robinson, 2013; Siebert & Wilson, 2013; Wood, 1997), a paradox of low skills required (Baum, 2015) but rising education levels (Stacey, 2015), contributions to poverty in work (Drier & Flaming, 2018; Horemans et al., 2016) and the neo-liberal-driven polarisation of the workforce (Kalleberg, 2011) come to the fore.

Granted, these are nuanced between different jurisdictions, developed and developing economies, and prevailing socio-politico-economic conditions (Baum, 2018a).

Table 3 maps evidence from our analysis and discussion to the SDG's. This summary presents a bleak assessment of the UN's SDs and suggests that in many contexts, the precarious nature of much tourism work makes a counter-contribution to the achievement of key SDGs despite being often celebrated as a key job driver within the SDGs (UN, 2015). Perhaps of most concern in this cross tabulation is that precarity, as a concept leading contemporary analyses of work relations, is borne out of reasonably recent post-Fordist industrial developments (Vallas & Prener, 2012). However, the compelling evidence is that while other industries may have become a locus for precarious work, tourism always has had such attributes (Orwell, 1933; Wood, 1997). The marginal worker thesis in tourism and hospitality (Robinson, 2008; Wood, 1992) significantly pre-dated this post-Fordist turn (Morgan et al., 2013). The effects of right wing populism, some are convinced (Cumming, Wood, & Zahra, 2016), will exacerbate the precarity of contingent workers via an erosive evolution of HRM practices and employment law. More than this, our analyses of global, regional and national data sources support the contention that contingent and non-standard employment increasingly attracts populations from the margins of society (Alberti et al., 2013; McDowell et al., 2009; Morgan et al., 2013), and so perpetuates, or sustains, their precarious lives.

Conclusion and future research

Our critical review in this paper presents a fundamental challenge to neo-liberal charged notions of tourism (Bianchi, 2009, 2017) and sustainable tourism (Gibson, 2009; Tribe et al., 2015) and the contribution which many writers believe tourism can make towards its attainment. By moving the conversation away from the dominant environmental—economic narrative in relation to sustainability and focusing on the social sustainability pillar, we have exposed significant flaws in the prevailing discourse about tourism existing in harmony with sustainable development goals. Our evidence points clearly to the (increasingly) precarious nature of much tourism employment and the manner in which this runs counter to; discursive notions of sustainability as captured in its progressive and developmental rhetoric, the objectives of sustainable HRM (Ehnert, 2009) and to the underpinning objectives of the UN's SDGs. Our findings also run counter to the ILO's (2012) aspirations for decent work in tourism (Baum, 2018a). As we have noted earlier, we do accept that notions of precarious work (and with it both the nature of job quality and the remedies available to improve it) are contested. Knox et al. (2015) point to inherent ambiguity with respect to interpretations of job quality in the sector while Knox (2014) further argues that, in the context of precarity, investment in employees working for temping agencies through enhanced training opportunities and higher levels of remuneration can pay dividends in terms of productivity and reduced turnover.

The conceptual contribution therefore, is to propose the need for a recalibration of sustainability in tourism relative to the social dimension, and specific to the workforce. The current discourse privileges the economic-environmental dimensions thus neglecting the social subsequently sustaining precarity via employment (Wacquant, 2014). Sustainable employment in tourism would offer opportunities for decent, rewarding, developmental work for all, without distinction on the basis of gender, ethnicity, age, disability or sexuality, work that allows employees to balance employment with family, social and leisure rights and obligations.

This aspiration also provides a route to the practice and policy implications of this narrative because stakeholders, whether governments, the tourism industry and the third sector must be charged with making this aspiration a reality and that will require tripartite collaboration but also commitment from all parties to the business and ethical advantages of change (cf. Gössling et al., 2016). Ensuring decent work and dignity within tourism employment, likewise, should be enshrined in existing CSR policies—eliminating the precarity in contingent work patterns is one key strand within this. Ultimately, flexible work need not be precarious work provided that organisations recognise all their employees, irrespective of their time or status commitment to the company, as valuable and contributing members of the team—and that flexibility is recognised as a reciprocal practice.

As our article demonstrates, the precarious nature of work in tourism has generated considerable rhetoric, even polemic in a general sense, but also in a more focused way that relates to the UN's SDGs. The *prima facie* case that good working conditions (in the sense of sustainable HRM practices) generate positive outcomes for both employees and businesses seems to be difficult to refute - but much more challenging to demonstrate empirically. And yet, as we also argue, practices across many sectors of tourism are frequently far removed from being sustainable. There is a need for research that interrogates issues of employment precarity across all its dimensions and within the full spectrum of tourism sector contexts in both the formal and informal/gig economies. Indeed, aspirations for change in the tourism workplace would be greatly enhanced by the availability of more accessible and definitive trend data within major social, employment and economic statistics, where currently issues of sector definition within Standard Occupational Classification (SOC) systems hinder comparative clarity. There is also need for an evidence-base which locates the consequences of precarity in the tourism workplace in a wider socio-economic context, scaling location-specific studies (cf. Drier & Fleming, 2018) to the level of the destination or sub-sector within tourism.

Our broad-brush analysis in this paper grounds provocative conclusions, setting the platform for future research. At the broadest level are the underpinning neo-liberal foundations, on which tourism has seemingly grown incompatible with an authentic sustainability vision, as manifest by tourism employment sustaining precarity? These data we address are, generally, high level and require careful drilling down on the basis of geographical location, sector variation and how intersectionality presents itself beyond the headlines. Within this study's scope, we were unable to engage with data in this way. In building the case for sustainability in tourism employment, there is also a need to dive much deeper into the polemics and the rhetoric about the jobs people do (Vallas & Prener, 2012) in the industry, as others are doing, for example in relation to migrants (McDowell et al., 2009) and intersectionality (Browne & Misra, 2003). This will provide a far greater understanding of the ambivalent relationship between sustainable development, and the triumvirate of precarious tourism employment *at work*, precarious tourism employment *of work*—and precarious lives.

ORCID

Richard N.S. Robinson (iD) http://orcid.org/0000-0001-9737-3812

References

Adler, P. A., & Adler, P. (2004). *Paradise laborers: Hotel work in the global economy*. Ithaca: Cornell University Press.

Alberti, G. (2016). Moving beyond the dichotomy of workplace and community unionism: The challenges of organising migrant workers in London's hotels. *Economic and Industrial Democracy, 37*(1), 73–94.

Alberti, G., Bessa, I., Hardy, K., Trappmann, V., & Umney, C. (2018). In, against and beyond precarity: Work in insecure times. *Work, Employment and Society, 32*(3), 447–457.

Alberti, G., Holgate, J., & Tapia, M. (2013). Organising migrants as workers or as migrant workers? Intersectionality, trade unions and precarious work. *International Journal of Human Resources Management, 24*(22), 4132–4148.

Anderson, B. (2010). Migration, immigration controls and the fashioning of precarious workers. *Work, Employment and Society, 24*(2), 300–317.

ANZ Research In-Depth. (2016). *Servicing Australia's future.* University of Queenland/AIBE. Retrieved from https://aibe.uq.edu.au/files/224/Servicing_Australias_Future_2030_June_2016.pdf

Armstrong, R. (2016). Modern slavery: risks for the UK hospitality industry. In H. Goodwin & X. Font (Eds.), *Progress in responsible tourism V* (pp. 67–78). Oxford: Goodfellow Publishers.

Arnold, D., & Bongiovi, J. (2013). Precarious, informalizing, and flexible work. transforming concepts and understandings. *American Behavioral Scientist, 57*(3), 289–308.

Asia-Pacific Economic Cooperation. (APEC) (2017). *Developing the Tourism Workforce of the Future in the APEC Region.* Retrieved from https://www.apec.org/Publications/2017/04/Developing-the-Tourism-Workforce-of-the-Future-in-the-APEC-Region

Australia Parliament House of Representatives. (2007). Standing Committee on Employment, Workplace Relations and Workforce Participation *Current vacancies: Workforce challenges facing the Australian tourism sector.* Canberra: Commonwealth of Australia. Retrieved from https://trove.nla.gov.au/work/5531434?selectedversion=NBD41895629

Barley, S. R., & Kunda, G. (2006). Contracting: A new form of professional practice. *Academy of Management Perspectives, 20*(1), 45–66.

Baum, T. (2018a). Sustainable human resource management as a driver in tourism policy and planning: A serious sin of omission? *Journal of Sustainable Tourism, 26*(6), 873–889. https://doi.org/10.1080/09669582.2017.1423318

Baum, T. (2018). Changing employment dynamics within the creative city: Exploring the role of 'ordinary people' within the changing city landscape. *Economic and Industrial Democracy,* 0143831X1774837. https://doi.org/10.1177/0143831X17748371

Baum, T. (2015). Human resources in tourism: Still waiting for change? A 2015 reprise. *Tourism Management, 50,* 204–212.

Baum, T., Cheung, C., Kong, H., Kralj, A., Mooney, S., Nguyễn Th Thanh, N., … Siow, M. L. (2016). Sustainability and the tourism and hospitality workforce: A thematic analysis. *Sustainability, 8*(8), 809.

Baum, T., Kralj, A., Robinson, R. N. S., & Solnet, D. J. (2016). Tourism workforce research: A review, taxonomy and agenda. *Annals of Tourism Research, 60,* 1–22.

Becker, W. S., Carbo, J. A., & Langella, I. M. (2010). Beyond self-interest: Integrating social responsibility and supply chain management with human resource development. *Human Resource Development Review, 9*(2), 144–168.

Berg, L., & Farbenblum, B. (2017). *Wage theft in Australia.* Sydney: Migrant Worker Justice Initiative: UNSW/UTS. Retrieved from https://static1.squarespace.com/static/593f6d9fe4fcb5c458624206/t/5a11ff31ec212df525ad231d/1511128887089/Wage+theft+in+Australia+Report_final_web.pdf

Bergene, A. C., Boluk, K., & Buckley, E. (2015). Examining the opportunities and challenges of union organisation within the hospitality industry. In D. Jordhus-Lier & A. Underthun (Eds.), *A hospitable world? Organising work and workers in hotels and tourist resorts* (pp. 195–212). London: Routledge.

Bertoli, S., Fernández-Huertas Moraga, J., & Keita, S. (2017). The elasticity of the migrant labour supply: Evidence from temporary Filipino migrants. *The Journal of Development Studies, 53*(11), 1822–1834.

Bianchi, R. (2017). The political economy of tourism development: A critical review. *Annals of Tourism Research, 70,* 88–102.doi.org/10.1016/j.annals.2017.08.005

Bianchi, R. (2009). The 'critical turn'in tourism studies: A radical critique. *Tourism Geographies, 11*(4), 484–504.

Biehl, K., & Kaske, R. (2011). *Tourismus in Östereich (mit einer Sonderauswertung des Österreichischen Arbeitsklimaindex).* Kammer für Arbeiter und Angestellte für Wien, Östereich.

Black, M. (1995). *In the Twilight Zone: Child workers in the hotel, tourism, and catering industry.* Geneva: International Labour Organization.

Bolton, S., & Houlihan, M. (2007). Beginning the search for the H in HRM. In S. Bolton & M. Houlihan (Eds.), *Searching for the human in human resource management: theory, practice and workplace contexts* (pp. 1–28). Basingstoke: Palgrave.

Boström, M. (2012). A missing pillar? Challenges in theorizing and practicing social sustainability: Introduction to the special issue. *Sustainability: Science, Practice and Policy, 8*(1), 3–14.

Browne, I., & Misra, J. (2003). The intersection of gender and race in the labor market. *Annual Review of Sociology, 29*(1), 487–513.

Brundtland, G., et al. (1987). *Our Common Future* (\'brundtland report\'). Retrieved from http://www.citeulike.org/group/13799/article/13602458

Cohen, S. A. (2011). Lifestyle travellers: Backpacking as a way of life. *Annals of Tourism Research, 38*(4), 1535–1555.

Coles, T., Fenclova, E., & Dinan, C. (2013). Tourism and corporate social responsibility: A critical review and research agenda. *Tourism Management Perspectives, 6,* 122–141.

Cumming, D., Wood, G., & Zahra, S. (2016). *The rise of right wing populism and its effect on HRM.* Retrieved from http://dx.doi.org/10.2139/ssrn.2879078

Cuthill, M. (2010). Strengthening the "social" in sustainable development: Developing a conceptual framework for social sustainability in a rapid urban growth region in Australia. *Sustainable Development, 18*(6), 362–373.

De Beer, A., Rogerson, C., & Rogerson, J. (2014). Decent work in the South African tourism industry: Evidence from tourist guides. *Urban Forum, 25*(1), 89–103.

Deloitte Access Economics (2015). *Australian Tourism Labour Force Report: 2015–2020*. Canberra: Australian Trade Commission, Austrade. Retrieved from https://www.tra.gov.au/ArticleDocuments/185/Australian_Tourism_Labour_Force_FINAL.PDF.aspx?Embed=Y

Dillard, J., Dujon, V. & King, M. C. (Eds.). (2008). *Understanding the social dimension of sustainability*. New York: Routledge.

Dredge, D., & Gyimóthy, S. (2015). The collaborative economy and tourism: Critical perspectives, questionable claims and silenced voices. *Tourism Recreation Research, 40*(3), 286–302.

Drier, P., & Flaming, D. (2018). *Working for the mouse: A survey of disneyland resort employees*. Occidental College Urban & Environmental Policy Institute and the Economic Roundtable. Retrieved from https://www.oxy.edu/urban-environmental-policy-institute.

Duffy, L. N., Kline, C. S., Mowatt, R. A., & Chancellor, H. C. (2015). Women in tourism: Shifting gender ideology in the DR. *Annals of Tourism Research, 52*, 72–86.

Duncan, T., Scott, D. G., & Baum, T. (2013). The mobilities of hospitality work: An exploration of issues and debates. *Annals of Tourism Research, 41*, 1–19.

Ehnert, I. (2009). *Sustainable human resource management*. Berlin: Springer.

Ehnert, I., Harry, W. & Zink, K. J. (Eds.). (2013). *Sustainability and human resource management: Developing sustainable business organizations*. Berlin: Springer Science & Business Media.

European Community. (2018). *Skills Panorama (Accommodation & food)*. Retrieved from http://skillspanorama.cedefop.europa.eu/bg/sectors/accommodation-food.

European Community. (2018). *Eurostat: Tourism industries employment*. Retrieved from http://ec.europa.eu/eurostat/statistics-explained/index.php/Tourism_industries_-_employment.

Florida, R. (2014). *The rise of the creative class revisited*. New York: Basic Books.

Garavan, T., Heraty, N., & Morley, M. (1998). Actors in the HRD process: An exploratory study. *International Studies of Management & Organization, 28*(1), 114–135.

Gibson, C. (2009). Geographies of tourism: Critical research on capitalism and local livelihoods. *Progress in Human Geography, 33*(4), 527–534.

Gill, R., & Pratt, A. (2008). In the social factory? Immaterial labour, precariousness and cultural work. *Theory, Culture and Society, 25*(7-8), 1–30.

Giousmpasoglou, C., Brown, L., & Cooper, J. (2018). Alcohol and other drug use in Michelin-starred kitchen brigades. *International Journal of Hospitality Management, 70*, 59–65.

Gössling, S., Ring, A., Dwyer, L., Andersson, A., & Hall, C. (2016). Optimizing or maximizing growth? A challenge for sustainable tourism. *Journal of Sustainable Tourism, 24*(4), 527–548.

Gursoy, D., Geng-Qing Chi, C., & Karadag, E. (2013). Generational differences in work values and attitudes among frontline and service contact employees. *International Journal of Hospitality Management, 32*(1), 40–48.

Homeshaw, J. (1995). Policy community, policy networks and science policy in Australia. *Australian Journal of Public Administration, 54*(4), 520.

Horemans, J., Marx, I., & Nolan, B. (2016). Hanging in, but only just: part-time employment and in-work poverty throughout the crisis. *Journal of European Labor Studies, 5*, 5.

Horney, N. (2016). The gig economy: A disruptor requiring HR agility. *People and Strategy, 39*(3), 20–27.

Hughes, E., & Scheyvens, R. (2016). Corporate social responsibility in tourism post-2015: A development first approach. *Tourism Geographies, 18*(5), 469–482.

International Labour Organization. (2010). *Developments and challenges in the hospitality and tourism sector*. Geneva: International Labour Office. Retrieved from http://www.ilo.org/wcmsp5/groups/public/@ed_norm/@relconf/documents/meetingdocument/wcms_166938.pdf

International Labour Organization (ILO). (2012). *Decent work indicators. Concepts and Definitions*. Geneva: ILO.

International Labour Organization. (2016). *Key indicators of the labour market* (Ninth ed.). Geneva: International Labour Office. Retrieved from http://www.ilo.org/wcmsp5/groups/public/—dgreports/—stat/documents/publication/wcms_498929.pdf

International Labour Organization. (2018). *ILOSTAT*. Geneva: International Labour Office. Retrieved from http://www.ilo.org/ilostat/faces/ilostat-home/download;ILOSTATCOOKIE=32tmgVPUVdWp5qM5Sn4IWqu9MFL3n6xwPBD0Y9m15S04F_mrh8ph!1506268203?_adf.ctrl-state=3h4bl1go1_388&_afrLoop=684984360524109&_afrWindowMode=0&_afrWindowId=null

Jafari, J., & Scott, N. (2014). Muslim world and its tourisms. *Annals of Tourism Research, 44*, 1–19.

Janta, H., Ladkin, A., Brown, L., & Lugosi, P. (2011). Employment experiences of Polish migrant workers in the UK hospitality sector. *Tourism Management, 32*(5), 1006–1019.

Jones, T., Ram, M., & Edwards, P. (2004). Illegal immigrants and the informal economy: workers and employer experiences in the Asian underground economy. *International Journal of Economic Development, 6*(2), 98–119.

Kalleberg, A. (2011). *Good jobs, bad jobs: The rise of polarized and precarious employment systems in the United States, 1970s to 2000s*. New York: Russell Sage Foundation.

King, N. (2004). Using templates in the thematic analysis of texts'. In: C. Cassell & G. Symon (Eds.), *Essential guide to qualitative methods in organizational research* (pp. 256–270). London: Sage.

Knox, A. (2006). The differential effects of regulatory reform: Evidence from the Australian luxury hotel industry. *Journal of Industrial Relations, 48*(4), 453–474.

Knox, A. (2014). Human resource management (HRM) in temporary work agencies: Evidence from the hospitality industry. *The Economic and Labour Relations Review, 25*(1), 81–98.

Knox, A. (2016). Coffee nation: an analysis of jobs in Australia's café industry. *Asia Pacific Journal of Human Resources, 54*(3), 369–387.

Knox, A., Warhurst, C., Nickson, D., & Dutton, E. (2015). More than a feeling: using hotel room attendants to improve understanding of job quality. *The International Journal of Human Resource Management, 26*(12), 1547–1567.

Kotera, Y., Adhikari, P., & Van Gordon, W. (2018). Motivation types and mental health of UK hospitality workers. *International Journal of Mental Health and Addiction, 16*(3), 751–763. https://doi.org/10.1007/s11469-018-9874-z.

Kramar, R. (2014). Beyond strategic human resource management: is sustainable human resource management the next approach? *The International Journal of Human Resource Management, 25*(8), 1069–1089.

Ladkin, A. (2011). Exploring tourism labor. *Annals of Tourism Research, 38*(3), 1135–1155.

Lashley, C. (2009). The right answers to the wrong questions? Observations on skill development and training in the United Kingdom's hospitality sector. *Tourism and Hospitality Research, 9*(4), 340–352.

Lee, D., Hampton, M., & Jeyacheya, J. (2015). The political economy of precarious work in the tourism industry in small island developing states. *Review of International Political Economy, 22*(1), 194–223.

Lim, A. (2017). Uber rolls out initiatives to give drivers more choice, flexibility in trips they accept, The Straits Times, 9th November. Retrieved from http://www.straitstimes.com/singapore/transport/uber-rolls-out-initiatives-to-give-drivers-more-choice-and-flexibility-in-trips

Longoni, A., & Cagliano, R. (2015). Environmental and social sustainability priorities: Their integration in operations strategies. *International Journal of Operations & Production Management, 35*(2), 216–245.

MacDonald, R. (1994). Fiddly jobs, undeclared working and the something for nothing society. *Work, Employment and Society, 8*(4), 507–530.

McDowell, L., Batnitzky, A., & Dyer, S. (2009). Precarious work and economic migration: Emerging immigrant divisions of labour in Greater London's service sector. *International Journal of Urban and Regional Research, 33*(1), 3–25.

McMillan, C. L., O'Gorman, K. D., & MacLaren, A. C. (2011). Commercial hospitality. *International Journal of Contemporary Hospitality Management, 23*(2), 189–208.

Melissen, F. (2013). Sustainable hospitality: A meaningful notion? *Journal of Sustainable Tourism, 21*(6), 810–824.

Methven O'Brien, C. M., & Dhanarajan, S. (2016). The corporate responsibility to respect human rights: A status review. *Accounting, Auditing & Accountability Journal, 29*(4), 542–567.

Miller, G., Rathouse, K., Scarles, C., Holmes, K., & Tribe, J. (2010). Public understanding of sustainable tourism. *Annals of Tourism Research, 37*(3), 627–645.

Mooney, S. (2018). Jobs for the girls? Women's employment and career progression in the hospitality industry. In: R. Burke & J. M. Christensen Hughes (Eds.), *Handbook of hospitality human resource management* (pp. 184–215). London and New York: Edward Elgar Publishing.

Moragra, C. (2017). *Nature and Determinants of Informal Employment among Grab and Uber Drivers in Metro Manila*, unpublished Master of Industrial Relations thesis, Manila: University of the Philippines Diliman.

Morgan, G., Wood, J., & Nelligan, P. (2013). Beyond the vocational fragments: Creative work, precarious labour and the idea of 'Flexploitation'. *The Economic and Labour Relations Review, 24*(3), 397–415.

Nickson, D., Warhurst, C., Cullen, A. M., & Watt, A. (2003). Bringing in the excluded? Aesthetic labour, skills and training in the 'new' economy. *Journal of Education and Work, 16*(2), 185–203.

Orwell, G. (1933). *Down and Out in Paris and London*, Victor Gollancz: London.

Osnowitz, D. (2010). *Freelancing expertise: Contract professionals in the new economy*. Ithaca: Cornell University Press.

Poulston, J. (2008). Rationales for employee theft in hospitality: Excuses, excuses. *Journal of Hospitality and Tourism Management, 15*(1), 49–58.

Quan, M. (2017). Precarious work in Europe: Assessing cross-national differences and institutional determinants of work precarity in 32 European countries. *Research in the Sociology of Work, 31*, 273–306.

Robinson, R. N. S. (2008). Revisiting hospitality's marginal worker thesis: A mono-occupational perspective. *International Journal of Hospitality Management, 27*(3), 403–413.

Robinson, R. N. S. (2013). Darker still: Present-day slavery in hospitality and tourism services. *Hospitality & Society, 3*(2), 93–110.

Robinson, R. N. S., Ritchie, B. W., Kralj, A., Solnet, D. J., Baum, T., & Ford, R. C. (2014). An Asia-Pacific core–periphery futures paradox: Divergent worker and tourist mobilities. *Journal of Travel Research, 53*(6), 805–818.

Ross, A. (2009). *Nice work if you can get it: Life and labor in precarious times*. New York: New York University Press.

Ruhanen, L., Weiler, B., Moyle, B. D., & McLennan, C. L. J. (2015). Trends and patterns in sustainable tourism research: A 25-year bibliometric analysis. *Journal of Sustainable Tourism, 23*(4), 517–535.

Santero-Sanchez, R., Segovia-Pérez, M., Castro-Nuñez, B., Figueroa-Domecq, C., & Talón-Ballestero, P. (2015). Gender differences in the hospitality industry: A job quality index. *Tourism Management, 51*, 234–246.

Siebert, S., & Wilson, F. (2013). All work and no pay: consequences of unpaid work in the creative industries. *Work Employment and Society, 27*(4), 711–721.

Smith, V. (2010). Enhancing employability: Human, cultural, and social capital in an era of turbulent unpredictability. *Human Relations, 63*(2), 279–300.

Solnet, D., Nickson, D., Robinson, R. N. S., Kralj, A., & Baum, T. (2014). Discourse about workforce development in tourism—An analysis of public policy, planning, and implementation in Australia and Scotland: Hot air or making a difference? *Tourism Analysis, 19*(5), 609–623.

Stacey, J. (2015). *Supporting Quality Jobs in Tourism*, OECD Tourism Papers. Paris: OECD Publishing. Retrieved from http://www.oecd-ilibrary.org/docserver/download/5js4rv0g7szr-en.pdf?expires=1516774043&id=id&accname=guest&checksum=CA4983ED67C6171AB1BA90BB74F74563

Standing, G. (2011). *The Precariat: The new dangerous class.* London: Bloomsbury Academic.

The Guardian. (2018). *Minimum wage: football clubs and Wagamama among worst underpayers. Name and shame list reveals 9,200 underpaid employees within total of 179 firms, 9th March:* Retrieved from https://www.theguardian.com/society/2018/mar/09/minimum-wage-marriott-hotels-and-wagamama-among-worst-underpayers

Timo, N. (1999). Contingent and retentive employment in the Australian hotel industry: Reformulating the core-periphery model. *Australian Journal of Labour Economics, 3*(1), 47.

The World Bank: IBRD-IDA. (2018). *Worldbank Indicators.* Retrieved from https://data.worldbank.org/indicator?tab=all

Tribe, J., Dann, G., & Jamal, T. (2015). Paradigms in tourism research: A trialogue. *Tourism Recreation Research, 40*(1), 28–47.

United Nations. (2015). *Transforming our World: The 2030 agenda for sustainable development.* New York: United Nations, Department of Economic and Social Affairs.

Vallance, S., Perkins, H. C., & Dixon, J. E. (2011). What is social sustainability? A clarification of concepts. *Geoforum, 42*(3), 342–348.

Vallas, S., & Prener, C. (2012). Dualism, job polarization, and the social construction of precarious work. *Work and Occupations, 39*(4), 331–353.

Wacquant, L. (2014). Marginality, ethnicity and penality in the neo-liberal city: An analytic cartography. *Ethnic and Racial Studies, 37*(10), 1687–1711.

Wood, R. C. (1992). Deviants and misfits: Hotel and catering labour and the marginal worker thesis. *International Journal of Hospitality Management, 11*(3), 179–182.

Wood, R. C. (1997). *Working in Hotels and Catering.* London: International Thomson Business Press.

World Economic Forum. (2016). *The future of jobs: Employment, skills and workforce strategy for the fourth industrial revolution.* World Economic Forum: Geneva, Switzerland.

WTTC. (2015). *Global talent trends and issues for the travel and tourism sector.* Oxford, UK: Oxford Economics. Retrieved from https://www.wttc.org/-/media/382bb1e90c374262bc951226a6618201.ashx

WTTC. (2017). *Travel & Tourism Economic Impact 2017 World.* Retrieved from https://www.wttc.org/-/media/files/reports/economic-impact-research/regions-2017/world2017.pdf.

Rethinking decent work: the value of dignity in tourism employment

Anke Winchenbach, Paul Hanna and Graham Miller

ABSTRACT

This paper focuses on establishing a conceptual grounding for the value of dignity in tourism employment for achieving decent work as part of the sustainable development agenda. Dignity is widely acknowledged as a key driver for 'good' work, but little conceptual grounding on the value of dignity in tourism employment has been established. This paper will contribute to the theoretical debate on sustainable tourism by providing a critical review of frameworks for decent work, workplace dignity (or its absence), and understandings of identity. We will explore how the context and conditions of tourism employment are conducive (or not) for offering dignified and sustainable employment. This paper makes two original contributions to knowledge. First, it introduces a psychosocial understanding of dignity in tourism employment, reflecting its deeply rooted individual, organisational, societal and policy aspects, and recognising the actors involved. Second, the critical importance of dignity in tourism employment for achieving the Sustainable Development Goals (SDGs) is discussed, with future research directions identified.

Introduction

This paper aims to present a conceptual grounding for the value of dignity in tourism employment, an area that to date has experienced limited attention in tourism studies. The authors argue for a critical engagement with the role of tourism in contributing to sustainable development. It is timely to address this neglect with focus on tourism's contribution to decent work as part of the United Nation's Sustainable Development Goals (SDGs) (United Nations [UN], 2015). Consequently, and in response to previous calls for critical engagement with sustainable tourism, ethics and decent work (Baum, 2018; Bramwell & Lane, 2014; Jamal & Camargo, 2014), this paper offers a theoretical and conceptual engagement with dignity at work. Further, this paper applies this theoretical engagement to illustrative examples of the tourism employment literature, developing a provisional conceptual framework and series of implications and suggestions for further research on dignity in tourism employment. Our approach and engagement with cross-disciplinary literature and examples from tourism practice was guided by Brookfield's 'Critical Thinking' (CT) (Brookfield, 1987), which allows a better understanding of tourism systems in the context of sustainable development (Boluk et al., 2017). Whilst the unit of analysis will be individual workers and groups of workers, there are implications for the sector at large, including sustainable Human Resource Management (HRM) studies (Zaugg et al., 2001), development studies and organisational studies.

The 2030 Agenda for Sustainable Development (UN, 2015) has made the International Labour Organisation's (ILO) Decent Work Agenda (ILO, 1999) an integral part of the vision for advancing a more sustainable future for all. The quest for dignity in the 17 SDGs, which combined address the environmental, social, and economic aspects of development from 2015 to 2030, is explicitly reflected in the UN Secretary General's Synthesis Report (UN, 2013) which states inclusion, dignity, prosperity and justice as four of the six 'essential elements' required for delivery of the SDGs. Thus, dignity and sustainable development are conceptually coupled.

Dignity, and respect for it, has been centre-stage in cross-disciplinary research on the quality of work (Bal, 2017; Bolton, 2007; Hodson, 2001; Sayer, 2007a). Workplace dignity is "the ability to establish a sense of self-worth and self-respect and to appreciate the respect of others" (Hodson, 2001, p. 3). Dignity is recognised as a fundamental part in the ILO's decent work agenda (ILO, 1999), which underpins Goal 8 of the SDGs (SDG8). The ILO defines decent work as "[p]roductive work under conditions of freedom, equity, security and dignity, in which rights are protected and adequate remuneration and social coverage are provided" (ILO, 1999, p. 15). While decent work touches on all SDGs (ILO, 2017), SDG8 combines the ILO's decent work agenda with economic growth into a goal of achieving "sustained, inclusive and sustainable economic growth, full and productive employment and decent work for all" (UN, 2017, p. 23). The ILO and the SDG documents convey that decent work, together with social justice and gender equality, are at the heart of sustainable tourism (ILO, 2017). However, others suggest that the notion of 'decent work' remains unclear, in terms of both meaning and practice (Sehnbruch et al., 2015), limiting the concept's application.

Although the meaning of 'decent work' remains unclear, most definitions broadly include aspects of respect and self-respect, as well as safe, fair, productive and meaningful work in conditions of freedom (Baum, 2018). Di Fabio and Maree (2016) draw together psychological, organisational and societal dimensions in their definition of decent work (Di Fabio & Maree, 2016, p. 9):

> Decent work helps all workers attain a sense of self-respect and dignity, experience freedom and security in the workplace, and (as far as possible) is afforded the opportunity to choose and execute productive, meaningful and fulfilling work that will enable them to construct themselves adequately and without restrictions and make social contributions.

This paper recognises all these dimensions, which enable a critical review of dignified work in tourism employment and its implications for sustainable tourism development. As Baum et al. (2016) argued, employees and work are at the heart of the sustainability debate in tourism.

Despite many references to it, dignity has experienced limited conceptual academic attention from the tourism community, unlike in other disciplines such as nursing and law (Gallagher, 2011; Rosen, 2012). This is particularly worrying for Baum et al. (2016), who argue that the tourism sector often falls short of meeting dignified working conditions and may occasionally operate contrary to the principles of decent work. To address this omission, this paper reviews the role of decent work in tourism employment as part of sustainable development, and then explores the relationship between dignity and identity, two conceptual strands unlinked in discussions on decent work in tourism. This approach facilitates our review of issues in tourism employment and how they relate to the theoretical underpinnings of dignity at work and identity. The paper then applies these concepts to illustrative examples from the tourism employment literature. By offering a preliminary psychosocial conceptualisation of dignity in tourism employment with examples, this paper aims to inform the debate and enhance understanding of dignity in tourism employment as part of the decent work and wider sustainable development agenda. Finally, the implications of the framework and potential avenues for future research are discussed. We conclude that a deeper understanding of, and engagement with the meaning and value of dignity in tourism employment might open a pathway for industry stakeholders to contribute meaningfully to decent work in tourism and, ultimately, to the SDGs as a "roadmap for peace, dignity and prosperity" (UNDP, 2016).

Decent work and sustainable tourism development

In the workplace, recognition of people's dignity is through the provision of decent work (Lucas, 2017). The ILO (1999) identified four pillars of decent work: employment creation, social protection, rights at work, and social dialogue, arguing that decent work involves:

- Productive work opportunities that deliver fair income.
- Secure workplaces and social protection for families.
- Better prospects for personal development and social integration.
- Freedom for individuals and groups of people to voice concerns, and to organise and participate in decisions affecting their lives.
- Equality of opportunity and treatment for all women and men.

Thus, decent work is not only about job creation, but also about the quality of such employment (ILO, 1999). However, while arguing that decent work is a global concept, the ILO report also acknowledges potential different interpretations of quality jobs in different societies, which "could relate to different forms of work, and also to different conditions of work, as well as feelings of value and satisfaction" (ILO, 1999, p. 4). Yet, from a dignity at work perspective, working conditions and feeling valued are at the heart of quality employment (Bolton, 2007).

There are many reasons for optimism due to the inclusion of decent work as part of the SDGs (UN, 2017), as this provides an opportunity to address some of the challenges and opportunities facing the tourism workforce. While the UN World Tourism Organisation's (UNWTO) outlook for tourism in relation to SDG8 primarily focuses on economic growth (UNWTO, 2018), and as such on 'business as usual' (Scheyvens et al., 2016), the ILO's guidelines on decent work and socially responsible tourism (ILO, 2017) go further. The guidelines cite tourism-specific targets, including emphasis on non-discriminatory working environments, fair wages and a good work–life balance, as well as worker involvement and social dialogue. The relevance for decent work in tourism lies in the labour intensity of the industry, as well as the opportunities for women, migrants and young people which are higher than in most other industry sectors (ibid). The guidelines make numerous suggestions for developing fairer working conditions and establishing policies and codes of practice for tackling the decent work deficits in the sector. Such deficits include extended working hours, limited social protection, gender discrimination and low wages; all of which the ILO argues are most prominent in the informal sector of the industry and affect women more severely than men (ILO, 2017). This is a concern for an industry with a considerable number of informal workers and where the workforce majority is female, particularly at the lower end of the occupational scale (UNWTO, 2011).

Whilst ILO guidelines propose paths towards sustainable tourism employment as part of the SDGs (Baum, 2018), the situation is rather complex. Firstly, we are some way off developing comparable data on objective measures and outcomes on the quality of work globally (Burchell et al., 2014). Second, critics argue that the concept lacks meaning (Lanari, 2005, as cited in Burchell et al., 2014). Additionally, some scholars have raised concerns about potential conflicts in the visions in SDG8 for economic growth on the one hand and full employment and decent work on the other (Baum, 2018; Frey, 2017; Scheyvens et al., 2016). For example, Selwyn (2013), like Scheyvens et al. (2016), discusses the co-opting of the Decent Work Agenda by powerful elite organisations. However, despite the widely held view that mechanisms that facilitate economic growth provide optimal outcomes, Harvey (2006) argues that neoliberal practices at work, emphasising competition, progress and profitability (Ayikoru et al., 2009), negatively affect job quality. Further, Crowley and Hodson (2014) found a correlation between neoliberalist organisational practices and reduced job security; increase in humiliation and meaningless work; and lower pay and benefits. Moreover, their study indicates that neoliberal approaches undermine organisational functioning due to increased labour turnover, thus eroding an organisation's foundations for success (Crowley & Hodson, 2014, p. 102).

Extensive research shows that a lack of dignity and respect, unequal power relations and poor working conditions create a sense of alienation and mistrust, negatively affecting the success of the business as well as workers and local communities (Jacobson, 2009; Korczynski & Ott, 2005; Paules, 1991). There are good examples of alternative economic structures addressing unequal power relations and enabling a more humane and fair system, a 'moral economy' (e.g. Bolton et al., 2016; Higgins-Desbiolles, 2012). However, Noronha et al. (2018) argue there is a need to reaffirm the meaning and value of decent work to equip employers in providing meaningful and dignified work.

Dignity features prominently in many tourism-related national and international policies; the Global Code of Ethics in Tourism (UNWTO, 2001) and the United Nations Declaration of Human Rights (UN, 1948) play a critical role in addressing dignity violations across the sector and beyond (for tourism human rights literature, see Cole & Morgan, 2010; Higgins-Desbiolles & Whyte, 2015). More recently, the Berlin Declaration (Transforming Tourism, 2017) specifically calls for respecting workers' dignity and the eradication of exploitation to meet the sustainable development agenda. However, while dignity has been widely embedded at policy level, the review of the literature suggests that what dignity means for decent work in tourism remains elusive. To address this shortcoming, this paper turns to the concept of dignity at work.

Dignity and work

Dignity has been conceptualised in multiple ways (Debes, 2009). However, while not uncontested (Macklin, 2003; Spiegelberg, 1971), there is wide support for the inherent, universal and unconditional dignity of humans simply by virtue of being human (Lucas, 2017; Misztal, 2013; Sayer, 2011). While this view implies that the meaning of dignity is self-evident (Lucas, 2015), several thinkers have investigated what constitutes a form of dignity that can be promoted or violated in social interactions at work.

Immanuel Kant, arguably the most commonly cited influencer of interpretations of dignity, set the moral case for equal treatment and the non-commodification of humans during modernity (Kant, 1998). According to Kant (1998), there is a moral obligation to treat people not as mere instrumental objects (with a finite value), but as ends in themselves, respecting the value and dignity of oneself (self-respect) and others (respect) (Kant, 1998). Thus, Kant makes the link between individual and societal aspects of dignity, and further explains that dignity is a value beyond price, a perspective that arguably conflicts with the predominant neoliberal structure of tourism. Kant's Categorical Imperative demands the respect of dignity as a moral law based on the inherent status of being human, and places responsibility for moral actions on the rational individual as a binding command with no exceptions. Ultimately, in a Kantian sense, a distinction is needed between economic value, that is the monetary exchange for something, and the intrinsic value of humans qua being human. However, modern thinkers established value, including compensation for work, as an intrinsic aspect of dignity (Bal, 2017; Berg & Frost, 2005).

Drawing on the Kantian understanding of the non-commodification of humans, post-modern thinkers of the industrial revolution such as Marx, Weber and Durkheim, and increasingly the global socio-economic challenges contemporary society faces, has led to questions about workplace quality via various cross-disciplinary inquiries concerned with dignity and work (Bal, 2017; Bal & de Jong, 2017; Bolton & Boyd, 2003; Bourdieu & Accardo, 1999; Fox, 1994; Gallagher, 2004;

Hodson, 1991, 1996, 2001). The seminal publication of Randy Hodson's *Dignity at Work* (2001) facilitated a renewed interest in dignity from the academic community, inspiring multiple publications (e.g. Bal, 2015; Bolton et al., 2016; Lucas, 2015, 2017; Lucas et al., 2013). In this context, dignity has been associated with, inter alia, value, worth, recognition, respect, self-respect, autonomy, freedom, rank, and equality (Bolton, 2007; Hodson, 2001; Lamont, 2009; Sayer, 2007a).

In his seminal analysis of over 100 workplace ethnographies, Hodson (2001) established four core behavioural domains for attaining and defending dignity at work: resistance to overwork and exploitation, organisational citizenship (taking pride in one's work and contributing successfully and efficiently), the pursuit of meaning through control and mastery, and group relations and social aspects of work life, including friendships and unions (Hodson, 2001, p. 19). Others have conceptualised dignity at work in terms of economic security, fair treatment, and satisfying work (Berg & Frost, 2005), taking subjective and objective dimensions of dignity into consideration (Bolton, 2007; Sayer, 2007b). Bolton (2007) makes an important contribution by distinguishing between dignity *at* work ("structures and practices that offer equality of opportunity, collective and individual voice, safe and healthy working conditions, secure terms of employment and just reward") and dignity *in* work (respect, autonomy, meaningful work and job satisfaction) (Bolton, 2007, p. 8). Thus, as Bolton explains, it is "not either material reward (dignity at work), or dignity in work that is required, but both; not either/or, but and" (Bolton, 2011, p. 378). Finally, for Sayer, dignity at work can emerge in conditions that foster "integrity, respect, pride, recognition, worth and standing or status" (Sayer, 2007a, p. 567). That moral management is good management has been argued elsewhere (Baum, 2006; The Guardian, 2015a). The multitude of definitions to describe workplace dignity discussed above, highlight the flexibility of the concept and illustrates the challenges of defining this powerful, yet "complex, ambiguous and multivalent"(Moody, 1998, p. 14) concept in other disciplines (Debes, 2009; Gallagher, 2011). Thus, there is a need for establishing a conceptual grounding for dignity in tourism employment.

In addition to links between work and dignity, scholars have outlined the beneficial characteristics of tourism employment (Airey & Nightingale, 1981; Baum et al., 2016). These benefits include opportunities during economic transition (Szivas & Riley, 1999) and livelihood diversification (Stead, 2005), offering opportunities for the less skilled, minorities, and women (Ashley et al., 2000), providing new knowledge and skills, meeting new people, and enabling social and labour mobility (Ladkin, 2011). Examples of studies on dignity in tourism employment include the research of Cockburn-Wootten (2012) on integrating dignity in hospitality workplace practice through communication and manager education, and highlighting the role of organisations in providing meaningful working environments. Further, Kensbock et al. (2016) established that room attendants find self-respect and dignity in employment by taking pride in their work as a meaningful contribution to the hotel's success. Here, individuals actively re-affirm their own values and capabilities to counter their low social standing inside and outside of work. Another insight is in Higgins-Desbiolles' (2012) study, showing how a more humanistic and collaborative approach to running a hotel created a powerful and dignified mode of employment, in which solidarity, equality and autonomy in business decisions went alongside respect for the contribution of individuals as well as care for the community. This case study demonstrates that, in addition to identity-affirming aspects such as being in work and feeling valued, various actors, and organisational and wider societal dimensions play a role in dignified work. The three examples resemble prominent features of dignified work established by Hodson (2001) and Bolton (2007), such as resistance, pursuit of citizenship and meaning, which are affected by, and affect individual, organisational and societal aspects of work life.

Undignified work

It has been argued that dignified employment is difficult to achieve in the unequal employment structures and relationships in neoliberal organisations and societies (Bolton, 2007; Sayer, 2007a), particularly for people working at the lower end of the hierarchy facing the indignities of precarious working conditions (Berg & Frost, 2005; Sayer, 2007a). Similarly, Jacobson (2009) established that dignity violations are more likely in settings of unequal power, including financial, educational, social, cultural, hierarchical and emotional disparities occurring on micro, meso, and macro levels. Denial of workplace dignity consists of one or all of the following: mismanagement and abuse, over-work, autonomy constraints, and contradictions of employee involvement (Hodson, 2001, p. 19), as well as discrimination, harassment and humiliation (Lucas, 2017).

Whilst the tourism sector is widely seen as a promising driver of economic growth and job creation globally, empirical studies on experiences of tourism employees paint a mixed picture of the perceived quality of work, working conditions and practices when viewed from a 'decent', or indeed 'dignified', work perspective (e.g. Higgins-Desbiolles, 2012; Kensbock et al., 2016; Wijesinghe, 2009). At an extreme profit maximisation end of a spectrum of responsibility, companies undertake unethical business practices by exploiting their workforce (Bal, 2017). Frequently cited negative features of tourism work are inadequate working schedules, insecure employment contracts, overwork, and insufficient pay, as well as lack of progression opportunity (Baum, 2015; Lindsay & McQuaid, 2004). Moreover, tourism workers report a lack of respect and recognition from managers and co-workers, limited workplace autonomy and monotonous tasks, poor communication, and inadequate fixtures and fittings, alongside issues relating to people's identity at work (Faulkner & Patiar, 1997; Kensbock et al., 2016). Robinson (2013) even claims that the labour requirements of commercial tourism transactions are structurally connected to human exploitation.

Examples of undignified work in tourism employment include: sexualised labour (Wijesinghe, 2009); sex tourism (Berkman, 1996); racism (Mbaiwa, 2005); gender discrimination; low wages, long shifts, narrow job functions (Choi et al., 2000), seasonality and low occupational standing (Richardson & Butler, 2012). Such issues can occur simultaneously and be supported by management (Orido, 2017). The UK trades union Unite show the breaching of basic human rights of hotel workers in global luxury hotel chains in London, with employees regularly missing mealtimes and being owed money (Unite, 2016). As reported elsewhere (e.g. The Guardian, 2015b, 2018), many workers described physical and emotional strains leading to stress and depression, and some reported feeling dehumanised altogether (Unite, 2016). These findings echo previous reports, which found that a low level of recognition of trade unions, income insecurity, split-shifts, unpaid overtime, physical violence, sexual harassment and stress are day-to-day experiences for hotel workers (Beddoe, 2004).

In such problematic working conditions, employees adopt strategies of emotional detachment to protect their dignity at work. Examples in tourism employment include Poulston's (2015) study with hospitality workers and Kensbock et al.'s (2016) research with Australian room attendants, with one interviewee describing her work as "walking into the Tardis" (Kensbock et al., 2016, p. 112), referring to a fictional time and space dimension. Further, in an example of how sexualised and commodified labour affects workers' experiences and perception of dignity at work, Wijesinghe (2009) describes a receptionist's experience of sexual harassment by a guest, highlighting the physical and emotional intimidation, how co-workers failed to support her, and, critically, how she felt unable to report the incident, indicating organisational acceptance of such a situation. The findings flag important issues relating to frontline tourism work and the commodification of attractive female workers to gain corporate competitive advantage (Folger⊘ & Fjeldstad, 1995). Another study found that mountain-porters largely perceive their occupation as humiliating and demeaning, feeling "their dignity remains constantly under attack because of the harsh physical working conditions and their acute awareness of being treated unfairly by the industry and its affluent consumers" (Arellano, 2011, p. 115). Arellano (2011) asserts that the porters' increased earnings from their participation in tourism activities do not compensate for their daily humiliation, a concern also flagged by Tourism Concern (2015).

Table 1. Spheres of dignity-promoting and dignity-violating features of work.

Sphere	Dignity-promoting features	Dignity-violating features
Individual worker	Self-respect, meaningful and satisfying work, pride, autonomy, mastery, efficiency, recognition of contribution, job satisfaction and flourishing	Humiliation and abuse, constraints on personal autonomy and voice, violations to physical and mental health
Organisational context	Respect, equal opportunity, safe and healthy working conditions, economic security, fair remuneration, collegiality and solidarity, participation and co-determination in organisational matters	Constraints on workplace autonomy (i.e. how to approach tasks), disrespect, hazardous working conditions, overwork and underpay, insecure work agreements, suppression of friendships and collective voice, constraints on co-worker relations, strict hierarchies
Wider socio-economic and policy context	Prestige and social standing of job, equality, economic growth as a means for achieving dignified work, minimum wage legislation, moral economy, dignified work recognised and promoted through international agendas and policies	Low social standing of job, inequality, treatment of people as a means to an end, and commodification of humans, weak legal and policy structures

While such issues and the inequalities between customers and employees (Sayer, 2007b) have long been acknowledged, examples continue to be reported (Ladkin, 2011). The Global Code of Ethics for Tourism (GCET) asserts that the exploitation of people "conflicts with the fundamental aims of tourism and is the negation of tourism" (UNWTO, 2001, article 2, section 3). More personally, the consequences of such exploitative employment practices are severe, often leading to employee dissatisfaction and disengagement, high absenteeism, and finally, resignation. Such a feeling negatively affects client satisfaction and indirectly affects economic viability (Bernhardt et al., 2000; Chi & Gursoy, 2009). Yet, dignity in employment is not considered as part of the claims about the number of jobs created by the tourism sector, albeit this threatens future recruitment, engagement and retention (Baum, 2015; Hoque, 2013). Lindsay and McQuaid (2004) identify people who felt they would prefer to be unemployed than join the hospitality workforce based on its negative image.

From the review of the literature above, three core areas of dignity can be identified, each with particular features (Table 1).

While dignity has received limited attention, many tourism studies implicitly give insight into workers' dignity, aligning with previous findings on features and dimensions of workplace dignity (Bolton, 2007; Hodson, 2001).

Dignity – A universal concept?

It has been argued that, in addition to an individual's values, norms and experiences, socio-economic, cultural, ethnic and political contexts play a role in how dignity and tourism employment might be experienced (Baum, 2018; Sayer, 2007a). Thus, it might be more difficult to achieve dignity at work for some people than for others, based on inequalities (Lucas, 2017). However, there is wide agreement on shared humanity of all people, with human rights, respect, fairness and equality recognised as universal human values that transcend groups, time and place (Hodson, 2001; Liu, 2003). Furthermore, there is considerable conceptual overlap between the dignity-promoting features presented in Table 1 and understanding of dignity in other cultures. For example, research within an African Ubuntu style of management found that "a sense of self-worth and dignity" (Browning, 2006, p. 1331) is achieved through supporting team spirit, fairness, autonomy and empowerment, and demonstrating respect (Browning, 2006). Thus, Ubuntu, similar to dignity, "tries to capture the essence of what it means to be human" (Murithi, 2007,

p. 281) and shares a concern for non-exploitative working conditions and emphasis on moral values, mutual respect and recognition (Pietersen, 2005).

Thus, while differences undoubtedly exist, the concept of dignity might have sufficient universal currency to contribute to a better understanding of decent work in tourism employment. This view aligns with interpretations of dignity in international frameworks which deem it globally applicable (e.g. UNDHR, SDGs) while also acknowledging vulnerable populations (e.g. ethnic and gender equality). To build understanding of dignity in tourism employment, and before investigating further the features and spheres of dignity in relation to tourism employment by way of engaging with exemplary tourism workplace studies, we turn to the concept of identity, which is widely established as a key aspect of dignity at work (Hodson, 2001; Jacobson, 2009; Sayer, 2007b).

Self, identity and the psychosocial subject

Attempts to understand the 'self' can be traced back as far as the late medieval period (11th–15th century), when 'self' was primarily realised through social relationships and religious beliefs. As traditional structures deteriorated through industrialisation, and religion became less centralised, social understandings of 'self' proliferated through an individual's social position in relation to production (Baumeister, 1987), and later also through goods consumed and practices adopted (Bourdieu, 1984). Within the social sciences, a number of theoretical perspectives have arisen conceptualising identity; for example, gender (e.g. Butler, 1990); class (e.g. Skeggs, 2004); and discourse (e.g. Billig, 1995); through to more specific theoretical models (e.g. Social Identity Theory; Tajfel & Turner, 1986).

Whilst production is no longer central to understanding and expressing the 'self' (Adams, 2007), there is a plethora of research exploring the relationship between notions of 'self', 'identity' and 'production/work' in marginalised roles (e.g. Crang, 1997; Snow & Anderson, 1987). In this paper, we adopt an understanding of the self that engages with the complexities involved in human behaviour, interaction, experience and choice (Gergen, 2009). We utilise the work of Kornberger and Brown (2007), which suggests that self and identity should not be understood as an 'essence'; rather, they are the result of complex power relationships within which an individual's identity is actively constructed yet also passively ascribed. Burkitt (2008, p. 242) provides a framework through which the individual can be understood in this way:

> ... the agent of resistance could be understood as the social self of everyday life, formed in the relations of the everyday world, both official and unofficial; a self that is a subject of power in some respects yet open to the possibility of immersion in alternative social worlds, or to the influence of the values and beliefs of various ideologies. A subject of power, certainly, but power that is heterogeneous, embedded in the relational contexts of everyday life with its various cultures and sub-cultures, social networks and groups, out of which emerge fully-rounded, if always unfinalized, selves.

Burkitt writes here about the individual, and its formation in the contemporary world acknowledging how individuals are positioned within neoliberal power relations that constitute the individual as a subject of work and consumerism. However, Burkitt also suggests that this is not a straightforward relationship, but rather involves the subjective interpretation of how one understands their own sense of self and potential alternative lifestyles and values in order to exercise their agency. It is on this understanding of the self that this paper is based; the self as a psychosocial subject (Adams, 2016) which is formulated through interpersonal exchanges whilst also emphasising subjective interpretations of 'right' and 'wrong', 'good' and 'bad' (Gergen, 2009), or, in our case, 'dignified' and 'undignified'.

Dignity of identity can be threatened by others when individuals are humiliated or treated as mere objects (Wainwright & Gallagher, 2008), but, it can also be protected and regained through actions of resistance (Hodson, 2001). One form of resistance for people to protect their self-worth and meaning is through identity work (Lucas, 2011); for example, Nelson and Lewis (2016) found that early childhood teachers negotiated their lack of professional recognition and low status through acting overly bureaucratic, which gave them a sense of high moral standards. Such standards serve as protection of dignity where economic aspects of success and external recognition are limited (Lamont, 2009; Lucas, 2011).

Thus, how people perceive dignity, even in marginalised occupations, is, like notions of the self, partly self-constructed, offering workers the opportunity for making sense of their lives (Dwyer et al., 2009). However, there is also a strong social aspect that plays a role in whether somebody experiences themselves as dignified or not (Statman, 2000). As Sayer (2007b) concludes: "being treated not purely as a means to someone else's end or as invisible, but as an end as oneself, a person in one's own right, is thus crucial" (2007b, p. 20), and makes a difference to people's experience of work. Therefore, we suggest that a perspective on dignity at work in tourism must be rooted in a holistic multilevel psychosocial analysis of tourism employment.

A missing piece?

In light of the examples presented above, it becomes clear that structural and psychological dimensions play a role in understanding dignity in tourism employment, which, taken together, point towards the potential benefits of an interlinked psychosocial understanding of dignity in tourism employment. It is therefore important to consider not only the identity-related aspects of dignity, but also the organisational setting and the overarching social, economic and political structures that influence employment culture, policy and practice (Bolton, 2007, p. 8; Sayer, 2007a). For example, the health scientist Jacobson (2009) suggests that interaction-based dignity, such as in work environments, is influenced by the positions of, and relationships between, various actors (individual or collective), features of the organisational setting, and the wider social order. While Jacobson's analysis largely resembles the features of dignity established by others (Bolton, 2007; Hodson, 2001); and in Table 1 she more clearly identified two levels of dignity violation and promotion: the individual and the collective. The 'dignity of self' benefits or harms the self (e.g. identity, self-respect, feeling valued etc.), moral agency, the body, and personhood (humanness). The other level, 'dignity in relation', which collectively affects groups of people or even humanity, is concerned with autonomy, status (e.g. visibility, social standing) and citizenship (the relationship between the state and an actor) (Jacobson, 2009, p. 7). Jacobson concludes that these dimensions are interconnected, in that a violation or promotion of dignity for one affects all and vice versa (Jacobson, 2009, p. 8). Taken together, dignity in tourism employment consists of psychological, physical, structural as well as socio-economic and policy aspects, involves different actors, and can affect individuals as well as groups of people or wider society; yet, circumstances on one level can influence the other. For example, in a neoliberal system, it is more likely that organisations operate within a competitive environment, which might put pressure on wages and working conditions, leaving workers in a vulnerable position where negative dignity encounters between the individual and different actors might occur, despite the individual having a strong sense of dignity of self. Alternatively, policies such as the ILO's decent work agenda and SDG8 can offer protective structures and guidance if a common understanding of the meaning of decent and dignified work is achieved, helping to counter the neoliberal context.

Drawing on the work of Jacobson (2009) and the spheres of dignity established in Table 1, Figure 1 proposes a theoretical framework of a psychosocial understanding of dignity in tourism employment.

Psychosocial in action

The interlink between psychological, organisational and social dimensions of workplace experiences in tourism has been established previously by Kensbock et al. (2016), as well as in other

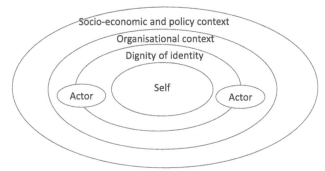

Figure 1. Conditions of a psychosocial understanding of dignity in tourism employment (adapted from Jacobson, 2009).

disciplines (Bolton & Laaser, 2013; Gallagher, 2004). One of such examples is Jacobson's (2009) taxonomy on the conditions in which dignity promotions or violations might occur in the context of health and human rights. Her model has been slightly modified, contextualised and theorised to reflect the multi-layered conditions and various actors in regard to dignity in tourism employment. While Jacobson (2009) also discusses implications for *the self* (italics in original), in the context of decent work and dignity in tourism employment the individual worker is at the forefront of the discussion; therefore, *the self* takes centre stage in our revised model. Second, the literature reviewed indicates that the individual's experience of dignity of identity is closely tied to, and to an extent dependent on, the organisational context and setting. Additionally, the positionality of and relationship with the actors involved play a role for dignity encounters; actors might include clients, managers and co-workers. Lastly, similar to Jacobson's (2009) graph, these elements are embedded in the wider social order; but the socio-economic and policy dimensions are drawn out more explicitly here. The following sections further explain the psychosocial view for achieving dignity in tourism employment; with a focus on the interplay between self, professional identity and actors, and the organisational and wider social contexts.

Dignity of identity

Several scholars have established the interconnectedness between dignity and self (Dwyer et al., 2009; Statman, 2000). The literature highlights the importance of considering workplace identity-affirming actions for tourism employees, as dignity is intrinsically linked to identity; acting as a "bridge [between] self and society" (Berger, 1970, p. 342). This explicit link has also been established in other studies. Defined as "the dignity that we attach to ourselves as integrated and autonomous persons, persons with a history and persons with a future with all our relationships to other human beings" (Nordenfelt, 2004, p. 75); dignity of identity then becomes a critical component of workers' experience, allowing feelings of self-respect and pride (Hodson, 2001). Mooney et al. (2016) found that positive professional identities play a key role in the decision to remain in the tourism sector.

As concept 'identity' does not flow in isolation; rather it has long been conceptualised as being inextricably linked to notions of the 'self' (Baumeister, 1987). Whilst there is much debate as to the extent to which 'self' and 'identity' are 'fixed' (McCrae & Costa, 1997) or 'fluid' (Potter and Wetherell, 1987), contemporary theorists largely agree that there is a social element to both (Burkitt, 2008). The questions arise whether customer-facing jobs in tourism face larger pressure from pleasing customers, and whether there is a greater risk of being dehumanised if people are more dependent on their job due to the absence of alternatives. Typically, people in more physically, mentally or economically constrained situations, or lower hierarchical or less skilled occupations, have less autonomy and choice, putting them at greater risk of being exploited and of experiencing undignified working conditions. For instance, Baum (2013) explained that people, especially women, are often forced to take up precarious work in the hospitality sector. While they might not challenge their situation overtly, their continued working under dehumanising conditions must not be interpreted as consent, but is a result of their choosing to provide for their families rather than feel greater indignity from being unable to do so (Baum, 2013). Further, questions of identity-related workplace dignity are particularly relevant in times of social change (Adams, 2007; Sennett, 1998), and when new types of employment such as tourism take the place of previous livelihood opportunities (Di Domenico & Miller, 2012; Morgan, 2013).

Organisational context

Viewed from a dignity perspective, the organisational context considers workplace characteristics such as level of respect, autonomy, trust, collaboration and worker democracy, as well as fair pay, recognition of contribution, manageable workload and interesting work (Bolton, 2007), which are all associated with positive work experiences for tourism workers (Higgins-Desbiolles, 2012; Kensbock et al., 2016). Thus, a work environment that enables positive social connections with managers, co-workers and clients, and the formation of a professional self-identity (self), contributes to lasting careers at all hierarchical levels (Mooney et al., 2016).

It could be argued that the purpose of any employment relationship is to compensate for goods and services with money (Sayer, 2007b); however, taking the example of the porters, who feel that being paid does not compensate for humiliation, it becomes clear that dignity is not something that can simply be bought. Instead, in line with Kantian ethics, Sayer (2007a) argues that dignity is above price, something that enables meaningful experiences for workers through relationships embedded in mutual respect and recognition. It is not only Kantian ethics that highlight mutual respect and recognition; indeed, central to Foucault's (1988) understanding of how individuals 'cultivate the self as an ethical subject', is an appreciation for reciprocal relation-ships with others. Thus, such an understanding appears imperative to consider in future tourism research. Then again, respect and reciprocity may be absent, for example when guests want more than money can buy or where respect for others is made obligatory regardless of their abusive behaviour (e.g. the 'customer is king' mantra). In these circumstances, a person is deval-ued and their dignity is under threat (Korczynski & Evans, 2013; Sayer, 2007b). There might then be a reciprocal benefit to create a client-employee relationship that is beyond the purely transac-tional, based on mutual respect and value of service. Thus, research on customer-employee encounters, and the role of dignity-impeding norms such as ownership structures, might benefit from taking a dignity perspective.

An example of psychosocial forces is Harris's (2009) study of a longstanding female Samoan executive housekeeper and her approach to managing staff in a luxury hotel. While housekeep-ing is widely considered as 'dirty work' (Hughes, 1971), symbolising a potential threat to workers' dignity and status, Harris (2009) provides an insightful account of how housekeepers build and retain a sense of pride and value in their work. Key factors are the executive's own progression within the hotel and her work-identity as 'Mama' (p. 156), as well as her commitment to nurtur-ing a sense of community amongst Samoan co-workers; respecting them as individuals, empow-ering decision-making, and recognising their contributions. In this way, workers experience a sense of belonging and meaningful work, which, in turn, positively influences emotional engage-ment and trust and, ultimately, staff turnover rates (Harris, 2009). Here, the interlink between spheres of identity, organisational structures and the wider sustainability agenda, in which decent work is concerned with economic security and opportunities for women and minorities, becomes apparent from possibly unlikely conditions.

Such research highlights that people might hold different values and perceptions of what comprises a 'good' or 'bad' job, including their understanding of dignity at work. This gives rise to the question as to what extent socio-economic and cultural contexts matter when talking about dignity at work, and whether tourism jobs relative to other possible employment, or to no employment, might indeed offer a sense of dignity.

Socio-economic and policy context

How individuals perceive the quality of their work might be contingent on the socio-economic and cultural setting (Baum, 2018), as well as the wider sustainability agenda and its practical applicability (Sharpley, 2000).

First, as highlighted in the 'decent work and sustainable tourism' section of this paper, we acknowledge that the current neoliberal approach in which tourism organisations operate can lead to alienation and exploitation, and a work situation in which the worker is deprived of their individuality. By prioritising commercial over human interests, a structural dehumanisation and disempowerment of workers, and indeed society takes place (Adams, 2007). Such concerns have previously been highlighted by writers such as Marx (1867), Foucault (1988), and Polanyi (1957), who all questioned dignified working conditions in hierarchical, profit- and consumption-driven societies, which is relevant to tourism. As such, an emphasis on a 'moral economy' might pave the way for achieving decent, and indeed dignified, tourism employment. While dignity and neo-liberalism may seem irreconcilable, it might be the non-monetary dimensions of dignity (e.g. mutual respect, self-respect, value and identity) that provide an opportunity for dignity to be experienced by tourism workers and translate into improved profit for companies; leading to increased staff retention, less absenteeism, and improved visitor experiences. In the words of Higgins-Desbiolles; "if proponents of the sector do not wish to face concerted criticism, opposition and resistance in a world increasingly characterised by insecurity and tension, then contemporary dynamics require a radical rethinking" (2006, p. 1206). Thus, an emphasis on moral values "must be fostered and protected against the harmful distortions which can be brought about by economic factors" (UNWTO, 1980, p. 3), thereby contributing to social stability and sustainable development as envisaged in the SDGs.

Second, Mattson and Clark (2011) assert that dignity can be of universal utility for appraising policy and identifying global interests. They also acknowledge the likely differences in how policies will be translated into local contexts, and further highlight that despite strong guiding policies and frameworks, "only real people in real places can provide the answers and actions" (Clarke, 2011, p. 316). As such, a renewed understanding of decent work, that promotes dignity-affirming actions and fosters mutual positive encounters in organisational settings, with the aim of protecting and enhancing dignified work identities of tourism workers, could be key for achieving decent tourism employment as part of the sustainable development agenda as envisaged in SDG8.

Conclusion

This article provides a critical review of publications on dignity and identity, and how these concepts are interlinked and applicable to tourism employment. The aim was to conceptually interrogate the grounding of the value of dignity in tourism employment for achieving 'decent work' in tourism, as envisaged in SDG8 as part of the wider sustainable development agenda. The review demonstrated that dignity is a powerful concept for assessing workplace experiences; such as respect, self-respect, professional identity and autonomy, but with limited application to issues in tourism employment and sustainable development. When applied to tourism studies at micro, meso and macro level, dignified work with an emphasis on the value of each individual and the contribution they make individually and collectively has been found to positively influence staff retention and customer satisfaction (Mooney et al., 2016), ultimately contributing to tourism businesses' success and SDG8 - economic growth and decent work.

The authors have established dominant features of the quality of tourism employment and linked the concepts of workplace dignity and identity to investigate how decent work in tourism employment can be understood and what can be done to achieve it. This has been achieved by introducing a multi-faceted psychosocial understanding of dignity in tourism employment, which considers employees' identity, the organisational context, and the wider socio-economic and policy context as well as the various actors involved at each of these levels. By applying examples, this article showed the interconnectedness between actions on various levels, but also showed how dignity encounters can appear in seemingly adverse conditions.

In conclusion, it is our contention that an engagement with the concept of dignity by the tourism community enables a deeper insight into the lived experiences of tourism workers and can help better define what decent work might mean for tourism employment and the wider global sustainability agenda. A next step should be to test the proposed model in empirical studies.

Furthermore, the authors indicated several promising future directions of tourism research. These include: research exploring dignity in relation to customer satisfaction and profit prioritisation; investigations seeking to understand the universal applicability of dignity in light of individual and cultural interpretations; and how a comprehensive understanding of *decent work* might inform tourism policy and practice. Moreover, as sustainable HRM (Zaugg et al., 2001) encompasses individual and social dimensions of sustainable development in relation to work, it offers another promising avenue to contribute to the limited body of tourism workforce research (Baum et al., 2016).

Finally, a dignity perspective in tourism employment could benefit the analysis of power in employment relations, and the debate on how the reputation of working in the sector could be enhanced, which can help address increasing skills shortages. Moreover, adopting dignity as a core value in tourism employment and considering its psychosocial dimensions has wider societal implications. For tourism to become a force for good, as envisaged by Higgins-Desbiolles (2006), people working in the industry will need to feel recognised as human beings, and feel valued both in monetary and non-monetary terms. Arguably, moving towards sustainable development is critically dependent on dignified work, as it forms the foundation of achieving both, decent work and economic success as envisaged in SDG8 and beyond, but more significantly is about recognising the lived experience of the person.

Disclosure statement

No potential conflict of interest was reported by the authors.

References

Adams, M. (2007). *Self and social change*. London: Sage.
Adams, M. (2016). *Ecological crisis, sustainability and the psychosocial subject*. Basingstoke: Palgrave.

Airey, D., & Nightingale, M. (1981). Tourism occupations, career profiles and knowledge. *Annals of Tourism Research*, *8*(1), 52–68. doi:10.1016/0160-7383(81)90067-0

Arellano, A. (2011). Tourism in poor regions and social inclusion: The porters of the Inca Trail to Machu Picchu. *World Leisure Journal*, *53*(2), 104–118. doi:10.1080/04419057.2011.580551

Ashley, C., Boyd, C., & Goodwin, H. (2000). *Pro-poor tourism: Putting poverty at the heart of the tourism agenda. Natural Resources Perspectives 51*. London: Overseas Development Institute.

Ayikoru, M., Tribe, J., & Airey, D. (2009). Reading tourism education: Neoliberalism unveiled. *Annals of Tourism Research*, *36*(2), 191–221. doi:10.1016/j.annals.2008.11.001

Bal, P. M. (2017). *Dignity in the workplace: New theoretical perspectives*. London: Palgrave Macmillan.

Bal, P. M. (2015). Beyond neoliberalism in work and organizational psychology: Human dignity and workplace democracy. *Gedrag & Organisatie*, *28*(3), 199–219.

Bal, P. M., & de Jong, S. B. (2017). From human resource management to human dignity development: A dignity perspective on HRM and the role of workplace democracy. In M. Kostera & M. Pirson (Eds.), *Dignity and organization* (pp. 173–195). London: Palgrave MacMillan.

Baum, T. (2006). *Human resource management for tourism, hospitality and leisure: An international perspective*. London: Thomson Learning.

Baum, T. (2013). *International perspectives on women and work in hotels, catering and tourism*. Geneva: ILO.

Baum, T. (2015). Human resources in tourism: Still waiting for change?—A 2015 reprise. *Tourism Management*, *50*, 204–212. doi:10.1016/j.tourman.2015.02.001

Baum, T. (2018). Sustainable human resource management as a driver in tourism policy and planning: A serious sin of omission? *Journal of Sustainable Tourism*, *26*(6), 873–889. doi:10.1080/09669582.2017.1423318

Baum, T., Cheung, C., Kong, H., Kralj, A., Mooney, S., Ramachandran, S., … Siow, M. L. (2016). Sustainability and the tourism and hospitality workforce: A thematic analysis. *Sustainability*, *8*(8), 809. doi:10.3390/su8080809

Baumeister, R. F. (1987). How the self became a problem: A psychological review of historical research. *Journal of Personality and Social Psychology*, *52*(1), 163. doi:10.1037//0022-3514.52.1.163

Beddoe, C. (2004). *Labour standards, social responsibility and tourism*. Retrieved from https://www.tourismconcern.org.uk/wp-content/uploads/2014/10/Labour-Standards-Report-2004.pdf

Berg, P., & Frost, A. C. (2005). Dignity at work for low wage, low skill service workers. *Relations Industrielles/Industrial Relations*, *60*(4), 657–682. doi:10.7202/012339ar

Berger, P. (1970). On the obsolecence of the concept of honor. *European Journal of Sociology*, *11*(02), 338–347. doi:10.1017/S0003975600002101

Berkman, E. T. (1996). Responses to the international child sex tourism trade. *Boston College International Comparative Law Review*, *19*, 397–422.

Bernhardt, K. L., Donthu, N., & Kennett, P. A. (2000). A longitudinal analysis of satisfaction and profitability. *Journal of Business Research*, *47*(2), 161–171. doi:10.1016/S0148-2963(98)00042-3

Billig, M. (1995). *Banal nationalism*. London: Sage.

Bolton, S. (2007). *Dimensions of dignity at work*. Oxford: Butterworth-Heinemann.

Bolton, S. (2011). Dimensions of dignity: Defining the future of work. In K. Townsend & A. Wilkinson (Eds.), *Research handbook on the future of work and employment relations* (pp. 370–384). Cheltenham, UK: Edward Elgar.

Bolton, S., Laaser, K., & McGuire, D. (2016). Quality work and the moral economy of European employment policy. *JCMS-Journal of Common Market Studies*, *54*(3), 583–598. doi:10.1111/jcms.12304

Bolton, S. C., & Boyd, C. (2003). Trolley dolly or skilled emotion manager? Moving on from Hochschild's managed heart. *Work, Employment and Society*, *17*(2), 289–308. doi:10.1177/0950017003017002004

Bolton, S. C., & Laaser, K. (2013). Work, employment and society through the lens of moral economy. *Work, Employment and Society*, *27*(3), 508–525. doi:10.1177/0950017013479828

Boluk, K., Cavaliere, C. T., & Higgins-Desbiolles, F. (2017). Critical thinking to realize sustainability in tourism systems: Reflecting on the 2030 sustainable development goals. *Journal of Sustainable Tourism*, *25*(9), 1201–1204. doi:10.1080/09669582.2017.1333263

Bourdieu, P. (1984). *Distinction: A social critique of the judgement of taste*. London: Routledge.

Bourdieu, P., & Accardo, A. (1999). *The weight of the world: Social suffering in contemporary society*. (P. Pankhurst Ferguson, trans.). Cambridge: Polity Press.

Bramwell, B., & Lane, B. (2014). The "critical turn" and its implications for sustainable tourism research. *Journal of Sustainable Tourism*, *22*(1), 1–18. doi:10.1080/09669582.2013.855223

Brookfield, S. (1987). *Developing critical thinkers*. Milton Keynes: Open University Press

Browning, V. (2006). 'The relationship between HRM practices and service behaviour in South African service organizations'. *The International Journal of Human Resource Management*, *17*(7), 1321–1338. doi:10.1080/09585190600756863

Burchell, B., Sehnbruch, K., Piasna, A., & Agloni, N. (2014). The quality of employment and decent work: definitions, methodologies, and ongoing debates. *Cambridge Journal of Economics*, *38*(2), 459–477. doi:10.1093/cje/bet067

Burkitt, I. (2008). *Social selves: Theories of self and society*. London: Sage.

Butler, J. (1990). *Feminism and the subversion of identity*. New York: Roudledge.

Chi, C. G., & Gursoy, D. (2009). Employee satisfaction, customer satisfaction, and financial performance: An empirical examination. *International Journal of Hospitality Management, 28*(2), 245–253. doi:10.1016/j.ijhm.2008.08.003

Choi, J.-G., Woods, R. H., & Murrmann, S. K. (2000). International labor markets and the migration of labor forces as an alternative solution for labor shortages in the hospitality industry. *International Journal of Contemporary Hospitality Management, 12*(1), 61–67. doi:10.1108/09596110010305154

Clarke, J. A. (2011). Beyond equality? Against the universal turn in workplace protections. *Indiana Law Journal, 86*(4), 1219–1287.

Cockburn-Wootten, C. (2012). Critically unpacking professionalism in hospitality: Knowledge, meaningful work and dignity. *Hospitality & Society, 2*(2), 215–230. doi:10.1386/hosp.2.2.215_1

Cole, S., & Morgan, N. (2010). Tourism and human rights. In S. Cole & N. Morgan (Eds.), *Tourism and inequality: Problems and prospects.* Wallingford, UK: CABI.

Crang, P. (1997). Performing the tourist product. In C. Rojek and J. Urry (Eds.), *Touring cultures: Transformations of travel and theory* (pp. 137–154). London: Routledge.

Crowley, M., & Hodson, R. (2014). Neoliberalism at work. *Social Currents, 1*(1), 91–108. doi:10.1177/2329496513511230

Debes, R. (2009). Dignity's gauntlet. *Philosophical Perspectives, 23*(1), 45–78. doi:10.1111/j.1520-8583.2009.00161.x

Di Domenico, M., & Miller, G. (2012). Farming and tourism enterprise: Experiential authenticity in the diversification of independent small-scale family farming. *Tourism Management, 33*(2), 285–294. doi:10.1016/j.tourman.2011.03.007

Di Fabio, A., & Maree, J. G. (2016). Using a transdisciplinary interpretive lens to broaden reflections on alleviating poverty and promoting decent work. *Frontiers in Psychology, 7,* 503.

Dwyer, L. L., Andershed, B., Nordenfelt, L., & Ternestedt, B. M. (2009). Dignity as experienced by nursing home staff. *International Journal of Older People Nursing, 4*(3), 185–193. doi:10.1111/j.1748-3743.2008.00153.x

Faulkner, B., & Patiar, A. (1997). Workplace induced stress among operational staff in the hotel industry. *International Journal of Hospitality Management, 16*(1), 99–117. doi:10.1016/S0278-4319(96)00053-9

Folgerø, I. S., & Fjeldstad, I. H. (1995). On duty-off guard: Cultural norms and sexual harassment in service organizations. *Organization Studies, 16*(2), 299–313. doi:10.1177/017084069501600205

Foucault, M. (1988). *The care of the self.* Harmondsworth: Penguin.

Fox, M. (1994). *The reinvention of work: A new vision of livelihood for our time.* San Franciso: Harper Collins.

Frey, D. F. (2017). Economic growth, full employment and decent work: The means and ends in SDG 8. *International Journal of Human Rights, 21*(8), 1164–1184. doi:10.1080/13642987.2017.1348709

Gallagher, A. (2004). Dignity and respect for dignity-two key health professional values: Implications for nursing practice. *Nursing Ethics, 11*(6), 587–599.

Gallagher, A. (2011). Editorial: What do we know about dignity in care? *Nursing Ethics, 18*(4), 471–473.

Gergen, K. (2009). *An invitation to social constructionism* (2nd ed.). London: Sage.

Harris, C. (2009). Building self and community: The career experiences of a hotel executive housekeeper. *Tourist Studies, 9*(2), 144–163. doi:10.1177/1468797609360598

Harvey, D. (2006). Neo-Liberalism as creative destruction. *Geografiska Annaler: Series B, Human Geography, 88*(2), 145–158. doi:10.1111/j.0435-3684.2006.00211.x

Higgins-Desbiolles, B. F. (2006). *Another world is possible: Tourism, globalisation and the responsible alternative* (Unpublished thesis). Flinders University.

Higgins-Desbiolles, F. (2012). The Hotel Bauen's challenge to cannibalizing capitalism. *Annals of Tourism Research, 39*(2), 620–640. doi:10.1016/j.annals.2011.08.001

Higgins-Desbiolles, F., & Whyte, K. P. (2015). Tourism and human rights. In C. M. Hall, S. Gössling, & D. Scott (Eds.), *The Routledge handbook of tourism and sustainability* (pp. 105–116). Oxon: Routledge.

Hodson, R. (1991). The active worker: Compliance and autonomy at the workplace. *Journal of Contemporary Ethnography, 20*(1), 47–78. doi:10.1177/089124191020001003

Hodson, R. (1996). Dignity in the workplace under participative management: Alienation and freedom revisited. *American Sociological Review, 61*(5), 719–738. doi:10.2307/2096450

Hodson, R. (2001). *Dignity at work.* Cambridge, UK: Cambridge University Press.

Hoque, K. (2013). *Human resource management in the hotel industry: Strategy, innovation and performance.* London: Routledge.

Hughes, E. C. (1971). *The sociological eye.* Chicago: Adline Atherton Inc.

International Labour Organization (ILO). (1999). *Decent work. Report of the Director General to the 87th meeting of the international labour conference.* Geneva: International Labour Office.

ILO. (2017). *ILO guidelines on decent work and socially responsible tourism.* Geneva: International Labour Office.

Jacobson, N. (2009). A taxonomy of dignity: A grounded theory study. *BMC International Health and Human Rights, 9*(1), 3.

Jamal, T., & Camargo, B. A. (2014). Sustainable tourism, justice and an ethic of care: Toward the just destination. *Journal of Sustainable Tourism, 22*(1), 11–30. doi:10.1080/09669582.2013.786084

Kant, I. (1998). *Groundwork for the metaphysics of morals.* Cambridge: Cambridge University Press.

Kensbock, S., Jennings, G., Bailey, J., & Patiar, A. (2016). Performing: Hotel room attendants employment experiences. *Annals of Tourism Research, 56*, 112–127. doi:10.1016/j.annals.2015.11.010

Korczynski, M., & Evans, C. (2013). Customer abuse to service workers: An analysis of its social creation within the service economy. *Work, Employment & Society, 27*(5), 768–784. doi:10.1177/0950017012468501

Korczynski, M., & Ott, U. (2005). Sales work under marketization: The social relations of the cash nexus? *Organization Studies, 26*(5), 707–728. doi:10.1177/0170840605051822

Kornberger, M., & Brown, A. D. (2007). 'Ethics' as a discursive resource for identity work. *Human Relations, 60*(3), 497–518. doi:10.1177/0018726707076692

Ladkin, A. (2011). Exploring tourism labor. *Annals of Tourism Research, 38*(3), 1135–1155. doi:10.1016/j.annals.2011.03.010

Lamont, M. (2009). *The dignity of working men: Morality and the boundaries of race, class, and immigration*. New York: Russell Sage.

Lindsay, C., & McQuaid, R. W. (2004). Avoiding the 'McJobs' unemployed job seekers and attitudes to service work. *Work, Employment & Society, 18*(2), 297–319. doi:10.1177/09500172004042771

Liu, Z. (2003). Sustainable tourism development: A critique. *Journal of Sustainable Tourism, 11*(6), 459–475. doi:10.1080/09669580308667216

Lucas, K. (2011). Blue-collar discourses of workplace dignity: Using outgroup comparisons to construct positive identities. *Management Communication Quarterly, 25*(2), 353–374. doi:10.1177/0893318910386445

Lucas, K. (2015). Workplace dignity: Communicating inherent, earned, and remediated dignity. *Journal of Management Studies, 52*(5), 621–646. doi:10.1111/joms.12133

Lucas, K. (2017). Workplace dignity. In C. Scott & L. Lewis (Eds.), *The international encyclopedia of organizational communication* (Vol. IV, pp. 2549–2562). Chichester: John Wiley & Sons.

Lucas, K., Kang, D., & Li, Z. (2013). Workplace dignity in a total institution: Examining the experiences of Foxconn's migrant workforce. *Journal of Business Ethics, 114*(1), 91–106. doi:10.1007/s10551-012-1328-0

Macklin, R. (2003). Dignity is a useless concept: It means no more than respect for persons or their autonomy. *British Medical Journal, 327*(7429), 1419–1420.

Marx, K. (1867). *Capital* (Vol. I). Harmondsworth: Penguin.

Mattson, D., & Clark, S. (2011). Human dignity in concept and practice. *Policy Sciences, 44*(4), 303–319. doi:10.1007/s11077-010-9124-0

Mbaiwa, J. E. (2005). The socio-cultural impacts of tourism development in the Okavango Delta, Botswana. *Journal of Tourism and Cultural Change, 2*(3), 163–185. doi:10.1080/14766820508668662

McCrae, R. R., & Costa, J. P. T. (1997). Personality trait structure as a human universal. *American Psychologist, 52*(5), 509. doi:10.1037//0003-066X.52.5.509

Misztal, B. A. (2013). The idea of dignity: Its modern significance. *European Journal of Social Theory, 16*(1), 101–121. doi:10.1177/1368431012449237

Moody, H. R. (1998). Why dignity in old age matters. *Journal of Gerontological Social Work, 29*(2-3), 13–38. doi:10.1300/J083V29N02_02

Mooney, S. K., Harris, C., & Ryan, I. (2016). Long hospitality careers—A contradiction in terms? *International Journal of Contemporary Hospitality Management, 28*(11), 2589–2608. doi:10.1108/IJCHM-04-2015-0206

Morgan, R. (2013). *Exploring how fishermen respond to the challenges facing the fishing industry: A study of diversification and multiple-job holding in the English Channel fishery* (Unpublished thesis). University of Portsmouth.

Murithi, T. (2007). A local response to the global human rights standard: The ubuntu perspective on human dignity. *Globalisation, Societies and Education, 5*(3), 277–286. doi:10.1080/14767720701661966

Nelson, J. L., & Lewis, A. E. (2016). I'ma teacher. Not a babysitter: Workers' strategies for managing identity-related denials of dignity in the early childhood workplace. *Research in the Sociology of Work, 29*, 37–71.

Nordenfelt, L. (2004). The varieties of dignity. *Health Care Anal, 12*(2), 69–81.

Noronha, E., Chakraborty, S., & D'Cruz, P. (2018). 'Doing Dignity Work': Indian Security Guards' Interface with Precariousness. *Journal of Business Ethics*. https://doi.org/10.1007/s10551-018-3996-x.

Orido, C. O. (2017). *Challenges faced by female chefs in the Kenyan hospitality industry: A study through an African oral tradition of storytelling* (Unpublished thesis). Auckland University of Technology.

Paules, G. F. (1991). *Dishing it out: Power and resistance among waitresses in a New Jersey restaurant*. Philadelphia: Temple University Press.

Pietersen, H. (2005). Western humanism, African humanism and work organizations. *SA Journal of Industrial Psychology, 31*(3), 54–61.

Polanyi, K. (1957). *The great transformation*. New York, NY: Rhinehart.

Potter, J., & Wetherell, M. (1987). *Discourse and social psychology: Beyond attitudes and behaviour*. London: Sage.

Poulston, J. (2015). Expressive labour and the gift of hospitality. *Hospitality & Society, 5*(2-3), 145–165. doi:10.1386/hosp.5.2-3.145_1

Richardson, S., & Butler, G. (2012). Attitudes of Malaysian tourism and hospitality students' towards a career in the industry. *Asia Pacific Journal of Tourism Research, 17*(3), 262–276. doi:10.1080/10941665.2011.625430

Robinson, R. N. (2013). Darker still: Present-day slavery in hospitality and tourism services. *Hospitality & Society, 3*(2), 93–110. doi:10.1386/hosp.3.2.93_1

Rosen, M. (2012). *Dignity: Its history and meaning*. Harvard University Press.

Sayer, A. (2007a). Dignity at work: Broadening the agenda. *Organization, 14*(4), 565–581. doi:10.1177/1350508407078053

Sayer, A. (2007b). What dignity at work means. In S. Bolton (Eds.), *Dimensions of dignity at work* (pp. 17–29). Oxford, UK: Butterworth-Heinemann.

Sayer, A. (2011). *Why things matter to people: Social science, values and ethical life*. Cambridge: Cambridge University Press.

Scheyvens, R., Banks, G., & Hughes, E. (2016). The private sector and the SDGs: The need to move beyond 'business as usual'. *Sustainable Development, 24*(6), 371–382. doi:10.1002/sd.1623

Sehnbruch, K., Burchell, B., Agloni, N., & Piasna, A. (2015). Human development and decent work: Why some concepts succeed and others fail to make an impact. *Development and Change, 46*(2), 197–224. doi:10.1111/dech.12149

Selwyn, B. (2013). Social upgrading and labour in global production networks: A critique and an alternative conception. *Competition & Change, 17*(1), 75–90. doi:10.1179/1024529412Z.00000000026

Sennett, R. (1998). *The corrosion of character: The personal consequences of work in the new capitalism*. New York: Norton.

Sharpley, R. (2000). Tourism and sustainable development: Exploring the theoretical divide. *Journal of Sustainable Tourism, 8*(1), 1–19. doi:10.1080/09669580008667346

Skeggs, B. (2004). *Class, self, culture*. London: Routledge.

Snow, D. A., & Anderson, L. (1987). Identity work among the homeless: The verbal construction and avowal of personal identities. *American Journal of Sociology, 92*(6), 1336–1371. doi:10.1086/228668

Spiegelberg, H. (1971). Human dignity: A challenge to contemporary philosophy. *World Futures: Journal of General Evolution, 9*(1-2), 39–64. doi:10.1080/02604027.1971.9971711

Statman, D. (2000). Humiliation, dignity and self-respect. *Philosophical Psychology, 13*(4), 523–540. doi:10.1080/09515080020007643

Stead, S. M. (2005). Changes in Scottish coastal fishing communities—Understanding socio-economic dynamics to aid management, planning and policy. *Ocean & Coastal Management, 48*(9), 670–692. doi:10.1016/j.ocecoaman.2005.08.001

Szivas, E., & Riley, M. (1999). Tourism employment during economic transition. *Annals of Tourism Research, 26*(4), 747–771. doi:10.1016/S0160-7383(99)00035-3

Tajfel, H. C., & Turner, J. C. (1986). The social identity theory of intergroup behavior. In S. Worchel and W. G. Austin (Eds), *Psychology of intergroup relations* (pp. 7–24). Chicago, IL: Nelson-Hall.

The Guardian. (2015a, July 28). *Can business make profits and improve employee rights and wellbeing?* Retrieved from https://www.theguardian.com/sustainable-business/2015/jul/28/business-profits-improve-employee-rights-workers-wellbeing

The Guardian. (2015b, May 30). Britain's hotel workers—Bullied, underpaid and with few rights. Retrieved from https://www.theguardian.com/business/2015/may/30/hotel-workers-bullied-underpaid-few-rights-uk

The Guardian. (2018, January 24). *Sexual harassment rampant in hospitality industry, survey finds*. [Online] Available at https://www.theguardian.com/world/2018/jan/24/sexual-harassment-rampant-hospitality-industry-unite-survey-finds (Accessed 3 February 2017).

Tourism Concern. (2015). *Where are we now on porters' rights?* Retrieved from https://www.tourismconcern.org.uk/where-are-we-now-the-latest-news-on-porters-rights/

Transforming Tourism. (2017). *Berlin declaration on "Transforming Tourism"*. Retrieved from http://www.transforming-tourism.org/berlin-declaration-on-transforming-tourism.html

Unite. (2016). *Unethical London: Global hotel chains—Making London an unethical tourist destination through 'standard industry practice'*. London: UniteWorks.

United Nations (UN). (1948). *Universal declaration of human rights*. New York: United Nations.

United Nations (UN). (2013). *A life of dignity for all: Accelerating progress towards the millennium development goals and advancing the United Nations development agenda beyond 2015*. New York: United Nations General Assembly.

United Nations (UN). (2015). *Transforming our world: The 2030 agenda for sustainable development*. Retrieved from https://sustainabledevelopment.un.org/content/documents/21252030%20Agenda%20for%20Sustainable%20Development%20web.pdf

UNDP. (2016). Sustainable development goals are a "roadmap for peace dignity and prosperity". Retrieved from http://www.undp.org/content/undp/en/home/presscenter/pressreleases/2016/09/23/sustainable-development-goals-are-a-roadmap-for-peace-dignity-and-prosperity-.html

Wainwright, P., & Gallagher, A. (2008). On different types of dignity in nursing care: a critique of Nordenfelt. *Nursing Philosophy: An International Journal for Healthcare Professionals, 9*(1), 46–54.

Wijesinghe, G. (2009). 'A display of candy in an open jar: Portraying sexualised labour in the hospitality industry using expressive phenomenology as methodology'. *Tourism and Hospitality Planning & Development, 6*(2), 133–143. doi:10.1080/14790530902981522

World Tourism Organization (UNWTO). (1980). *Manila declaration on world tourism*. Madrid: World Tourism Organization.

World Tourism Organization (UNWTO). (2001). *Global code of ethics for tourism*. Madrid: World Tourism Organization.

World Tourism Organization (UNWTO). (2011). *Global report on women in tourism 2010*. Madrid: World Tourism Organization.

World Tourism Organisation (UNWTO). (2018). *Tourism and the sustainable development goals—Journey to 2030*. Retrieved from https://www.e-unwto.org/doi/book/10.18111/9789284419401

Zaugg, R. J., Blum, A., et al. (2001). Sustainability in *human resource management* (Working paper No. 51). Institute for Organisation und Personel. Bern: University of Bern.

Constructing sustainable tourism development: The 2030 agenda and the managerial ecology of sustainable tourism

C. Michael Hall (iD)

ABSTRACT

The UN 2030 Agenda for Sustainable Development sets a series of sustainable development goals (SDGs) "to end poverty, protect the planet and ensure prosperity for all" by 2030. The Agenda influences tourism policy even though the Agenda resolution only mentions tourism three times. A "heterogeneous constructionism" approach is adopted to examine the managerial ecology of tourism and the SDGs. Managerial ecology involves the instrumental application of science and economic utilitarian approaches and in the service of resource utilisation and economic development. A managerial ecological approach is integral to UNWTO work on the SDGs, as well as other actors, and is reflected in policy recommendations for achievement of the SDGs even though tourism is less sustainable than ever with respect to resource use. This situation substantially affects capacities to do "other," and create alternative development and policy trajectories. It is concluded that a more reflexive understanding of knowledge and management is required to better understand the implications of knowledge circulation and legitimisation and action for sustainable tourism. More fundamentally, there is a need to rethink human–environment relations given the mistaken belief that the exertion of more effort and greater efficiency will alone solve problems of sustainable tourism.

Introduction

It has become something of a truism that sustainable development is a major focus of tourism policy makers, including industry and destination marketing organisations, and of tourism researchers. In the case of the former, for example, the lead UN agency the World Tourism Organisation (UNWTO) has sustainable development as one of the key headings on its website for what it does (together with mainstreaming tourism, ethics and social responsibility, tourism and development, competitiveness and fostering knowledge). With respect to the latter, there is a designated journal focussing on sustainable tourism, and numerous texts and journal articles, accounting for possibly as much as around five percent of journal output (Hall, Lew, & Williams, 2014). The policy significance of sustainable tourism is such that 2017 was the official UN International Year of Sustainable Tourism for Development. Yet despite such interest and overt attention, empirical measures suggest the tourism is actually less sustainable than ever at the global scale (Hall, 2011; Rutty, Gössling, Scott, & Hall, 2015; Scott, Hall, & Gössling, 2016a, Scott,

Gössling, Hall, & Peeters, 2016b). Concerns as to tourism's contribution to sustainable develop-ment have also become an issue at the local scale following a series of high profile negative reactions to tourism growth in destinations such as Barcelona, Iceland and Venice, which have become part of a wider industry and policy maker response to the supposed "success" of tour-ism, perhaps best illustrated by the high profile World Travel and Tourism Council (WTTC) and McKinsey & Company (2017) report on *Coping with Success: Managing Overcrowding in Tourism Destinations.*

The UN 2030 Agenda for Sustainable Development sets a series of sustainable development goals (SDGs) "to end poverty, protect the planet and ensure prosperity for all" by 2030 "as part of a new sustainable development agenda." Given the emphasis of the UNWTO on sustainable tourism and the economic significance of the sector the SDGs and the associated millennium development goals (MDGs) have become focal points for the study of tourism's contribution to sustainable development and the sustainability of tourism overall (Christie & Sharma, 2008; Saarinen, Rogerson, & Manwa, 2011; Saarinen & Rogerson, 2014). This is despite the United Nations 2030 Agenda for Sustainable Development resolution only mentioning tourism three times – in the context of natural resource use and conservation, employment generation and the promotion of local culture and products, and the sustainable use of marine resources so as to increase the economic benefits to small island developing states and least developed countries. Nevertheless, despite some critiques of the means to achieving the goals (Ferguson, 2011; Scheyvens, Banks, & Hughes, 2016), the dominant discourse tends to reflect the approaches and themes of the UNWTO and UNDP's (2017) account of tourism's "journey" to achieving the SDGs. As the UNDP and UNDP (2017) suggest, without any irony following their review of national reporting on tourism and the SDGs, "Evidently, if tourism is not well managed, it can have a negative impact on people, the planet, prosperity and peace" (p. 31). Key factors regarded as crucial to the success of the SDG journey to 2030 include enhanced competitiveness (Ruhanen, 2007), the significance of the private/corporate sector, and improved management and use of technology in becoming more efficient in responding to environmental/economic/social prob-lems (Herrera-Cano & Herrera-Cano, 2016; Henriques & Brilha, 2017; Imon, 2017; Koide & Akenji, 2017; Lima, Eusébio, Partidário, & García Gómez, 2012; Novelli & Hellwig, 2011), often in relation to specific local case studies (Lapeyre, 2011; Matarrita-Cascante, Brennan, & Luloff, 2010; Mbaiwa, 2011).

The nature and achievement of sustainable development can be considered in a variety of ways (Hopwood, Mellor, & O'Brien, 2005), including with respect to tourism (Hall, Gössling, & Scott, 2015). This therefore raises a critical question: Why then are the SDGs predominantly framed in a particular growth and business way in a tourism context that emphasise the import-ance of market oriented approaches and managerialism, when the SDGs are also concerned with broader social and environmental concerns as well as economic change? And, therefore, poten-tially other ways of framing, seeing and doing. For example, Taleb Rifai, Secretary-General of the UNWTO suggests, "The 2030 Agenda for Sustainable Development with its 17 [SDGs] sets the path that we all must embrace. ... the private sector, which is the key player in tourism, ... is beginning to recognise that the SDGs offer true business opportunities as sustainable business operations can spur competitiveness and increase profit" (UNWTO-UNDP, 2017, pp. 6–7). Achim Steiner, UNDP Administrator, states, "The role of the private sector and access to financing are paramount to building a more sustainable tourism sector. Long-term competitiveness depends on the willingness to manage industry vulnerabilities and invest in new markets and services ... " (UNWTO-UNDP, 2017, p. 9). At the Official Closing ceremony of the International Year of Sustainable Tourism for Development 2017 which discussed the "roadmap" for advancing the contribution of tourism towards the 2030 Agenda for Sustainable Development, Gloria Guevara, President and CEO, WTTC, similarly commented, "Sustainability remains the bedrock of our activ-ity. We will continue to drive the conversation on planning for and managing tourism growth, define a sector-wide response to climate change, work on how the sector can reduce illegal trade in wildlife and contribute to inclusive job creation" (UNWTO, 2017a). In the same official UNWTO press release for the event, Talal Abu-Ghazaleh, Chairman, Talal Abu-Ghazaleh Organisation in Jordan was quoted as saying, "I personally believe that the future of tourism lies in enabling ICT capacities. Accordingly, we should harness those powers for smart tourism... I believe that the way forward in our journey to 2030, is smart tourism. I call on all of you to guide me and support me in this endeavor"; while Marie-Gabrielle Ineichen-Fleisch, State Secretary Economic Affairs (SECO) of Switzerland states, "In the future, a strong international cooperation of all relevant actors involved in the tourism sector should become the driving force to promote sustainable tourism and to implement tourism policies efficiently" (UNWTO, 2017a). So, are we all meant to follow, cooperate and work with the UNWTO and UNDO focus on SDGs in order to be relevant or does relevance lie beyond official agendas and the seeming synchronicity of approaches that appear to dominate sustainable tourism discourse?

Grounded in research on natural resource management practices (Bavington, 2001, 2011; Bavington & Banoub, 2016; Jenkins, 2015; Oelschlaeger, 2014; Thornton & Hebert, 2015), this paper draws upon critiques of managerial ecology to highlight the way in which the development and implementation of the SDGs in the context of tourism, reflects the main actors "mutual coercion mutually agreed upon through the self-organising disciplinary power of the market's invisible hand" (Bavington, 2011, p. 9). Importantly, researchers themselves are often part of the system of natural resource management by which nature, as well as human activity, is valorised in terms of property, services, and private rights (Bavington, 2011). As Wynn (2011, p. xvii) suggests, "conveniently, these strategies proved entirely congruent with prevailing neoliberal economic doctrines emphasising the challenges of complexity, conflict and uncertainty in economic systems." Just as significantly, the critique of managerial ecology claims that much natural resource management could best be described as a form of "managed annihilation" (Bavington, 2001, 2011) by which natural resources decline as a result of "people too much given to framing the world as a set of problems they have the capacity to fix" (Wynn, 2011, p. xvii).

This paper provides a counter-institutional perspective on the tourism sector's approach to the SDGs and the framing of sustainable tourism. This is primarily undertaken in relation to the received view of the dominant social paradigm within tourism that defines the basic belief structures and practices of tourism marketplace actors as manifested in existing exchange structures as well as the actions of actors that serve to reinforce the paradigm within associated institutional structures. Lead international agencies, such as the UNWTO and the World Travel and Tourism Council (WTTC), together with larger corporate actors and national industry associations and destination marketing organisations are key actors in the promotion of the value of the market, growth, competition and the "management" of problems. Such a paradigm is also strongly reinforced by many universities and the academics within them. This is despite the growing contradictions between such positions and sustainability, as evidenced by increased biodiversity loss, growing concentration of economic wealth in the hands of a few, and the increasing realities of a changing climate (Rutty et al., 2015). Instead, knowledge is inherently multiple, with multiple claims to representing reality and multiple ways of knowing (Sandercock, 1998). This constructionist position is in contrast to positivist claims that examination of the facts will reveal the truth that can be rationally responded to by management practices. Accordingly, a "heterogeneous constructionism" approach is taken to the construction of the SDGs and tourism in terms of existing exchange structures. The nature of this approach is discussed first, before examining tourism and the SDGs, particularly as constructed by the UNWTO.

Heterogeneous constructionism

Sustainability is an environmental problem. But how is our notion of the environment that we respond to in personal, economic, management and policy terms constructed?

The problem of tourism and the SDGs, and sustainable tourism overall, raises questions about the significance of biophysical processes for tourism production systems, and therefore requires addressing dualistic notions about the natural world and its relationship to socio-economic processes. As Mansfield (2003) questioned, "How can we treat nature, biophysical processes, and the 'organic' as analytically significant without treating them as a mechanistic function or a materiality that is outside of social existence?" (p. 10). Taylor (1995a, 1995b, 1999) used the term "heterogeneous constructionism," to capture an emphasis on the heterogeneity of components, elements or resources drawn into the practice of knowledge making. Taylor (1995a) used the qualifier "heterogeneous" to establish some distance from standard views about social construction, which imply that scientists' accounts reflect or are determined by their social views.

Demeritt's (2001) examination of the construction of global warming and the politics of science used a heterogeneous constructionism approach to refers to the "mutual construction of nature, science, and society. Rather than taking these phenomena as given, this approach is concerned with how they are constructed through the specific and negotiated articulation of heterogeneous social actors" (Demeritt, 2001, p. 311). From this approach, the facts of nature are not given as such but emerge artefactually as the heterogeneously constructed result of contingent social practices (Demeritt, 1998, 2001). Heterogeneous constructionism is ontologically realist about entities, but epistemologically antirealist with respect to theories and how they are framed with respect to relations (Demeritt, 1998), i.e. what we designate as "carbon dioxide" has an ontologically objective existence, but our conception and classification of it are socially contingent. Heterogeneous constructionism therefore provides a way of acknowledging "that the world 'matters' without taking for granted either the particular configuration of its matter or the processes by which it may be realised for us" (2001, p. 311). As Rouse (1987) stated with respect to the physical sciences

> Practices are not representations that can be understood abstractly. They are always ways of dealing with the world. The ontological kinds they make manifest are determinable only through our purposive interactions with things of those kinds, and thereby with the other things that surround us. And those other things are as essential to the existence of meaningful ontological possibilities as our practices are ... Another way to put this is that for there to be things of any particular kinds, there must be a world to which they belong. But the reality of that world is not a hypothesis to be demonstrated; it is the already given condition that makes possible any meaningful action at all, including posing and demonstrating hypotheses. (Rouse, 1987, pp. 159–60)

A heterogeneous construction approach seeks to avoid dualistic categories that treat nature either as an external realm that acts as resource for, limit to, determinant of, or backdrop to human society, or as a pure social construction with no independent reality. Instead, for the heterogeneous constructionist, nature and the environment are artifactual and their understanding an active and ontologically transformative practice. For example, the development of nature-based industries, such as the ecotourism sector, highlights that biophysical processes provide both barriers and opportunities for production systems, and as such, they play a key role in structuring some industries, especially those that are biologically based (Boyd, Prudham, & Schurman, 2001). As Castree (2005, p. 16) comments, "without knowledges of nature we can never really come to know the nature to which these knowledges refer... we use tacit and explicit knowledges to organise our engagements with those phenomenon we classify as 'natural'. There is, in short, no unmediated access to the natural world free from frameworks of understanding."

The classical empiricist approach has been extremely significant in research on tourism and the environment, and is integral to the SDGs as they seek to enable growth while simultaneously conserving nature and natural resources, but the framework it provides is often taken for granted without consideration of the "assumptions that organise and, importantly, circumscribe the field of analysis" (Castree, 2002, pp. 116–117). The clearest example of this comes with the notion of impact, a metaphor derived from the material realist ontology of classical empiricism that is widely used with respect to tourism and sustainability, including with respect to the SDGs and concepts of "overtourism." For example, the UNWTO-UNDP (2017) report notes, "Both countries and companies lack frameworks to capture, aggregate and report on the full economic, social and environmental impacts of tourism" with respect to "Improving performance by measuring impact and sharing knowledge" (p. 14). While the report defines sustainable tourism itself in relation to impacts as "tourism that takes full account of its current and future economic, social and environmental impacts" (UNWTO-UNDP, 2017, p. 17).

The metaphor of human impacts is a major focus of sustainable tourism and "has come to frame our thinking and circumscribe debate about what constitutes explanation" (Head, 2008, p. 374). The metaphor has certain features:

1. The emphasis on *the moment(s) of collision between two separate entities* (e.g. the "impact" between tourism and the economic/social/physical environment as part of the "three pillars" of sustainability) has favoured explanations that depend on correlation in time and space (Weyl, 2009), and methodologies that are fully focussed on dating and/or particular moments in time, to the detriment of the search for mechanisms of connection and causation rather than simple correlation (Head, 2008).
2. The emphasis on the moment(s) of impact *assumes a stable natural, social or economic baseline, and an experimental method in which only one variable is changed* (Head, 2008). Such an approach is also inappropriate for understanding complex and dynamic socio-environmental systems (Hall, 2013a).
3. Third, and perhaps most profoundly influential, is the way the terms "tourism impacts" or "tourist impacts" ontologically *positions tourism and tourists as "outside" the system under analysis*, as outside of nature (or whatever it is that is being impacted) (Hall, 2013a). This is ironic given that research on global environmental change demonstrates just how deeply entangled tourism is in environmental systems (Rutty et al., 2015), yet the metaphor remains in widespread use in official documents and in tourism research.
4. Putting a significant explanatory divide between humans and nature requires the *conflation of bundles of variable processes* under such headings as "human," "climate," and "environment" (Demeritt, 2001; Head, 2007, 2008). To which we could add "tourism."
5. A further characteristic of dichotomous explanations is their *veneer of simplicity and elegance*. Yet, "the principle that preference should be given to explanations that require the fewest number of assumptions has been incorrectly conflated with the idea that simpler explanations are more likely to be true than complex ones … In fact, the view that causality is simple takes many more assumptions than the view that it is complex" (Head, 2008, p. 374).

As Demeritt (2001) was at pains to point out, his approach was not a claim that anthropogenic climate change was not real, rather that very little attention has been paid to the cultural politics of scientific practice and its consequential role in framing and, in that sense, constructing knowledge. Instead, he contended that the demand for and expectation of policy relevance on scientific research has subtly shaped the formulation of research questions, choice of methods, standards of proof, and the definition of other aspects of what constitutes "good" scientific practice. This pattern of reciprocal influence between the science and politics of climate change, Demeritt (2001, pp. 308–309) argues, "belies the categorical distinction so often made between science, based purely on objective fact, and politics, which involves value-laden decision making that is separable from and downstream of science." In a similar fashion, the argument developed here asserts that a heterogeneous constructionist interpretation, in revealing "complexity" and the entangled interaction of society-environment-technology, raises serious questions about the implications of the relationship between tourism and the SDGs being dominated by a particular economic-political discourse and the policy responses which it legitimates (Bickerstaff & Walker, 2003).

Tourism and the SDGs as managerial ecology

Managerial ecology, as expressed in environmental and resource management, involves the instrumental application of science and utilitarian economic approaches in the service of resource utilisation and economic development (Bavington & Slocombe, 2002). According to Merchant (1980, p. 238): "Managerial ecology seeks to maximise energy production, economic yields and environmental quality through ecosystem modelling, manipulation, and prediction of outcomes," and is characterised by an "unquestioned faith in management as the solution to deep seated ecological and social problems" (Bavington, 2002, p. 5). Merchant (1980) argued that the historical roots of managerial ecology lay in reductionist utilitarian approaches to the human–nature relationship, while Zwier and Blok (2017) see the Anthropocene concept as an outcome of managerial ecology thinking. Nevertheless, while complexity science focuses on uncertainty and there being limits on predictability and control, what Sardar and Ravetz (1994) described as resulting in the demolition of "the notion of control and certainty in science," there has not been "a wholesale rejection of the idea of management, rather it has resulted in redefinition, redeployment and relocation of management, managers and the managed" (Bavington, 2002, p. 7).

Management is significant in its perceived capacity to solve complex problems, such as those tackled by the SDGs, because it seeks to eliminate indeterminism and emphasises the role of science and technology in addressing crises (Alvesson & Willmott, 2012). In contrast, more recent developments in socio-ecological thinking have highlighted not only the multi-scale dynamic complexity of sustainability issues but also the way in which policy-making is influenced by values and the political ecology of decisions. However, the consequences of complexity from a managerial ecology framework depend on perspective. If complexity is seen from an ontological perspective as an inherent characteristic of nature then this clearly suggests that there must be limits to control and, instead, adaptive and coping strategies are required. In contrast, if complexity is regarded as an epistemological problem, then complexity is not an inherent "fact," but instead an outcome of perspective, level of knowledge and the tools that are used for analysis (Bavington, 2010). For example, even though the UNWTO and UNDP (2017) acknowledge that tourism value chains are characterised by their "immense size and complexity" (p. 44), they go on to argue, *"Effective management requires consistent measurement of impact*: While the tourism private sector can contribute to all 17 SDGs – in particular to SDGs 12, 13, 1, 4 and 8 on 'Responsible Consumption and Production', 'Climate Action', 'No Poverty', 'Quality Education', and 'Decent Work and Economic Growth', respectively – its impact is still difficult to measure given that there is no universal means by which travel and tourism businesses and destinations can measure and monitor their progress or contribution towards the SDGs" (UNWTO & UNDP, 2017, p. 56). Nevertheless, measurement, surveillance, control, and regulation lie at the core of managerialist values developed in an economic and philosophical context where process is subordinated to output (and profit) (Lynch, 2014).

Another reason for the maintenance of managerialist positions is that the notion of complexity may be recognised as relevant at some scales or situations and not in others. Complexity, for example, may be recognised as occurring in large scale environmental systems but not in the behaviours of individual communities, policy actors or people, which from a managerial ecology perspective may continue to be framed from neo-classical economic perspectives as rational actors (Bavington, 2011). This becomes especially significant given the emphasis on the role of the private sector and market solutions in the SDGs. For example, in SDG 9 "Build resilient infrastructure, promote inclusive and sustainable industrialisation and foster innovation," the UNWTO and UNDP (2017, p. 27) emphasise suggested relationships between technology, sustainability, and the market stating that "The rise in innovation and new technologies has changed the tourism business model, benefitting nations through efficiency gain, enhanced customer engagement and knowledge transfer. By embracing new technologies, countries can create market awareness, provide location-based services and enrich travel experience." Such statements are remarkable for the lack of analysis behind them as to what, for example, "efficiency gains" and technologically driven business models may mean for changes in tourism employment, especially the use of zero-hour and part-time contracts, or how the actions of large disruptive informal sector companies such as Airbnb and Uber affect housing and transport services (Corporate Europe Observatory, 2018; Mann, 2018; McCurry, 2018; Wachsmuth & Weisler, 2017). Indeed, sustainability itself is strongly positioned as an economic or competitive value rather than an ethical or environmental one: "many companies already seem to acknowledge that their contribution [to the SDGs] should be integrated into core business and form an inherent part of the creation of value to succeed on today's markets" (UNWTO & UNDP, 2017, p. 41).

A key issue of the UNWTO and UNDP (2017) analysis of the SDGs is the extent to which tourism's relationship to the SDGs is treated as a social problem. For example, that in regard to the 2030 Agenda's five key themes – people, planet, prosperity, peace and partnerships – it is suggested that tourism is mostly contributing to issues that relate to "prosperity" and "planet" (UNWTO & UNDP, 2017, pp. 30–31). Although there is attention to the economic returns from tourism there is little focus on the distribution of income and economic capital, i.e. who benefits? Similarly, attention to climate change and marine and coastal issues is primarily invoked as a physical change, rather than in terms of the social and economic injustices that give rise to the socio-economic and environmental issues that the SDGs try and address. However, it has long been recognised that designing interventions and policies without considering the role of existing institutions or societal responses will likely lead to policy failure (Taylor 1997a, 1997b), yet this continues to be done. As Taylor (1997a, p. 172) suggested with respect to poverty issues, that resonate strongly with tourism's supposed role in poverty reduction and SDG 1 (End poverty in all its forms everywhere) in particular, "Acknowledging the statistics of inequality does not, however, constitute an analysis of the dynamics of inequality. In the absence of serious intellectual work – conceptual and empirical – heartfelt caveats about the rich and the poor do not substantially alter the politics woven into this research."

In the same way discussion regarding the supposed benefits of tourism to reduce poverty is limited in policy terms. The UNWTO and UNDP (2017, p. 16) state that the tourism public policy focus of SDG 1 is "Tourism provides income through job creation at local and community levels. It can be linked with national poverty reduction strategies and entrepreneurship. Low skills requirement and local recruitment can empower less favoured groups, particularly youth and women." The option of a more progressive tax system is not raised and neither are issue of the tax avoidance and minimisation strategies of many large corporations with significant interests in travel and tourism (Bryan, Rafferty, & Wigan, 2017; Schneider, 2018). This is perhaps all the more surprising given that "tax income from tourism" is explicitly identified by the UNWTO and UNDP (2017, p. 16) as a means of investing in health care services, although it is possible that they differentiate between taxes on tourists (in some circumstances) versus taxes on tourism companies. The UNWTO has previously come out publicly in opposition to proposals to tax tourism, including in Africa (UNWTO, 2014) with then UNWTO Secretary-General, Taleb Rifai, arguing, "A tourism tax in Africa is a threat to the competitiveness of the region and to all African economies which increasingly have tourism as a key pillar to their development." Indeed, the press release stated, that taxation is "one of the main obstacles to the sustainable development of tourism and aviation in the region" (UNWTO, 2014).

The example of taxation highlights the tensions that exist with respect to how the relationship between sustainable development and tourism is understood. While the UNWTO emphasise the sustainable development of tourism, the SDGs are about the contribution of tourism to a broader notion of sustainable development. These are related but they are certainly not the same thing. For example, potential CSR actions for companies identified by UNWTO and UNDP (2017) for the SDGs focus on market-oriented actions, i.e. purchasing strategies, improved human resource management, efficiency improvements and donations. There is little in the form of state intervention in terms of greater regulation of the sector or direct charging for environmental subsidies that are currently borne by residents. Instead, the UNWTO and UNDP (2017) focus on the development of partnerships to finance sustainable tourism initiatives, suggesting that "public–private and multi-stakeholder partnerships can strengthen private sector engagement and galvanise the support needed to achieve the SDGs" (UNWTO & UNDP, 2017, p. 13).

Public–private partnerships are "working arrangements based on a mutual commitment (over and above that implied in any contract) between a public sector organisation with any other organisation outside the public sector" (Bouvaird, 2004, p. 200). Austerity measures, funding uncertainty and changes in philosophies of governance have led to greater use of private sector organisations for public service delivery, including tourism (Hall, 2014), to improve governance, broaden donor networks, and/or increase income streams. Although public–private partnerships have long been criticised in a tourism context for their capacities to exclude local stakeholders (Hall, 1999), they remain a favoured governmental strategy for tourism development, despite concerns over equity, cost-effectiveness and long-term liability (Frost & Laing, 2018). In particular, although they remain criticised for: (a) the problematic ways in which "communities," "partnership" and "stakeholders" are defined, delineated and constructed; (b) the lack of align-ment and integration with local and national development planning policies and processes; (c) top-down governance, and the absence or erosion of participatory processes and empowerment goals; and (d) the tendency towards highly conservative development visions (McEwan, Mawdsley, Banks, & Scheyvens, 2017), they remain a legitimisation strategy of international agen-cies and government for market oriented policies (Bäckstrand & Kylsäter, 2014). Indeed, such issues reflect broader debates surrounding the way tourism is used for development, and discus-sions on the value of pro-poor tourism and more inclusive forms of tourism.

Notions of inclusive tourism, for example, are usually framed as part of CSR strategies and activities. Zapata Campos, Hall, and Backlund (2018) suggest that the incorporation of inclusive tourism concerns within the CSR agenda-setting process is primarily a response to customer con-cerns, the activities of NGOs, and/or because of negative publicity as these may affect brand reputation and consumer behaviour. They conclude that sustainability policies and standards, can be loosely coupled, or decoupled, from internal practices, and have the potential to trigger further engagement with CSR and some aspects of inclusive tourism, by stimulating both intra- and inter-firm learning through collaborative processes among competitors. However, they argue that such measures cannot lead to profound changes in the sustainability practices of the mass tourism industry if the area is underinstitutionalised. Instead, they stress that sustainability stand-ards compliance is improved in countries with strong labour and other forms of regulation (Toffel, Short, & Ouellet, 2015):

> Powerful players in the industry, such as large tour operators, have the ability to enable greater sustainability and more inclusive forms of tourism. But if more coercive institutional pressures, in the form of laws, regulations and incentives, are not enacted to accelerate this process, it risks perpetuating a limited adoption of inclusive practices in the mass tourism industry (Zapata Campos et al., 2018, p. 16).

Instead, the ongoing message of international tourism bodies in relation to tourism and sus-tainable development is that continued focus on improved competitiveness, efficiency, the mar-ket and growth is the answer, even though it must be done "better" (Zurab Pololikashvili, Secretary-General of the UNWTO, in UNWTO, 2018).

> Tourism's sustained growth brings immense opportunities for economic welfare and development', said the UNWTO Secretary-General, while warning at the same time that it also brings in many challenges. 'Adapting to the challenges of safety and security, constant market changes, digitalization and the limits of our natural resources should be priorities in our common action' … The UNWTO Secretary-General stressed education and job creation, innovation and technology, safety and security; and sustainability and climate change as the priorities for the sector to consolidate its contribution to sustainable development and the 2030 Agenda, against the backdrop of its expansion in all world regions and the socio-economic impact this entails. To address these issues, Mr. Pololikashvili concluded that 'public/private cooperation as well as

public/public coordination must be strengthened, in order to translate tourism growth into more investment, more jobs and better livelihoods (UNWTO, 2018).

Similarly, the previous UNWTO Secretary-General, Taleb Rifai, stated with respect to the tourism and the SDGs: "As the world comes together to implement the 2030 Agenda for Sustainable Development, the exponential growth of our sector provides tremendous hope that our sector will remain one that has a truly positive change in the world. It should inspire us all to act, together, to make this world a better place" (in UNWTO, 2017b, p. 5). The remarkable thing with these comments is that even though Rifai emphasises the significance of growth in introducing the relationship between tourism and the SDGs: "2016 was a momentous year for tourism. International tourist arrivals continued their upward trajectory in their seventh straight year of above-average growth despite many challenges, reaching 1.2 billion. A comparable sequence of uninterrupted solid growth has not been recorded since the 1960s" (in UNWTO, 2017b, p. 5). There is no recognition that despite such growth tourism's contribution to development goals is extremely uneven, while also contributing to environmental change, including climate change (Rutty et al., 2015). This would suggest that tourism growth by itself is insufficient to achieve many of the SDGs, instead attention needs to be paid to the social, economic and political processes behind development, rather than just the greater marketisation and financialisation of tourism development, assets and services that the UNWTO advocates.

Managerial ecology and the neoliberalisation of sustainable tourism and the SDGs

The discussion above highlights that the managerial ecology of the main tourism bodies to the SDGs is profoundly neoliberal in emphasis. Shaping both the relationship of the individual to the environment as well as its management and, it can be argued, how research should be framed. Neoliberalism is premised on the assumption that the citizen's relationship to the state and others is mediated via the market (Harvey, 2005). Neoliberal managerialism, also referred to as new managerialism (Clarke, Gewritz, & McLaughlin, 2000; Lynch, 2014), involves governing through enacting and institutionalising technical changes imbued with market values. In the case of the UNWTO, there has been a profound shift towards market values over time while retaining the guise of sustainability. This, of course, also reflects shifts elsewhere in governmentality, but critically it has not made tourism any more sustainable, indeed, as noted at the beginning of this paper, tourism has become less sustainable in absolute terms by most empirical measures. The focus on greater efficiency in tourism, in terms of per tourist consumption, for example, makes little difference to the overall absolute sustainability of tourism and the achievement of the environmental goals of the SDGs if growth in visitor numbers, their total consumption, and the rebound effects from interventions outweighs greater material efficiency per tourist.

Language defines the world. This is more than issues of defining what constitutes sustainable tourism, as significant as that might be, it also structures how we are to understand tourism and its relationship to the SDGs. Neoliberal approaches, such as those portrayed in the UNWTOs approach to the SDGs, are often presented as apolitical, while at the same time neoliberalism is the dominant political, economic and social imaginary of contemporary society (Hursh, Henderson, & Greenwood, 2015), understood as "a way of thinking shared in a society by ordinary people, the common understandings that make everyday practices possible, giving them sense and legitimacy" (Rizvi & Lingard, 2010, p. 34). Although there are varieties of neoliberalism, there is clearly enough commonality between them to observe that the UNWTO and UNDP (2017) report and associated UNWTO activities in relation to the SDGs are serving to re-embed sustainable tourism in different political, legal, and cultural arrangements that privilege business and corporate interests and the financialisation and marketisation of sustainable development. As an agency of corporate interest, the activities of the WTTC that promote such a position is perhaps understandable. In contrast, the UNWTO is meant to have a wider mandate. The UNWTO and UNDP (2017) nevertheless reinforce the notion that the private sector and competitive markets should have greater responsibility in the provision of tourism infrastructure and services and, as such, act to further reinforce the commodification of the environment by tourism (Büscher, Dressler, & Fletcher, 2014). Indeed, Dauvergne and Lister (2013, p. 25) suggest: "Turning sustainability into eco-business ... is altering the nature of environmentalism, increasing its power to accelerate some forms of change, but limiting what is on the table to question, challenge, and alter. Sustainability as an idea can be radical: not just calling for changes in the rules of the game (i.e. market dynamics), but also to the game itself (i.e. the global economy)." Furthermore, adoption of the language of resilience, especially in relation to SDG13 "climate action" to further justify certain forms of sustainable development act as a form of "neoliberal environmentalism addresses the depletion of ecosystems as a global security problem, the only solution to which is the securitisation and financialization of the biosphere" (Walker & Cooper, 2011, p. 155). Indeed, the overall sense of crisis engendered by the SDGs, sustainable tourism and, the more recent, overtourism, only appear to encourage the UNWTO and the WTTC to advocate "more of the same" neoliberal strategies, even though they are not working.

Discussion and conclusions: What hope?

> Above all, however, tourism is a sector of hope. With its manifold socio-economic benefits and broad influence on a diverse range of sectors, tourism is a valuable part of global solutions to these global challenges and can be even more so. With more than 1.2 billion international tourists today and 1.8 billion predicted by 2030, the sector keeps on providing opportunities for each traveller and everyone involved in tourism to contribute to a more responsible, sustainable and inclusive future for all (UNWTO Secretary-General, Taleb Rifai, in UNWTO, 2017b, p. 5).

The framing of the SDGs through the undifferentiated appeal of sustainable development talks to a sense of global citizenship. Such appeals are not necessarily illegitimate, particularly in areas such as human rights, but it does "steer attention away from the difficult politics that result from differentiated social groups having different interests in causing and alleviating" economic, environmental and social problems (Demeritt, 2001, p. 313), which the SDGs are ostensibly seeking to address. The approach, shared in much of the research on sustainable tourism, serves to "tune out" positions that are not in keeping with neoliberal management ecology, such as those challenging certain assumptions surrounding problem framing and the relative roles of the market, corporations and the state (Hall, 2011).

Knowledge, and the representation of knowledge in relation to the UNWTO's official position on the SDGs and the roadmap for sustainable development to 2030, is not politically neutral and reflects a particular approach to issues of sustainability and sustainable tourism. As Evans and Marvin (2006) observe from their research on sustainable cities, knowledges are not additive and so reducing them to a *lingua franca*, in this case market-oriented neoliberal managerialism (Knafo, Dutta, Lane, & Wyn-Jones, 2018; Lawrence, 2017; Peck, 2010), will not of itself enable a resolution to that engagement. Instead, to be effective, agreement may need to be generated between actors whose knowledge of an issue is rooted in very different experiences. Indeed, some resource managers have recognised the potential value of communitarian strategies that seek to embrace Local Ecological Knowledge, empowering local people, and sought to reduce socio-economic inequities that have resulted from previous management regimes. However, "much discussed, it has not been widely implemented" (Wynn, 2011, p. xvi). Nevertheless, such an approach does not fundamentally question the "need for, or the usefulness of, management" (Bavington, 2011, p. 10) while stressing the importance of "achieving 'buy-in' from resource users to achieve consensus, avoid conflict, and permit ongoing economic growth" (2011, p. 107). Engaging different knowledges is therefore fundamentally different to engaging different voices. To explore this, Rydin (2007) suggests that it is helpful to recast knowledge as knowledge claims, i.e. a claim to understanding certain causal relationships. Such a situation is extremely important with respect to the sustainability – tourism relationship, because the UNWTO response both implicitly and explicitly presents knowledge claims by which tourism is expected to become "a more sustainable tourism sector by aligning policies, business operations and investments with the SDGs" (UNWTO & UNDP, 2017, p. 12).

Several reasons may exist for the relative lack of critical assessment of tourism's role in the SDGs. First, perhaps many researchers actually believe the stance taken by the UNWTO and others or, at least, do not actually care, with sustainability not actually being a significant interest of tourism researchers. If this were the case, then the epistemic community of tourism is dominated by neoliberal market orientations in which sustainability is more often than not framed by market and private sector oriented solutions in which individuals are "responsible *and* rational, moral yet calculating" (Bavington, 2011, p. 10; see also Reade, et al., 2017) in their agency. However, as discussed elsewhere in relation to the realities of individual capabilities to be sustainable (Whitmarsh, Seyfang, & O'Neill, 2011), there are substantial differences in the governmental and decision-making assumptions surrounding approaches that stress the sovereignty of individual agency versus those that regard people as holistic elements of larger systems (Hall, 2016). Second, research may be subject to "policy-palatability" (Buttel & Taylor, 1992) in which research and publications seek to accommodate the dominance of neo-liberal economics and managerial thinking. Third, policy makers may not only reject the results of research from outside of their paradigmatic thinking, they may also not fund such research (Shove, 2010). Policymakers, along with policy partnerships, legitimise lines of enquiry that generate results that can be accepted and managed, even if they do not necessarily provide the "solution" to policy problems. The result is a self-fulfilling cycle of credibility (Latour & Woolgar, 1986) in which evidence of the relevance and value of knowledge and research method to policymakers helps in securing additional resources for that approach (Hall, 2013b). Fully understanding the role that knowledge plays in expropriation requires expanding the focus of analysis to include not just the application of research, but also its production and circulation. Indeed, it is notable that the UNWTO and UNDP (2017) report on tourism and the SDGs contains reference to only three academic publications (and three BSc/masters theses), although it did receive some academic peer review. Instead, the vast majority of references are from institutional and industry sources. Similarly, the endnotes of the high profile report on tourism and overcrowding by WTTC and McKinsey and Company (2017) contained no academic sources, although some were used in the text for definitions and three academics were acknowledged for their "contributions." This is not to denigrate such contributions but rather to demonstrate the highly restricted nature of what is incorporated in such works, especially when there is a very long-standing literature on the overcrowding and carrying capacity issues in tourism (e.g. Ovington, Groves, Stevens, & Tanton, 1974; Skinner, 1968). Indeed, the conclusion to the foreword of the WTTC and McKinsey and Company (2017, p. 5) report:

> This work is only the beginning; the research is a starting point for ongoing conversations. To solve this challenge, leaders must be willing to identify and address the barriers (including beliefs, norms, and structures) that are holding us back from effectively managing overcrowding. And they must look for ways to compromise: when overcrowding goes too far, the repercussions are difficult to reverse.

Only serves to reinforce the neoliberal managerial stance that frames such complex problems in terms of management solutions and individual agency.

Haraway (1991) claims that knowledge (science) is about "interpretation, translation, stuttering and the partly understood. Translation is always interpretive, critical and partial. Here is a ground for conversation, rationality, and objectivity—which is power-sensitive, not pluralist, 'conversation'" (1991, p. 195). This stands in stark contrast to the approaches of lead tourism agencies to the SDGs in which the complexity of socio-ecological systems is regarded as manageable, through neoliberal means, and measurable, and therefore available for use. However, if tourism along with socio-ecological systems are genuinely regarded as (irreducibly) complex, and therefore uncertain, then this position cannot hold (Taylor, 2005). Instead, greater recognition needs to be given to constraints, including the effects of growth, as well as ethics. Bavington (2011), among others (Oelschlaeger, 2014), suggests the need for a fundamental rethink of human–environment relations so that the dominant notion of natural resource stewardship of the last 150 years moves away from the drive to manage and control nature to one that commits "to living within the limits of the ecosystems of which we are a part" (Wynn, 2011, p. xvii). Such a position is particularly apt given that this reinforces the need to treat sustainable development as a qualitative measure as opposed to a metric of growth. However, to change such thinking is extremely difficult given the dominance of neoliberal perspectives on governance and management ecology, and its self-fulfilling cycle of credibility as noted above. To achieve "third order" change the norms of governance structures require a substantial shift. As Hall (2011) argued, too much attention is given to the assumption that an institution is "good" because it facilitates partnership and network development rather than focus on norms and institutionalisation as first and necessary steps in the assessment of what institutional arrangements are promoting and their outcomes. This has resulted in enabling certain types of responses to global environmental problems consistent with this situation, "such as possibilities for the privatisation of environmental governance in some areas or the increasing use of market mechanisms. But at the same time it has made trade-offs much more difficult because it denies that they may be necessary among values of efficiency, economic growth, corporate freedom, and environmental protection" (Bernstein, 2002, p. 14). In such a context, research on the policy contradictions and failures resulting from current approaches may open up the possibilities of informing paradigm change and new ways of policy learning (Hall, 2011).

Initiatives such as the SDGs fail because they do not confront the way in which neoliberal rationalities are embedded in many tourism policy practices. The managerial approach advocated by the UNWTO and others is rooted in the political and economic context of capitalistic resource extraction by which success means failure, i.e. continued growth in tourism leads to grossly uneven development. Destination and resource managers, mediated by state agencies, corporate interests and economic rationality, may "manage" resources into oblivion (Bavington, 2011; Wynn, 2011). In some ways this could be construed as "Brundtland-as-usual" in the sense that Brundtland's ambiguity allowed business and policy-makers to promote sustainable development by using Brundtland's support for rapid growth to justify the phrase "sustainable growth" (Hopwood et al., 2005) or, in the case of the UNWTO and others, "sustainable tourism." However, it is possible, if not likely, that given the hegemonic position of neoliberal discourse neither much of the tourism industry, especially its international leadership, nor many tourism academics, can see other (Or, if they do, then they are not saying or writing). Instead, there is a need to encourage greater embrace of post-normal science and governmentalities in order to respond to the world for the complex place that it is. Embedded in such an approach is recognition that tourism policy work and research are inherently political when dealing with the uneven distribution of economic capital and social and environmental justice as well as a need to incorporate not just a range of voices in tourism policy making for the SDGs but a greater range of knowledge(s). To do so requires ontological shifts as well as more practical turns with respect to knowledge generation and transfer processes and increased pressure from researchers, NGOs and other interested parties to highlight policy failure and hold policy-makers responsible. Indeed, there may be benefits in greater research on the practices of prefigurative politics, i.e. those forms of social relations, decision-making, culture, and human experience that are the ultimate goal of a movement (Boggs, 1977). What otherwise may be framed as being the change you want to see (Pickerill & Chatterton, 2006).

Responding to complexity, relationality and uncertainty in the policy environment requires skills of adaptation and coping as well as new knowledge transfer skills. Things become what they are through interaction with other things—through translation. One strategy from planning is to develop an "epistemology of multiplicity" (Sandercock, 1998, p. 76) that include different ways of knowing: through dialogue; from experience; from local knowledge; by learning to read symbolic and non-verbal evidence; and through contemplative or appreciative knowledge, as well as more traditional means of acquiring scientific knowledge. Associated with such post-positivist thinking is the insight that knowledge is not just the domain of the expert, whether a scientist or policy maker, but rather is associated with a variety of actors and knowledges in a variety of social locations (Bavington, 2011; Rydin, 2007). This means that notions of collaboration need to extend well beyond the narrowly envisaged public-private partnerships that are emphasised by the UNWTO and UNDP in their assessments of tourism's contribution to the SDGs.

Demystifying managerial ecology, tourism knowledge and policy making and "demonstrating the social relations its construction involves does not necessarily imply disbelief in either that knowledge or the phenomena it represents" (Demeritt 2001, p. 310). As Demeritt went on to note, "Given its vital role in helping to make sense of environmental problems such as climate change, there simply can be no question of doing without science. Rather, the challenge is how to understand and live with it better" (2001, p. 310). As part of this process the holy grail of manageability espoused by the UNWTO and others, the belief that all problems can be solved by exerting greater effort and demanding greater efficiency within the status quo of continued tourism growth and consumption, necessitates challenge. Indeed, the fundamental challenge the SDGs and their tourism advocates face if they really want tourism to be a "sector of hope" is shifting from a growth mentality to one that explicitly commits humanity to prospering and travelling within the limits of the ecosystems of which we are a part.

Acknowledgements

The author would like to thank the anonymous referees for their valuable comments as well as those of the editors of the special issue.

Disclosure statement

No potential conflict of interest was reported by the author.

ORCID

C. Michael Hall ⓘ http://orcid.org/0000-0002-7734-4587

References

Alvesson, M., & Willmott, H. (2012). Making sense of management: A critical introduction. Thousand Oaks: Sage.
Bavington, D. (2001). From jigging to farming. Alternatives, 27(4),16–21.
Bavington, D. (2002). Managerial ecology and its discontents: Exploring the complexities of control, careful use and coping in resource and environmental management. Environments, 30(3),3–21.
Bavington, D. (2010). From hunting fish to managing populations: Fisheries science and the destruction of Newfoundland cod fisheries. Science as Culture, 19(4),509–528. doi:10.1080/09505431.2010.519615

Bavington, D. (2011). *Managed annihilation: An unnatural history of the Newfoundland cod collapse*. Vancouver: UBC Press.

Bavington, D., & Banoub, D. (2016). Marine fish farming and the blue revolution: Culturing cod fisheries. *London Journal of Canadian Studies, 31*(1),35–44.

Bavington, D., & Slocombe, S. (2002). Theme issue introduction: Moving beyond managerial ecology: Contestation and critique. *Environments, 30*(3),1–2.

Bernstein, S. (2002). Liberal environmentalism and global environmental governance. *Global Environmental Politics, 2*(3),1–16. doi:10.1162/152638002320310509

Bickerstaff, K., & Walker, G. (2003). The place(s) of matter: Matter out of place–public understandings of air pollution. *Progress in Human Geography, 27*(1),45–67. doi:10.1191/0309132503ph412oa

Boggs, C. (1977). Revolutionary process, political strategy and the dilemma of power. *Theory and Society, 4*(3),359–393.

Bouvaird, T. (2004). Public–private partnerships: From contested concepts to prevalent practice. *International Review of Administrative Sciences, 70*(2),199–215.

Bäckstrand, K., & Kylsäter, M. (2014). Old wine in new bottles? The legitimation and delegitimation of UN public–private partnerships for sustainable development from the Johannesburg Summit to the Rio + 20 Summit. *Globalizations, 11*(3),331–347. doi:10.1080/14747731.2014.892398

Boyd, W., Prudham, W. S., & Schurman, R. A. (2001). Industrial dynamics and the problem of nature. *Society and Natural Resources, 14*(7),555–570. doi:10.1080/08941920120686

Bryan, D., Rafferty, M., & Wigan, D. (2017). Capital unchained: Finance, intangible assets and the double life of capital in the offshore world. *Review of International Political Economy, 24*(1),56–86. doi:10.1080/09692290.2016.1262446

Buttel, F. H., & Taylor, P. J. (1992). Environmental sociology and global environmental change: A critical assessment. *Society and Natural Resources, 5*(3),211–230. doi:10.1080/08941929209380788

Büscher, B., Dressler, W., & Fletcher, R. (2014). *NatureTM Inc: Environmental conservation in the neoliberal age*. Tuscon: University of Arizona Press.

Castree, N. (2002). False antitheses? Marxism, nature and actor networks. *Antipode, 34*(1),111–146. doi:10.1111/1467-8330.00228

Castree, N. (2005). *Nature*. London: Routledge.

Christie, I. T., & Sharma, A. (2008). Millennium development goals – What is tourism's place? *Tourism Economics, 14*(2),427–430. doi:10.5367/000000008784460346

Clarke, J., Gewirtz, S., & McLaughlin, E. (2000). *New managerialism new welfare?* London: Sage.

Corporate Europe Observatory . (2018). *UnFairbnb: How online rental platforms use the EU to defeat cities' affordable housing measures*. Brussels: Corporate Europe Observatory.

Dauvergne, P., & Lister, J. (2013). *Eco-business: A big-brand takeover of sustainability*. Cambridge, MA: MIT Press.

Demeritt, D. (1998). Science, social constructivism and nature. In B. Braun & N. Castree (Eds.), *Remaking reality: Nature at the millennium* (pp.173–193). New York: Routledge.

Demeritt, D. (2001). The construction of global warming and the politics of science. *Annals of the Association of American Geographers, 91*(2),307–337. doi:10.1111/0004-5608.00245

Evans, R., & Marvin, S. (2006). Researching the sustainable city: Three modes of interdisciplinarity. *Environment and Planning A, 38*(6),1009–1028. doi:10.1068/a37317

Ferguson, L. (2011). Promoting gender equality and empowering women? Tourism and the third Millennium development goal. *Current Issues in Tourism, 14*(3),235–249. doi:10.1080/13683500.2011.555522

Frost, W., & Laing, J. (2018). Public–private partnerships for nature-based tourist attractions: The failure of Seal Rocks. *Journal of Sustainable Tourism, 26*(6),942–956. doi:10.1080/09669582.2017.1423319

Hall, C. M. (1999). Rethinking collaboration and partnership: A public policy perspective. *Journal of Sustainable Tourism, 7*(3-4),274–289. doi:10.1080/09669589908667340

Hall, C. M. (2011). Policy learning and policy failure in sustainable tourism governance: From first and second to third order change? *Journal of Sustainable Tourism, 19*(4-5),649–671. doi:10.1080/09669582.2011.555555

Hall, C. M. (2013a). The natural science ontology of environment. In A. Holden & D. Fennell (Eds.), *The Routledge handbook of tourism and the environment* (pp.6–18). Abingdon: Routledge.

Hall, C. M. (2013b). Framing behavioural approaches to understanding and governing sustainable tourism consumption: Beyond neoliberalism, "nudging" and "green growth"? *Journal of Sustainable Tourism, 21*(7),1091–1109. doi:10.1080/09669582.2013.815764

Hall, C. M. (2014). *Tourism and social marketing*. Abingdon: Routledge.

Hall, C. M. (2016). Intervening in academic interventions: Framing social marketing's potential for successful sustainable tourism behavioural change. *Journal of Sustainable Tourism, 24*(3),350–375. doi:10.1080/09669582.2015.1088861

Hall, C. M., Gössling, S., & Scott, D. (Eds.). (2015). *The Routledge handbook of tourism and sustainability*. Abingdon: Routledge.

Hall, C. M., Lew, A. A., & Williams, A. (2014). Tourism: Conceptualizations, disciplinarity, institutions, and issues. In A. A. Lew , C. M. Hall , & A. Williams (Eds.), *The Wiley Blackwell companion to tourism* (pp.3–24). Chichester: Wiley Blackwell.

Haraway, D. (1991). *Simians, cyborgs, and women: The reinvention of nature.* New York: Routledge.

Harvey, D. (2005). *A brief history of neoliberalism.* Oxford: Oxford University Press.

Head, L. (2007). Cultural ecology: The problematic human and the terms of engagement. *Progress in Human Geography, 31*(6),837–846. doi:10.1177/0309132507080625

Head, L. (2008). Is the concept of human impacts past its use-by date? *Holocene, 18*(3),373–377. doi:10.1177/0959683607087927

Henriques, M. H., & Brilha, J. (2017). UNESCO Global Geoparks: A strategy towards global understanding and sustainability. *Episodes, 40*(4),349–355.

Herrera-Cano, C., & Herrera-Cano, A. (2016). Maldivian disaster risk management and climate change action in tourism sector: Lessons for the sustainable development agenda. *Advances in Sustainability and Environmental Justice, 19*,113–131.

Hopwood, B., Mellor, M., & O'Brien, G. (2005). Sustainable development: Mapping different approaches. *Sustainable Development, 13*(1),38–52. doi:10.1002/sd.244

Hursh, D., Henderson, J., & Greenwood, D. (2015). Environmental education in a neoliberal climate. *Environmental Education Research, 21*(3),299–318. doi:10.1080/13504622.2015.1018141

Imon, S. S. (2017). Cultural heritage management under tourism pressure. *Worldwide Hospitality and Tourism Themes, 9*(3),335–348. doi:10.1108/WHATT-02-2017-0007

Jenkins, D. (2015). Impacts of neoliberal policies on non-market fishing economies on the Yukon River, Alaska. *Marine Policy, 61*,356–365. doi:10.1016/j.marpol.2014.12.004

Knafo, S., Dutta, S. J., Lane, R., & Wyn-Jones, S. (2018). The managerial lineages of neoliberalism. *New Political Economy, 1.* doi:10.1080/13563467.2018.1431621.

Koide, R., & Akenji, L. (2017). Assessment of policy integration of sustainable consumption and production into national policies. *Resources, 6*(4),48. doi:10.3390/resources6040048

Lapeyre, R. (2011). The Grootberg Lodge partnership in Namibia: Towards poverty alleviation and empowerment for long-term sustainability. *Current Issues in Tourism, 14*(3),221–234. doi:10.1080/13683500.2011.555521

Latour, B., & Woolgar, S. (1986). *Laboratory life: The construction of scientific facts.* Princeton: Princeton University Press.

Lawrence, J. C. (2017). Managing the environment: Neoliberal governmentality in the Anthropocene. In P. Heikkurinen (Ed.), *Sustainability and peaceful coexistence for the anthropocene* (pp.88–104). Abingdon: Routledge.

Lima, S., Eusébio, C., Partidário, M. R., & García Gómez, C. S. (2012). Knowledge and development for tourism. In E. Fayos-Solà (Ed.), *Knowledge management in tourism: Policy and governance applications* (pp.95–113). Cheltenham: Emerald Group Publishing.

Lynch, K. (2014). New managerialism, neoliberalism and ranking. *Ethics in Science and Environmental Politics, 13*(2),141–153. doi:10.3354/esep00137

Mann, A. (2018). The human toll of falling taxi licence values. *ABC News,* 5 August. Available at http://www.abc.net.au/news/2018-08-05/falling-taxi-licence-values-sparks-suicide-fears/10060558

Mansfield, B. (2003). Fish, factory trawlers, and imitation crab: The nature of quality in the seafood industry. *Journal of Rural Studies, 19*(1),9–21. doi:10.1016/S0743-0167(02)00036-0

Matarrita-Cascante, D., Brennan, M. A., & Luloff, A. E. (2010). Community agency and sustainable tourism development: The case of La Fortuna, Costa Rica. *Journal of Sustainable Tourism, 18*(6),735–756. doi:10.1080/09669581003653526

Mbaiwa, J. (2011). The effects of tourism development on the sustainable utilisation of natural resources in the Okavango delta, Botswana. *Current Issues in Tourism, 14*(3),251–273. doi:10.1080/13683500.2011.555525

McEwan, C., Mawdsley, E., Banks, G., & Scheyvens, R. (2017). Enrolling the private sector in community development: Magic bullet or sleight of hand? *Development and Change, 48*(1),28–53. doi:10.1111/dech.12283

McCurry, J. (2018). 'Tourism pollution': Japanese crackdown costs Airbnb $10m. *The Guardian,* 15 June. Available at https://www.theguardian.com/world/2018/jun/15/tourism-pollution-backlash-japan-crackdown-costs-airbnb-10m-kyoto

Merchant, C. (1980). *The death of nature: Women, ecology and the scientific revolution.* New York: Harper & Row.

Novelli, M., & Hellwig, A. (2011). The UN millennium development goals, tourism and development: The tour operators' perspective. *Current Issues in Tourism, 14*(3),205–220. doi:10.1080/13683500.2011.555523

Oelschlaeger, M. (2014). Deep ecology and the future of the wild in the Anthropocene. *Trumpeter, 30*(2),231–246.

Ovington, J. D., Groves, K. W., Stevens, P. R., & Tanton, M. T. (1974). Changing scenic values and tourist carrying capacity of national parks. An Australian example. *Landscape Planning, 1*,35–50. doi:10.1016/0304-3924(74)90004-5

Peck, J. (2010). *Constructions of neoliberal reason.* Oxford: Oxford University Press.

Pickerill, J., & Chatterton, P. (2006). Notes towards autonomous geographies: Creation, resistance and self-management as survival tactics. *Progress in Human Geography, 30*(6),730–746. doi:10.1177/0309132506071516

Reade, B., Davis, R., Bavington, D., & Baird, C. (2017). Industrial aquaculture and the politics of resignation. Marine Policy, 80, 19–27.

Rizvi, F., & Lingard, B. (2010). Globalizing education policy. New York: Routledge.

Rouse, J. (1987). Knowledge and power: Toward a political philosophy of science. Ithaca, NY: Cornell University Press.

Ruhanen, L. (2007). Destination competitiveness: Meeting sustainability objectives through strategic planning and visioning. In Á. Matias , P. Nijkamp , & P. Neto (Eds.), Advances in modern tourism research: Economic perspectives (pp.133–151). Heidelburg: Physica-Verlag HD.

Rutty, M., Gössling, S., Scott, D., & Hall, C. M. (2015). The global effects and impacts of tourism: An overview. In C. M. Hall , S. Gössling , & D. Scott (Eds.), The Routledge handbook of tourism and sustainability (pp.36–63). Routledge, Abingdon.

Rydin, Y. (2007). Re-examining the role of knowledge within planning theory. Planning Theory, 6(1),52–68. doi: 10.1177/1473095207075161

Saarinen, J., & Rogerson, C. M. (2014). Tourism and the Millennium Development Goals: perspectives beyond 2015. Tourism Geographies, 16(1),23–30. doi:10.1080/14616688.2013.851269

Saarinen, J., Rogerson, C., & Manwa, H. (2011). Tourism and Millennium Development Goals: Tourism for global development? Current Issues in Tourism, 14(3),201–203. doi:10.1080/13683500.2011.555180

Sandercock, L. (1998). Towards cosmopolis. London: Wiley.

Sardar, Z., & Ravetz, J. R. (1994). Complexity: Fad or future? Futures, 26(6),563–567. doi:10.1016/0016-3287(94)90028-0

Scheyvens, R., Banks, G., & Hughes, E. (2016). The private sector and the SDGs: The need to move beyond 'business as usual'. Sustainable Development, 24(6),371–382. doi:10.1002/sd.1623

Schneider, I. (2018). Big data-based capitalism, disruption, and novel regulatory approaches in Europe. In A. R. Saetnan , I. Schneider , & N. Green (Eds.), The politics and policies of big data: Big data, big brother? Abingdon: Routledge.

Scott, D., Hall, C. M., & Gössling, S. (2016). A review of the IPCC 5th Assessment and implications for tourism sector climate resilience and decarbonization. Journal of Sustainable Tourism, 24(1),8–30.

Scott, D., Gössling, S., Hall, C. M., & Peeters, P. (2016). Can tourism be part of the decarbonized global economy? The costs and risks of carbon reduction pathways. Journal of Sustainable Tourism, 24(1),52–72. doi:10.1080/09669582.2015.1107080

Shove, E. (2010). Beyond the ABC: Climate change policy and theories of social change. Environment and Planning A, 42(6),1273–1285. doi:10.1068/a42282

Skinner, D. N. (1968). Landscape survey with special reference to recreation and tourism in Scotland. Planning Outlook, 4(1-2),37–43. doi:10.1080/00320716808711396

Taylor, P. J. (1995a). Building on construction: An exploration of heterogeneous constructionism, using an analogy from psychology and a sketch from socio-economic modeling. Perspectives on Science, 3(1),66–98.

Taylor, P. J. (1995b). Co-construction and process: A response to Sismondo's classification of constructivisms. Social Studies of Science, 25(2),348–359. doi:10.1177/030631295025002015

Taylor, P. J. (1997a). How do we know we have global environmental problems? Undifferentiated science-politics and its potential reconstruction. In P. Taylor , S. Halfon , & P. Edwards (Eds.), Changing life: Genomes-ecologies-bodies-commodities (pp.149–174). Minneapolis: University of Minnesota Press.

Taylor, P. J. (1997b). Appearances notwithstanding, we are all doing something like political ecology. Social Epistemology: A Journal of Knowledge, Culture and Policy, 11(1),111–127. doi:10.1080/02691729708578833

Taylor, P. J. (1999). What can agents do? Engaging with complexities of the post-Hardin commons. Advances in Human Ecology, 8,125–156.

Taylor, P. J. (2005). Unruly complexity: Ecology, interpretation, engagement. Chicago: University of Chicago Press.

Thornton, T. F., & Hebert, J. (2015). Neoliberal and neo-communal herring fisheries in Southeast Alaska: Reframing sustainability in marine ecosystems. Marine Policy, 61,366–375. doi:10.1016/j.marpol.2014.11.015

Toffel, M. W., Short, J. L., & Ouellet, M. (2015). Codes in context: How states, markets, and civil society shape adherence to global labor standards. Regulation & Governance, 9(3),205–223. doi:10.1111/rego.12076

UNWTO . (2014). UNWTO cautions against potential tourism tax in Africa. PR No.: PR14033, 13 May 14. Madrid: UNWTO.

UNWTO . (2017a). Press release: A roadmap towards 2030: The legacy of the International Year of Sustainable Tourism for Development 2017. PR 17137, 19 Dec 17. Madrid: UNWTO.

UNWTO . (2017b). UNWTO annual report 2016. Madrid: UNWTO.

UNWTO . (2018). Press release: Tourism can and should lead sustainable development: UNWTO Secretary-General opens ITB 2018. PR 18020, 06 Mar 18. Madrid: UNWTO.

UNWTO & UNDP . (2017). Tourism and the sustainable development goals – Journey to 2030. Madrid: UNWTO.

Wachsmuth, D., & Weisler, A. (2017). Airbnb and the rent gap: Gentrification through the sharing economy. Environment and Planning A: Economy and Space, 50(6), 1147-1170. doi:0308518X18778038.

Walker, J., & Cooper, M. (2011). Genealogies of resilience: From systems ecology to the political economy of crisis adaptation. Security Dialogue, 42(2),143–160. doi:10.1177/0967010611399616

Weyl, H. (2009). *Philosophy of mathematics and natural science* (rev. ed.). Princeton: Princeton University Press.

Whitmarsh, L., Seyfang, G., & O'Neill, S. (2011). Public engagement with carbon and climate change: To what extent is the public 'carbon capable'? *Global Environmental Change, 21*(1),56–65.

WTTC and McKinsey & Company. (2017). *Coping with success: Managing overcrowding in tourism destinations.* London: WTTC.

Wynn, G. (2011). Foreword. This is more difficult than we thought. In D. Bavington (Ed.), *Managed annihilation: An unnatural history of the Newfoundland cod collapse* (pp.xi–xxxiii). Vancouver: UBC Press.

Zapata Campos, M. J., Hall, C. M., & Backlund, S. (2018). Can MNCs promote more inclusive tourism? Apollo tour operator's sustainability work. *Tourism Geographies*, 20(4), 630–652. doi:10.1080/14616688.2018.1457074

Zwier, J., & Blok, V. (2017). Saving Earth: Encountering Heidegger's philosophy of Techné. *Research in Philosophy and Technology, 21*(2/3),222–242. doi:10.5840/techne201772167

Can tourism help to "end poverty in all its forms everywhere"? The challenge of tourism addressing SDG1

Regina Scheyvens (iD) and Emma Hughes (iD)

ABSTRACT

SDG1 presents the global community with an important, but highly challenging goal. When discussing tourism's potential to contribute to SDG1 to "end poverty in all its forms everywhere", the multidimensional nature of poverty must be considered rather than focusing solely on economic deprivation. Specifically, we need to shift the focus beyond how tourism can foster economic growth, provide jobs and income, to considering sociopolitical aspects of poverty and how structural inequalities are impeding people's development. The contradictions involved in poor people, in poor locations, with poor labour rights, putting on smiling faces to serve rich guests of former colonial powers and to clean up their messes, should not be overlooked if we are genuinely interested in challenging the negative aspects of global tourism and making it more equitable and sustainable in the future. Thus, if governments and tourism industry players wish to do more than pay lip service to SDG1, they will need to make some significant changes to the way in which they work. This article will draw inspiration from tourism businesses in Fiji that are addressing SDG1 and related goals, and discuss how they have the potential to contribute to longer-term sustainable development.

Introduction

Tourism has long been purported to make significant contributions to alleviating poverty, and since the late 1990s, work in this area has coalesced around the concept of "pro-poor tourism". Whether tourism can be a key driver to "end poverty in all its forms everywhere" as required by SDG1, however, is a big question. Many proclamations have been made about the actual and potential contributions tourism can make to developing countries, perhaps none more audacious than that of the president of Counterpart International, Lelei LeLaulu, who asserted that tourism represents "the largest voluntary transfer of resources from the rich to the poor in history, and for those of us in the development community - *tourism is the most potent anti-poverty tool ever*" (eTurbo News, 2007 – emphasis added).

In this article, concerns are raised about the dominant narrative which suggests that tourism is, inherently, a tool for poverty alleviation. Given the scale of poverty and its entrenched and multidimensional nature, we must seriously consider whether a fickle and somewhat frivolous industry like tourism can hope to significantly improve the well-being of over a billion of the world's population that are poor (Scheyvens, 2011). Certainly tourism can bring much desired investment, employment and tax revenue; however, we challenge the notion of tourism as a panacea for sustainable development and instead critically interrogate both the potential and constraints facing those who wish to ensure that tourism contributes effectively to poverty alleviation.

To begin, we consider the multidimensional nature of poverty and the critical components of a successful approach to poverty alleviation. Next, we discuss changing views of scholars on the relationship between tourism and poverty, noting that tourism has been criticized by some for entrenching – rather than alleviating – poverty. This is followed by an analysis of the specifics of SDG1. While retaining a focus around SDG1, this article will also cross-refer other SDGs where relevant synergies exist, including goals on gender (SDG5), decent work (SDG8), and inequality (SDG10). Drawing from our own research, a case study illustrates some of the ways in which tourism businesses in Fiji can be said to address SDG1 and related goals. Finally, the discussion considers the potential for tourism businesses to move beyond *ad hoc* donations to local communities to instead contribute to poverty alleviation through more long-term, sustainable development efforts.

Understanding the multidimensional nature of poverty

When discussing tourism's potential to contribute to SDG1 on ending poverty, we first need to appreciate the multidimensional nature of poverty. Thus, it is essential that we look beyond those definitions of poverty that focus only on economic deprivation. This thousands of people consulted during the World Bank's Definitions of Poverty study revealed that being poor meant four things to them: lack of assets (physical, environmental, social, human); lack of basic resources (e.g. food, shelter, land); the absence of basic infrastructure (e.g. health clinics, transport), and last but definitely not least, lack of voice, power and independence, making them vulnerable to exploitation and humiliation (Narayan, Patel, Schafft, Rademacher, & Koch-Schulte, 2000). This last point underlines why Frenzel (2013), in his work on slum tourism, stresses that we need to understand qualitative indicators of poverty alleviation rather than being fixated on quantitative measures. This may also be why Bebbington (2007, p. 813) asserts that " ... chronic poverty is a socio-political relationship rather than a condition of assetless-ness".

A rights-based approach to development corroborates this view. As laid out in the 1986 UN Declaration on the Right to Development: "A fundamental human freedom is freedom from want. *Poverty is a human rights violation*, and freedom from poverty is an integral and inalienable right" (emphasis added). A rights-based approach to development builds on this right:

> A rights-based approach holds that someone, for whom a number of human rights remain unfulfilled, such as the right to food, health, education, information, participation, etc., is a poor person. Poverty is thus more than lack of resources – it is the manifestation of exclusion and powerlessness (Mikkelsen, 2005, p. 204).

We thus assert that in order to discuss how tourism can help to "end poverty in all its forms everywhere", rather than focusing only on whether tourism can foster economic growth, provide jobs and income, we need to consider whether tourism:

- provides alternative livelihood strategies which help to reduce the vulnerability of poor communities, and enhance their well-being
- helps poor people to build their capabilities and assets
- facilitates the empowerment of poor people and helps them to lead dignified lives in which they have greater control over their own wellbeing
- leads to poor people to securing their rights (Scheyvens, 2011, p. 25).

These points align quite closely with the targets associated with SDG1, as will be shown below (see section on "Agenda 2030: unpacking SDG1").

The relationship between tourism and poverty

Scholarly views on the relationship between poverty and tourism have varied widely since the mid-1900s, with the industry being soundly criticised for a number of years. While in the 1950s and 1960s tourism was identified as a modernisation strategy that could help newly independent developing countries to create jobs and earn foreign exchange, by the 1970s and 1980s many social scientists were arguing that poor people and poorer countries were typically excluded from or disadvantaged by what tourism can offer. Thus, Turner and Ash, in their landmark book on *The Golden Hordes: International Tourism and the Pleasure Periphery,* warned that "tourism has proved remarkably ineffective as a promoter of equality and as an ally of the oppressed" (1975, p. 53, cited in Higgins-Desbiolles, 2006, p. 1193). During this time, tourism was widely critiqued as an industry dominated by large corporations which exploit the labour and resources of developing countries, cause environmental degradation, commodify traditional cultures, entrench inequality, and deepen poverty (Britton, 1982; Pleumarom, 1994). Given the strength and vigour of this critique, the reversal of this thinking in the past twenty years – coinciding with the development industry's global focus on poverty alleviation from the 1990s onwards – has been quite remarkable.

Tourism has been identified as a promising economic sector through which to develop poverty alleviation strategies thanks to some persuasive statistics. In the face of threats and shocks which impact on global economic development – including terrorist incidents, natural disasters, and political instability – tourism as a sector continues to grow, outpacing general growth of the global economy. Travel and Tourism generated over 10 per cent of global GDP in 2016 and provided 292 million jobs (i.e. one in every 10 jobs); tourism growth supported an additional 6 million jobs in the sector in 2016 alone (World Travel & Tourism Council, 2017). Developing countries have a market share of over 40 per cent of worldwide international tourism arrivals, up from 34 per cent in 2000 (UNWTO, 2007, p. 4). Twenty of the world's Least Developed Countries can count tourism as their first or second source of export earnings, and many small island developing states get over a quarter of their GDP from the tourism industry (UNWTO, 2018). As a sector, tourism is also seen as a strong performer when compared with many other sectors; for example, 20 years of data revealed that the real value of primary product exports from the South Pacific had declined and "the only sector to demonstrate a continuous upward trend has been tourism" (Sofield, Bauer, De Lacy, Lipman, & Daugherty, 2004, p. 25–26). Furthermore, it is suggested that the approximately $68 billion given in aid annually pales in significance compared with revenues from tourism which are around $153 billion (Ashley and Mitchell, 2005, cited in Christie & Sharma, 2008, p. 428).

On the back of such positive figures, it should not be surprising that "pro-poor tourism" (PPT) emerged from the late 1990s onwards. In part, it evolved out of UK-sponsored research on sustainable livelihoods in southern Africa (see e.g. Ashley & Roe, 1998). Tourism was put forward as an industry which could not only contribute to a country's economic growth, but which had considerable potential to improve the well-being of rural communities (Goodwin, 1998; IIED, 2001, p. 41). The Overseas Development Institute (ODI) and Department for International Development (DFID) in the UK subsequently funded a number of studies and projects (see e.g. Ashley & Roe, 2002; Roe, Goodwin, & Ashley, 2002). Soon after, the UN World Tourism Organization (UNWTO) came on board. Together with UNCTAD, it initiated the ST-EP programme ("Sustainable Tourism–Eliminating Poverty") in 2002, funding projects and doing capacity building. A range of other donors and agencies, including universities and multilaterals, showed commitments to PPT in the first decade of the new millennium – some were influenced by alternative development thinking in line with enhancing people's control over tourism and the benefits they gained from the industry, while others were more neoliberal in focus in line with pro-poor growth (Scheyvens, 2007a). While generally supported, some important questions have also been raised about tourism's potential as a tool for poverty alleviation.

Critiques of tourism as a tool for poverty alleviation

In the face of strong enthusiasm for tourism's potential to contribute to development in recent years, we need to openly acknowledge the ways in which tourism has caused or entrenched poverty and to challenge the associated ways of operating within the industry. This section thus provides an important prelude to exploring the potential of tourism to contribute to SDG1. Hall, for one, seriously refutes some of the purported benefits of tourism:

> The notion espoused by the UNWTO that "tourism exchanges benefit primarily the countries of the South" is a ridiculous one and hides the reality that not only is the consumption of tourism the domain of the wealthy, but in many ways so is its production (Hall, 2007: p.116).

Some of the main critiques of tourism in terms of its impacts on poverty are discussed below.

Tourism highlights inequalities between the wealthy and the impoverished

Fundamentally, can PPT help to overcome the inequalities between tourists and local people, when international tourism is to some extent based upon, and highlights, the vast inequalities between the wealthy and the impoverished? This is immediately apparent than when viewing tourists' leisure pursuits: "Golf courses and enormous pools are an insult to more than 1.3 billion people denied access to clean water" (UNDP, 1999, cited in Richter, 2001, p. 50). It is also clear in the following example of the differing mobility experiences of tourists and local peoples:

> For the majority of the Andean poor, migrating is a better and quicker way to escape poverty than waiting for tourists. But they arrive unknown and unloved at their destinations, in stark contrast to what tourists experience when visiting exotic destinations (Zoomers, 2008: p.981).

Tourism is structured around differences, between people, places, and environments, but also differences in wage rates and labour laws. Thus, poor countries may be attractive to resort developers partly because they offer cheap labour, which both lowers construction costs and ongoing labour costs when running a resort. This leads Plüss and Backes to surmise that, "to some extent tourism always feeds off the poverty of host regions" (2002, p. 12).

The challenge of reaching the poorest of the poor

Rather than suggesting that tourism might "solve" poverty, the available data in some cases show that tourism has impacted negatively on the lives of the poor. Thus, for example, Manyara and Jones (2007) cite evidence that in Kenya, the incidence of poverty is greater in those areas with high tourist activity. Even tourism endeavours with a pro-poor focus have struggled to reach the poorest of the poor, as found in recent research in Peru (Llorca-Rodriguez, 2017). Similarly, Ghimire and Li (2001, p. 102) have noted that tourism has brought economic benefits to rural communities in China, as evidenced by a proliferation of televisions and satellite dishes. However, living conditions have not improved on the whole. Ghimire and Li thus question whether poverty can be seen to have been alleviated in this context where there is still a lack of potable water, energy sources are unreliable, and sanitation and health-care facilities are poor (2001, p. 102). Another study comparing 13 countries that were highly dependent on tourism found that growth in tourism did not lead to a reduction in income inequality, and nor did it reduce the overall number of poor people; however, it can improve the economic well-being of the poor such that they are less poor than before tourism (Mahadevan & Suardi, 2017).

For something to be called pro-poor tourism then, Schilcher argues that the poor should capture disproportionate benefits:

> The tourism industry must be "moulded" so that "the poor" and "poorest" receive a proportionately higher share of tourism's benefits than people above the poverty line in order to reduce poverty-enhancing inequalities" (2007, p. 68).

The profit imperative

It is argued that tourism can benefit poor people *and* big business, or that tourism growth can bring profits to the industry *and* result in a bigger slice of the tourism pie for the poor (Roe et al., 2002). However, maximising profits and alleviating poverty are not necessarily a win-win connection. Major players in the tourism industry, as in any industry, are centrally concerned with profit maximisation (Ashley & Haysom, 2006; Zhao & Ritchie, 2007). Should we assume that they might have some ethical commitment to ensuring their business contributes to poverty alleviation? In reality, there is likely to be a need for trade-offs (Kontogeorgopoulos, 2005). Yet, Chok, Macbeth, and Warren (2007, p. 51) suggest that many advocates of pro-poor types of tourism have not been realistic about the types of trade-offs required to ensure that tourism benefits the poor:

> Tourism development that generates net benefits for the poor and protects the environment... will place restrictions on human activity and challenge our current rapid expansion development model. In other words, there may be strong moral imperatives but weak profit margins.

When we look closely at what is being proposed by business actors, self-interest is a clear driver, which is why we see a focus on voluntary change rather than regulation, and soft measures to reduce environmental impacts rather than fundamental changes in production and consumption (Pingeot, 2014, p. 29). This leads Luke to suggest that corporates are more interested in the "sustainability of profitable corporate growth" rather than the SDGs (Luke, 2013, p. 89). Ghosh (2015) asserts that the global development agenda post-2015 should focus, first and foremost, on benefitting the citizenry, rather than putting corporate capital at the heart of sustainable development initiatives.

The need for fundamental structural changes

The neoliberal policy environment in which most tourism businesses operate typically promotes trade liberalisation, market-led growth and private sector development, while calling for minimum government "interference" in market mechanisms. The role of governments is seen as smoothing the way for outside investors and assisting them with gaining access to prime tourism sites. Providing such an "enabling environment" can lead to exploitation of local environments and alienation of land. It can also result in a development landscape that is dominated by powerful corporations, financial institutions and local elites (Kumi, Arhin, & Yeboah, 2014). When it is widely acknowledged that neoliberal mechanisms have led to social inequalities (see Fletcher, 2012; Murray & Overton, 2011), it follows that these same mechanisms should not be relied on to try to solve inequalities (Kumi et al., 2014, p. 549). As Moore (2015, p. 801) argues, "... the post-2015 development agenda should go beyond just re-writing goals and targets that adhere to 'sustaining' the same old economic and social models".

Challenging patterns of distribution and structural inequality should thus be priorities in order to comprehensively address poverty. It may, for example, be very difficult for well-designed pro-poor tourism initiatives to be implemented effectively if corruption and cronyism are rife, there is racism and sexual discrimination, and if powerful elites typically capture the benefits of development interventions (Chok et al., 2007). For tourism to contribute to ending poverty in all its forms, everywhere, it would need to challenge major power brokers such as local elites, company directors and government leaders.

Agenda 2030: unpacking SDG1 and its relationship to tourism

Clearly, there is still solid debate between proponents of tourism as a tool for poverty alleviation and the critics. Not surprisingly, the global goals for achieving sustainable development by 2030, often referred to as Agenda 2030 or the Sustainable Development Goals (SDGs), fall strongly on the side of proclaiming the potential of the tourism industry in efforts to achieve sustainable development. The SDGs were agreed to by 190 countries in New York in September 2015. They are unique in one sense because they are universal, applying to all signatory countries rather than designed specifically for the "developing" world. A number of commentators have lauded the extensive consultation with a wide range of stakeholders that went into developing the 17 SDGs. The trope of "partnership" in SDG discussions has been strong (Scheyvens, Banks, & Hughes, 2016).

In terms of both these consultations and expectations for delivery of the global goals, the private sector assumed a greater role than in past UN-led discussions. The convergence of attention on the private sector's roles in development since Rio +20 in 2012 has seen the emergence of business-driven forums and sectoral initiatives aimed at more ethical, sustainable and responsible business practices. Many assert that the private sector has particular strengths to bring to bear in delivering on the SDGs, including innovation, responsiveness, efficiency and provision of specific skills and resources (Lucci, 2012; Porter & Kramer, 2011). Examples abound of companies working together with both governments and non-profit organisations to deliver on development goals (Chakravorti, Macmillan, & Siesfeld, 2014, p. 6).

Concerns have been raised, however, about the dominance of large Western transnational companies, especially those representing oil/gas/mining, in the consultations and negotiations over development of the SDGs meant that private sector gained a much stronger role over agenda setting than in previous UN processes (Koehler, 2017; Pingeot, 2014). These corporate actors suggested repeatedly that to end poverty and achieve inclusive development, it will be necessary to grow the economy, which will lead to shared prosperity: no need for trade-offs is suggested. In addition, in line with the discussion on neoliberalism above, business representatives argued that the role of governments is to create an enabling environment so that the private sector can deliver on sustainability goals: governments are seen as having "a key role to play in realizing a business-friendly trade system, pricing incentives, transparent procurement, and to encourage and support responsible business" (Pingeot, 2014, p. 18). Note that there is nothing here on the place of careful government regulations to control business, nor on compromises that need to be made in order to respect the integrity of the natural environment.

SDG1

While many development commentators have been pleased to see poverty alleviation as the first of the SDG's 17 goals, others are not so enthused by this, recognising that according to earlier UN development declarations, extreme poverty should have been eradicated by 1990, or at least 2005, or otherwise – via the Millennium Development Goals – by 2015. Now, we must wait until 2030: thus, says " … we observe a distressing procrastination in the UN's poverty agenda" (Koehler, 2017, p. 212). From a positive perspective in terms of tackling poverty, however, the 2030 agenda recognises that inequality is a major issue within and between countries, and it thus identifies the importance of addressing redistribution, social rights, and resource consciousness (Koehler, 2017).

The SDG1 targets speak of enhancing the resilience of poor people, putting in place effective policies and social protection systems, and ensuring that the poor and vulnerable have equal rights to economic resources and access to basic services. These targets, and other associated goals, are discussed below in turn with respect to the tourism industry.

1.1

By 2030, **eradicate extreme poverty** for all people everywhere, currently measured as people living on less than $1.25 a day

1.2

By 2030, **reduce** at least by half the proportion of men, women and children of all ages living in **poverty in all its dimensions** according to national definitions

These first two targets have an explicit economic focus, with two of the three indicators for measuring them based on poverty lines (usually a dollar value). Even though we know there are limits to perceiving poverty purely in economic terms, it is important to recognize that provision of jobs, or small business activities within the tourism sector, can definitely contribute to poverty alleviation efforts (Mitchell & Ashley, 2010). However, this issue of employment in the tourism sector and connections to poverty alleviation needs to be linked to the discussion below on SDG8 which calls for "decent work for all". It is pleasing to see, meanwhile, that it is not only economic development that is considered through target 1.2, with indicator 1.2.2 specifically focusing on multidimensional poverty "according to national definitions", thus enabling countries to devise definitions reflective of their own values and contexts.

1.3

Implement nationally appropriate **social protection systems** and measures for all, including floors, and by 2030 achieve substantial coverage of the poor and the vulnerable

The third target represents a progressive move within Agenda 2030 in terms of the introduction of social protection, including policy recommendations regarding social protection floors to assist those living in extreme poverty. Such systems could start with provision of basic income security and essential health care, and extend to more comprehensive forms of support (Kaltenborn, 2017). This target is backed up by target 5.4 (under SDG5 on women's empowerment), "recognize and value unpaid care and domestic work through the provision of public services, infrastructure and social protection policies" and target 10.4 (within SDG10 on reducing inequality within and between countries), "Adopt policies, especially fiscal, wage and social protection policies, and progressively achieve greater equality" (Koehler, 2017, p. 215). It will require substantial inputs of resources for all governments to be able to implement the social protection systems required by SDG1 (Kaltenborn, 2017).

While provision of social protection policies would not normally be considered the core mandate of tourism industry players, they can nevertheless make contributions towards this target by, for example, providing health care insurance or superannuation payments for their employees, or through corporate social responsibility initiatives that support local health clinics or hospitals from the medium to long term. Tourism business can also contribute to target 1.3 by avoiding tax dodging, a behaviour sometimes associated with big business. When governments earn adequate taxes from tourism and other industries, they are in a better position to provide social services for their people.

1.4

By 2030, ensure that all men and women, in particular the poor and the vulnerable, have **equal rights to economic resources, as well as access to basic services, ownership and control over land** and other forms of property, inheritance, natural resources, appropriate new technology and financial services, including microfinance

The fourth target of SDG1 is about rights to economic resources and services. The poorest of the poor is often excluded from accessing tourism opportunities, for example the ability to access work opportunities or establish a business (Zhao & Ritchie, 2007). Credit is an economic resource that is especially important for small-scale entrepreneurs who do not have collateral and thus find it difficult to access capital to build their business. The ability to set up small businesses to benefit from tourism can also be impeded by large hotels offering all-inclusive holidays and selling imported crafts rather than those that are locally manufactured (Mowforth & Munt, 2009). The issue of ownership and control over land issue is one that governments can directly address by putting in place an appropriate legislative environment. Governments can, furthermore, set up systems to ensure that fair rents/lease monies are paid when businesses are located on customary land and that land on which businesses are operating has been acquired legally.

Beaches are a highly prized economic resource closely linked to tourism opportunities, yet local access to beaches and the foreshore can be restricted by resorts which want to claim exclusive rights of access to their customers. This can directly impinge on local livelihood options, e.g. fishing as a subsistence or market-based activity, selling cut fruit to tourists, or offering horse-riding or hair-braiding services.

1.5

By 2030, build the **resilience** of the poor and those in vulnerable situations and reduce their exposure and vulnerability to climate-related extreme events and other economic, social and environmental shocks and disasters

The fifth target focuses on decreasing exposure and increasing resilience of the poor and vulnerable in the face of climate change as well as other shocks and disasters. Its association with more frequent, extreme events, means that climate change is already impacting severely on some tourism-based communities. For example, in 2016 the tourism-dependent economy of Fiji faced tropical cyclone Winston, a category 5 event that made it the most severe storm in Fiji's history. Neighbouring them, Vanuatu also faced a category 5 event in tropical cyclone Pam in 2015, and in 2017 cyclone, Gita devastated parts of Tonga and Samoa. Tourism businesses undoubtedly already contribute to protecting their staff, providing emergency relief supplies locally, and assisting with rebuilding in their area when such events strike, but more work is needed to reduce exposure of people to these extreme events. This includes acknowledging and mitigating harmful impacts of tourism development on the environment which can exacerbate disasters. For example, the removal of mangroves on Denarau Island in Fiji has been identified as a contributing factor to the regular flooding events experienced by Nadi town (Bernard & Cook, 2015); the April 2018 flooding there led to several fatalities as well as millions of dollars worth of property and infrastructural damage. Ensuring that proper environmental assessments are undertaken and adhered to in the construction of resorts and facilities would serve as a protective factor for communities.

1.a

Ensure significant mobilization of resources from a variety of sources, including through enhanced development cooperation, in order to provide adequate and predictable means for developing countries, in particular least developed countries, to implement programmes and policies to end poverty in all its dimensions

One of the reasons for the drive to get private sector entities on board as development actors in the SDG process was the need to secure more resources for development (Lucci, 2012). Certainly tourism businesses do commit resources to development, often through CSR programmes (see Ashley & Haysom, 2006; Hughes & Scheyvens, 2015). However, sometimes the funding is *ad hoc* or one-off, rather than enduring and contributing to longer-term goals of the country concerned. Ideally, larger tourism businesses especially would ensure that their CSR policies align with government policy to deliver support to the poor, including social protection measures. For example, they might contribute to hospital refurbishment or teaching resources in schools in poorer areas.

1.b

Create sound policy frameworks at the national, regional and international levels, based on pro-poor and gender-sensitive development strategies, to support accelerated investment in poverty eradication actions.

Target 1.b sits firmly in the realm of government responsibility. Good tourism policies, aligned with other relevant national policies (e.g. on environmental protection, inclusive economic development and social well-being), can help to direct more sustainable forms of development. A more inclusive policy environment can certainly help to spread the benefits of tourism (Mbaiwa,

2017; Scheyvens & Biddulph, 2017). Also needed here are opportunities for destination communities to have a voice in development plans and processes, so that their concerns are not overlooked in resultant policies. In addition, sound policies can influence action and resource allocation by tourism corporates. Specifically, Ramani, Parihar, and Sen (2017) argue that well-designed policies can "nudge" multinational companies to contribute to achieving SDG1.

Links to other SDGs

A challenge to considering SDG1 is that none of the global goals exist in isolation. It has been suggested that SDG1 has a "synergistic relationship with most of the other goals" (Pradhan, Costa, Rybski, Lucht, & Kropp, 2017, p. 1169), and these synergies need to be leveraged to enhance chances of achieving the global goals. Thus, other goals will also be noted even though SDG1 is the primary focus of discussion in this article.

For example, SDG8 addresses "decent work for all", which is closely associated with poverty alleviation because the ability to earn an income from tourism can undoubtedly raise people out of poverty. To date, the tourism industry has certainly provided some opportunities for the poor, especially small-scale entrepreneurs working in countries with weak regulatory system that allow low-capital start-ups, such as selling crafts at a roadside stall. However, SDG8 also promotes "economic growth", something which should not be an uncontested goal in an agenda so clearly concerned with the environmental impacts of human development, including climate change (Koehler, 2017). It is also of concern to see how target 8.9 focuses on growth in jobs rather than decent work for all: "By 2030, devise and implement policies to promote sustainable tourism that creates jobs and promotes local culture and products". The associated indicators are tourism's share of GDP and the number of jobs. Unfortunately, this target and indicator is weaker than the goal as they do not speak about decent work or labour rights. In a service-oriented, female-dominant industry with high rates of casual employment (Cañada, 2018), it is important to ask questions about the quality of any jobs that are created and about whether employees have fair contracts and good working conditions. Other issues might include whether staff receive good remuneration and training. Pay rates and labour conditions of tourism workers have often been compromised in the past to enhance competitiveness of a business (James, 2004). This is something that needs attention throughout tourism research: "workforce and workplace considerations are widely neglected in the growing volume of debate relating to sustainable tourism" (Baum et al., 2016, p. 809).

Similarly, SDG5, "achieve gender equality and empower all women and girls", is associated with SDG1 because women make up a large proportion of the tourism workforce, but often in low-level, precarious jobs (Berno & Jones, 2001; Enloe, 2000). The United National World Tourism Organization (UNWTO) asserts:

> Tourism can empower women in multiple ways, particularly through the provision of jobs and through income-generating opportunities in small and larger-scale tourism and hospitality related enterprises. As one of the sectors with the highest share of women employed and entrepreneurs, tourism can be a tool for women to unlock their potential, helping them to become fully engaged and lead in every aspect of society (UNWTO, 2015, p. 3).

The wording "become fully engaged" shows a lack of understanding of the domestic and sharing economy in which women in many societies are so fully engaged already, and thus, the UNWTO does not consider whether childcare and other support structures will be available for women who want to "unlock their potential" in tourism. Also in terms of work, there is a need to challenge stereotypes by not just getting women involved in tourism work – as so many are already – but by employing men and women across a variety of roles in the tourism sector, for example, opening up housekeeping work to men and maintenance work to women. Further, women's perspectives in tourism are frequently marginalized, while developers, government officials, chiefs/community leaders and corporate managers who are most often male dominate when decisions are made (Scheyvens, 2007b). A stronger goal would involve proactively provide opportunities for female staff to get training and be promoted to supervisory and management positions. Questions should also be asked about whether the tourism industry is discouraging sex tourism and adopting no tolerance policies for sexual harassment of staff.

SDG10, "reduce inequality within and among countries", is also closely linked to SDG1, given that tourism can both reduce and exacerbate poverty in tourism destinations. As noted earlier, there is evidence that tourism can raise overall incomes, while simultaneously entrenching poverty. Research in Thailand revealed that tourism growth did increase household income, but led to worsened distribution (Wattanakuliarus & Coxhead, 2008). It is positive then to see that target 10.1 aims to "sustain income growth of the bottom 40 per cent of the population at a rate higher than the national average". However, some researchers believe further efforts are needed in the policy domain: " ... tourism growth is not a panacea for other goals of development policy; to address inequality, additional policy instruments are required" (Wattanakuliarus & Coxhead, 2008, p. 929). This supports the need for target 10.4, which calls for "fiscal, wage and social protection policies".

Tourism opportunities tend to principally benefit the population in tourism areas, with areas distant from the tourist trail excluded from those opportunities. The ability of governments to ensure that benefits are shared equitably is contingent on their will to implement an effective policy and regulatory framework (Goodwin, 2007). For developing countries, this can be limited by the power of multinational tourism companies to shift operations to alternative destinations if they feel the economic environment is more conducive elsewhere.

Inequality among countries is also an issue: developing countries have limited influence on decisions on industry regulations at a global level. It would be helpful to allow governments more agency to influence international frameworks and institutions, for example the World Trade Organisation, World Bank, and IMF (Schilcher, 2007). This aligns with target 10.6 on "enhanced representation and voice of developing countries in decision making in global international economic and financial institutions".

This discussion has shown that, while there are some shortfalls, there is definitely promise in terms of some of the Agenda 2030 goals and targets associated with poverty alleviation. The following case study discusses examples identified from research in Fiji that align with SDG1 in particular.

Case study: tourism as a tool for poverty alleviation in Fiji

While Fiji is classed as an "upper-middle income country" by the World Bank, almost a third of the population of approximately 900,000 remain below the poverty line (Ministry of Economy, 2017), with many others vulnerable to falling below the poverty line (Pacific Islands Forum Secretariat, 2015). Despite the fact that Fiji had already met the Millennium Development Goal target of halving the proportion of people suffering from hunger by 2010, the proportion of the population living in poverty increased across the period of the MDGs to an estimated 40 per cent in 2008 (Ministry of National Planning, 2010, p. 10). By 2015, this figure had dropped to 28 per cent, but this increases to 36 per cent in rural areas (Ministry of Economy, 2017). As one of Fiji's main economic sectors, tourism is a significant contributor to employment and consequently national and household incomes. Tourism contributes 23 per cent to Fiji's GDP (Harrison & Prasad, 2013, p. 744), with the total contribution of travel and tourism to employment estimated to be 33 per cent of employment in 2014 and predicted to rise to 40 per cent by 2025 (WTTC, 2015). It is in this context that we examine the potential for tourism to address SDG1.

The authors were both part of a Royal Society Te Aparangi-funded project between 2013 and 2016 which examined the potential for tourism businesses to generate locally meaningful development outcomes. The research in Fiji was primarily undertaken across 5 months in 2014. The second author was based within two indigenous Fijian communities neighbouring five-star international resorts in two of the main tourist locations: one adjacent to Denarau Island and the other on the Coral Coast, accounting respectively for fifty per cent (Bernard & Cook, 2015, p. 306) and 18 per cent (Pratt, McCabe, & Movono, 2016) of Fiji's visitor arrivals. Data were gathered through interviews, focus groups, and observation with community members, hotel management and staff, recipients of hotel donations (including schools and hospitals), tourism bodies, government ministries, and locally based non-governmental organisations. A household survey was also undertaken in each village to better understand the level of employment in tourism. The following section is organised around the commitments of SDG1 to explore the ways in which hotels can be said to address each of the targets and some of the challenges that remain.

Reducing poverty – targets 1.1 and 1.2

SDG targets for poverty reduction focus specifically on "national definitions" of poverty; in the Pacific, this is measured as the proportion living below the basic needs poverty line (Pacific Islands Forum Secretariat, 2015, p. 9). The ability of tourism to contribute in economic terms to reducing the proportion of the population in Fiji living in poverty is reflected in employment statistics. Tourism in Fiji provides more than 12 per cent of jobs; when the supply chain and indirect employment are included, this share is 33 per cent (WTTC, 2015). Associated income earning opportunities include procurement of food, entertainment and services, and other small business opportunities. Together, this makes a significant contribution to household incomes. Household surveys undertaken in the two tourism villages in our study demonstrate the reliance of local communities on tourism. Surveys of 50 households in each village (comprising approximately one third of Village A and two thirds of Village B) show that almost every household surveyed in Village A and three quarters of households in Village B have a member currently employed in tourism, either directly by a hotel or indirectly, for example, in a taxi-driving business or selling handicrafts. Almost two-thirds of the population of the villages have been employed at some point in tourism with half of these in tourism employment for more than ten years and around 20 per cent for over 20 years (see Table 1).

As noted above, however, the most effective way for employment to address poverty is through offering work which is secure, safe, and sustainable, in line with SDG8. Fiji has a large informal sector, estimated at around 65 per cent of those in employment (Narayan, 2010) with the limited protection this affords workers. Tourism sector workers are impacted by a climate where many hotels maintain a flexible workforce in order to weather fluctuations associated with seasonality any downturn in tourist numbers, some employing up to 85% of the workforce on casual contracts. In the case study hotels, approximately 40 per cent of the staff were employed on permanent full time contracts, with the remainder on contracts with variable hours according to hotel needs. Trending against this norm, after many years of action from the National Union of Hospitality, Catering & Tourism Industries Employees, the Warwick Hotel (not one of our case studies) agreed to move towards 70% of staff on secure contracts over a period of three years

Table 1. Village residents employed in tourism.[a]

	Village A		Village B		Total	
Total households (approx.)	150		75		225	
Number of households surveyed	50		50		100	
Total adults in survey households	153		154		307	
Households with tourism employment	45	90%	36	72%	81	81%
Adults currently employed in tourism	67	44%	52	34%	119	39%
Adults previously employed in tourism	37	24%	28	18%	65	21%
Length of employment over 20 years[b]	10	10%	25	31%	35	19%
Length of employment over 10 years[b]	48	46%	44	55%	92	50%

[a]Either directly as a hotel employee, or indirectly, for example as a taxi driver.
[b]Percentage of adults employed currently or previously in tourism.

(personal communication, union official, 24 September 2014). This is a significant achievement for workers' rights: in addition to providing security of income, this also enables staff to save, take out bank loans, and in turn support other enterprises in their communities.

In an environment where women are under-represented across all industries in Fiji, the hotel, retail, and restaurant industry also has one of the highest proportions of female employees (at 41 per cent) (Ministry of National Planning, 2010, p. 31) with implications for SDG 5, achieving gender equality. There is a gender segregation of employment within the tourism sector, with women often occupying the lower hierarchy of jobs, in addition to a predominance in frontline roles, in keeping with images promoted through marketing campaigns (Berno & Jones, 2001; Naidu, 2013). A breakdown of roles in the household survey shows the gender divisions in the type of employment, with women most likely to work in housekeeping and waiting roles (see Table 2). Equal numbers of women and men were employed in Village A with almost twice the number of women than men employed in the hotel in Village B. Both women and men held management roles (in small numbers); however, more women were concentrated in informal sector roles such as babysitting and selling handicrafts. In addition to their paid responsibilities, many community and caring responsibilities also fall to women: the women who work in the hotels are able to do so because of the mothers, mothers-in-law, aunties, and sisters caring for the children and elderly. Research findings showed that women are in a position where they must constantly respond to community demands; cultural obligations in particular fall heavily on women, such as hospitality, communal cleaning, and organising, often resulting in a combination of a high level of responsibilities with a low level of income security.

Social protection – target 1.3

The constraints outlined in the previous section limit the extent to which tourism is able to meet the social protection targets within SDG1, including the income security and health care provision that accompanies secure work contracts. The tourism industry mitigates some of these gaps through Corporate Social Responsibility programmes that support the long-term sponsorship of health and education projects that can in turn lead to the creation of greater social protection for local communities. For example, one hotel in our study committed to sponsoring schools

Table 2. Employment by gender and role.[a]

	Village A		Village B		
	Women	Men	Women	Men	Total
Food & Beverage staff	12	5	8	9	34
Housekeeping	16		7	3	26
Chef/cook	3	4	5	5	17
Taxi driver		15			15
Babysitter	4		8		12
Clerk/cashier	1		7	1	9
Handicraft seller	5		4		9
Manager	2	3	2	1	8
Sports & recreation		3	3	2	8
Grounds staff		4		2	6
Porter		5		1	6
Accountant/IT		2	1	2	5
Professional trade (electrician/plumber)		2		2	4
Front office	2		2		4
Entertainer		3			3
Training officer			2		2
Retail outlet	1				1
Landscaper		1			1
Dishwasher			2		2
	46	47	51	28	

[a]Includes both current and previous roles.

over a 5–10-year period and another funded school infrastructure and equipment with a view to creating long-term value. Where support is coordinated with government plans, this can create further added value. For example, the Coral Coast chapter for the Fijian Hotel and Tourism Association has established a health and safety fund supported by guest donations from five resorts in the region. The chapter collaborates closely with the Ministry of Health, recently co-funding the construction of a brand new maternity unit which cost FJ$2.6million (US$1.3 million), FJ$600,00 of which came from the tourism fund (Bainimarama, 2015). The unit was opened by President Bainimarama in January 2015. Initial data indicate fewer women are travelling outside the region to give birth (personal communication, Fiji Hotel and Tourism Association official, 1 May 2015). The tourism industry has also taken steps to combat a rise in prostitution and in child sex tourism (Save the Children Fiji, 2005) with both case study hotels signing up to the Ending Exploitation of Children in Travel and Tourism (ECPAT) initiative.

A limitation to the social protection enabled by tourism results from unequal access to the benefits of tourism, connected to SDG10 reducing inequalities. Tourism is concentrated in four main areas of Fiji (Harrison & Prasad, 2013, p. 747), creating a geographical imbalance in access to tourism opportunities and benefits, with remote, rural communities in particular often excluded from these benefits. Collaboration with other third sector organisations can assist in generating positive outcomes for communities outside tourism areas. Rise Beyond the Reef (RBTR) is a non-governmental organisation that works with remote, rural villages in Fiji to identify their development needs and connect them with support from the tourism industry. In this way, they enabled the financing and construction of an early learning centre with hotel support. RBTR has also created the opportunity for women artists and artisans to sell their products in high-end hotels and gift shops and on cruise ships, providing them with a sustainable, alternative income source. A percentage of profits goes to the artists, a percentage to the women's cooper-atives involved, and a percentage to expanding the programme. The success of the programme means that village coordinators now also receive a monthly stipend (personal communication, Executive Director of Rise Beyond the Reef, 17 October 2014).

Access to economic resources and services and control over land – target 1.4

Beyond an income focus on poverty reduction, SDG1 recognises the rights to economic resour-ces. One way to ensure ongoing and fair access to economic resources is to provide the infra-structure to enhance income earning potential through procurement and small business opportunities. There are key challenges for hotels in purchasing local produce in Fiji, namely quality, quantity, and reliability of supply. A recent value chain analysis suggests 67 per cent of food and beverages are still imported (Harrison & Pratt, 2015, p. 13). Through our research, we identified a number of initiatives which facilitate these types of opportunities for communities through enabling greater access to resources. These include the University of the South Pacific's "farm to table" initiative and the Pacific Agribusiness Research for Development Initiative (PARDI) which provide access to markets for smallholder vegetable farmers. As a result, farmers supplying tomatoes were able to earn 40 per cent more on their shipment by providing hotels with high-quality graded tomatoes year-round (PARDI News, 2013).

Target 1.4 also incorporates the right to ownership and control over land. For hotels on indi-genous-owned land, which makes up around 87 per cent of all land in Fiji, fair leases can make a critical difference to poverty levels. Past evidence has demonstrated a wide variation in leases in terms of the amounts of lease money paid to landowners and the additional provisions that benefit communities such as preferential employment or business opportunities (Boydell & Baya, 2014). The iTaukei Land Trust Board, the body that manages leases, is now encouraging older lease holders to identify wider ranging benefits for the landowners in addition to lease income. Where there is evidence of redistribution of wealth, this can reduce inequality and provide a means to tackle the conditions that create poverty.

Government plays an important role in ensuring the benefits of tourism are shared; thus, a fundamental component of target 1.B recognises the need for sound policy frameworks. In 2014, the Fijian government implemented the Equal Rent Distribution Policy which meant that, after many years of traditional leaders getting large slices of the pie before it was distributed among landowners, now lease money is shared equally among all registered landowners. Reports from TLTB suggested that some community members were receiving the lease money they were entitled to for the first time and women in particular viewed the change as positive (Rokosuka, 2015).

Resilience to climate-related extreme events and other economic, social, and environmental shocks and disasters – target 1.5

Addressing poverty goes hand in hand with decreasing vulnerability and increasing resilience (target 1.5). In Fiji, as in the Pacific Islands more widely, communities are vulnerable to the impacts of natural disasters such as floods and cyclones; in 2016, for example, Fiji faced its most extreme event in recorded history, the category 5 tropical cyclone Winston. Both hotels in our study demonstrated many examples of disaster relief provided after an adverse event: these include monetary payments, food or equipment donations, and assistance to rebuild severely affected areas. Examples of enhancing preparedness of communities before disasters were less common. At a national level, lack of coordination between donors and national strategies became particularly evident after Fiji's 2009 floods. The Ministry of Education reported that multiple donors were assisting schools and individual students in different ways across the country with no shared knowledge or planning. In response, the Ministry initiated a system to coordinate donors centrally, which has since worked effectively in cyclone responses and they are keen to expand their network to include additional tourism industry stakeholders (personal communication, Acting Deputy Secretary - Primary and Secondary Education, 21 August 2014).

In terms of building resilience to economic and social shocks, effective partnerships with local organisations can create an important buffer for communities. One tour organisation, Talanoa Treks, supports local communities in a respectful way with food, accommodation, and tour guides sourced from local villages, who also receive a contribution to the village development fund. Some large hotels market these tours to guests which increases the uptake of the tours. By promoting community ventures such as this, either through marketing or business mentoring, this supports ongoing community development and builds resilience of communities to environmental or economic shocks (Hughes, 2016).

Discussion

SDG1, with its emphasis on complete eradication of poverty by 2030, presents the global community with an important, but highly challenging goal (Kaltenborn, 2017; Koehler, 2017). While there is a great deal of rhetoric on the virtues and promise of tourism as a tool for poverty alleviation, strenuous efforts will be needed to deliver on its potential in countries like Fiji. In reality, there are still major barriers to those in extreme poverty gaining direct benefits from tourism, not least because they do not fit the image or skill set associated with catering for tourists seeking luxurious, hedonistic holidays. The contradictions involved in poor people, in poor locations, with poor labour rights, putting on smiling faces to serve rich guests of former colonial powers and to clean up their messes, should not be overlooked if we are genuinely interested in challenging the negative aspects of global tourism and making it more equitable, and sustainable, in the future. Whether an industry so driven by the image of luxury and hedonism can make significant headway in addressing this goal remains to be seen.

A key challenge for those advocating for tourism as a tool for poverty alleviation is to ascertain how tourism can contribute not just to the economic well-being of the poor, but how it can challenge poverty more generally. As noted earlier in this article, poverty is a complex, multidimensional concept. Thus, in addition to ensuring that tourism brings economic benefits, efforts to achieve SDG1 by tourism players should seek to enhance people's access to resources and build their resilience; empower poorer people and help them to secure their rights; and provide more opportunities for the poor and vulnerable to participate in decision-making about tourism development. The examples from Fiji effectively demonstrate that tourism can readily contribute to incomes, and therefore poverty reduction, via employment; however, addressing the issues of decent work with clear career pathways, social protection, and overcoming inequalities in the distribution of resources and opportunities is more complex.

The tourism industry is singled out for special attention in the SDGs, as if it is able to magically deliver on a number of key goals. It is unrealistic to expect this. The norm in terms of tourism industry initiatives related to poverty alleviation is that there are a range of *ad hoc* donations from tourists or hotels which may contribute to addressing an immediate need, but there is little in the way of comprehensive strategies (Hughes & Scheyvens, 2015). However, the case of Fiji also illustrates positive examples that provide a welcome change from this norm and show that other approaches are possible, even if those that exist are somewhat isolated examples. This includes the Warwick Hotel's efforts to get more staff employed on secure contracts, and the Fiji Hotel and Tourism Association's collaboration with the Ministry of Health to upgrade facilities at the local hospital. In order for resources to be effectively mobilised at a scale that would allow lower income countries to implement policies to end poverty, these types of examples would have to be standard practice across the industry.

Innovative approaches are required in order to move beyond simply ameliorating the symptoms of poverty. Early case studies of tourism attempting to contribute to poverty alleviation showed that "a proactive interventionist approach is needed" whereby governments target the poor and establish legislation to back up affirmative action strategies (Briedenham and Wickens, 2004; Sofield, 2003, p. 351). Signs of governments challenging inequitable structures would include the following: regulating large-scale businesses and international trade (e.g. requiring clear performance standards of foreign companies to maximise benefits for the country through local procurement or joint ventures); controlling negative impacts, e.g. on the environment; implementing good labour rights legislation along with appropriate incentives for upskilling employees or employing vulnerable peoples (e.g. youth at risk); providing social safety nets; recognising unpaid care work; and creating an environment that supports freedom of expression, allowing strong NGOs, media, and advocacy groups which can play a watchdog role regarding tourism development.

Meanwhile, tourism businesses could show serious commitment to SDG1 by fully recognizing the rights and protecting well-being of their workers (including providing permanent contracts, quality training, health and retirement schemes); using local suppliers of goods and services wherever possible; and by using CSR funds for longer-term partnerships to deliver social services to communities. In addition, if industry associations want to demonstrate a commitment to sustainable tourism and poverty alleviation, rather than making platitudes about the need to build capacity among communities and to find ways in which they can gain more of the benefits of tourism, they could influence members to support local procurement, to endorse acceptable labour standards in the industry, and to ensure fair lease arrangements are in place for customary land.

The discussion above demonstrates that to effectively address poverty, initiatives must be both long term in order for sustained and sustainable outcomes, and coordinated, in order to dovetail with government strategies and existing non-governmental or community-based interventions. Positive examples include coordinating emergency response procedures with local and national government, and participating in initiatives to provide better uptake of local produce can ensure that tourism benefits local populations in an equitable way. Similarly, local voices should be part of the planning process as Carbone (2005, p. 562) argues: "tourism planning should be based on 'bottom-up globalization', which engages in distributive justice by entrusting more decision making power in local communities". Stakeholders must also be willing to address structural inequalities through, for example, policy and regulatory changes; this was evident in the Fijian government's Equal Rent Distribution Policy supporting customary landowners. This could be quite a challenge when guided by the SDGs as some commentators believe that Agenda 2030 is remedial rather than challenging the structural causes of poverty (Koehler, 2017). Koehler thus asserts that we need to aim beyond Agenda 2030: "build on what is useful, and at the same time, imaginatively but realistically transcend the agenda where it lacks ambition and supplement the missing analysis and critique" (2017, p. 211).

Disclosure statement

No potential conflict of interest was reported by the authors.

ORCID

Regina Scheyvens http://orcid.org/0000-0002-4227-4910
Emma Hughes http://orcid.org/0000-0001-9762-6074

References

Ashley, C., & Haysom, G. (2006). From philanthropy to a different way of doing business: strategies and challenges in integrating pro-poor approaches into tourism business. *Development Southern Africa, 23*(2), 265–280. doi: 10.1080/03768350600707553

Ashley, C., & Roe, D. (2002). Making tourism work for the poor: Strategies and challenges in southern Africa. *Development Southern Africa, 19*(1), 61–82. doi:10.1080/03768350220123855

Ashley, C., & Roe, D. (1998). *Enhancing community involvement in wildlife tourism: Issues and challenges. IIED Wildlife and Development Series No.11*. London: International Institute for Environment and Development.

Bainimarama, V. (2015). *PM Bainimarama speech at the opening of Sigatoka Hospital new extension*. The Fijian Government. Retrieved from http://www.fiji.gov.fj/Media-Center/Speeches/PM-BAINIMARAMA-SPEECH-AT-THE-OPENING-OF-SIGATOKA-H.aspx?feed=news

Baum, T., Cheung, C., Kong, H., Kralj, A., Mooney, S., Nguyễn Thị Thanh, H., ... low, M. L. (2016). Sustainability and the tourism and hospitality workforce: A thematic analysis. *Sustainability, 8*(8), 809. doi:10.3390/su8080809

Bebbington, A. (2007). Social movements and the politicization of chronic poverty. *Development and Change, 38*(5), 793–818. doi:10.1111/j.1467-7660.2007.00434.x

Bernard, K., & Cook, S. (2015). Luxury tourism investment and flood risk: Case study on unsustainable development in Denarau island resort in Fiji. *International Journal of Disaster Risk Reduction, 14*, 302–331.

Berno, T., & Jones, T. (2001). Power, women and tourism development in the South Pacific. In G. Apostolopulos, S. F. Sönmez, & D. J. Timothy (Eds.), *Women as producers and consumers of tourism in developing regions* (pp. 93–109). Westport, CT: Praeger.

Boydell, S., & Baya, U. (2014). *Using trust structures to manage customary land in Melanesia: what lessons can be learnt from the iTaukei Land Trust Board in Fiji*. Paper presented at the 2014 World Bank Conference on Land and Poverty Washington DC, 24–27 March.

Briedenham, J., & Wickens, E. (2004). Tourism routes as a tool for the economic development of rural areas – Vibrant hope or impossible dream? *Tourism Management, 25*(1), 71–79. doi:10.1016/S0261-5177(03)00063-3

Britton, S. (1982). The political economy of tourism in the third world. *Annals of Tourism Research, 9*(3), 331–358. doi:10.1016/0160-7383(82)90018-4

Cañada, E. (2018). Too precarious to be inclusive? Hotel maid employment in Spain. *Tourism Geographies, 20*(4), 653–674. doi:10.1080/14616688.2018.1437765

Carbone, M. (2005). Sustainable tourism in developing countries: poverty alleviation, participatory planning, and ethical issues. *The European Journal of Development Research, 17*(3), 559–565. doi:10.1080/09578810500209841

Chakravorti, B., Macmillan, G., & Siesfeld, T. (2014). *Growth for good or good for growth? How sustainable and inclusive activities are changing business and why companies aren't changing enough.* Massachusetts: Citi Foundation; Fletcher School; Monitor Institute. Retrieved from http://www.citifoundation.com/citi/foundation/pdf/1221365_Citi_Foundation_Sustainable_Inclusive_Business_Study_Web.pdf.

Chok, S., Macbeth, J., & Warren, C. (2007). Tourism as a tool for poverty alleviation: a critical analysis of 'pro-poor tourism' and implications for sustainability. In C. M. Hall (Ed.), *Pro-poor Tourism: Who Benefits?* (pp. 34–55). Clevedon: Cromwell Press.

Christie, I. T., & Sharma, A. (2008). Research note: Millennium Development Goals – what is tourism's place? *Tourism Economics, 14*(2), 427–430. doi:10.5367/000000008784460346

Enloe, C. H. (2000). *Bananas, beaches and bases: Making feminist sense of international politics.* Berkeley: University of California Press.

eTurbo News (2007). 'Aerial highway' critical for poor countries'. November 18. Retrieved from http://forimmediater-elease.net/pm/853.html

Fletcher, R. (2012). Using the master's tools? Neoliberal conservation and the evasion of inequality. *Development and Change, 43*(1), 295–317. doi:10.1111/j.1467-7660.2011.01751.x

Frenzel, F. (2013). Slum tourism in the context of the tourism and poverty (relief) debate. *Die Erde: Zeitschrift Der Gesellschaft Für Erdkunde, 144*(2), 117–128.

Ghimire, K. B., & Li, Z. (2001). The economic role of national tourism in China. In Ghimire, K. (Ed.), *The native tourist: Mass tourism within developing countries* (pp. 86–108). London: Earthscan.

Ghosh, J. (2015). Beyond the Millennium Development Goals: A southern perspective on a global new deal. *Journal of International Development, 27*(3), 320–329. doi:10.1002/jid.3087

Goodwin, H. (1998). Background paper for the workshop on Sustainable Tourism and Poverty Eliminiation. In *preparation for the 1999 session of the Commission on Sustainable Development*. London: Department for International Development and DTER.

Goodwin, H. (2007). Indigenous tourism and poverty reduction. In R. Butler & T. Hinch (Eeds.), *Tourism and iIndigenous pPeoples* (pp. 84–94). Oxford, England: Elsevier: pp. 84-94.

Hall, C. M. (2007). Pro-poor tourism: do 'tourism exchanges benefit primarily the countries of the South'?. *Current Issues in Tourism, 10*(2–3), 111–118. doi:10.1080/13683500708668426

Harrison, D., & Prasad, B. (2013). The contribution of tourism to the develoment of Fiji and other Pacific Island countries. In C. A. Tisdell (Ed.), *Handbook of tourism economics: analysis, new applications and case studies* (pp. 741–761). Singapore: World Scientific.

Harrison, D., & Pratt, S. (2015). Tourism in Pacific islands: Current issues and future challenges. In S. Pratt & D. Harrison (Eds.), *Tourism in Pacific islands. Current issues and future challenges* (Vol.48, pp. 3–21). Oxford: Routledge.

Higgins-Desbiolles, F. (2006). More than an 'industry': the forgotten power of tourism as a social force. *Tourism Management, 27*(6), 1192–1208. doi:10.1016/j.tourman.2005.05.020

Hughes, E. L. (2016). *The tourist resort and the village: Local perspectives of corporate community development in Fiji* (Doctoral Thesis). Massey University, Palmerston North.

Hughes, E., & Scheyvens, R. (2015). Prospects for sustainable development in the Pacific: a review of Corporate Social Responsibility in Tourism. *The Journal of Pacific Studies, 35*(1), 47–65.

International Institute for Environment and Development (IIED). (2001). *The future is now.* London: Author.

James, G. (2004). Riding the wave: Working within a globalised tourism economy. *Tourism in Focus, 52*, 12–13.

Kontogeorgopoulos, N. (2005). Community-based ecotourism in Phuket and Ao Phangnga, Thailand: Partial victories and bittersweet remedies. *Journal of Sustainable Tourism, 13*(1), 4–23. doi:10.1080/17501220508668470

Kaltenborn, M. (2017). Overcoming extreme poverty by social protection floors - approaches to closing the right to social security gap. *Law and Development Review, 10*(2), 237–273.

Koehler, G. (2017). The 2030 Agenda and eradicating poverty: New horizons for global social policy? *Global Social Policy*, *17*(2), 210–216. doi:10.1177/1468018117703440

Kumi, E., Arhin, A., & Yeboah, T. (2014). Can post-2015 sustainable development goals survive neoliberalism? A critical examination of the sustainable development–neoliberalism nexus in developing countries. *Environment, Development and Sustainability*, *16*(3), 539–554. doi:10.1007/s10668-013-9492-7

Llorca-Rodriguez, C. M. (2017). Tourism and poverty alleviation: An empirical analysis using panel data on Peru's department. *International Journal of Tourism Research*, *19*(6), 746–756.

Lucci, P. (2012). *Post-2015 MDGs: What Role for Business?* London: Overseas Development Institute.

Luke, T. W. (2013). Corporate social responsibility: An uneasy merger of sustainability and development. *Sustainable Development*, *21*(2), 83–91. doi:10.1002/sd.1558

Mahadevan, R., & Suardi, S. (2017). Panel evidence on the impact of tourism growth on poverty, poverty gap and income inequality. *Current Issues in Tourism*, 1–12. doi:10.1080/13683500.2017.1375901

Manyara, G., & Jones, E. (2007). Community-based tourism enterprises development in Kenya: An exploration of their potential as avenues of poverty reduction. *Journal of Sustainable Tourism*, *15*(6), 628–644. doi:10.2167/jost723.0

Mbaiwa, J. E. (2017). Poverty or riches: Who benefits from the booming tourism industry in Botswana. *Journal of Contemporary African Studies*, *35*(1), 93–112. doi:10.1080/02589001.2016.1270424

Mikkelsen, B. (2005). *Methods for development work and research: A new guide for practitioners*. London: Sage.

Ministry of Economy. (2017). *5-year and 20-year national development plan. Transforming Fiji*. Suva: Government of Fiji.

Ministry. of National Planning (2010). *Millennium Development Goals 2nd Report 1990-2009*. Report for the Fiji Islands. Suva: Government of Fiji.

Mitchell, J., & Ashley, C. (2010). *Tourism and poverty reduction*. London: Earthscan.

Moore, H. L. (2015). Global prosperity and sustainable development goals. *Journal of International Development*, *27*(6), 801–815. doi:10.1002/jid.3114

Mowforth, M., & Munt, I. (2009). *Tourism and sustainability: Development and new tourism in the Third World* (3rd ed.). London: Routledge.

Murray, W. E., & Overton, J. D. (2011). Neoliberalism is dead, Long live neoliberalism. Neostructuralism and the new international aid regime of the 2000s. *Progress in Development Studies*, *11*(4), 307–319. doi:10.1177/1464993410011004 03

Naidu, V. (2013). *Fiji: The challenges and opportunities of diversity*. London: Minority Rights Group International.

Narayan, P. (2010). *Green jobs in the South Pacific. A preliminary study*. Suva, Fiji: International Labour Organization.

Narayan, D., Patel, R., Schafft, K., Rademacher, A., & Koch-Schulte, S. (2000). *Voices of the poor: Can anyone hear us?* Oxford: Published for the World Bank by Oxford University Press.

Pacific Islands Forum Secretariat. (2015). 2015 Pacific regional MDGs tracking report. Retrieved from http://www.forumsec.org/resources/uploads/embeds/file/2015%20Pacific%20Regional%20MDGs%20Tracking%20Report.pdf

PARDI News (2013). Pacific Agribusiness Research for Development Initiative. Retrieved from https://lrd.spc.int/pardi-publications/pardi-newsletter/doc_download/2151-pardi-newsapril-2013highresolution

Pingeot, L. (2014). Corporate Influence in the Post-2015 Process. Working paper. Misereor; GPF; Brot fur die Welt. Retrieved from http://www.cid.org.nz/assets/Key-issues/Beyond-2015/Corporate-influence-in-the-Post-2015-process.pdf

Pleumarom, A. (1994). The political economy of tourism. *The Ecologist*, *24*(4), 142–148.

Plüss, C., & Backes, M. (2002). *Red Card for Tourism? 10 Principles and Challenges for a Sustainable Tourism Development in the 21st Century*. Freiburg: DANTE (NGO network for sustainable tourism development).

Porter, M. E., & Kramer, M. R. (2011). The big idea: Creating shared value. How to reinvent capitalism – and unleash a wave of innovation and growth. *Harvard Business Review*, *89*(1–2), 62–78.

Pradhan, P., Costa, L., Rybski, D., Lucht, W., & Kropp, J. P. (2017). Systematic study of Sustainable Development Goal (SDG) interactions. *Earth's Future*, *5*(11), 1169–1179. doi:10.1002/2017EF000632

Pratt, S., McCabe, S., & Movono, A. (2016). Gross happiness of a 'tourism' village in Fiji. *Journal of Destination Marketing & Management*, *5*(1), 26–35. doi:10.1016/j.jdmm.2015.11.001

Ramani, S. V., Parihar, R., & Sen, S. (2017). On nudging MNE toward SDG1: A policy perspective. *International Business and Management*, *33*, 89–129.

Richter, L. K. (2001). Tourism challenges in developing nations: continuity and change at the millennium. In D. Harrison (Ed.) *Tourism and the less developed world: Issues and case studies* (pp. 47–59). New York: CABI Publishing.

Roe, D., Goodwin, H., & Ashley, C. (2002). *The tourism industry and poverty reduction: A business primer. PPT Briefing No. 2*. London: Pro-Poor Tourism Partnership.

Rokosuka, E. (2015). *Positive feedback on equal distribution of lease payment*. fijivillage.com, 23 June, 2016. Retrieved from http://fijivillage.com/news/Positive-feedback-on-equal-distribution-of-lease-payment-s2rk59/

Save the Children Fiji. (2005). The commercial sexual exploitation and sexual abuse of children in Fiji: a situational analysis. Retrieved from http://resourcecentre.savethechildren.se/sites/default/files/documents/3232.pdf

Scheyvens, R. (2011). *Tourism and poverty*. New York: Routledge.

Scheyvens, R. (2007a). Exploring the tourism-poverty nexus. *Current Issues in Tourism, 10*(2–3), 231–254. doi:10.2167/cit318.0

Scheyvens, R. (2007b). Ecotourism and Gender Issues. In J. Higham (Ed.) *Critical issues in ecotourism. Understanding a complex tourism phenomenon* (pp. 185–213). Oxford: Elsevier.

Scheyvens, R., Banks, G., & Hughes, E. (2016). The private sector and the SDGs: The need to move beyond 'business as usual'. *Sustainable Development, 24*(6), 371–382. doi:10.1002/sd.1623

Scheyvens, R., & Biddulph, R. (2017). Inclusive tourism development. *Tourism Geographies, 20*, 1–21. doi:10.1080/14616688.2017.1381985

Schilcher, D. (2007). Growth versus equity: The continuum of pro-poor tourism and neoliberal governance. *Current Issues in Tourism, 10*(2–3), 166–193. doi:10.2167/cit304.0

Sofield, T. (2003). *Empowerment for sustainable tourism development*. Oxford: Pergamon.

Sofield, T., Bauer, J., De Lacy, T., Lipman, G., & Daugherty, S. (2004). *Sustainable tourism ∼ Eliminating poverty: An overview*. Australia: Cooperative Research Centre for Sustainable Tourism.

UNWTO (2007). *United Nations World Tourism Organization 2007, UNWTO ST-EP Programme: An Initiative of the World Tourism Organization (UNWTO) in conjunction with the UNWTO ST-EP Foundation*. Madrid: UNWTOAuthor,.

UNWTO (2015). *Tourism and the Sustainable Development Goals*. Brochure. Retrieved from https://www.e-unwto.org/doi/pdf/10.18111/9789284417254

UNWTO (2018). Tourism and pPoverty aAlleviation. Retrieved from http://step.unwto.org/content/tourism-and-poverty-alleviation-1

Wattanakuliarus, A., & Coxhead, I. (2008). Is tourism-based development good for the poor? A general equilibrium analysis for Thailand. *Journal of Policy Modeling, 30*(6), 929–955. doi:10.1016/j.jpolmod.2008.02.006

World Travel and Tourism Council (2015). *Travel and tourism. Economic impact 2015*: Fiji. Retrieved from https://www.wttc.org//media/files/reports/economic%20impact%20research/countries%202015/fiji2015.pdf

World Travel and Tourism Council (2017). *Travel and Tourism Economic Impact 2017*. WTTC, London: Author. Retrieved from https://www.wttc.org/-/media/files/reports/economic-impact-research/regions-2017/world2017.pdf

Zhao, W., & Ritchie, J. (2007). Tourism and poverty alleviation: An integrative research framework. *Current Issues in Tourism, 10*(2–3), 119–143. doi:10.2167/cit296.0

Zoomers, A. (2008). Global travelling along the Inca Route: Is international tourism beneficial for local development? *European Planning Studies, 16*(7), 971–983. doi:10.1080/09654310802163769

The critical capacities of restaurants as facilitators for transformations to sustainability

Freya Higgins-Desbiolles and Gayathri Wijesinghe

ABSTRACT

The United Nations released the Sustainable Development Goals (SDGs) following the 2012 Rio +20 UN Conference on Sustainable Development. This articulated 17 SDGs that balance the environmental, social and economic aspects of development, setting a timespan between 2015 and 2030 to end global poverty through sustainable development approaches.

According to the World Travel and Tourism Council, the tourism industry as a critical component of the global economy can play an important role in influencing consumers to participate in sustainability through their food consumption choices. Research shows restaurants and cafés around the world have offered sustainability best practice initiatives drawing attention to the political consequences of personal eating habits. This article presents the findings from case study research of twenty Australian restaurants featuring sustainability in their business concept and in their practices. Findings indicate that restaurants make surprising and valuable contributions to the SDG agenda. These restaurants' efforts range from: implementation of specific SDGs; using food as a way to unite and empower people; educating their stakeholders about environmental and community impacts of sustainability practices; and modelling alternatives that in some cases address critical questions of how are we to live.

Introduction

The way humanity manages or mismanages its food supply will in many ways define the 21st century— currently we know that we are not doing a great job ... (Nick Nuttall, Global Director of Communications, United Nations Environment Programme cited OzHarvest, 2014)

As the global community encounters the full impacts of the ecological limits to growth, food sovereignty, food justice and food ethics have become important considerations. The tourism industry, which is at the forefront of wealth and employment creation in the global economy, can play an increasingly influential role in getting consumers to participate in sustainability efforts through their consumption choices, particularly in relation to food (World Travel & Tourism Council, 2017). Tourism analysts have explored emerging intersections between food justice issues and regional tourism development strategies, exploring topics such as local food movements, slow food and volunteers on organic farms highlighting intersections between tourism niches and food justice (e.g. Mair, Sumner, & Rotteau, 2008; Sims, 2009).

Simultaneously, restaurants and cafés around the world have offered sustainability best practice initiatives drawing attention to 'the political consequences of personal eating habits' (Johnston & Baumann, 2015, pp. 8–9). Recognising these transitions in the attitudes of restaurateurs, who are often important to the development of the tourism industry through growth in food tourism, researchers and a restaurateur undertook a study of the pedagogy of sustainability employed by this restaurateur in Adelaide (Moskwa, Higgins-Desbiolles, & Gifford, 2014). The findings inspired this research into how restaurateurs' beliefs behind their daily practices and long-term visions, foster a food tourism industry based on holistic sustainable practices. This article is based on twenty case studies of restaurants and cafés in Australia, which featured various aspects of sustainability in their mission and approaches.

Sustainability is an increasing focus of communities around the globe. The United Nations released the Sustainable Development Goals (SDGs) as an outcome of the 2012 Rio +20 UN conference on Sustainable Development, which followed up the Millennium Development Goals (MDGs). 'The 17 SDGs balance the environmental, social and economic aspects of development and run from 2015 to 2030. SDGs exceed the MDGs in scale, scope and ambition, seeking to eliminate rather than reduce global poverty' (Bramwell, Higham, Lane, & Miller, 2017, p. 4). As Bramwell et al. (2017) noted, since the release of the SDGs, there has been patchy engagement with them in the tourism discipline. Literature searches suggest there is even less in the domain of hospitality as shown in the recent analysis offered by Higgins-Desbiolles, Moskwa, and Wijesinghe (2017) concerning the lack of engagement with holistic sustainability in hospitality and tourism literature.

This research began under a clear understanding that cafés are sites of privileged and commodified consumption and intuited that a healthy scepticism is required on any assertions that tourism and hospitality can readily contribute to the SDGs the global community is working towards by the 2030 target date. At first glance, an analysis of 'sustainable cafés and restaurants' would seemingly best connect to Goal 12 of the SDGs: 'Responsible Consumption and Production' that ensures sustainable consumption and production patterns. However, the details found in the twenty case studies undertaken showed much greater efforts and impacts than this one goal. The restaurants studied were addressing social inclusion, poverty, women's rights, refugee rights, urban planning and regeneration, workers' cooperative structures and indeed much more. In fact, this article indicates that among these twenty restaurants and cafés studied, most of the 17 SDGs were being addressed in some ways. This illustrates two important points: restaurants are moving past standard business boundaries and are playing an influential role in fostering more sustainable futures; as sites of conviviality, cafés can foster engagement that may expand the influence of sustainability advocacy beyond the usual channels.

The capacity of food, food cultures and food tourism to open up dialogue and connect people is increasingly clear. There is no greater conversation to hold today than how we are to create a sustainable future, where everyone eats, enjoys a good life and lives a little more lightly on the planet. The Australian restaurants and cafés presented in this article demonstrate that some restaurateurs in this sector are showcasing much more than good food.

Literature review

This article critically examines the capacity of the enjoyment of food consumed at restaurants to contribute to the attainment of sustainable development and sustainable tourism. It does this specifically by looking at this through the tools provided by the SDGs. There is a multitude of literature on sustainable development and sustainable tourism, including in this journal, and so this literature review will focus necessarily only on the topic of food and sustainability due to word limitations. Using the Brundtland report's definition of sustainable development, which describes it as 'satisfying the needs of the present generation without compromising the ability of future generations to meet their needs' (WCED, 1987, ch 2, sec. 1, para. 1), this article considers in what ways the consumption of food may support efforts to secure long-term sustainability.

The triple bottom line (TBL) approach is one way that sustainable development has been better understood. This approach suggests that examining the environmental, social and economic aspects of phenomenon such as tourism provides an in-depth and more holistic approach to better inform understanding and practice (see Elkington, 1999). As the *Economist* has noted:

> The triple bottom line (TBL) thus consists of three Ps: profit, people and planet. It aims to measure the financial, social and environmental performance of the corporation over a period of time. Only a company that produces a TBL is taking account of the full cost involved in doing business. (Economist, 2009)

The TBL offers a useful lens from which to analyse the sustainability practices of restaurants.

In terms of the economics of sustainability, it often proves less difficult to get businesses to engage with this aspect because this is the core of their concern. The restaurant sector is known for its competitiveness and high rate of business failure. However, the folklore that some 90% of restaurants fail in their first year has been proven fallacious by research (Parsa, Self, Njite, & Kig, 2005). Using quantitative and qualitative methods, Parsa et al. (2005) found instead a rate closer to 26% in the first year and identified critical factors from the external environment such as the competitive environment, restaurant density and the business size and factors from the internal environment due to management capability and leadership. In more recent times however, it seems that competition resulting from proliferation of restaurants due to the promotion of eating out as a key aspect of leisure and a critical component of tourism, may be adding to business vulnerability. For instance in the United Kingdom, it was reported that mid-market restaurant chains such as Jamie's Italian were restructuring in the face of financial difficulties and a decline in customers (Naylor, 2018). Stefan Chomka, the editor of Restaurant magazine, noted that 'brands go through a natural life cycle' (cited in Naylor, 2018) and so chains like Jamie's Italian may fall out of fashion. However, the research of Parsa et al. (2005, p. 314) uncovered from qualitative interviews with restaurateurs that 'a successful restaurant requires focus on a clear concept that drives all activities'. Their research indicated that this together with passion, focus and commitment underpinned success and longevity. These insights suggest that the economic sustainability of restaurants may in fact be supported by having a sustainability concept at their core that when authentically promoted may resonate with restaurant stakeholders and communities.

Many restaurants have now embraced the need to support efforts at environmental sustainability also. As the movement for 'green dining' indicates, consumers increasingly care about restaurant environmental practices (Hu, Parsa, & Self, 2010) and this has resulted in the development of the Green Restaurant Association (GRA, n.d.). If one looks at one issue, food waste, one can understand the importance of greater concern for the environmental impacts of our food consumption. The Food and Agriculture Organization (FAO) provides data to underscore just how significant food waste is as an issue for the global community. 'Food loss and waste … amount to a major squandering of resources, including water, land, energy, labour and capital and needlessly produce greenhouse gas emissions, contributing to global warming and climate change' (FAO, n.d.). When restaurants such as the ones studied here tackle this issue, they play an important role in attaining greater environmental sustainability. But this focus on environmental aspects of sustainability in restaurants may not be without problems. Higgins-Desbiolles et al. (2017) undertook a systematic review covering 25 years of tourism and hospitality literature, which suggested previous research has predominately focused on the environmental aspects of sustainability. This work suggested that social sustainability through restaurants is the neglected pillar of the TBL approach but also we may be missing opportunities for more holistic analysis if we become myopically focused on green dining.

While arguably under-studied in tourism and hospitality, the social sustainability potential of food consumed in restaurants is very significant. Food, food tourism and the socio-cultural capacities of food to provide meaning and shape relationships have recently gained greater attention. No longer limited to scientific studies of food nutrition or concerns with food distribution and access, food has become a site of cultural and social significance. Analytic approaches have included economic geographies of food (Goodman, 2008), food pedagogies (Flowers & Swan, 2012), food justice (Alkon & Agyeman, 2011) and food as critically reflexive leisure (Mair et al., 2008), for instance.

The consumption of food may activate multiple levels of social engagement. Montanari (2009) argues:

> Depending on production methods, food can also become a cultural reference point, an element of regional development and a tourist resource. This occurs with 'local' food, representing a model of production and consumption that suggests a strong link with the region in which the food is produced (p. 91).

Nilsson, Svard, Widarsson, and Wirell (2011) researched slow food as 'eco-gastronomic heritage' in three Italian towns, finding that while the movement purports to improve quality of life for local residents and tourists, there are tensions with commercialisation. Hall and Gossling (2013) published an edited volume focused on 'sustainable culinary systems'. Spurred by the growing interest in the ethical consumption and production of food, their work particularly focused on the drive for consuming local foods, slow food, slow tourism and sustainable culinary systems. Everett and Aitchison (2008) have examined how development of food tourism can contribute to building regional identities and support sustainability by fostering local food.

Consumption of food can also reveal wider, structural issues facing the global community. For example, Fonte (2006) explored the way the slow food movement offers a critique of the food supply in relation to the ecological injustice of global food production systems. Peace (2008) applied an anthropological analysis to the Terra Madre movement and the slow food approach. Peace (2008) asserted that the slow food movement 'strives to establish a critical analysis of the power exercised by global forces over the local production and consumption of food, and seriously asks what can be done in response' (p. 39). While Peace argued that the slow food movement fetishizes tradition and community food systems, the proponents of slow food argue they are presenting alternatives to negative forms of globalization (Peace, 2008). Mair et al. (2008) used critically reflexive leisure approaches to analyse the politics of food found in three contemporary movements: slow food, food justice and organic farming. By using this approach they argued that food practices can be understood as 'a motivator for civic engagement, a source of knowledge, and a catalyst for change' (Mair et al., 2008, p. 399). The questions raised in the sphere of food and its consumption get to the very heart of considerations of how are we to live. As Clarke, Barnett, Cloke, and Malpass (2007, p. 233) explained, the growth of the slow food movement supports a behaviour involving 'new forms of citizenly action … being configured through the creative redeployment of the repertoires of consumerism'. In this research, illustrative cases were identified that were gaining great attention, including Kinfolk using the social enterprise format for social inclusion (see Kinfolk, n.d.) and the Moroccan Soup Bar employing Muslim women and offering creative events such as 'speed date a Muslim' to challenge prejudice and societal tensions in Australia (see Taguchi, 2017).

This brief review indicates that restaurants are an important site for implementation of sustainability goals and that research is demonstrating interesting insights based on TBL evaluations. It is also important to recognise the work of hospitality industry associations to advance practice.

The Sustainable Restaurant Association (SRA) based in the United Kingdom is at the forefront of this work. This not-for-profit, membership organisation was founded in 2009 and works to promote more sustainable practices in the restaurant and catering sector. Its main focus is on offering an accreditation system, so that diners can identify which restaurants they wish to patronise by turning to the information provided by an independently verified Sustainability

Rating system helping diners choose a restaurant that matches their sustainability priorities (SRA n.d.-a). This rating system assesses restaurants as one, two, or three star sustainability champions depending on how they rate against a wide range of criteria. This rating system allows for assessment of restaurants across a range of consumer concerns for sustainability from responsible fisheries to local provenance (see SRA n.d.-a).

The SRA framework sets out three focus areas of sourcing, society and environment and divides these up into 10 areas for consideration. Under sourcing, they encourage restaurants to: 'celebrate local and seasonal, serve more veg and better meat, source fish responsibly and support global farmers' (SRA, n.d.-b). The facet on society recommends: 'treat people fairly, support the community and feed people well' (SRA, n.d.-b). Lastly, the programme on environment highlights three key areas: 'value natural resources; reduce, reuse and recycle; and waste no food' (SRA, n.d.-b). This framework represents a well-balanced approach to TBL criteria and supports efforts to implement more holistic forms of sustainability in the sector (as per Higgins-Desbiolles et al., 2017).

Recent research has demonstrated that some sustainable restaurants and cafés are operating much more holistically now in their efforts towards sustainability. Moskwa et al. (2014) positioned the sustainability efforts undertaken by restaurateur Stuart Gifford as contributing to social and environmental justice. They stated:

> This sustainability activism encourages the sustainability of the tourism and hospitality industries on a pragmatic level, but it also is about creating thriving and engaged local communities and enhancing the local environment, economy and culture in ways that can be enjoyed by locals and visitors alike. (Moskwa et al., 2014, p. 130)

As a result of these insights from the literature, when restaurant cases were identified and selected within Australia for this study, a variety of types of restaurants demonstrating the TBL aspects of sustainability were selected rather than only those narrowly focused on environmental initiatives.

Research has shown that some restaurateurs creatively use their restaurants as models of sustainability in order to foster learning, engagement and change among their stakeholders (Higgins-Desbiolles, Moskwa, & Gifford, 2014). In undertaking the literature review, it was found that the history of food cultures is demonstrative of this use of the restaurant as a model to foster transformations. For instance, Alice Waters who founded Chez Panisse, located in Berkley, California, was clearly one of the first to use her restaurant as a model of sustainability practice. As Johnston and Baumann (2015) describe her impact:

> Alice Waters was one of the first chefs to openly recognize the political consequences of personal eating habits. Her restaurant, Chez Panisse, which opened in 1971, featured seasonably available California foods, and has been widely credited with inspiring culinary interest in local ingredients and farm-to-table connections ... (p. 9)

Co-founder of Sustainable Table, Cassie Duncan also articulated this in her interview with us:

> Cafes and restaurants play an important role in shaping our food culture. They are on the front line, serving food to the masses each and every day and by nature of this, have millions of touch points to influence how and where someone chooses to buy food. (personal communication, 21 January 2015)

This research paid close attention to this phenomenon for cases where the restaurateur viewed her/his restaurant as a tool for modelling sustainability.

Employing critical approaches to this topic, it is clear that some scepticism is called for as most restaurants are sites of privileged consumption. This needs to be critically thought about in terms of movements for food justice and also in terms of how effective privileged restaurants are in supporting the goals of the SDGs. It is important to acknowledge the hard work underway on food justice, which is challenging the race and class issues of access to healthy and nourishing foods. Food justice is 'communities exercising their right to grow, sell, and eat [food that is] fresh, nutritious, affordable, culturally appropriate and grown locally with care for the well-being of the land, workers and animals' (Just Food cited in Alkon & Agyeman, 2011, p. 5). As Alkon and Agyeman demonstrated, food justice needs to be understood in light of advocacy for environmental justice as marginalised communities assert their rights to safe and positive futures. The emphasis that these concerns bring to understandings of the food system is a concern with '…food injustice in the wider political, economic, and cultural systems that produce both environmental degradation and racial and economic inequality' (Alkon & Agyeman, 2011, p. 9).

It is also important to be critically reflexive on how restaurants can help support implementation of the SDGs. This is particularly the case for restaurants located in developed countries such as Australia, the site of our twenty case studies. The SDGs are often associated erroneously with development efforts only undertaken in developing countries. Unlike the MDGs, the SDGs have universal applicability:

> Building on the success and momentum of the MDGs, the new global goals cover more ground, with ambitions to address inequalities, economic growth, decent jobs, cities and human settlements, industrialization, oceans, ecosystems, energy, climate change, sustainable consumption and production, peace and justice. The new Goals are universal and apply to all countries, whereas the MDGs were intended for action in developing countries only. (United Nations, n.d.)

Nonetheless, the SDGs have been the subject of significant criticism, including on the practicality of their universal applicability (see Swain, 2018). Criticisms have ranged from the philosophical concerning the incompatibility between ecological limits and the economic development goals, to specific difficulties in measurement and monitoring, to a key concern with their non-binding nature. Swain's (2018) critical analysis indicated that developed countries should remain focused on their social and environmental policies, while developing countries should be focused on their economic and social policies. Swain (2018) asserted: 'While being a transformative agenda that is universal, people-centric and comprehensive, SDGs are also constrained by these characteristics' (p. 354). This suggests a disjuncture between what can be expected of developed countries versus what can be expected of developing countries and suggests the problematic nature of the SDG agenda. Our study makes a contribution by considering what roles restaurants in developed countries such as Australia might play in promoting aspects of sustainability that contribute to a number of SDGs.

The analysis that follows indicates the ways that certain restaurants may foster engagement and implementation of certain SDGs through their business practices, their provision of food to their customers and through their pedagogies. Considering how consumption focused our societies are becoming, how large our food consumption's eco-footprint is and how rapidly food tourism is growing, it is essential that the tourism and hospitality disciplines consider the ways in which restaurants play their responsible roles in implementing the SDGs.

Methods

This work is an expansion of a pilot study conducted in 2011 with one restaurateur (Higgins-Desbiolles et al., 2014). Using a semi-structured interview technique, 20 restaurateurs in Adelaide and Goolwa in South Australia and Melbourne, Victoria were interviewed between 2014 and 2015. The cities of Adelaide and Melbourne were selected because they are known for their vibrant and creative food scenes and Goolwa was selected as the location of Australia's first Cittaslow, or 'Slow Town'.

Interviews were undertaken under a formal consent for interview process requesting interviewees to forego anonymity and allow attribution of quotes to interviewees in the reporting of findings; all agreed to these requests. Restaurants were selected through purposive sampling based on expert recognition of the enterprise as a site of sustainable restaurant practices and/or membership in associations like Green Table, the Sustainable Table and Cittaslow Goolwa. Interview data was supplemented with primary and secondary data and participant observation to identify and critically analyse the sustainability practices at each site.

This research was based on case study approaches, adhering to Yin's (2014) conceptualisation of multiple, embedded case study design (pp. 50–69). As Yin (1994) claims, 'a case study is an empirical enquiry that investigates a contemporary phenomenon within its real-life context, especially when the boundaries between phenomenon and context are not clearly evident' (p. 13). The twenty gathered case studies were conducted as if each could stand alone because each of the individual restaurants had entirely, unique contexts and circumstances. As Yin (2014) suggested, replication does not have to be the target of multiple case studies and the research was not seeking to compare and contrast between the case studies. As Stake (1995) argued, the goal of case study research does not have to be 'producing generalizations', as the 'uniqueness' and 'particularization' of the case with its rich insights and lessons teach us deep understanding about the case itself and also that from which it differs (pp. 7–8). The strengths case study approaches offers are the descriptive insights and rich context-specific knowledge (Flyvberg, 2006). The selected case studies were chosen as 'exemplars' of sustainable restaurants in order to identify leading practices and this designation was based on third party certification (e.g. with Sustainable Table or Cittaslow), expert recommendation, and/or snowball sampling approaches (see Pagell & We, 2009).

Qualitative approaches were used in the interviews to elicit narratives enabling rich insights into what restaurateurs' experiences can tell us about the influence of sustainable eateries on public awareness and participation in aspects of sustainability. Data analysis was based on inductive techniques which Thomas (2006) describes as 'approaches that primarily use detailed readings of raw data to derive concepts, themes, or a model through interpretations made from the raw data by an evaluator or researcher' (p. 238).

Ensuring validity in qualitative research is a key concern and so a number of strategies were undertaken to ensure findings were sound. Analyst triangulation (Miles & Huberman, 1994) was employed whereby data analysis was carried out independently by two of the researchers to minimise subjectivity. Each interviewee was given an opportunity to review the transcript from their interview to ensure accuracy of the content and address any inadvertent misconceptions that may have occurred. Additional validation was secured by corroborating restaurateur interviews with primary data from social media and supporting documents (e.g. sustainability reporting, grant applications, etc.) and secondary data such as media reporting on the restaurant or restaurateur.

The twenty cases included:

- Adelaide: The Organic Market and Café, Red Lime Shack, Café Troppo, Good Life Modern Organic Pizza, Locavore, Co-op Coffee Shop, Nove on Luce, Etica, Sarah's Sister's Sustainable Café and Experience Café.
- Goolwa: The Australasian Circa 1858, Bombora, Motherduck and Rankines at The Whistle Stop.
- Melbourne: Lentil as Anything, STREAT, Charcoal Lane, Brothl, Mesa Verde and The Grain Store.

These twenty case studies included: upmarket restaurants and local cafés; social enterprises and for-profit businesses; restaurants that were part of a chain or singular businesses; restaurants featuring specialty cuisines including vegetarian and native foods; restaurants using alternative models such as cooperative structures; and restaurants with a 'mission', including animal rights and ethics, zero-waste philosophy and vegetarian eating. Appendix 1 provides short briefs on each of the twenty restaurants studied.

The findings from the research are provided in the next section.

Findings and discussion

> *The hospitality industry is shockingly wasteful and I wanted to show that it could be done differently.* (Joost Bakker, creator of Brothl, cited in Prior, 2015)

This research project demonstrated that the roles of restaurants and cafés in contributing to sustainable development and sustainable food tourism is diverse and complex and well worth considering (see Table 1). The research revealed that there are restaurants and cafés in these three locations making valuable contributions through layered forms of sustainability practices, including addressing the various components of the TBL approach, through pedagogically performing sustainability for their stakeholders and in some cases, contributing to wider dialogue about societal choices concerning how we are to live. Findings confirmed the early insights offered by Higgins-Desbiolles et al. (2014), reinforcing that a number of restaurateurs are using the restaurant as a model of sustainable practice with a view to influencing others in multiple ways. Here we will offer brief insights into illustrative examples. These brief vignettes on the restaurants studied indicate that restaurants and cafés are doing much more to contribute to the attainment of the SDGs than may be first recognized. This is followed by analysis of the case studies considered as a whole.

Nurturing sustainability: Motherduck in Goolwa

Motherduck in Goolwa, South Australia is focused on providing good, healthy, local food and nutritional insights to customers. Motherduck is located in the main street of this small tourist town and has brought a point of difference to what otherwise are mainly take-away vendors and fish and chip shops. As Melissa Howard noted:

> My vision was when we opened up this place – it's because myself as a chef I found there was nowhere for me in Goolwa to go out and have … a nice dinner and with good customer service … So I was like 'Okay something needs to happen here in Goolwa'. (personal communication, 3 October 2014)

Goolwa is the first Cittaslow town in Australia and it features quality local producers and has a town committed to thinking through the merits of slow food. Motherduck offers a restaurant that exemplifies the spirit of this movement and a model of a transition to thoughtful engagement with food.

Melissa's keypoint of difference was her focus on customer nutrition and education of the customer on healthy food choices:

> On my menu I have exactly what foods you are eating, why they are good for you and what they're doing to benefit you. Ninety-nine percent of people love the fact that I've put what the health benefits there are for them in the food that they are eating because a lot of them don't understand. (Melissa Howard, personal communication, 3 October 2014)

This effort indicates ways restaurants can support SDG 3 focused on good health and well-being. As the world's population finds fast foods and processed foods being heavily promoted by industrialised food systems, restaurants can take up the challenge to inform their customers about the nutritional values of foods and what eating them offers in terms of health.

Australasian Circa 1858 participating in the Cittaslow project of Goolwa, SA

The Australasian was the only interviewee in our sample representing a restaurant associated with a five star accommodation. Co-owner Deb Malley defined sustainability as 'a circular flow between things, between businesses and people' (personal communication, 17 December 2014). Her work together with Chef and business partner Juliet Michell showcased this ethos as their business was built by being embedded in this regional, tourist town. They were ardent supporters of the local Cittaslow initiative and their business promoted other businesses such as

Table 1. Summary of restaurant sustainability practices.

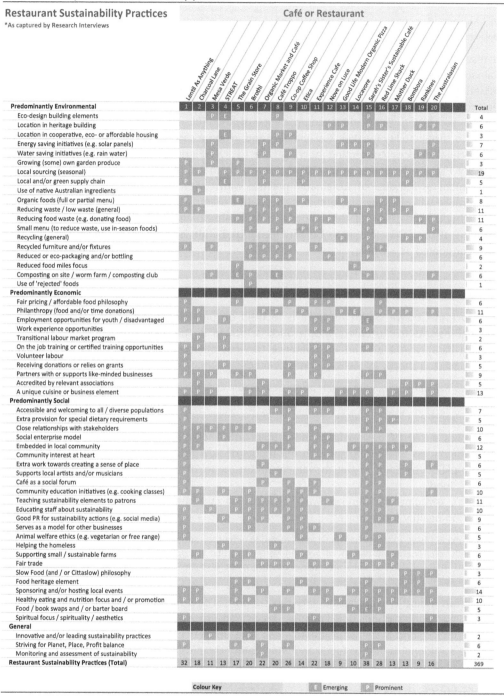

Restaurant Sustainability Practices — *As captured by Research Interviews* — Café or Restaurant

Columns: 1 Lentil As Anything, 2 Charcoal Lane, 3 Mesa Verde, 4 STREAT, 5 The Grain Store, 6 Broth!, 7 Organic Market and Cafe, 8 Café Troppo, 9 Co-op Coffee Shop, 10 Etica, 11 Experience Cafe, 12 Nove on Luce, 13 Good Life Modern Organic Pizza, 14 Locavore, 15 Sarah's Sister's Sustainable Cafe, 16 Red Lime Shack, 17 Mother Duck, 18 Bombora, 19 Rankines, 20 The Australasian.

Practice	Total
Predominantly Environmental	
Eco-design building elements	4
Location in heritage building	6
Location in cooperative, eco- or affordable housing	3
Energy saving initiatives (e.g. solar panels)	7
Water saving initiatives (e.g. rain water)	6
Growing (some) own garden produce	3
Local sourcing (seasonal)	19
Local and/or green supply chain	5
Use of native Australian ingredients	1
Organic foods (full or partial menu)	8
Reducing waste / low waste (general)	11
Reducing food waste (e.g. donating food)	11
Small menu (to reduce waste, use in-season foods)	6
Recycling (general)	4
Recycled furniture and/or fixtures	9
Reduced or eco-packaging and/or bottling	6
Reduced food miles focus	2
Composting on site / worm farm / composting club	6
Use of 'rejected' foods	1
Predominantly Economic	
Fair pricing / affordable food philosophy	6
Philanthropy (food and/or time donations)	11
Employment opportunities for youth / disadvantaged	6
Work experience opportunities	3
Transitional labour market program	2
On the job training or certified training opportunities	6
Volunteer labour	3
Receiving donations or relies on grants	5
Partners with or supports like-minded businesses	9
Accredited by relevant associations	5
A unique cuisine or business element	13
Predominantly Social	
Accessible and welcoming to all / diverse populations	7
Extra provision for special dietary requirements	5
Close relationships with stakeholders	10
Social enterprise model	6
Embedded in local community	12
Community interest at heart	5
Extra work towards creating a sense of place	6
Supports local artists and/or musicians	5
Café as a social forum	6
Community education initiatives (e.g. cooking classes)	10
Teaching sustainability elements to patrons	11
Educating staff about sustainability	10
Good PR for sustainability actions (e.g. social media)	9
Serves as a model for other businesses	6
Animal welfare ethics (e.g. vegetarian or free range)	5
Helping the homeless	3
Supporting small / sustainable farms	6
Fair trade	9
Slow Food (and / or Cittaslow) philosophy	3
Food heritage element	6
Sponsoring and/or hosting local events	14
Healthy eating and nutrition focus and / or promotion	10
Food / book swaps and / or barter board	5
Spiritual focus / spirituality / aesthetics	3
General	
Innovative and/or leading sustainability practices	2
Striving for Planet, Place, Profit balance	6
Monitoring and assessment of sustainability	2
Restaurant Sustainability Practices (Total)	369

Totals per café/restaurant (columns 1–20): 32, 18, 11, 13, 17, 20, 22, 20, 26, 14, 22, 18, 9, 10, 38, 28, 13, 13, 9, 16.

Colour Key: E Emerging   P Prominent

Bombora at the Beach (a beachside café), Coorong Kayaking and Spirit of the Coorong river cruises. In Australian regional towns such as Goolwa, businesses may struggle and such cooperative approaches help build more sustainable futures. This is one example of SDG 17, which emphasises partnerships for sustainability. Current economic systems often promote business competition whereas Cittaslow philosophy invites participant businesses to view their enterprise as part of a community and a community economy.

Valuing heritage and what matters: The Grain Store in Melbourne

The Grain Store is a high-end restaurant in Melbourne's central business district. Not only have Melanie Stolpe and Ingo Meissner preserved the physical heritage of the building it occupies, but they have also tried to engage customers with a dialogue on food heritages and our food choices. Chef Meissner emphasises the value of enjoying local, seasonal and freshly obtained food (personal communication, 10 December 2014). Low-key education was a feature of the Grain Store, as Meissner promotes healthy, sustainable and local foods to customers, suppliers, staff and the community, through the hosting of community events, talks and activities. The Grain Store actively supports CERES fair food and organic food network and acts as a site where people can pick up organic produce boxes for their home shopping needs. This represents important work in bringing healthy foods to urban dwellers and connecting them to producers in ways that build relationships. This supports SDG 11 focused on sustainable cities and sustainable communities, as rapidly growing urban populations must be informed and connected to the lives of rural communities if sustainable agriculture models are to continue.

Designed for Sustainability: Café Troppo in Adelaide

Café Troppo was developed by Phil Harris, founder of Troppo Architects, and his family. Café Troppo won the City of Adelaide prize in the 2014 South Australian Architecture Awards. This is not surprising considering that the origins of the café are rooted in a competition run by the Adelaide City Council for an eco-housing development in the early 2000s. Architect Phil Harris of Troppo Architects won the competition to build a three-story apartment block featuring ecological and equity commitments in its planning and design as he built Adelaide's first 'affordable eco-housing'. Harris left a space for a café on the bottom level of the complex, and when it remained un-letted, he and his family took up the challenge in creating a sustainable café in this urban space. The café was envisioned as a key social feature of his design of this urban building on Whitmore Square. As a result the café uses sustainable and innovative design to save on resource use and is a source of community-building in its diverse neighbourhood. 'Just like the eco-housing building we are nestled underneath, our ethos here at the café centres around sustainability, the environment and the community. Every decision involved in creating this place has been made with this in mind' (Café Troppo, n.d.). As a result of these unique origins, Café Troppo can be argued to be contributing to SDG goals 7 on Affordable and Clean Energy with its use of passive design techniques, SDG 9 on Innovation in its cutting edge design approaches, SDG 11 on Sustainable Cities and Communities, SDG 13 on Climate Action, as well as others among the 17 SDGs.

Locavore in the Adelaide Hills, SA

Chris March co-founded this restaurant in Stirling, SA following the principles of the locavore movement. The basic premise of the locavore is to only consume sustenance from within the local area, often designated as from within a one hundred mile radius. For Adelaide's Locavore restaurant, the commitment to promoting local features in the food and drinks menu, in as much of the supply chain as possible and in the hiring of local staff. March's focus is on raising the consciousness of his customers and encourages them to 'know the origin of your food and read the labelling' (personal communication, 15 January 2015). March noted when he first opened his restaurant local provenance did not have the high profile it has today and he and his staff had to fully explain the concept and the ways this shaped the menu.

Locavore's website explained the locavore focus as follows:

> A recent Australian survey by Choice Magazine found that the average basket of food has travelled up to 70,000 kms, or 3 times around the world! So if a locavore basket only travels 1000 km, and we serve four baskets a day, then we save 100 000 000 km a year! (Locavore, 2015)

Now that eating local has a strong profile, March envisioned developing a chain of locavore restaurants to advance the concept further and ' ... we could see people being able to do a whole tour of Australia with Locavore Restaurants' (personal communication, 15 January 2015). Locavore can be credited with contributing to SDG 12 on Responsible Consumption and Production.

Everyone deserves a place at the table: Lentil as Anything in Melbourne

Lentil as Anything is a 'pay as you feel', not-for-profit chain of popular vegetarian restaurants, including four restaurants and a catering business. Its first restaurant was established in St Kilda, Melbourne in 2000, and the most recent in Newtown, Sydney in 2014. The unique character of this restaurant chain is that whilst the menu contains no set prices, it offers a wide range of choices of vegetarian foods, desserts and drinks, all served on a donation basis with patrons asked to give what they can afford or what they feel the experience is worth (Commonwealth of Australia, 2009, p. 26). The other key feature is offering work experience and training in hospitality, to groups such as new migrants and refugees who work on a voluntary basis [noting refugee visas may block them from paid employment]. Their mission statement stated these operative values:

- Caring for people: Provide a wholesome and nutritious meal where money is not a concern.
- Promoting multiculturalism: Fostering an environment of inclusion and not exclusion.
- Reforming society: Acting on the structures of society to restore justice.
- Extending/Spreading its ethos and values: Hiring volunteers, the long-term unemployed and the marginalised.
- Encouraging: Young people to be active citizens and get involved in community based initiatives. (Lentil as Anything, n.d.)

Their values are centered on mutual respect, generosity, trust, equality, freedom and kindness (Lentil as Anything, n.d.). It is a social experiment that involves reciprocity; demonstrating that both 'giving' as well as 'receiving' generosity can be a successful model for economic sustainability (Shanaka Fernando, personal communication, 23 July 2014). This social enterprise operates on a financial model involving donations and volunteering. The concept encourages people to 'think carefully about their own values and ethics' (Commonwealth of Australia, 2009, p. 26). The founder, Shanaka Fernando, said that he wants to:

> ... communicate to people that this is their space, there is no owner, there is no businessman making a profit out of it. It is our own space and we make of it, what we give to it, and we imperil it by what we take out of it — when we don't regard our contribution in the right context. (personal communication, 23 July 2014)

This has led, for example, to a sense of ownership and solidarity, even to the extent that when the restaurants are short-staffed customers have been known to volunteer their services. In this aspect, both the customers and staff have a role in contributing to the kind of culture the restaurants promote. Lentil as Anything restaurants have modelled the fact that a 'commercial business can be financially successful and popular with the public while being operated on a socially responsible basis where the main priority is not profit' (Commonwealth of Australia, 2009, p. 26). Shanaka Fernando hoped this concept will inspire other restaurateurs and lead to a global movement (Fernando & Hill, 2012, p. 175); with signs this is already happening with the openings of similar restaurants including Bon Jovi's 'Soul Kitchens', Fernando offers Lentil as Anything as a model to challenge the 'hubris, greed and heedlessness' that sit behind recent financial crises (Fernando & Hill, 2012, p. 6). The restaurants have a growing involvement in schools and community education on social sustainability issues, ethics and values (Lentil as Anything, n.d.).

Founder Shanaka Fernando held ambitious social and cultural visions behind his efforts through Lentil as Anything:

> I wanted to make food available to people in our community without having to worry about money ... I really wanted to see how this notion of sitting and eating together and celebrating our kinship would play out in a society where there is a heavy focus on an individual separating themselves from community through material and title driven aggrandisement and to see if we can create a situation at least in the space of the restaurant where people's character and their sense of individuality was something that complemented the group rather than threatened the unity of it. (personal communication, 23 July 2014)

Fernando's vision through Lentil has excited interest; for example, in 2014 research was undertaken to estimate the 'social return on investment' delivered through the three Melbourne restaurants (see Lentil as Anything, n.d.). This case study demonstrates all 17 SDGs and most unusually for the restaurant sector SDG 1 on no poverty and SDG 2 on zero hunger. This vision also indicates that unusually these restaurants are making significant contributions to SDG 16 on peace and justice, as they work to transform the values and lifeways of their stakeholders. Most importantly, Fernando's vision through his Lentil restaurants demonstrates that restaurants can be effectively used as tools to model alternative approaches to sustainable living.

Cooperatives building value: The Co-op Coffee Shop of Adelaide

The Co-op Coffee Shop opened in Adelaide in mid-2014 as the first café co-op in South Australia. Greens Member of the South Australian Parliament Tammy Franks drew attention to the Co-op Coffee shop as a model of co-operative businesses saying in a speech that it offered a different paradigm and could pave the way for other co-operative enterprises in the state (Franks, 2014). They sought capital for the project from the crowd-sourcing site Pozible, which secured more than $11,000 for the project. In this campaign, the Co-op expressed their vision:

> We will create a 'third space': a place where people come to meet, relax, share ideas and socialise outside of the home and workplace. Adelaide cries out for a space where local community groups and progressive groups in general can organise and hold events, and as well as this, the space will be accessible to the general public - especially you! Your contributions will allow you to join us in creating this concept for all. (Co-op Coffee Shop, 2013)

Co-op member Sam Shelter gave a sense of its purpose prior to its opening when it was seeking support through crowd-funding:

> Essentially we're trying to create real fair trade all the way through production to consumption. So you think of fair trade normally you pay a fair wage to the people who produce it but those who are in the service industry or the hospitality industry aren't treated fairly so it doesn't make it all the way down the line. So that's what we want to try and do is create real fair trade. To do that we want to make the most stable, ethical jobs so people don't feel like they're being taken advantage of and they don't feel like they'll lose their jobs during an economic downturn. (Heckler, 2013)

The features of the workers cooperative model include the fact that workers are their own bosses and they create their own workplace environment, decisions are made by consensus, and workers create a fair and equitable working environment featuring fair and adequate pay and conditions. Since its inception, the Co-op Coffee Shop had committed to fulfilling the seven values of cooperatives, including openness, democratic practices, supporting other cooperatives and concern for their communities (see Co-op, n.d.).

The Co-op Coffee shop had additional features of sustainability in its operations, including strong environmental and social priorities; but a predominant feature was a focus on social relationships and community. Co-operative member Ian Law stated:

> cooperatives ... provide that opportunity to create a small community and then build on it and in an environment where we have what I consider governments that have been fairly hostile to individuals creating that sense of community, this is one way of cutting out a bit of that harshness and providing a sense of connection and building up community that can make the ill effects that come from there perhaps less than what they might otherwise be (personal communication, 1 August 2014).

Unfortunately, the Co-op Coffee Shop closed in 2015 because the building's owner did not renew their lease on the building, instead opening his own café in the venue. During its year of operation, this café modelled SDG 8 particularly as through its cooperative model it offered an example of decent work.

Ethics at the forefront: Etica- Ethical Pizzeria and Mozzerella Bar in Adelaide

Etica was created by Federico and Melissa Pisanelli as a result of their concern to foster greater consumer awareness and engagement with animal welfare ethics. The vision of Etica is: 'To promote animal welfare ... we do that by considering all animal derived products and making sure that they come from farms that practice the highest animal welfare standards' (Federico Pisanelli, personal communication, 27 February 2015).

This couple had studied animal law and were very interested in how animals are treated in Australia. In the decision to open a pizzeria, they were concerned to promote the cause of animal welfare and to raise consumer awareness of issues in the production of animal derived products (Federico Pisanelli, personal communication, 27 February 2015). On their website, they provided a brief outline of the issue of animal welfare ethics in our modern factory farming system and stated 'we want to help consumers understand where our food comes from' and also 'we want to influence other restaurants in subscribing to the importance of animal welfare' (Etica Pizzeria, n.d., [archived website]).

Etica's example indicates restaurateurs are not afraid to use their restaurant to raise ethical issues and work to provoke thought in their customers. In fact, Etica caused a storm of controversy in 2017 when it decided to make an installation at its second restaurant out of a taxidermied cow in order to highlight the ethics of the dairy industry (see Koehn, 2017). Etica's efforts can be viewed as contributing to SDG 12 concerning responsible consumption and production, among others.

Native foods and recognizing First Nations: Charcoal Lane in Melbourne

Charcoal Lane in Melbourne is a social enterprise featuring a collaboration between Mission Australia (a non-government organization supporting the disadvantaged), Accor Hotels Group and William Angliss Training Institute. The aim of this social enterprise is to provide holistic support to enable disadvantaged young Indigenous Australians a successful transition to sustainable mainstream employment. The enterprise provides trainees with on-the-job hospitality industry skills training, accredited certified education from the William Angliss Institute, professional work placements in the hospitality industry, as well as personal support. Charcoal Lane models what is possible in terms of hospitality's commitment to corporate social responsibility when non-profits work together with the hospitality sector. As Manager Ashan Abeykoon articulated the vision: 'our number one goal is to create employment ... for the First People's, the traditional owners to make sure they can survive and get a job, and be in an economically, financially sustainable position' (personal communication, 25 July 2014). Charcoal Lane holds a unique positioning with its commitment to support Indigenous Australian advancement. Its mission stated:

[t]o develop a safe and supportive environment for our trainees we have strong relationships with the local Koorie community. Cultural development is at the heart of what we do ... As a social enterprise we aim to operate a business that provides a social benefit or outcome to both individuals and the community. Ultimately we achieve this by helping young Aboriginal people develop a pathway to ongoing education or employment and paying respect to their culture. (Charcoal Lane, 2014)

Charcoal Lane models the partnerships advocated in SDG 17, the decent work of SDG 8, the innovation of SDG 9, the sustainable cities and communities of SDG 11 and responsible consumption of SDG 12.

Modelling profitable sustainability: Sarah's Sister's Sustainable Café in Adelaide

Sarah's Sister's Sustainable Café in Semaphore was established in 2005. It is co-owned by a couple with more than 35 years in the restaurant sector indicating an economic sustainability than many in the industry envy; they first started with Sarah's Café in 1978 on Hutt Street in Adelaide's CBD. It is a vegetarian café and works to address food waste through a degustation menu. As the title of Sarah's Sister's suggests, it is all about sustainability with strong commitments to environmental sustainability and service to the local community. Co-owner Stuart Gifford explained:

We were quite disciplined ... we adopted the name with the word sustainable in our title only when we knew we could commit to (and this was our own rules) ... making a 50% reduction overall [in waste and energy reductions] in comparison to taking the route of a normal café. (personal communication, 12 January 2015)

Inspired by 'cradle to grave sustainability' thinking, Sarah's Sister's has been carefully designed and managed. This starts with the creative re-use of a heritage building and builds with the principles of 'passive design' using the natural environment and design concepts to reduce the business' ecological footprint.

Gifford communicated a concept of his work through the café as providing 'a model of profitable sustainability' (personal communication, 12 January 2015) which he noted is very important in influencing the hospitality sector to embrace sustainability more fully. Describing the cost savings that energy efficiency and waste reductions can deliver makes sound business sense and can deliver an edge in business competitiveness. While he is motivated by a passion for sustainability, he pragmatically realises that the wider transitions necessary in the hospitality sector can be nudged by this sound business logic (Stuart Gifford, personal communication, 12 January 2015). This case clearly focuses on the essential nature of the economic pillar of the TBL model for sustainability to be achieved.

Sarah's Sister's also supports the social sustainability of its community and stakeholders. It has supported local events, exhibitions and workshops playing host to reclaim the night events (about safe cities), SALA living artists' festivals and the Adelaide Fringe. In the past three years, Sarah's Sister's has developed partnerships with local primary schools. This features the development of community gardens by the students, which become foundations for building on-going relationships between the school, the restaurant and the community. As produce is exchanged in one direction, waste for composting goes in the other direction and conversations are generated about our food, its supply and our larger choices. This development demonstrates Gifford's commitment to building a more sustainable future through the use of the café as a tool to start conversations.

As Table 1 demonstrates, a thorough analysis of Sarah's Sister's actions designated it as the most accomplished among the twenty cases selected. In terms of the SDGs, Sarah's Sister's is making remarkable contributions to SDG 4 on quality education, SDG 11 on sustainable cities and communities and SDG 12 responsible consumption and production.

Table 2. The SDGs and the role of restaurants and cafes in the hospitality sector.

SDG	Found in frameworks and codes[a]	Found in restaurants in this literature review[b]	Found in restaurants in this study[b]	Identified potentials[b]
1. No poverty End poverty in all its forms everywhere	ST 'donate leftover food' [advice for businesses; noting foodbanks give these foods to people experiencing homelessness]; ST supports OrphFund in Uganda	Using restaurants to raise funds for development projects, non-profits, etc. (Shebeen bar in Melbourne, a 100% not for profit bar; Kinfolk restaurant)	Restaurants with a mission to contribute to non-profits in one-off cases or on-going (Sarah's Sister's)	Embedded in communities, restaurants could identify and support segments such as the homeless
2. Zero hunger End hunger, achieve food security and improved nutrition and promote sustainable agriculture	ST 'food co-ops, food swaps and community supported agriculture'	Restaurants give to food banks (e.g. Oz Harvest)	Restaurants with a pay what you can ethos (Lentil as Anything)	Restaurants are sites of privileged consumption and could do more for food justice and sustainability
3. Good health and well-being Ensure healthy lives and promote well-being for all at all ages	SRA 'feed people well'	Restaurants featuring native foods and promoting protection of diverse foods	Restaurants educate for healthy nutrition (Motherduck)	Educating for nutrition and broader health could feature on menus
4. Quality education Ensure inclusive and equitable quality education and promote lifelong learning opportunities for all	Could view ST and SRA frameworks as education tools for consumers and other stakeholders	Training institutes in collaboration with Chefs and Restaurants to train disadvantaged individuals in the hospitality sector	Restaurants used for training and qualifications (Charcoal Lane. Lentil as Anything, and STREAT)	Sustainable restaurants could offer cooking classes to educate on sustainable home-cooking
5. Gender equality Achieve gender equality and empower all women and girls	SRA's 'treat people fairly'	Restaurant used to empower migrant and marginalised women (Moroccan Soup Bar)	Not clearly highlighted in the 20 cases however women clearly dominated workforce	Restaurants have more to do on ensuring equal pay, equal rights and workplace free of harassment
6. Clean water and sanitation Ensure availability and sustainable management of water and sanitation for all	ST 'resources are used unsustainably: water' [agriculture is water intensive so must avoid food waste]; SRA 'value natural resources: manage water usage to save money and reduce environmental impact'	Entrepreneur Joost Bakker showcasing waste water recycling at Melbourne's Federation Square and Flemington Race meets	Water saving initiatives and technologies used (Sarah's Sister's washing dishes by hand)	Development of technologies and practices to reduce water waste; implement policy of no use of bottled water
7. Affordable and clean energy Ensure access to affordable, reliable, sustainable, and modern energy for all	SRA 'value natural resources: improving energy efficiency'	Restaurants showcase the logic of using sustainable energy	Restaurants using design for sustainability (Café Troppo, Sarah's Sister's)	Restaurants could be subsidised with funding for sustainable infrastructure e.g. solar panels

(continued)

Table 2. Continued.

SDG	Found in frameworks and codes[a]	Found in restaurants in this literature review[b]	Found in restaurants in this study[b]	Identified potentials[b]
8. Decent work and economic growth Promote sustained, inclusive, and sustainable economic growth, full and productive employment, and decent work for all	SRA's 'treat people fairly: providing equal opportunities, training and clear policies to keep employees happy and productive'	Issues reported in Australia concerning minimum wage rate and fair work conditions	Restaurants run by workers cooperatives (Co-op Coffee Shop)	Essential to address fair workplaces and career opportunities in hospitality
9. Industry, innovation and infrastructure Build resilient infrastructure, promote inclusive and sustainable industrialization, and foster innovation	SRA's 'innovating to reduce food waste'	Entrepreneur Joost Bakker showcasing zero waste at Melbourne's Federation Square and Flemington Race meets	Restaurants showcasing sustainable technologies and practices (Brothl); Restaurants showing innovation is creative (Etica)	Restaurants could be subsidised with funding for sustainable infrastructure e.g. solar panels, water saving devices
10. Reduced inequalities Reduce inequality within and among countries	SRA's 'treat people fairly: providing equal opportunities, training and clear policies to keep employees happy and productive'	Growth in social enterprise models in restaurant sector	Restaurants with pay what you can (Lentil as Anything); Restaurants with a pay it forward scheme such as meals or coffees for disadvantaged (Red Lime Shack)	Social tourism principles could be expanded to restaurants to assist people on low-incomes to benefit from dining out- levelling of class privilege in hospitality
11. Sustainable cities and communities Make cities and human settlements inclusive, safe, resilient, and sustainable	SRA 'support the community'; ST 'City dweller's guide to sustainable food'	The City of Melbourne's Food Policy 'vision of a food system that is secure, healthy, sustainable, thriving and socially inclusive'	Restaurants used to create community and build connections (Sarah's Sister's, Lentil as Anything, Nove on Luce, Experience Café)	Restaurants act as third space for people to come together in dialogue; could see food system's wider capacities to regenerate environment and community [e.g. through community gardens]
12. Responsible consumption and production Ensure sustainable consumption and production patterns	SRA 'celebrate local and seasonal', 'serve more veg and better meat'	Growing relationships between consumers and producers in the food systems through things like slow food movement, farmer's markets	Restaurants featuring ethical values such as fair trade products or vegetarian focus (Sarah's Sister's); restaurants supporting food relationships (Grain Store supporting CERES food box distribution)	Likely greater consumer interest in local sourcing and transparency of all foods throughout their supply chain
13. Climate action Take urgent action to combat climate change and its impacts	ST recognises food waste as contributing to serious environmental problems	Restaurants are dealing with specific issues of global climate change through their efforts, e.g. reducing	Restaurants modelling holistic sustainable approaches to spark consumer engagement with	Food system challenges likely due to climate change; food justice will get more difficult

(continued)

Table 2. Continued.

SDG	Found in frameworks and codes[a]	Found in restaurants in this literature review[b]	Found in restaurants in this study[b]	Identified potentials[b]
14. Life below water Conserve and sustainably use the oceans, seas, and marine resources for sustainable development	SRA 'source fish responsibly'; ST 'choose sustainable seafood'	food waste, considering their eco-footprint Promotion of sustainable fisheries; alliances between green groups and fisheries	sustainability (Sarah's Sister's) Joost Bakker discussing putting the despised European carp on Australian menus as a sustainability measure (a fish causing problems as an introduced species)	Collapse of fisheries is a key challenge facing the future requiring restaurants to consider their supply chain on this issue
15. Life on land Protect, restore, and promote sustainable use of terrestrial ecosystems, sustainably manage forests, combat desertification, and halt and reverse land degradation and biodiversity loss	SRA 'value natural resources' and 'serve more veg and better meat'; ST argues food choices can drive change to more sustainable food systems	Movements of farmers markets, slow food, organic foods; linking urban and rural communities through food and food tourism	Restaurants thinking through impacts on environment (Organic Market and Café)	The role of our food systems in ecological degradation and need to change (e.g. need to reduce meat production)
16. Peace, justice and strong institutions Promote peaceful and inclusive societies for sustainable development, provide access to justice for all, and build effective, accountable, and inclusive institutions at all levels	SRA 'support global farmers'	Examples of restaurants used to bring polarised sections of the community together (Speed date a Muslim run by Moroccan Soup Bar)	Restaurants used for advocacy, community meetings and social change (Co-op Coffee Shop, Sarah's Sister's); Restaurants are promoting alternative socialities (Lentil as Anything)	Food justice will be a key challenge in the future and restaurants must engage with this issue
17. Partnerships for the goals Strengthen the means of implementation and revitalize the Global Partnership for Sustainable Development	ST's advice to businesses 'Develop relationships and ask questions' [of your supply chain and others]	Sustainable Table and its networks in Australia illustrate cooperative networks	Partnerships for transformations in the hospitality sector (Charcoal Lane working with Mission Australia, Accor Hotels and William Angliss Institute)	Hospitality sector must engage with wider food justice, food sustainability issues to play their part in building sustainable futures

[a]ST refers to Sustainable Table of Australia and SRA refers to the Sustainable Restaurant Association of the UK
[b]Information in column 2 is derived from SRA (n.d.) and ST (n.d.); information in columns 3–5 derived from the research project.

Using a restaurant to disrupt thinking: Brothl in Melbourne

Brothl was a creative effort by innovation and sustainability leader Joost Bakker, who has become nationally and internationally renowned for his efforts in promoting zero waste and infinite recyclability in pop-up initiatives like Greenhouse and Silo restaurant. Brothl's key focus was on zero waste and Bakker clearly used it as a tool to model innovative thinking in the restaurant sector. Bakker explained:

> My philosophy is everything is related, it's holistic. You can be passionate about doing one thing a certain way and not worry about the rest of things in your life. That's why a restaurant is so good, because I can nail every single component and put my philosophy on it. I believe it is possible to have a completely zero-waste world. It's not far-fetched … people will change very quickly when they see it can work. (Bakker cited in Tippet, 2012)

Bakker observed how wasteful the hospitality sector could be and he resolved to model a zero waste business. At Brothl, he had implemented this vision. Using the meat offcuts and bone waste of top restaurants such as Neil Perry's Rockpool and Ben Shrewry's Attica, he created a menu based on broths that showcased ways to achieve zero food waste; thus giving Brothl its name.

While Baker had undertaken numerous initiates in modelling waste reduction, the most significant had been his influential closed loop composting system which Bakker claimed some 100 restaurants had adopted, diverting some 4000 tonnes of organic waste away from landfill each year (personal communication, 4 December 2014).

This composter was situated in the adjacent laneway to Brothl so that customers could see it and understand its purpose. This was the source of Brothl's demise as a conflict ensued with Melbourne City Council (see Worrall, 2015). The fact that Bakker chose to let Brothl close rather than give in over the composter issue indicates most clearly his driving purpose was to use the restaurant as a model of best practice 'zero waste'. Bakker employed Brothl as model of sustainability to transform current practices rather than simply as a commercial enterprise. With this zero waste focus, Brothl particularly highlighted SDG 9 on innovation and SDG 12 on responsible consumption.

Analysis of the twenty cases together

While many restaurants and cafés may be sustainable in specific and even multiple aspects, what is different in these cases is that these restaurants are not only working to be more sustainable in their practices but also visibly modelling these practices in order to foster engagement and change in their customers, suppliers and even other restaurants. This research also indicated emergent themes to consider on the ways restaurants are contributing to sustainability efforts.

Cafés as third spaces

Cafés have been studied by sociologists for decades for the roles they may play in fulfilling political, cultural and social functions (see Warner, Talbot, & Bennison, 2012). For instance, sociologist Ray Oldenburg (1999) argued cafés can provide a 'third place' of social connection that offers another alternative to work and home environments. This is well-illustrated in Ben Hewitt's (2010) description of Claire's Restaurant in his book *The town that food saved*. Referring to Oldenburg's concept of 'the third space', Hewitt (2010) argued a restaurant like Claire's:

> [P]rovides a venue for people to come together, a place that's not work and not home, but something in-between … third places are cornerstones of community life and facilitate the sort of social engagement essential to any healthy community. They are the places where ideas are born and debated, where groundswells arise in discussions over food and drink. (p. 141)

Moskwa et al. (2014, p. 138) argued that their case study of Sarah's Sister's Sustainable Café also illustrated this activation of the café as a 'third space': 'a site for people to gather together

to strengthen community bonds leading to community activism'. They also quoted the restaurateur, Stuart Gifford who claimed: 'cafés have been a place where new ideas and revolutions have
started' (Gifford, cited in Moskwa et al., 2014, p. 138).

This research has supported this view of cafés serving as third spaces for people to come
together and to connect in a time when communities have been undermined by the dynamics
of globalisation. As described above, the Co-op Coffee Shop in Adelaide expressly set out in its
founding ethos to create a third space for community in its urban location. Additionally, the case
of Lentil as Anything in Melbourne indicated that Fernando had a vision to bring all kinds of
people together over food for a radical agenda of inclusion, care ethics, justice and sustainability.
In the case of Charcoal Lane in Melbourne the appreciation of native foods offers a pathway to
reconciliation efforts needed in Australia between Indigenous and non-Indigenous Australians.

Food as a tool for critical pedagogy

Higgins-Desbiolles et al. (2014) provided a case study analysis of a 'sustainable café' and offered
an analysis of food as a tool for critical pedagogy. They noted:

> Gifford's pedagogy through the café emphasizes that sustainable approaches to food consumption are
> actually better and more enjoyable than the mainstream food industry. Gifford suggests that this can be a
> segue into inviting customers into deeper and more complex sustainability issues as it opens up a space for
> dialogue and reflection. (Higgins-Desbiolles et al., 2014, pp. 276–277)

We found that a number of the restaurateurs we interviewed held aspirations to be a role
model for others in terms of sustainability practices. Using the term employed in the work by
Higgins-Desbiolles et al., they can be characterized as 'sustainability pedagogues' or teachers, as
they work to inform some or all stakeholders about environmental and social impacts of food
consumption choices. Tactics to educate the patrons and other stakeholders were diverse and
included: creative thought provocations such as Etica's use of a prominently displayed cow car-
cass in its pizzeria (see Cook, 2017); conventional education through printed materials such as
menus, brochures and social media; hosting cooking classes, tours and exchanges to disseminate
sustainability messages; creating sustainable supply chain linkages by supporting suppliers to
transition to sustainable practices; engaging in activism by lobbing for policy changes, holding
educational events, and communicating through mainstream and social media channels; and
engaging in cooperation rather than competition, evident through the clear willingness to share
their models and practices with others.

While it might be argued that all restaurants inform their customers, we found these case
studies different in that the restaurant becomes a tool to model and promote sustainability practices. The most clear case was Joost Baaker through Brothl when he closed this restaurant when
he was prevented from modelling its zero waste practices. The Co-op Coffee Shop saw itself as a
model of a workers' cooperative and shared the experience with others in the hopes in inspiring
other to develop cooperatives that could support fair and empowering workplaces. This
approach of partnerships, cooperation and sharing has been reported as a characteristic of more
socially responsible forms of entrepreneurship (see Choi & Gray, 2008).

Layers of sustainability

Another clear theme of this multi-case study research is that different restauranteurs are advancing on different approaches to sustainability through their cafés and restaurants. The research by
Moskwa et al. (2014) suggested that the life story of the restaurateur would, in part, explain her/
his use of the restaurant as a tool to foster engagement with sustainability. For instance, it was
the experience of learning about top-end restaurants and their food wastage when he supplied
cut flowers to Rockpool and Attica Restaurants, that inspired Joost Bakker to base Brothl's menu
on the meat offcuts of such restaurants. Similarly, it was the experience of growing up in

privilege in his home country of Sri Lanka that inspired Shanaka Fernando to focus Lentil as Anything on radical equity and inclusion (Fernando & Hill, 2012).

This research advances understanding of TBL approaches to sustainability in tourism by indicating sustainability might be achieved in layers of action. Kane (1999) has presented a view that sustainability needs to be approached in layers because of the complexity and contradictions that are inherent in sustainable development as a concept (true also of the SDGs). While Kane's point is to address how analysis must focus on layers of hierarchy when analysing complex systems for sustainability because addressing the diverse strands of the TBL approach involves trade-offs, and her insight does have relevance here. The key point for this work is that there are tensions in working towards TBL or holistic sustainability and to be attuned to efforts in moving in the 'right direction' (Kane, 1999, p. 23).

Our findings indicate that achieving holistic sustainability across all three pillars of the TBL can be difficult and often trade-offs are made. Arguably, Baaker was so focused on zero-waste modelling that he failed in terms of the long-term sustainability of Brothl. Many of the studied restaurants focused on certain key visions: Etica on animal welfare, the Co-op Coffee Shop on cooperative arrangements; Brothl on zero waste; and STREAT addressing youth issues through a social enterprise model. However, some of our restaurants did score highly on all aspect of the TBL, including Sarah's Sister's, Lentil as Anything and the Red Lime Shack, as Table 1 demonstrates.

The findings here demonstrate multiple layers of practice and impacts, ranging from implementation of specific SDGs, pedagogical performance to engage stakeholders in wider considerations of their choices that might enhance greater sustainability and indeed even critical questioning of how are we to live and what futures do we want to build. It has not been possible to report here on all the cases undertaken or identify the multiple practices and contributions each restaurant has made as revealed in the research for this project. A fuller report of these is provided in the public report presented from this research (see Higgins-Desbiolles, Wijesinghe & Moskwa, 2014). Additionally Table 1 summarises the practices of the twenty restaurants in a chart structured according to TBL criteria to help inform readers. Table 2 specifically considers the roles that restaurants can and do play in supporting each of the 17 SDGs and underscores their importance in this regard. It also identifies as yet unfulfilled potential that could guide future efforts.

In closing this analysis we note that the findings of this research align with findings made in other studies such as that of Higgins-Desbiolles et al. (2014) in terms of restaurateurs using their restaurants as models of sustainability in order to foster learning, engagement and change among their stakeholders. While there is an array of foci in the twenty case studies studied, from animal welfare, to zero waste, to workers' rights, to fostering social connection, what is held in common is a belief that a restaurant can be used as model or efficacious tool for transformation towards sustainability. Our research has supported the findings of Moskwa et al. (2014) who found that their restaurateur's ' … approach rejects a model of business and society based on endless capital accumulation and economic growth no matter what the ecological, social or even political consequences. It engages alternative approaches and explores possibilities' (p. 140).

Conclusion

Food, food tourism and food cultures are now a key component of people's leisure time and thus this space marks a very promising opportunity to engage all stakeholders in understanding the ways the choices they make can contribute to achieving the 17 SDGs. Many of the cases studied in this research project indicated that restaurateurs are excited by the opportunities to use their restaurants to foster engagement with sustainability. Parsa et al.'s (2005) research showed that restaurateurs who have a driving concept and a passion hold an edge in this competitive business sector. Our research suggests that restaurateurs who embed their restaurant in the life of their local community and/or restaurants that embody an ethos that can move their customers to develop a meaningful relationship with them in some way may find themselves more sustainable in the future. As Parsa et al. (2005) stated: 'interestingly, successful restaurant owners all had a well-defined concept that not only provided a food product but also included an operating philosophy, which encompassed business operations as well as employee and customer relations' (p. 315). From this research, it is clear that restaurateurs who show a commitment to sustainability and underpin their business with a balanced 'profit, people and planet' concept and approach, achieve a committed following and make important contributions to efforts to secure the goals of the SDGs. It is accepted widely that sustainability is an increasing concern. Research has shown that food and food practices can be employed as catalysts for change in addressing sustainability concerns. This study examined how cafés and restaurants through their food practices are leading the way for others to reflect on the politics of food and sustainability.

However, applying a critical reading of the employment of restaurants as tools to promote engagement with the SDGs, conduct sustainability pedagogy and/or contribute to building alternative futures does reveal serious limitations. As the analysis of Alkon and Agyeman (2011) indicated, food justice must move beyond white, middle-class privilege expressed through organic markets, local provenance and slow foods. This positionality of privilege may cause proponents to overlook the ways in which people of colour and disadvantaged communities struggle for access to food and also how the privilege of some may come at the expense of the nourishment of others. Among our case studies, only the case of Lentil as Anything offered insights into a fully radical challenge through food justice approaches.

However, if one subscribes to the argument that all stakeholders must play their part in the transitions to sustainability, our study clearly reveals some exemplars of current practice. It has revealed important developments occurring in the restaurant sector and the work of inspiring restaurateurs leading the way in innovative and high impact use of the restaurant space to foster sustainability among their stakeholders. Harnessing businesses such as restaurants in the efforts to attain the SDGs is a key plank in the 2030 Agenda for Sustainable Development. As Co-Founder of the Sustainable Table Cassie Duncan stated: 'cafes and restaurants play an important role in shaping our food culture' (personal communication, 21 January 2015). The twenty cases studies reported on here point the way to exciting possibilities of the roles restaurants can play as facilitators of transitions to more sustainable futures as articulated in the SDG agenda.

Disclosure statement

The authors report no conflicts of interest. The authors alone are responsible for the content and writing of this article.

Acknowledgement

The authors would like to acknowledge and thank Dr Emily Moskwa or her research assistance on this project. We also acknowledge fundingsupport from the Le Cordon Bleu - University of South Australia Research Grant Program.

References

Alkon, A. H., & Agyeman, J. (2011). *Cultivating food justice: Race, class and sustainability*. Cambridge: MIT Press.

Bramwell, B., Higham, J., Lane, B., & Miller, G. (2017). Twenty-five years of sustainable tourism and the Journal of Sustainable Tourism: Looking back and moving forward. *Journal of Sustainable Tourism, 25*(1), 1–9. doi:10.1080/09669582.2017.1251689.

Café Troppo. (n.d.). *A little about us*. Retrieved from http://cafétroppoadelaide.com/a-little-about-us/

Charcoal Lane. (2014). *Charcoal Lane: A social enterprise of Mission Australia*. Retrieved from http://www.charcoallane.com.au/

Choi, D. Y., & Gray, E. R. (2008). Socially responsible entrepreneurs: What do they do to create and build their companies? *Business Horizons, 51*(4), 341–352.

Clarke, N., Barnett, C., Cloke, O., & Malpass, A. (2007). Globalising the consumer: Doing politics in an ethical register. *Political Geography, 26*(3), 231–249. https://doi.org/10.1016/j.polgeo.2006.10.009

Commonwealth of Australia. (2009). *I am Australian: Exploring Australian citizenship – Lower secondary unit teacher resource manual*. Belconnen, ACT: National Communications Branch.

Cook, C. (2017, September 26). Social media backlash as Adelaide pizza restaurant Etica hangs stuffed cow from ceiling. *The Advertiser*. Retrieved from Retrieved from https://www.adelaidenow.com.au/business/small-business/social-media-backlash-as-adelaide-pizza-restaurant-etica-hangs-stuffed-cow-from-ceiling/news-story/17dbf1e49c779b26d35588d8ca225910

Co-op. (n.d.). *Co-operative identity, values and principle*. Retrieved from https://ica.coop/en/whats-co-op/co-operative--identity-values-principles

Co-op Coffee Shop. (2013). *Co-op Coffee Shop start-up fund*. Retrieved from http://www.pozible.com/project/173266.

Economist. (2009, November 17). Triple bottom line. Retrieved from http://www.economist.com/node/14301663

Elkington, J. (1999). *Cannibals with forks: The triple bottom line of 21st century business*. Oxford: Capstone.

Etica Pizzeria. (n.d.). *Etica website*. Retrieved from http://www.eticapizzeria.com.au [website no longer available].

Everett, S., & Aitchison, C. (2008). The role of food tourism in sustaining regional identity. *Journal of Sustainable Tourism, 16*(2), 150–167.

Fernando, S., & Hill, G. R. (2012). *Lentil as Anything: Everybody deserves a place at the table*. Fremantle, Western Australia: Vivid Publishing.

Flowers, R., & Swan, R. (2012). Pedagogies of doing good: Problematisations, authorities, technologies and teleologies in food activism. *Australian Journal of Adult Learning, 52*(3), 532–572.

Flyvberg, B. (2006). Five misunderstandings about case-study research. *Qualitative Inquiry, 12*(2), 219–245.

Fonte, M. (2006). Slow Food's Presidia: What do small producers do with big retailers? In T. Marsden & J. Murdoch (Ed.), *Between the local and the global* (pp.203–240). Research in Rural Sociology and Development, Vol. *12*. Bingley, UK: Emerald Group.

Food and Agriculture Organization (FAO). (n.d.). *Key facts on food loss and waste you should know!* Retrieved from http://www.fao.org/save-food/resources/keyfindings/en/

Franks, T. (2014, May 7). *Co-op Coffee Shop, statement to South Australian Legislative Council*. Retrieved from http://www.tammyfranks.org.au/2014/05/07/co-op-coffee-shop/

Goodman, M. (2008). *Towards visceral entanglements: Knowing and growing economic geographies of food*. Environment, politics and development working paper series, Department of Geography, King's College London, Paper 5, pp. 1–25.

Green Restaurant Association (GRA). (n.d.). *Green Restaurant Association*. Retrieved from https://www.dinegreen.com

Hall, C. M., & Gossling, S. (Eds.) (2013). *Sustainable culinary systems: Local foods, innovation, tourism and hospitality*. London: Routledge.

Hewitt, B. (2010). *The town that food saved: How one community found vitality in local food*. New York: Rodale Inc.

Heckler. (2013). *Interview – The Co-op Coffee Shop*. Retrieved from http://www.heckler.com.au/2013/12/06/interview-the-co-op-coffee-shop/

Higgins-Desbiolles, F., Moskwa, E., & Gifford, S. (2014) The restaurateur as a sustainability pedagogue: The case of Stuart Gifford and Sarah's Sister's Sustainable Café. *Annals of Leisure Research, 17*(3), 267–280.

Higgins-Desbiolles, F., Wijesinghe, G. & Moskwa, E. (2014). A taste of sustainability: Case studies of sustainable cafes in Australia.e Retrieved from http://apo.org.au/node/74066.

Higgins-Desbiolles, F., Moskwa, E., & Wijesinghe, G. (2017). How sustainable is sustainable hospitality research? A review of sustainable restaurant literature from 1991 to 2015. *Current Issues in Tourism*, pp. 1–30. doi:10.1080/13683500.2017.1383368.

Hu, H. H., Parsa, H. G., & Self, J. (2010). The dynamics of green restaurant patronage. *Cornell Hospitality Quarterly, 51*(3), 344–362. doi:10.1177/1938965510370564.

Johnston, J., & Baumann, S. (2015). *Foodies: Democracy and distinction in the gourmet foodscape* (2nd ed.). New York, NY: Routledge.

Kane, M. (1999). Sustainability concepts: From theory and practice. In J. Kohn, J. Gowdy, F. Hinterberger & J. van der Straaten (eds.) *Sustainability in question* (pp. 15–30). Cheltenham, UK: Edward Elgar.

Kinfolk. (n.d.). *Who is Kinfolk?* Retrieved from http://kinfolk.org.au/about/

Koehn, E. (2017). *Adelaide pizzeria called "deranged psychopaths" as storm continue over decision to hang cow from venue ceiling.* Smart Company. Retrieved from https://www.smartcompany.com.au/industries/hospitality/etica-cow-controversy/

Lentil as Anything. (n.d.). *About us.* Retrieved from https://lentilasanything.com/about/

Locavore. (2015). *Locavore website.* Retrieved from http://locavore.com.au/

Mair, H., Sumner, J., & Rotteau, L. (2008). The politics of eating: Food practices as critically reflexive leisure. *Leisure/Loisir, 32*(2), 379–405.

Miles, M. B., & Huberman, A. M. (1994). *Qualitative data analysis: An expanded sourcebook.* Thousand Oaks, CA: Sage.

Montanari, A. (2009). Geography of taste and local development in Abruzzo (Italy): project to establish a training and research centre for the promotion of enogastronomic culture and tourism. *Journal of Heritage Tourism, 4*(2), 91–103.

Moskwa, E., Higgins-Desbiolles, F., & Gifford, S. (2014) Sustainability through food and conversation: the role of an entrepreneurial restaurateur in fostering engagement with sustainable development issues. *Journal of Sustainable Tourism, 23*(1), 126–145.

Naylor, T. (2018, February 22). The casual dining crunch: Why are Jamie's Italian, Strada, Byron (and the rest) all struggling? *The Guardian.* Retrieved from https://www.theguardian.com/lifeandstyle/2018/feb/22/casual-dining-crunch-jamies-italian-strada-byron-struggling?CMP=fb_gu

Nilsson, J. H., Svard, A. C., Widarsson, A., & Wirell, T. (2011). "Cittaslow" eco-gastronomic heritage as a tool for destination development. *Current Issues in Tourism, 14*(4), 373–386.

Oldenburg, R. (1999). *The great good place: Cafés, coffee Shops, bookstores, bars, hair salons, and other hangouts at the heart of a community.* New York, NY: Marlowe & Company.

OzHarvest. (2014). *OzHarvest: Our Story.* Retrieved from http://www.ozharvest.org/what-we-do/our-story/

Pagell, M., & We, Z. (2009). Building a more complete theory of sustainable supply chain management using case studies of 10 exemplars. *Journal of Supply Chain Management, 45*(2), 37–56.

Parsa, H. G., Self, J. T., Njite, D., & Kig, T. (2005). Why restaurants fail. *Cornell Hotel and Restaurant Administration Quarterly, 46*(3), 304–322. doi:10.1177/0010880405275598.

Peace, A. (2008). Terra Madre 2006: Political theater and ritual rhetoric in the Slow Food Movement. *Gastronomica, 8*(2), 31–39.

Prior, D. (2015). The trash collector. *New York Times.* Retrieved from. http://tmagazine.blogs.nytimes.com/2015/02/13/joost-bakker-interview/?smid=fb-share

Sims, R. (2009). Food, place and authenticity: local food and the sustainable tourism experience. *Journal of sustainable tourism, 17*(3), 321–336.

Stake, R. E. (1995). *The art of case study research.* Thousand Oaks, CA: Sage.

Sustainable Restaurant Association (SRA). (n.d.-a). *Our rating.* Retrieved from https://thesra.org/rating

Sustainable Restaurant Association (SRA). (n.d.-b). *Our sustainability framework.* Retrieved from https://thesra.org/framework/

Swain, R. B. (2018). A critical analysis of the Sustainable Development Goals. In L. Filho & W. Cham (Eds.), *Handbook of sustainability science and research* (pp. 341–356). New York, NY: Springer. Retrieved from https://doi.org/10.1007/978-3-319-63007-6_20

Taguchi, K. (2017). Speed date a Muslim. *ABC Compass.* Retrieved from http://www.abc.net.au/compass/s4661624.htm

Thomas, D. R. (2006). A general inductive approach for analysing qualitative evaluation data. *American Journal of Evaluation, 27*(2), 237–246.

Tippet, G. (2012, January 29). All he is saying, is give pee a chance, *The Sunday Age.* Retrieved from http://www.theage.com.au/victoria/all-he-is-saying-is-give-pee-a-chance-20120128-1qne5.html

United Nations. (n.d.). The sustainable development agenda. Retrieved from http://www.un.org/sustainabledevelopment/development-agenda/

Warner, J., Talbot, D., & Bennison, G. (2012). The cafe as affective community space: Reconceptualizing care and emotional labour in everyday life. *Critical Social Policy, 33*(2), 305–324.

World Commission on Environment and Development (WCED). (1987). *Our common future.* Retrieved from http://un-documents.net/ocf-02.htm

World Travel and Tourism Council. (2017). *5 Ways tourism can support local economies.* Retrieved from https://medium.com/@WTTC/5-ways-tourism-can-support-local-economies-8cc8ded47370.

Worrall, A. (2015, February 26). Waste-free cafe to close over compost dispute. *The Age Online.* Retrieved from https://www.theage.com.au/national/wastefree-cafe-to-close-over-compost-dispute-20150226-13pvm3.html

Yin, R. K. (1994). *Case study research: Design and methods* (2nd ed.). Thousand Oaks, CA: Sage.

Yin, R. K. (2014). *Case study research: Design and methods* (5th ed.). Los Angeles, CA: Sage.

Appendix 1

Restaurants and cafés studied in the taste of sustainability research project

Adelaide: The Organic Market and Café, Red Lime Shack, Café Troppo, Good Life Modern Organic Pizza, Locavore, Co-op Coffee Shop, Nove on Luce, Etica, Sarah's Sister's Sustainable Café and Experience Café.

Goolwa: The Australasian Circa 1858, Bombora, Motherduck and Rankines at The Whistle Stop.

Melbourne: Lentil As Anything, STREAT, Charcoal Lane, Brothl, Mesa Verde and The Grain Store.

- **The Organic Market and Café** is located in Stirling, a suburb in the Adelaide Hills. It serves locally-grown organic produce. This business was established in 1982 as a fresh organic market for local growers and was extended in 1992 to include an organic café. This family-run business includes an export arm, as well as facilities for online shopping and home delivery. This popular business has a competitive advantage, due to its established brand and the uniqueness of being a market and café combined.
- **The Red Lime Shack** opened in 2012 in Port Adelaide and features a vegan and vegetarian menu. The restaurant is on one of the main thoroughfares and is located in one of the heritage buildings that are now being revitalized in this maritime area. The owner, Steph Taylor, is leading the way in efforts to revitalise and renew Adelaide's rundown inner Port area. She and her work team have helped create markets at nearby Hart's Mill, clean up derelict areas, support pop-ups and projects of Renewal SA in the precinct and events and other activation measures.
- **Café Troppo** is family-run, trendy café Whitmore Square in the southwest corner of Adelaide's CBD; it opened in May, 2012. Café Troppo won the City of Adelaide prize in the 2014 South Australian Architecture Awards. The origins of the café were rooted in a competition run by the Adelaide City Council for an eco-housing development in the early 2000s. Architect Phil Harris of Troppo Architects won the competition to build a three-story apartment block featuring ecological and equity commitments in its planning and design as part of Adelaide's first 'affordable eco-housing'. Harris left a space for a café on the bottom level of the complex, and when it remained un-letted, he and his family took up the challenge in creating a sustainable café in this urban space. Manager and chef Maddie Harris works on the principle of a dynamic, seasonal menu with the weekday menu being changeable and displayed on a blackboard.
- **Good Life Modern Organic Pizza** began selling pizza from 2003 featuring organic ingredients before it became trendy. In fact it is credited with offering Australia's first certified organic pizza and the business markets itself as the 'world's first carbon neutral pizza'. The business is owned and run by two brothers, Jake and Marty Greenrod, running organic pizza restaurants in three Adelaide locations (the CBD, the seaside suburb of Glenelg and the upmarket location of North Adelaide).
- **Locavore** is an award-winning wine and tapas bar located in Stirling, in the Adelaide Hills. The term locavore refers to someone committed to eating foods procured within a range of 100 miles (160 kilometres). It was inspired by the 100 mile diet which was derived by the example of Alisa Smith and Bill MacKinnon. Owner Chris March noted his Locavore restaurant was 'Locavore before it was a word in Australia' (personal communication, 15-January 2015).
- **The Co-operative Coffee Shop, or Co-op Coffee Shop** for short, was established in mid-2014 after two years of planning and organising by people with a vision for creating a worker-owned and controlled café in the Adelaide CBD. It was located on Currie Street across from a large TAFE campus and in a building shared with Co-West and Mad Mouse Alley, which offered community spaces for writers, artists and social groups. The Co-op Coffee Shop began with the energy and commitment of ten cooperative members who were determined to create a positive work environment for themselves and to offer a model of a cooperative café which would demonstrate how things could be done differently. They additionally sought capital for the project from the crowd-sourcing site Pozible, which secured more than $11,000 for the project. It closed after a year of operations as the owner of the building took back the premises after the lease ended.
- **Nove on Luce** was a social enterprise situated on Light Square in the Adelaide CBD. It ran on a not-for-profit basis using the café space to offer solutions to youth unemployment, address family disintegration, help integrate international students and other migrants into the community, and foster social cohesion through social interaction. It offered 'startup training initiatives for those who are ready to break the cycle of poverty and apathy in our community'. It started out with funding from the Coastlands Church who wanted to offer support for community service and engagement. It also received inspiration from other leading social enterprise café, particularly STREAT in Melbourne. It offered a simple and affordable menu in a central location. It changed ownership in 2017 to KIK Coffee, a social enterprise supporting disadvantaged youth.
- **Etica: Ethical pizzeria and mozzarella bar** in Adelaide has the motto: 'We have sourced what we regard as the most ethically available food in Australia'. It was created by Federico and Melissa Pisanelli as a result of their concern to foster greater consumer awareness and engagement with animal welfare ethics and a desire to honour the Neapolitan food traditions of their heritage. In terms of the former, Federico Pisanelli states the aim of Etica is, 'To promote animal welfare … we do that by considering all animal derived products and

making sure that they come from farms that practice the highest animal welfare standards' (personal communication, 27 February 2015).

- **Sarah's Sister's Sustainable Café** in Semaphore was established in 2005. It is co-owned by a couple with more than 35 years in the restaurant sector; they first started with Sarah's Café in 1978 on Hutt Street in Adelaide's CBD. It is a vegetarian café located on the main street of the coastal suburb of Semaphore. As the title of Sarah's Sister's suggests, it is all about sustainability. The menu has a la carte and a degustation menu.
- **Experience Café** opened in late 2013 on the east side of Adelaide's CBD. It is a not-for-profit, Christian café with a focus on helping new migrants, refugees and students obtain vital local work experience, English language skills and preparation for work. Reverend Ruthmary Bond has been the catalyst to this visionary use of the café which resulted from her work at the state office for the Uniting Church in a program entitled Fresh Expressions of Church; she has innovatively developed this concept of Experience Café bringing the church into the marketplace in an effort to foster holistic thriving. The menu offered is simple, healthy and affordable.
- **The Australasian Circa 1858** is an award-winning luxury hotel in the holiday town of Goolwa. It stands out from our other case studies as it is firstly a luxury accommodation and its restaurant is only open to non-resident guests on Saturday evenings. The owners have been supporters of Cittaslow Goolwa since its inception and have contributed to the sense of place established in Goolwa. Co-owners Deb Smalley and Juliet Michell have a commitment to providing their guests with a unique experience which is based on a sense of aesthetics which restores the spirit and soul. They have won awards such as the 2012 South Australian Tourism Award for luxury accommodation, the 2013 SA Tourism Award for hosted accommodation and also placing in these same categories in the national tourism awards of Tourism Australia.
- **Motherduck** is located in Goolwa and is focused on providing good, healthy, local food and nutritional insights to customers. Motherduck is located in the main street of this small tourist town, bringing a point of difference to a street otherwise filled with takeaway vendors and fish and chip shops. Melissa Howard opened her health focused restaurant named 'Motherduck' in 2014. The name comes from her children's reference to her as a mother duck. Melissa wanted to create a point of difference, by offering 'healthy nutritious good food' cooked from the heart 'with love', whilst also caring for the environment as well as the people who grow the food.
- **Bombora @ Goolwa Beach Café** is a seaside café that is a local icon in Goolwa, well known for its seafood and seasonal local produce. Bombora is located right on the beachfront. Bombora is at the forefront of the Cittaslow movement in Goolwa. Co-owner Olaf Hanson was supportive of Goolwa's application to become the first Australian Cittaslow township after having seen Cittaslow operate successfully in Europe. Olaf and his co-owners support the year-long programme of Goolwa Cittaslow activities and work to build the community and economy being developed through this initiative.
- **Rankines at The Whistle Stop Café, Bar & Restaurant** offers local food by the river in Goolwa. It has been open for more than 20 years and is run by co-owners Peter and Sue Rankine; this couple has over forty years of experience in the hospitality sector. Rankines at The Whistle Stop is a member of the food and wine group Cittaslow Goolwa. Peter Rankine noted that his restaurant adheres to the code of ethics of Cittaslow Goolwa's food and wine group
- **Lentil as Anything** is a 'pay as you feel', not-for-profit chain of popular vegetarian restaurants. The unique character of this restaurant chain is that whilst the menu contains no set prices, an array of premium vegetarian meals and desserts are offered on a donation basis. Patrons are asked donate what they can afford or feel the experience is worth. Its first restaurant was established in St Kilda, Melbourne in 2000, and the most recent in Newtown, Sydney in 2014. Melbourne is its largest operation with venues in Abbotsford, Thornbury and St Kilda. Lentil as Anything's philosophy is based on giving a 'wholesome and nutritious meal where money is not a concern'. This social enterprise operates on a financial model involving donations and volunteering. Their values are centred on mutual respect, generosity, trust, equality, freedom and kindness.
- **STREAT** is a social enterprise with a vision to, 'stop youth homelessness and disadvantage, one mouthful at a time'. Inspired by KOTO, a training program and restaurant providing street youth with job opportunities in Vietnam, Rebecca Scott and Kate Barrelle, founded STREAT in 2010 with a class of nine trainees and two small food carts, in Melbourne's Federation Square. By 2014 STREAT had expanded within Melbourne to four cafés, one coffee roastery and one production kitchen (for catering business), and helped over 180 young people aged between 16 and 25 years to break the cycle of homelessness. Its outstanding contribution to social sustainability has been recognised with many accolades, such as the 2014 Australia's most prestigious specialty coffee GOLD award, 2013 Most Innovative Australian Social Enterprise, David Clarke Scholarship for outstanding leadership in social change, 2013 Business 3000+ Award in the Social Enterprise category, and Youth Now award for Best Employer of Students with Additional Needs. STREAT claims they strive for holistic sustainability through 'People, Planet and Profit'.
- **Charcoal Lane** is a social enterprise offering hospitality training and social support to Indigenous Australian youth. It is located in the inner city suburb of Fitzroy, Melbourne. It is a unique high-end restaurant featuring modern Australian, seasonally inspired cuisine infused with native ingredients. It is a commercially viable social enterprise established in July 2009 by Mission Australia (a national community service organisation) in

partnership with the Victorian Aboriginal Heath Service (VAHS), William Angliss Institute, and Accor. The aim of this social enterprise is to provide holistic support to enable disadvantaged young Indigenous Australians a successful transition to sustainable mainstream employment. The enterprise provides trainees with on-the-job hospitality industry skills training, accredited certified education from the William Angliss Institute, professional work placements in the hospitality industry, as well as support for social and emotional well-being.

- **Brothl** was a restaurant created by Joost Bakker in Melbourne's CBD to showcase a zero waste philosophy. Joost Bakker's work is synonymous with sustainable practice in eateries. Known for his 2008 pop-up restaurant in Melbourne's Federation Square, which featured cutting-edge sustainability, he followed it up with other pop-up ventures in Perth and Sydney and then permanent restaurants including Silo on Hardware Street in Melbourne's CBD. With, Brothl, which built on the work of Silo, Joost Bakker invited us 'to imagine a world without waste' (menu Brothl). Brothl's cheeky name came from the broths that are featured on the menu, that were developed from the bones and meat offcuts that high-end restaurants like Rockpool generated. Bakker closed Brothl in 2015 because of a dispute with Melbourne City Council over the siting of his compost machine in the adjacent laneway.
- **Mesa Verde Restaurant and Bar** is located in Melbourne's CBD and features a rooftop garden and Australia's first rooftop worm farm. Mesa Verde is a Mexican restaurant and stylish. Mesa Verde means 'green table' in Spanish and brands the 'green restaurant' ethos it supports. Located on the level just below the rooftop of an inner city building, Mesa Verde's unique feature is that it houses Australia's first rooftop worm farm. The worm farm uses up kitchen waste and supplies fertiliser to grow difficult to source Mexican herbs and speciality chillies and vegetables for the restaurant and bar.
- **The Grain Store** is located in Melbourne's CBD. Opened by Chef Ingo Meissner (previously of Sydney's Hilton and Melbourne's Crown Casino) and Melanie Stolpe, this couple have created a high-end restaurant featuring local and seasonal food. Drawing on their German heritage, which featured seasonal, wholesome, family cooking, they offer 'honest cooking' in a beautiful and comfortable setting. The design features actual barn doors in the restaurant to evoke the farms and the farmers that provide the ingredients for the menu. The owners support CERES fair food program supplying organic and nutritional foods to urban dwellers and educational workshops where their customers can meet local producers.

Index